Turner's Modern World

Turner's Modern World

David Blayney Brown, Amy Concannon, James Finch and Sam Smiles

First published 2020 by order of the Tate Trustees
by Tate Publishing, a division of Tate Enterprises Ltd,
Millbank, London SW1P 4RG
www.tate.org.uk/publishing

on the occasion of the exhibition
Turner's Modern World organised by Tate Britain
in association with the Kimbell Art Museum and the
Museum of Fine Arts, Boston

Tate Britain, London
28 October 2020 – 7 March 2021

Kimbell Museum of Art, Fort Worth
9 May – 5 September 2021

Museum of Fine Arts, Boston
11 Oct 2021 – 17 Jan 2022

The exhibition at Tate Britain is supported by

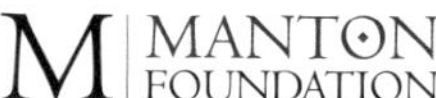

With additional support from the
Turner's Modern World Exhibition Supporters Circle:
Tavolozza Foundation

Tate Americas Foundation, Tate Patrons and
Tate Members

ISBN 978 1 84976 713 2 (hardback)
ISBN 978 1 84976 712 5 (paperback)

Library of Congress Control Number applied for

David Blayney Brown is Senior Curator, Historic British
Art, at Tate
Amy Concannon is Curator, British Art 1790 – 1850,
at Tate
James Finch is Assistant Curator, 19th Century British
Art, at Tate
Sam Smiles is Honorary Professor, University of Exeter

Senior Editor: Alice Chasey
Production: Elizabeth Stanton / Juliette Dupire
Picture Researcher: Emma O' Neill
Designed by The Studio of Williamson Curran
Colour reproduction by DL Imaging, London
Printed and bound in Italy by Graphicom

Front cover: J.M.W. Turner, *Peace – Burial at Sea* 1842
(detail of no.162)

Measurements of artworks are given in centimetres,
height before width

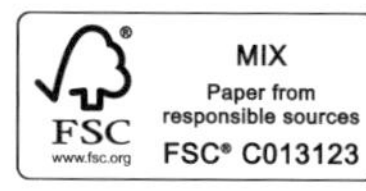

Director's Foreword

The lifetime of J.M.W. Turner (1775–1851) spanned the steam age, Napoleonic Wars, the expansion of empire, political reform and technological advances that transformed society and shaped the modern world. Historians have long held that Britain's industrial revolution and political revolution in France inaugurated profound modernisation. *Turner's Modern World* places his art at the heart of these developments.

Turner's contemporary interests are well known, but they are often seen independently of each other. Despite many exhibitions on particular themes in his work at Tate and elsewhere, none has presented the spectrum of his modern subjects. This exhibition can be seen as a sequel to *Late Turner: Painting Set Free* first shown at Tate Britain in 2014 and curated by David Blayney Brown, Amy Concannon and Sam Smiles, who are also the present exhibition's curators. There, they argued for Turner's late-career modernity on his own terms, rather than as a proto-modernist validated by later artists and critics; and against John Ruskin's reductive positioning of Turner as the foremost 'modern painter' on the basis of his understanding of the natural world. Now, they extend these arguments to Turner's whole career, emphasising subjects as much as style.

This exhibition is calibrated to *his* modern world, not ours. Connections between them can be overdone. Nothing stays modern for long and certainly did not during his lifetime of dizzying change. The urbanised industrial powerhouse of 1851 would have been unrecognisable to the Georgian Britain where Turner grew up. Yet just as Turner knew he was living in extraordinary times, where everything was in flux, few of us now feel certain of what lies ahead.

That being said, much in Turner's life and work, as inspiration or provocation, will surely resonate today. Moreover, from our vantage point there are aspects of Turner's own times, which he depicts, that we understand better than he could have done. Turner's 'steam pictures' are a case in point. Uniquely, these pictures put as much emphasis on emissions as on the new machines doing the emitting. In doing so, Turner could not

have known that he was offering testimony to the beginnings of global warming or what geologists call the era of the Anthropocene (some prefer the term Capitalocene to suggest that culpability rests with the socio-economic system rather than on human populations equally). Britain in Turner's day was the world's leading industrial power and, as such, the leading CO_2 emitter in the eighteenth and nineteenth centuries by a long stretch. Those emissions that he painted remain in the atmosphere today and their effect on global warming has been accumulative. Given Turner's deep interest in science, in particular theories of light and colour, it is likely he would have suspected that the extraordinarily vivid sunsets he was capturing in watercolour and oils late in his career were influenced by the refraction of light through particles of pollution.

As well as a witness, Turner became an interpreter who, the wider his observations became, seemed to feel a responsibility to create images that spoke for and defined his age. His pictures of steam power in the 1840s were unique for placing steamboats and rail in serious works of art and being painted with what looked to some observers like steam itself. They were not his first pictures to challenge critics and collectors. An undercurrent of radicalism, social as well as painterly, entered his work. His pictures of warfare focused on its victims. He took up humanitarian and libertarian causes and painted tragic pictures of human suffering as if asking for a new morality to match the material advances of the age.

Turner was not the painter-equivalent of a photo-journalist, yet on occasions a newspaper story would serve as the initial inspiration for a sublime and universalising treatment of a specific topical event (as, for example, with the early topical protest songs of Bob Dylan, which have themselves transcended their era). *A Disaster at Sea* (no.116) is an example of the works by Turner that the curators have chosen to identify as 'cause paintings'. One hundred and twenty female convicts and children on board the *Amphitrite* bound for Australia (probably from Millbank Prison, whose demolition paved the way for what is now Tate Britain) were left to drown by the captain on account of their criminalised status when the ship hit a storm in the Channel. The painting was triggered by a newspaper report, while its epic pyramidal composition was suggested by Géricault's *Raft of the Medusa* (no.117) – which also wrought sublime drama from a contemporary tragedy at sea.

We should not idolise Turner. His investment in 1805 in a Jamaican cattle ranch worked by enslaved labour suggests he had reset his own moral compass by 1840 when he painted *Slave Ship* (no.119) as an indictment of the slave trade. As problematic as that picture is for commentators who see its visual splendour as mitigating the horror of its subject, Turner was the only artist to reveal Middle Passage history in a London exhibition. There are no precedents or comparisons for many of his other pictures either, unless we look to European contemporaries like Delacroix, Géricault or Goya, and none at all for his pictures of steam. In painting these themes, in a new way, he stood alone.

Of all Turner's modern subjects, *Slave Ship* is surely the most salient today, as Black Lives Matter demands that we confront histories of enslavement, exploitation and genocide whose legacies live on. The painting – and the notorious *Zong* massacre on which it may be based – have an especially powerful afterlife in contemporary works of art and literature that speak back to the inexpressible horror of the transatlantic slavery from what Paul Gilroy has characterised as the Black Atlantic perspective. These include reimaginings by artists The Otolith Group, Sondra Perry and Kara Walker, and in literature like David Dabydeen's book-length poem *Turner*, Winsome Pinnock's play *Rockets and Blue Lights* (named after another Turner picture) and M. Nourbese Philip's book *Zong!* These contemporary works of art are surely located 'in the wake' of the slave ship – a powerful notion introduced by Christina Sharpe in her eponymous 2016 study. The painting itself is now too fragile to travel to London. Perhaps its absence will make its subject more present, inviting reflection rather than looking. At Tate Britain The Otolith Group's film *Hydra Decapita* (2010), in Tate's Collection,

will be screened for the duration of Turner's Modern World. Folding the past into future, and the Atlantic Ocean into the galaxy, its soundtrack combines Ruskin's famous description of the painting, sung like an ancestral lament, with the intoned astrological and hydrological speculations of Gerald Donald, previously of Drexciya, the seminal Detroit techno band and influential afrofuturist touchstone, and now one half of Dopplereffekt.

Also absent in London are loans from other American collections that we judged should stay stateside during the covid pandemic. They will now join the exhibition in the Kimbell Art Museum, Fort Worth, which then moves to join *Slave Ship* in the Museum of Fine Arts, Boston. We thank Eric M. Lee and George Shackelford in Fort Worth and Matthew Teitelbaum, Frederick Ilchman and Julia Welch in Boston for their enthusiastic response to this exhibition. For Tate it has been curated by David Blayney Brown, Amy Concannon and Sam Smiles, working as equal partners with James Finch and organised by Hattie Spires, covering Amy's maternity leave. Andrea Schlieker, Carolyn Kerr, Kiko Noda, Wendy Lothian and the late Gillian Buttimer have given generously of their experience and support. We are very grateful to the Tavolozza Foundation as part of the Turner's Modern World Exhibition Supporters Circle, and to Tate Americas Foundation, Tate Patrons and Tate Members for their additional support of the exhibition. We thank HM Government, the Department for Digital, Culture, Media and Sport and Arts Council England for providing and arranging Government Indemnity for the exhibition in London.

As always, we are deeply indebted to our lenders for so generously sharing important works. The National Gallery, director Gabriele Finaldi, Susan Foister and Christine Riding, and the Museu Calouste Gulbenkian and director Penelope Curtis have made extraordinary contributions to the London exhibition. To all our lenders, our profound thanks.

Alex Farquharson
Director Tate Britain, London

Curators' Acknowledgements

We are deeply grateful to all those colleagues, scholars and friends who have supported this exhibition and publication. Eric M. Lee and George Shackelford at the Kimbell Art Museum, Fort Worth, and Matthew Teitelbaum, Frederick Ilchman and Julia Welch at MFA Boston turned their enthusiasm for the project into an active partnership. It has been a pleasure and a privilege to work with them. At Tate, Maria Balshaw, Alex Farquharson, Andrea Schlieker and Carolyn Kerr have sustained and encouraged us.

Any Turner exhibition must draw on previous scholarship and we would like to acknowledge particular debts to Anthony Bailey, Leo Costello, Jason Edwards, Gillian Forrester, James Hamilton, Elizabeth Jacklin, Pieter van der Merwe, Jan Piggott, Cecilia Powell, Eric Shanes, Ian Warrell and Andrew Wilton. David Dabydeen, David Dibosa, Kodwo Eshun, Delia Jarrett-Macauley, Mark Miller and the BAME Network at Tate have offered fresh insights and helped steer crucial aspects of the project. Our thanks also to Lord Bragg, Timothy Clode, Susan Foister, Matthew Hargraves, Colin Harrison, Ranjit Hoskote, Nirmalya Kumar, Lowell Libson, William Mirza, Jane Munro, Martin Myrone, Christine Riding and Inigo Thomas for their assistance. Courtauld Curatorial Intern Guillaume Fabius made an important contribution to the research and administration of the exhibition in its early stages.

Within the Tate project team we thank Kiko Noda, Exhibition Registrar and Wendy Lothian, Senior Programme Manager, International Collaborations for their calm professionalism in difficult circumstances; Andy Shiel, Liam Tebbs, Kwai Lau and Juleigh Gordon-Orr in Art Handling for developing socially distanced ways to install works; David Hingley, Emma Garrett and Renata Smialek for helping us to open the exhibition safely. Jacqueline Moon, Vivian Yip, Rosie Freemantle, Rachel Crome, Natasha Trenwith, Rebecca Hellen, Amy Griffin, Gabriella Macaro, Gates Sofer, Roger Murray and Adrian Moore have worked, often through lockdown, to conserve and prepare works for display.

Thanks to Kirsteen McSwein, Sam McGuire, Richard Martin and Ese Jade Onojeruo in Interpretation and Learning; Tate Library and Archive; La Kingsbeer, Mark Crowley and Abi Laughton in Marketing; Cecily Carbone and Kathy Maniura in Press; Scott Morris in Digital and Sam Mackay in Development. Tate Senior Editor Alice Chasey and Picture Researcher Emma O'Neill, copyeditor Colin Grant, and designer Geoff Williamson at The Studio of Williamson Curran have made a beautiful reality of this book against what have sometimes seemed almost insuperable odds. To everyone who has stood by us, our heartfelt thanks.

David Blayney Brown
Amy Concannon
James Finch
Sam Smiles

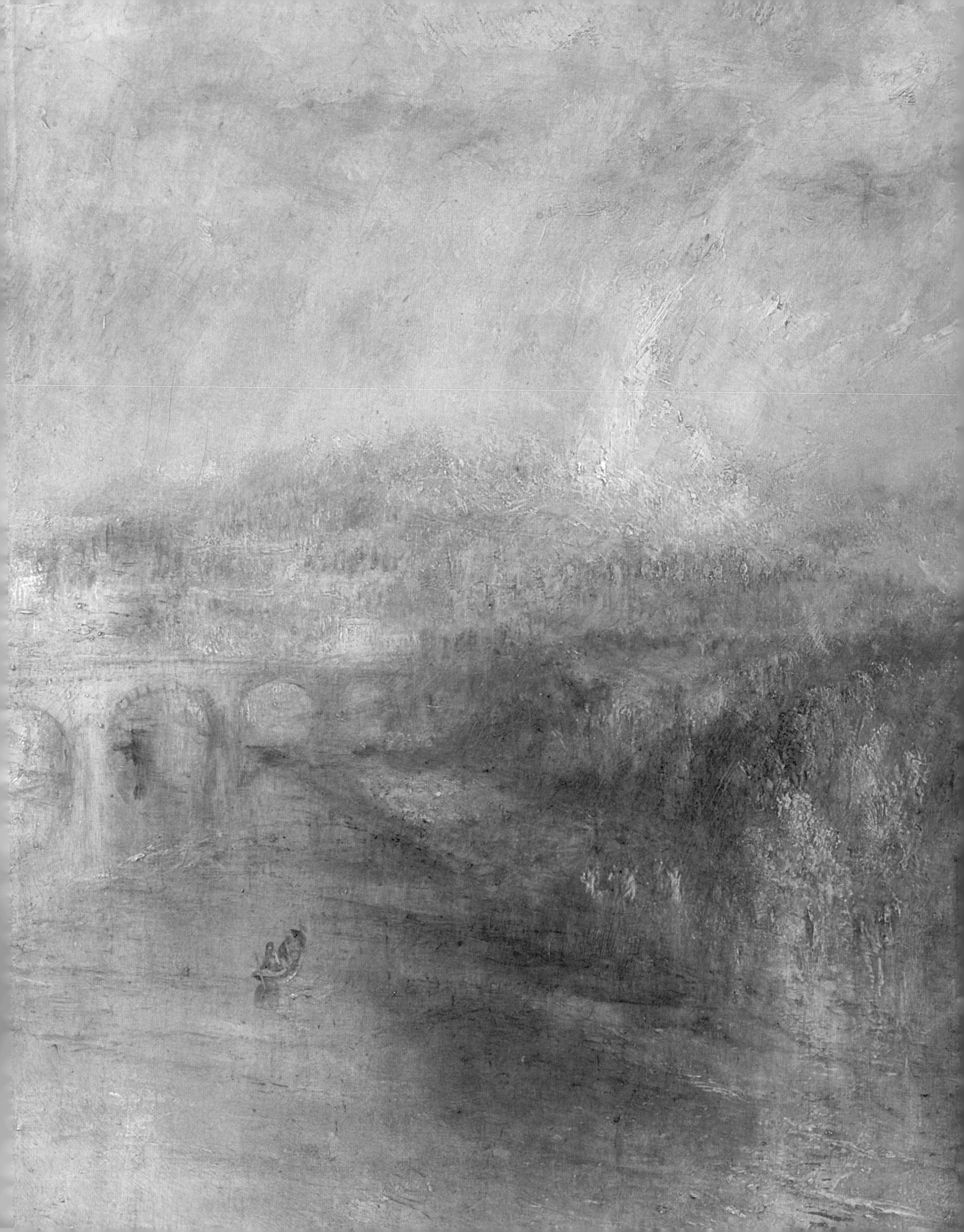

Introduction

David Blayney Brown
and Sam Smiles

'The world has never seen anything like this picture.'[1] The novelist William Makepeace Thackeray, reviewing Turner's *Rain, Steam, and Speed – The Great Western Railway* (no.135), was not exaggerating. Turner's lifelong interest in the inventions, events, politics, society, culture and science of his time – the focus of this exhibition – resulted in many of his most original works and transformed his way of painting. None of his British contemporaries came near to matching him, and it is even more remarkable that this artist, who began as a topographical watercolourist, regarded himself as essentially a landscape painter and was so enthused by the history and art of the past, created such a vivid and comprehensive testament to his own era – not just as a witness but an interpreter and tribune for his generation.

Turner's Britain did not suffer the existential traumas that impelled Théodore Géricault and Eugène Delacroix in France, Francisco de Goya in Spain and Karl Friedrich Schinkel in Germany to reinvent themselves and their art. Nevertheless, he lived through a truly volatile age. Born just before the American War of Independence began, he lived to see the construction of the Crystal Palace for the Great Exhibition of 1851, a spectacular display of technological innovation and Britain's new-found sense of itself as a global superpower. His early adulthood coincided with the wars against Revolutionary and Napoleonic France (1793–1815). Freed from serious competition by the allied victory, Britain's empire entered a long expansionary phase. Elsewhere, the post-war period was marked by the Greek War of Independence (1821–32), and revolutions in France and Belgium (1830) and more widely across Europe (1848). They did not reach Britain, although pent-up demand for social and political reform flared up in many regions and in 1848 guns were stationed in Hyde Park.

Meanwhile, the nation's economic and political fabric underwent continual and far-reaching alterations. Industrial development brought machines to the workplace, the spread of steam power and a massive redistribution of the rapidly growing population from the country to newly industrialised cities. The speed of change was dizzying and led the philosopher and political economist John Stuart Mill to observe that 'the nineteenth century will be known to posterity as the era of one of the greatest revolutions of which history has preserved the remembrance, in the human mind, and in the whole constitution of human society'.[2] Mill was right to recognise a rolling and (largely) bloodless revolution but not everyone was sanguine about progress and its causes. There was widespread unrest in the 1810s as mechanisation destroyed jobs and familiar working practices. Successive administrations resisted what they perceived to be dangerous ideas, legislating to curb revolutionary sympathies in the 1790s, opposing campaigns for electoral reform – most notoriously, sending militia to crush a peaceful demonstration in Manchester in 1819 (the Peterloo Massacre) – passing the Six Acts to suppress free speech soon afterwards and putting Chartist leaders, also agitating for electoral reform, on trial in the 1830s and 1840s. While creating immense wealth, the nation was blighted by dire conditions in factories, mills and urban slums, poor education and public health. Soot and smoke filled the air, blackening buildings and rotting lungs. Cholera ravaged cities. Amidst all this, a manufacturing elite and burgeoning middle class emerged to challenge the old landed aristocracy. Progressive legislation, often disputed by those whose privileges it diminished, mitigated religious discrimination, widened the electoral franchise, improved working conditions and ended first the slave trade and then slavery itself in British territories.[3] Arguments seethed about the state's treatment of the poor as well as the winners and losers from free trade, with far-reaching legislation enacted in each case.[4]

Art, science and literature flourished but the response of many painters to such tumultuous, transformative times was simply to turn away. Established genres and modes of representation struggled to accommodate current realities. As a student at the Royal Academy, Turner was taught to avoid the contemporary and political. Art rose in seriousness to the extent that it elevated itself above the temporal. Only recently it had been thought normal, even preferable, to

     Previous page: *Rain, Steam, and Speed – The Great Western Railway* 1844 (no.135)

depict recent events in idealised terms, even employing the classical nude for contemporary figures. William Hazlitt, the radical critic and sometime painter, found the 'spirit of the age' in its writers and politicians and argued, paradoxically, that 'we are so far advanced in the Arts and Sciences, that we live in retrospect, and doat [sic] on past achievements'.[5] He found painting resistant to modernity and lacking the 'gusto' he admired in his favourite old masters. Hazlitt died in 1830, never saw Turner's most modern pictures and was selective in his critique of art. Moreover, he had ignored the fact that some of Turner's predecessors and contemporaries found inspiration in the contemporary world. Interest in William Hogarth's morality pictures of earlier Georgian England revived with the publication of John Ireland's *Hogarth Illustrated* (1794–9), their inclusion in a retrospective of eighteenth-century artists at the British Institution in 1814 and expensive purchases by the Prince Regent and Turner's friends and patrons including William Beckford and John Soane. P.J. de Loutherbourg painted modern subjects from

battles to industry and created a paradigm of an engaged contemporary artist for Turner to adopt and extend. Others mentioned in this book include Joseph Wright of Derby, William Hodges, Robert Ker Porter, Benjamin Robert Haydon – and Géricault and Delacroix when they exhibited in London, a city they found far more culturally stimulating and receptive than post-Napoleonic Paris. David Wilkie's scenes of everyday life – and sometimes modern history – made him the most genuinely influential artist of the younger generation. Print-shop windows were full of scabrous skits on current events and people in the news by brilliant caricaturists like James Gillray and George Cruikshank. Paul Pry (William Heath) and Shortshanks (Robert Seymour) turned their comic genius on the 'March of Intellect' (no.2) or the 'small inconveniences' of steam locomotion (no.1).

Turner took up modern subjects, as he did everything else, competitively. What were other artists missing or doing that he might do better? But his modern outlook cannot be explained

1
Robert Seymour,
Locomotion, Plate 2nd,
c.1830.
Hand-coloured etching on
paper, 16.2 × 22.8,
Wellcome Collection

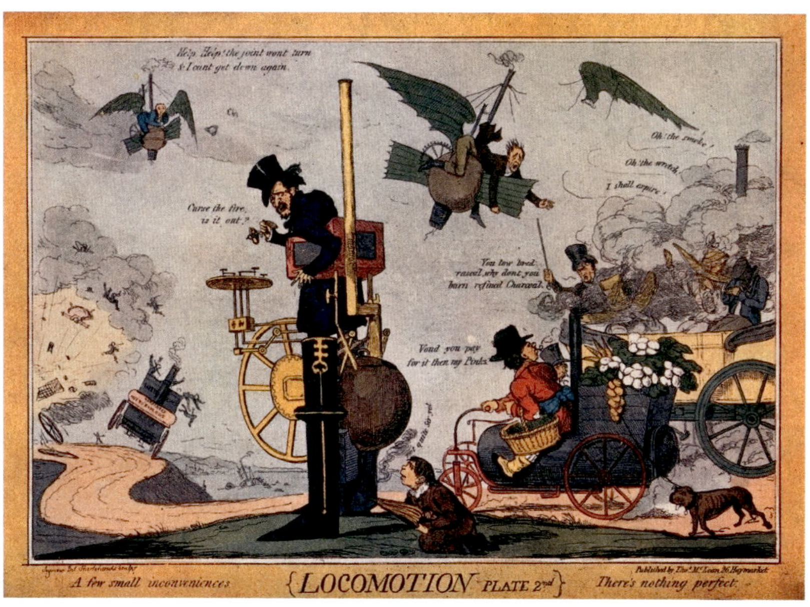

by art alone, any more than by the London upbringing to which John Ruskin attributed it in his first book *Modern Painters*. Clients, patrons, and friends in many fields must have played a part. The aristocrats and landed gentry who supported his early career were often also entrepreneurs, mining magnates, canal-builders and pioneering agriculturalists. Later, he was employed principally by merchants and industrialists who had made their fortunes from trade. If he had little encouragement from British royalty – not for want of trying – a long acquaintance with the progressively minded King of France, Louis-Philippe, was some compensation. Working with writers, poets and publishers widened his perspectives. One of the most scientifically connected of artists, he had friends whose research was upending former certainties about the age of the earth, the nature of the physical world and the forces acting on it. He attended their lectures at the Royal Institution, *conversaziones* where the arts and sciences met, and was a founder member of the Athenaeum, the club whose membership was based on intellectual achievement rather than inherited privilege.

In these enlightened circles what had seemed fixed and ordered, socially or physically, was now seen as dynamic and evolutionary. Analysts like Mill and Thomas Carlyle remarked the 'mighty change in our whole manner of existence' in a 'mechanical age' marked by 'transition [and] intellectual anarchy'.[6] Turner, whose 'wonderful range of mind' impressed his contemporary John Constable,[7] must have been in his element, but the implications of all this for art were rarely discussed. Critics who talked about modern painters to distinguish them from old masters seldom argued for modern subjects. Typically forthright, Ruskin did so in *Modern Painters*:

> All classicality, all middle-age patent reviving, is utterly vain and absurd; if we are to do anything great, good, awful, religious, it must be got out of our own little island and out of these very times, railroads and all; if a British painter, I say this in all seriousness,

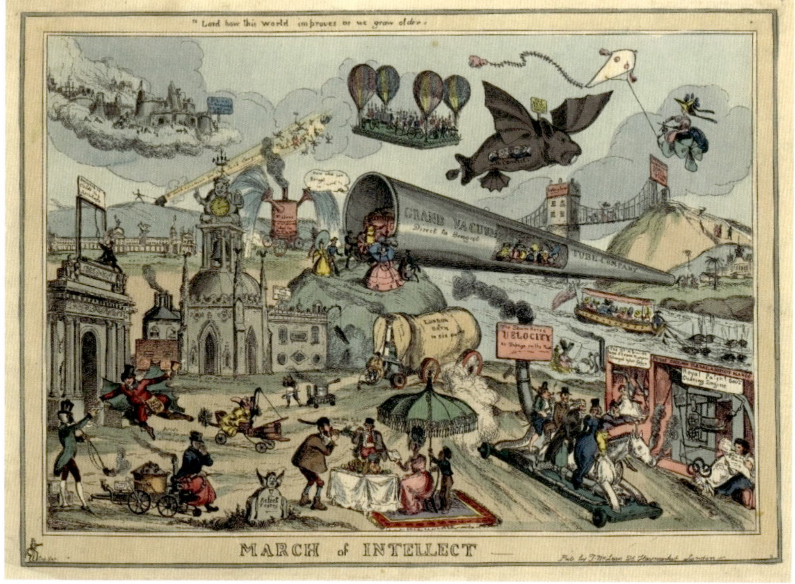

2
William Heath,
March of Intellect 1829,
print. Hand-coloured
etching on paper, published
by Thomas McLean,
The Trustees of the
British Museum

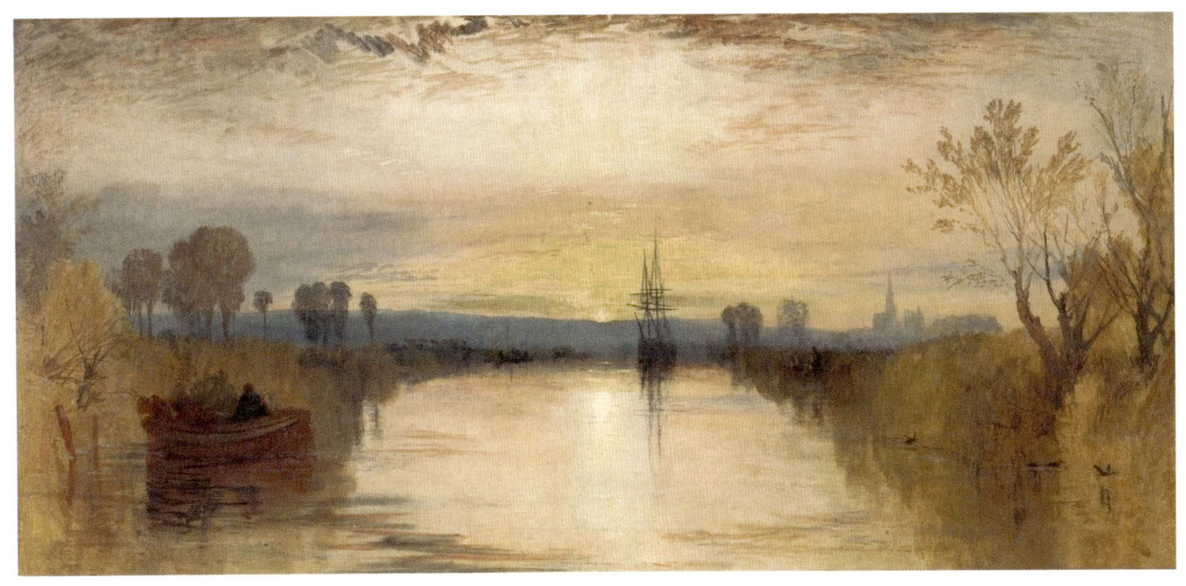

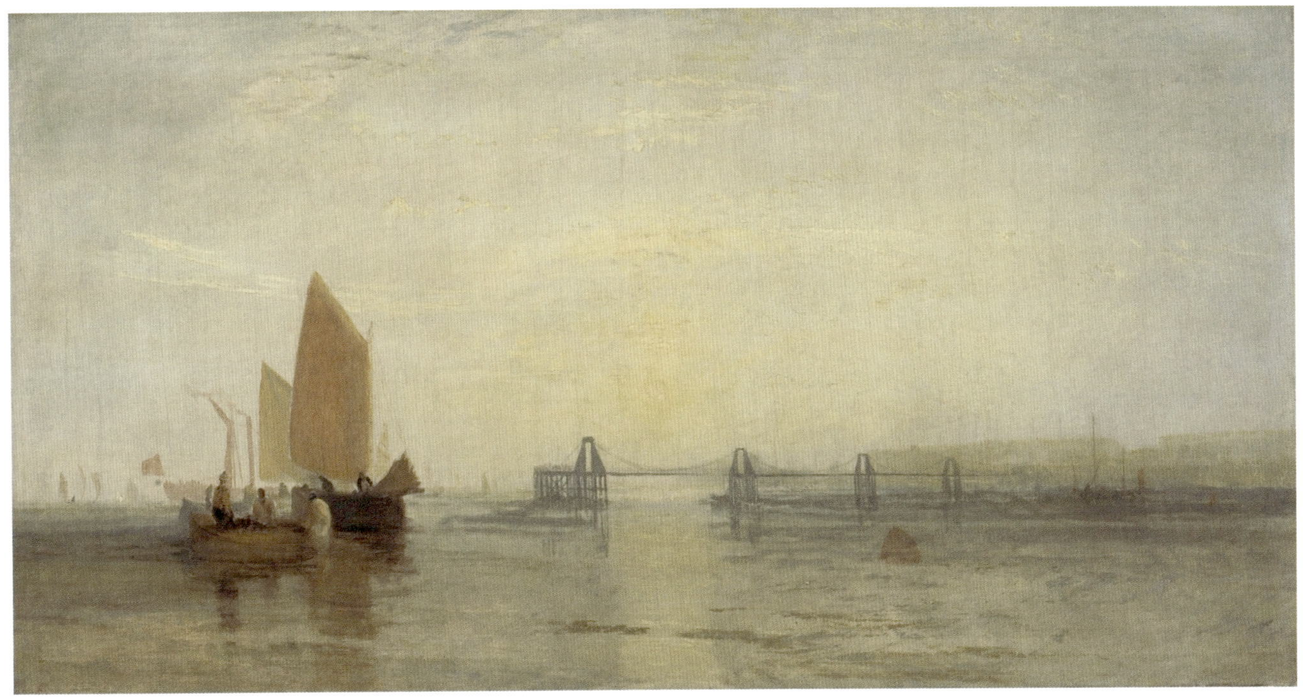

3 *Chichester Canal* c.1828. Oil paint on canvas, 65.4 × 134.6, Tate
4 *The Chain Pier, Brighton* c.1828. Oil paint on canvas, 71.1 × 136.5, Tate

cannot make historical characters out of the British House of Peers, he cannot paint history; and, if he cannot make a Madonna of a British girl of the nineteenth century, he cannot paint one at all.[8]

Typically inconsistent, Ruskin disliked or ignored many of Turner's most modern pictures, especially those containing things he loathed like trains and steamboats, and his counter-claim that Turner's greatest achievement was his understanding of the natural world has been a major impediment to appreciating how modern he really was. Emphasising subject pictures at least on this occasion, Ruskin omitted landscape painting and it was left to an anonymous writer to extend the argument, asking if those who prefer travelling abroad to what is on their doorstep are 'more absurd, nay... *so* blind and ridiculous' as painters who persist 'in *not* seeing the subjects everywhere presented for their pencils in modern life, social and otherwise, as it exists among us?'[9]

Turner began to observe his modern world while still a boy, travelling round the country as a topographical draughtsman and watercolourist. When war came, he painted some of its key battles, its impact on the home front, and state-of-the-nation surveys of Britain and the British, which he continued during the ensuing peace with pictures of canals (no.3), piers (no.4), steamboats and the railway. First topography, then landscape he transformed into media flexible and responsive enough to accommodate an array of contemporary impressions, rural and urban, at home and abroad: agriculture, architecture, travel on land and sea, work at, in Ruskin's words, 'forge and furnace, helm and plough',[10] leisure, industry, inventions, defence, war and its aftermath, and social and political events. His watercolours and exhibition pictures show a world in flux, often wreathed in smoke and smog. A sailing vessel converted to steam plies the water off Dover (no.139); steamboats take over the Thames, Seine and Rhine (nos.133, 143, 161); a new tug tows the old *Temeraire* to be broken up (no.134); a road bridge is superseded by one for the Great Western Railway (no.135). Soon after the Poor Law is amended to deny able-bodied

men assistance outside the workhouse, the old Houses of Parliament burn down (no.109). Ruskin's claim that the fire was Turner's 'only new sensation' in an uninspiring decade[11] was nonsense when others were arriving all the time and generating the pictures of 'old England and new England combined' that made a lasting impression on the painter Ford Madox Brown.[12] The transitions Turner portrayed were matched in the dynamic way he conceived and painted them. *The Fighting Temeraire* evolved from an oil sketch, including the Nore lightship moored near the naval anchorage (no.141). Pictures of Louis-Philippe's visit to Queen Victoria (nos.157–9) and Antarctic whaling (nos.154–6) probably emerged from the stock of sketches he kept in his studio, awaiting some immediate stimulus to give them subjects or complete them for exhibition. An industrial scene started many years earlier was repainted as the casting of a statue of the Duke of Wellington (no.12).

What Turner thought or wanted others to think about the new world he depicted – the '64,000 dollar question' for one recent commentator[13] – is difficult to establish. His political views, which he never made explicit but have been variously interpreted, are discussed elsewhere in this book. Were his pictures of social and technological change elegies for a vanishing past or celebrations of the new – or both? He was clearly the most observant artist of the Georgian and Victorian eras, enjoyed friendships with some of the best minds of the day, and appreciated practical improvements, using steamboats and trains and installing a plumbed lavatory at home. His paintings are an extraordinary record of his time. But can we detect his personal opinions about many of their subjects or, more difficult, point to a consistent approach in his treatment of them? Verses he wrote for them, or drafted for a topographical survey of England's southern coast, are indicative, but although the latter comment on the Napoleonic blockade and other issues facing coastal communities, they were too incoherent for publication, and thereafter he worked through visual allusions and associations, sometimes suggesting various things at once and not easily decoded even by contemporaries who shared

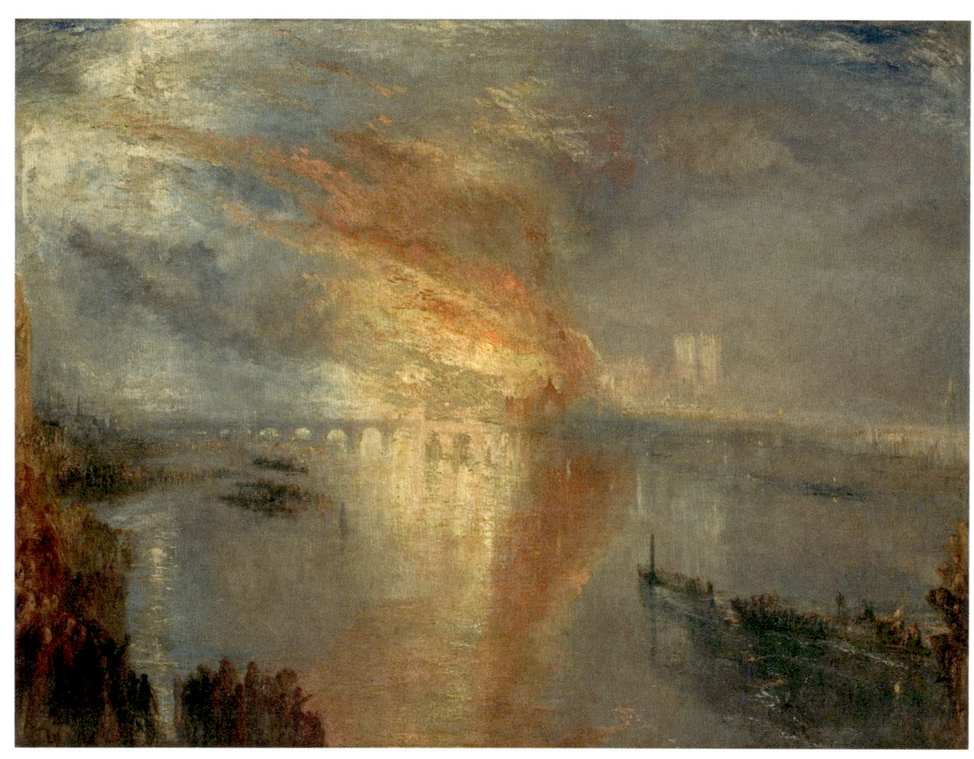

more of his frame of reference than we can today. He seems to have enjoyed teasing Ruskin with hidden meanings. As a professional artist whose major commissions came from wealthy patrons, he had learned to be circumspect; it would have been unwise to openly support causes they might consider contentious. In any case, his understanding of the world seems to have been highly nuanced, never promoting doctrinaire positions in his paintings but, instead, putting human experience at the centre of his interest.

It is surely significant that Turner's deepest adult friendship with a patron was with the radically minded Yorkshire landowner Walter Fawkes, but whether they were drawn to each other because they thought alike or the patron influenced the painter in a liberal direction is moot. Turner's admiration for Byron's poetry was encouraged by Fawkes but probably also self-directed, and he was as happy to work for Fawkes's Tory opponents in the Lascelles family and for the very conservative writer Walter Scott. Early patrons included 'West India merchants' – the favoured euphemism for plantation and slave owners – as well as abolitionists. In 1805 he bought a £100 share in a tontine scheme to fund a cattle-breeding ranch in Jamaica worked by slave labour.[14] Although he later sided with the abolitionists, in the early 1800s his clients' ethics and incomes are unlikely to have perturbed him any more than his own. But many of the allegiances he made and pictures he painted on his own initiative about great liberal causes of the day – political reform, religious toleration, Greek independence, ending the slave trade – as well as those taking the side of victims of war, colonial deportation and man-made and natural disasters suggest he became progressively reformist in much of his thinking. He never flaunted the wealth he made through his own efforts, lived modestly and sympathised with those less fortunate. More often than royal or state ceremonial he pictured places and events – in modern parlance – from below, locating a turnip harvest in sight of Windsor Castle as 'near Slough' (no.83), as if answering the same 'levelling muse' to whom Hazlitt credited Wordsworth's poetry.[15] When the interest on his investments fell, he told his friend and fellow painter George Jones, 'I like 5% for my money and the quartern loaf at a shilling. Ask the poor man what he likes: he would say, "I like the quartern loaf at 8 pence & interest at 4%."'[16]

Just as there had been little encouragement for artists to champion modern subjects, Turner's attempts met with a mixed reception. Some he never sold, others he deliberately kept, and critics were slow to pay attention. A notable exception was the engraver, editor and polemicist John Landseer – father of the painter Edwin – who praised *The Battle of Trafalgar* (no.35) as a pioneering '*British epic picture*' and recorded the actual subject of *Spithead: Boat's Crew Recovering an Anchor* (no.41) as 'Danish ships seized at Copenhagen'.[17] While in 1799 Turner's first picture of modern warfare, *The Battle of the Nile* (location unknown), was said to have 'compleatly [sic] failed' to live up to its main motif, an exploding warship,[18] sometimes his subjects were obscure, or just too convoluted to be readily understood. For example, *A Country Blacksmith Disputing upon the Price of Iron* (no.85) was not just anodyne rustic genre, or humorous like Edward Penny's *Gossiping Blacksmith* (Tate) shown in the Royal Academy's first exhibition in 1769, but was about the impact of a new tax to pay for the war effort; yet as a contemporary critic noted, this was 'too much to express in a picture, nor is it reasonable to expect that such a story should be clearly told on canvas'.[19] *The Field of Waterloo* (no.37), which threw critics because it neither celebrated the victory nor took the British side, was described as 'allegorical' rather than 'a particular battle'[20] or belittled as a 'drunken hubbub on an illumination night'.[21] Turner's critics liked to make fun of his profoundly serious pictures such as *Slave Ship (Slavers Throwing Overboard the Dead and Dying – Typhon Coming on)* (no.119) because these contentious subjects made them feel uncomfortable. Snobbery was another favourite tactic: *Keelmen Heaving in Coals by Night* (no.6), apparently painted for the Manchester industrialist Henry McConnell as a celebration of British muscle to contrast with Venetian lassitude, was 'glorious moon-light wasted on dingy coal-whippers'.[22]

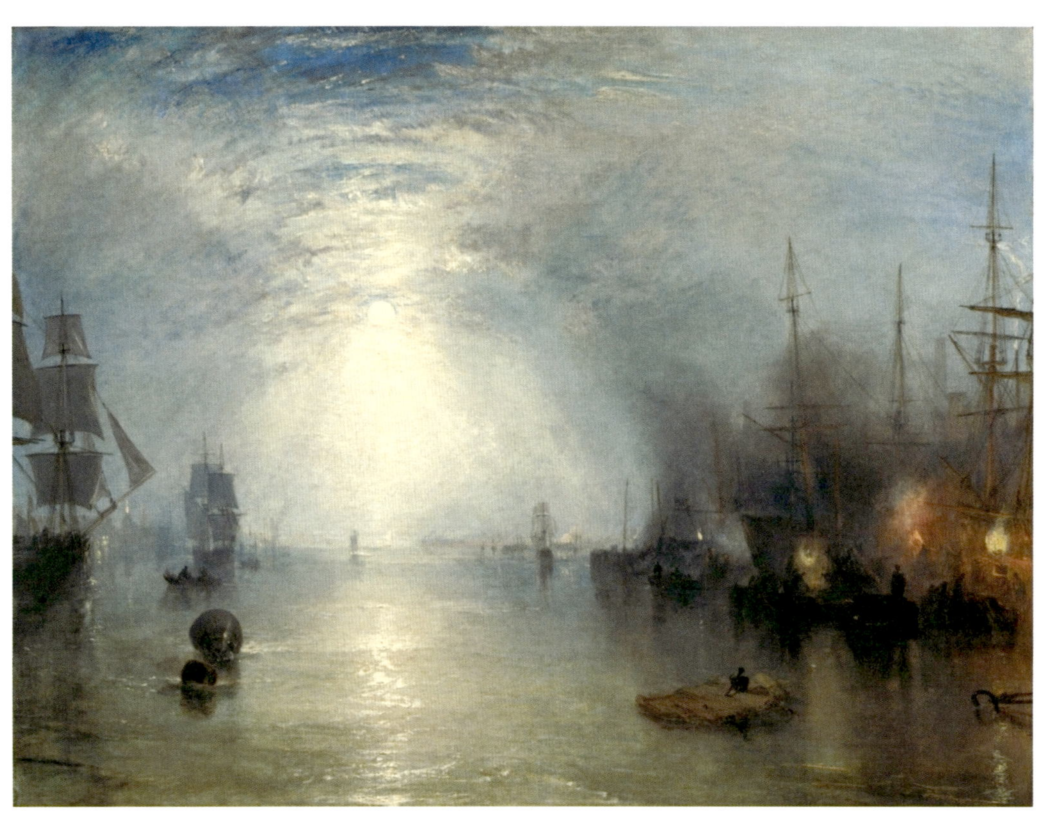

 Keelmen Heaving in Coals by Moonlight 1835. Oil paint on canvas, 92.3 × 122.8, National Gallery of Art, Washington, DC

Yet if workmen were unworthy subjects for
that reviewer, others personalised *The Fighting
Temeraire* (no.134) as 'a noble human being',[23] a
'superannuated veteran led by a sprightly boy'[24]
or a 'venerable victor in a hundred fights'.[25] For
the last critic it was 'the most wonderful of all
the works of the greatest master of the age' and,
for a correspondent of Ruskin's, Turner's 'first,
almost prophetic idea of smoke, soot, iron, and
steam'.[26] Steam, used to greater ends in early
Victorian Britain than anywhere else and 'almost
an Englishman' in the eyes of the American Ralph
Waldo Emerson,[27] 'fills mankind with schemes'
according to Turner's scientist friend Mary
Somerville.[28] Constable thought Turner painted
with 'tinted steam',[29] and his pictures of steam
power between 1831 and 1844 brought elemental
and mechanical energies into perfect fusion
with his late style. While it often caused derision
and painting a train at all seemed 'insane', *The
Times* recognised that 'railways have furnished
Turner with a new field for the exhibition of his
eccentric style'[30] and said much the same about
his pictures of the whaling industry (nos.153–6).
Turner's virtuoso handling and swirling, vortical
compositions that sweep us into his pictorial
world or send a train bursting out of it at 50 or
60 miles an hour can be seen as allegories of
the accelerating tempo of the age. Allegory was
not a dead language for the critic who wrote in
1839 that the *Temeraire* was treated 'historically
and allegorically'[31] or for Turner who must
have painted the Parliament fire at least partly
because, like the radical *Examiner*, he realised
that the 'calamity reads like an allegory'.[32]

What would Turner be making art about today?
Climate change, pandemic disease, pollution,
migration, deportation, refugees, trafficking,
his country's identity and place in Europe and
the world, fires, floods, whatever is to replace
vehicle and air travel, AI? That our crises and
preoccupations come so readily to mind is a
measure of his breadth of vision. How would he be
working now? Unphased by new daguerreotypes
brought from Paris by his friend Samuel Rogers
and an 'inquisitive' visitor himself to J.J.E. Mayall's
photographic studio, he would probably not be
a painter or photographer but communicating in

other media. He would know he was not living in
the most modern place in the world and that the
future was arriving elsewhere. He would find new
ways to define the present, address its concerns
and stir its conscience. Writing about the launch
of a merchant ship at Greenwich, Turner set
himself and his nation a challenge:

> Why not in Britain Novelty is found
> Why should not novelty again resound
> Then try on Thamias fertile shore.[33]

His pictures more than justified his hopes but
not in a narrow, nationalist sense. He began
as a British artist, became European and now
belongs to the world. To paraphrase Hazlitt on
Wordsworth's poetry, Turner's art was a 'pure
emanation of the Spirit of the Age [and] one of
the innovations of the time'.[34]

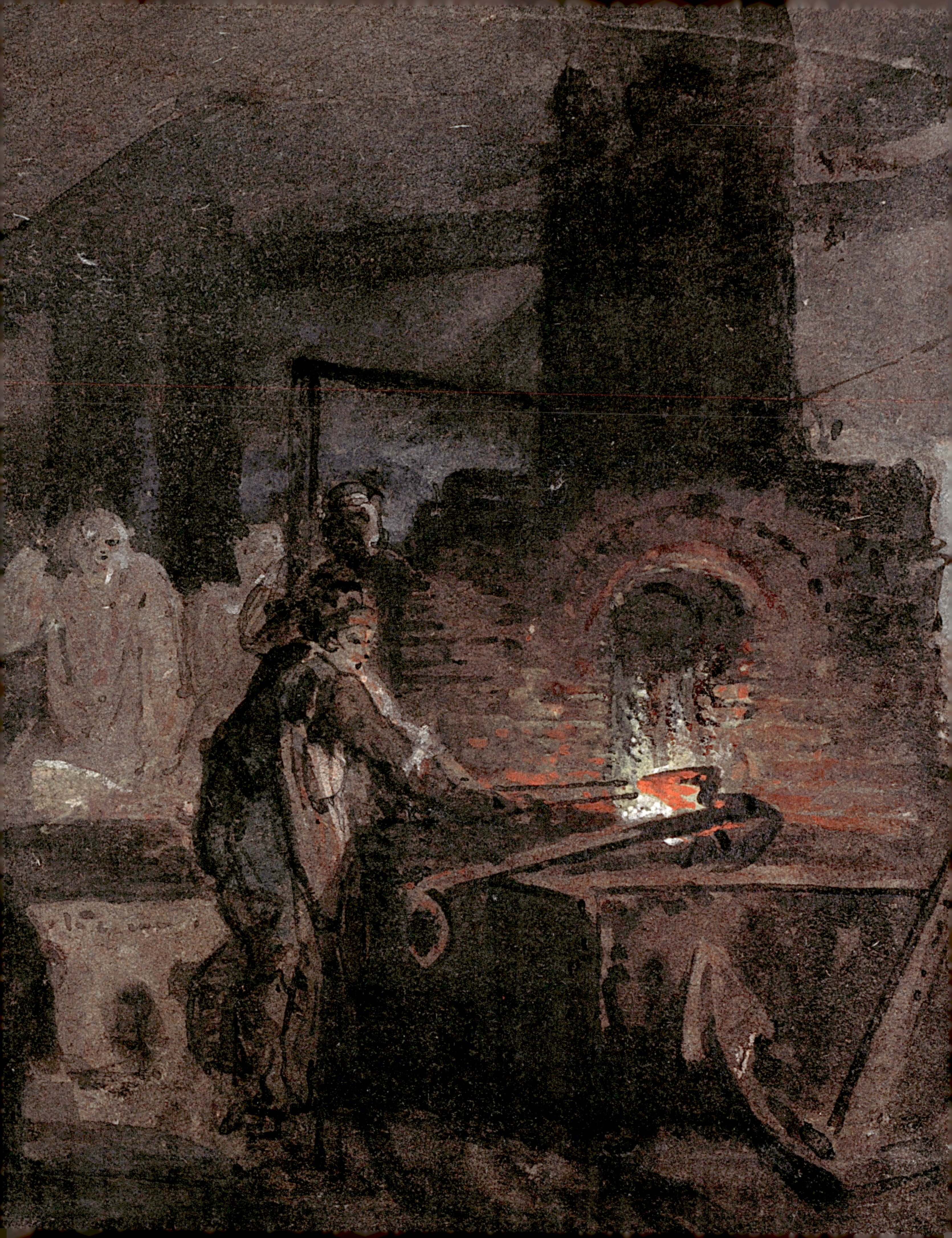

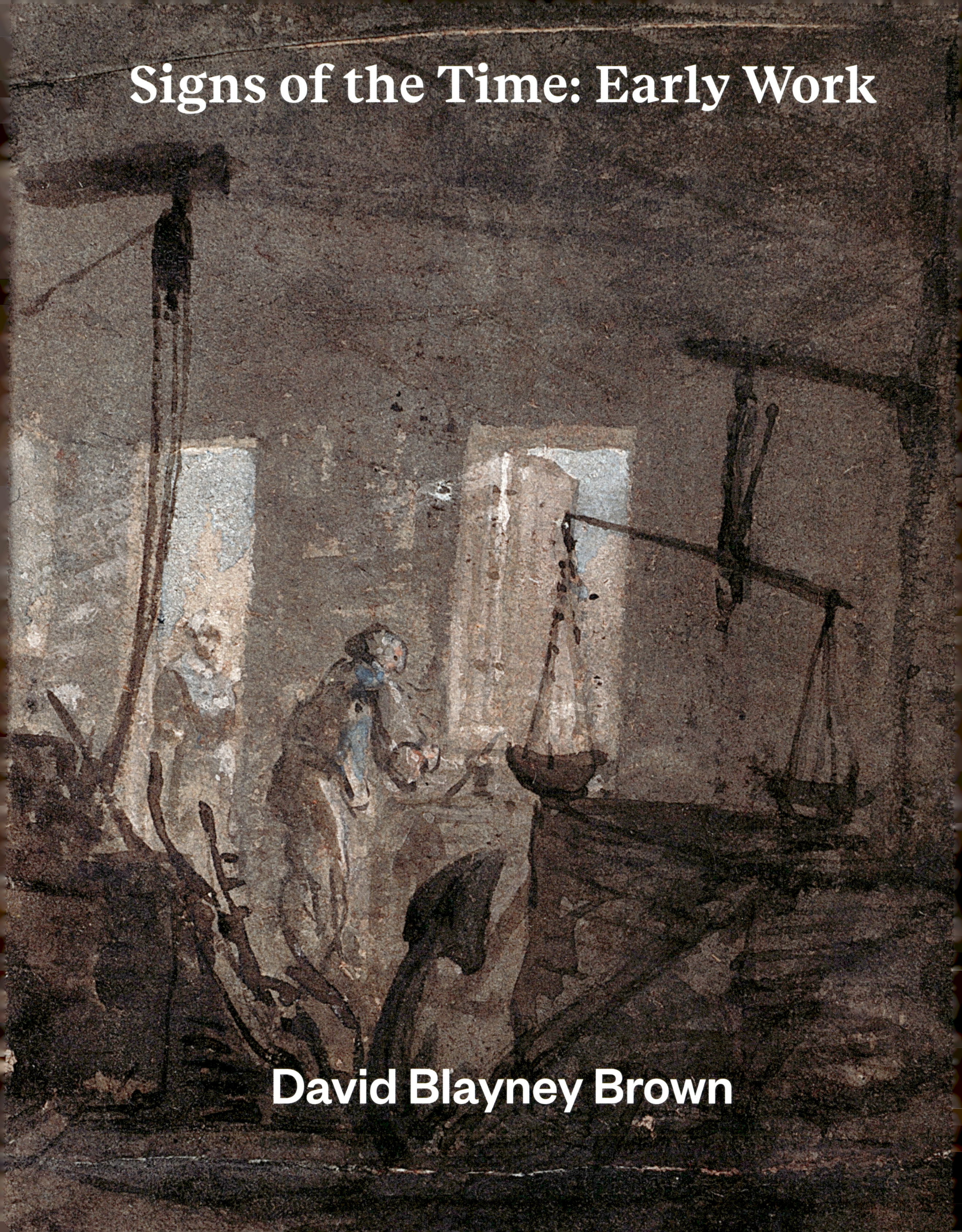
Signs of the Time: Early Work
David Blayney Brown

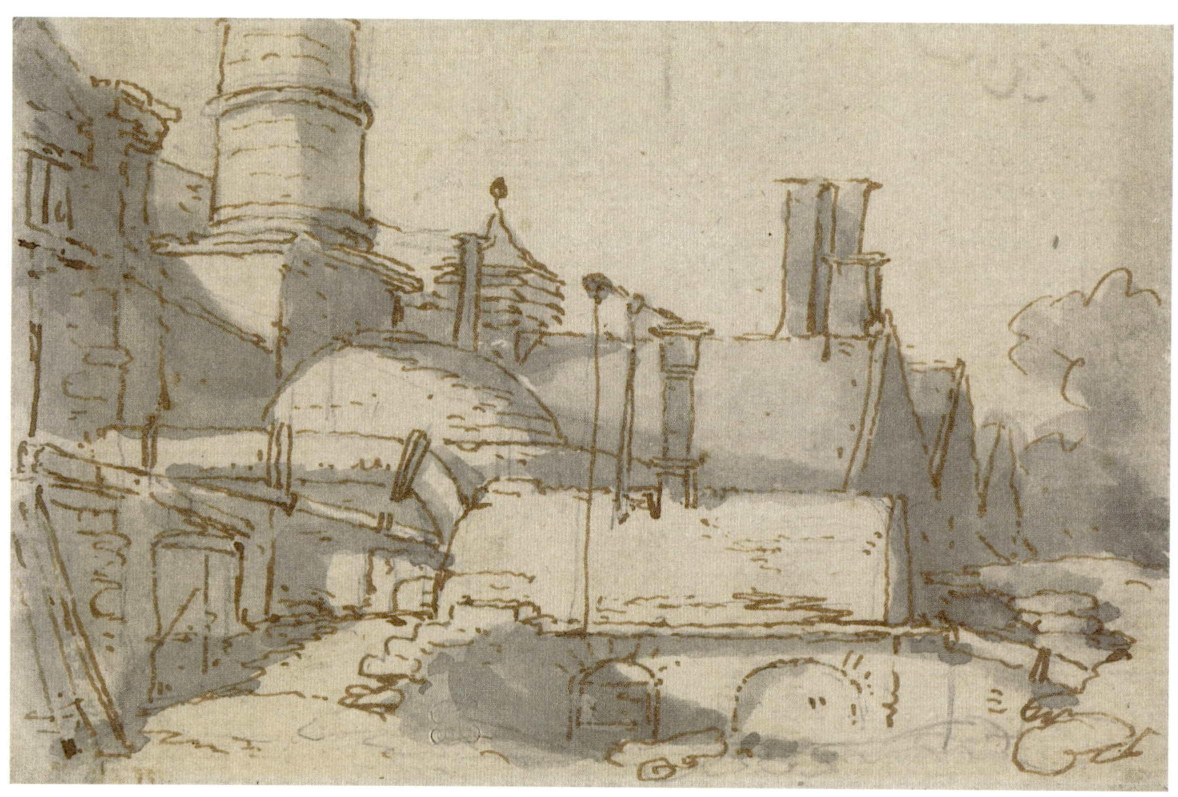

Previous Page: *Interior of a Forge: Making Anchors* 1796–7 (no.14)
7 Philip James de Loutherbourg, *The Boiler House and Casting House of a Furnace, Probably Bedlam Furnace, at Coalbrookdale* 1786 or 1800.
Pen and ink, graphite and watercolour on paper, 7.3 × 9.5, Tate

Glimpses of contemporary life appeared in Turner's earliest topographical watercolours of picturesque landscapes and historic buildings. They came into sharper focus in urban scenes and in sketches of industrial activity in the Midlands, the North and Wales and of fishermen and mariners around the coast. While he devoted much of his energy to historical subjects in the academic grand style, his first exhibited picture, shown in 1796, was a modern marine. His first picture of modern naval warfare followed in 1799. Tentatively at first, then more confidently, he introduced modern features into imaginary subjects and, conversely, historical interventions to reflect on current concerns.

Turner's studies at the Royal Academy from the age of fourteen contributed little to his contemporary outlook. Modern subjects were not recommended in an institution where students drew from antique sculpture and were encouraged to read Greek and Roman history. Turner supplemented the Academy's curriculum by working for architects, attending the informal 'academy' hosted by the collector Dr Monro and cultivating established artists he could learn from or compete with. For Ruskin, however, it was not so much London's opportunities as the city itself that made Turner the foremost 'modern painter'. In an eloquent if subjective coda to his book *Modern Painters* he contrasted the 'Two Boyhoods' of Turner in the capital and Giorgione in Venice. While Giorgione studied in a 'school' free of 'ignoble care … common and poor … foulness [and] tumult', Turner was surrounded by 'the present work of men' in a 'darksome Vanity Fair'. Near his childhood home, 'Covent Garden after the market' so opened his eyes that 'he not only could endure, but enjoyed and looked for *litter*' and developed 'understanding of and regard for the poor'.[35] Describing a dystopian London that might have come from Hogarth's darkest moral subjects, Ruskin managed simultaneously to argue that Turner had abandoned its vices and chaos to paint nature – his main justification for Turner's modernity – and become, as Ruskin himself wanted to be, a social critic addressing 'human truth'.

Ruskin's remarks notwithstanding, London was never a dominant subject for Turner. His first watercolours of it are conventional topography influenced by architectural draughtsmen like Thomas Malton – whom he called his 'real master', having worked in his studio in 1789 – and including rather stilted versions of the figures in city scenes by Paul Sandby, Edward Dayes and Thomas Rowlandson. But he was a fast learner and soon made watercolour – the hottest medium of the 1790s, exhibited in its own right – the vehicle for original work. *The Pantheon, the Morning after the Fire*, shown at the Academy in 1792 (no.16) when he was sixteen, is more animated than the aquatint views published in Malton's *Picturesque Tour through London and Westminster* that year. It drew on his drawing skills and personal contacts depicting a topical, newsworthy incident. He was soon working for the Pantheon's architect, James Wyatt, and made a watercolour of its burnt-out interior for another architect, Thomas Hardwick. The Pantheon in Oxford Street was a London landmark, recently used as an opera house. Living near the theatres in Covent Garden and Drury Lane, Turner cannot have missed the significance of this, the first of his London fires. As he shows, it attracted a crowd, still watching the firemen at work the following morning.

High Green, Wolverhampton (no.17) appeared at the Academy in 1796, one of nine varied exhibits including, for the first time, an oil painting, *Fishermen at Sea* (Tate). During a tour of the Midlands and South Wales in 1794 Turner had visited Wolverhampton's summer fair. While the event dated back to 1258, he fixes it in real time – 11.30 in the morning according to a clock on a wall. A banner bears the loyalist slogan 'King and Constitution', invoked during the French wars and stamped on metal buttons made in nearby Birmingham. Among the stalls and entertainments are signs of poverty and hardship. A mother with a child on her back and an old woman seem to be begging while a young man leans on a crutch. He looks like a wounded or disabled sailor, reminding us that Britain has been at war for three years. That the fair takes place on High Green in front of half-timbered buildings and the medieval St Peter's church makes it no less current, but an hourglass beside the old woman shows that time passes. The layered content and meanings of Turner's mature topography – above all in his later *Picturesque Views in England and Wales* – are already prefigured here.

'Grim WOLVERHAMPTON lights her smouldering fires.' Had Turner read this line by the 'Swan of Lichfield', Anna Seward, in her recent poem about industrial Coalbrookdale?[36] Unless smoking domestic chimneys hint at fouler emissions nearby, he gives no sign of Wolverhampton's transformation from a market to a manufacturing town. The industrial Midlands, Black Country and South Wales with their mills, mines, ironworks, coal pits and kilns hardly register in Turner's 1794 sketchbooks and seldom in those used in northern England in 1797. At first, like many artists, he preferred them contrasted with picturesque scenery and historic buildings or glowing sublimely after dark like the lime kiln he saw beside the River Tywi near Llanstephan Castle in 1795. A coloured sketch contrasts moonlight and firelight and adds a boat bringing material

to and from the kiln (no.21). Lime produced by heating and calcinating limestone was used for construction and agriculture, and kilns sprang up wherever the stone could be found – often small-scale operations like this one. An old label on a drawing made around 1799 (no.22) locates another to Surrey and says it was drawn to 'show the effect of moonlight on fire light … when the moon was visible'. Similar contrasts of moon, fire and lamplight rather than the process of production appear in a painting of a lime kiln (?1797; Yale Center for British Art, New Haven) seen at Coalbrookdale according to a later print (no.23). This most famous of all early industrial sites, where the Darby family had perfected iron-smelting using 'coking' coal, is transformed into a modern transcription of a Rembrandt *Flight into Egypt* and a study in light and shade.

Never just a documentary reporter, Turner was attracted to industry for aesthetic reasons – at least at first. It supplied him with effects and sparked his imagination. He seems to have made no on-the-spot sketches of Coalbrookdale

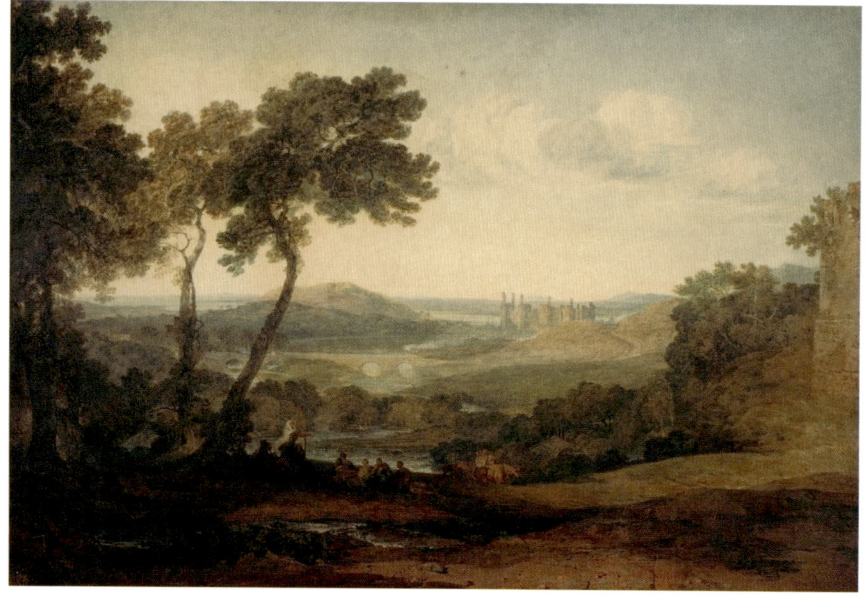

8
Caernarvon Castle, North Wales exh. 1800.
Watercolour on paper
70.6 × 105.5
Tate

during his early Midlands tours. Perhaps he preferred to commit its chimneys and furnaces to memory or had already seen drawings by P.J. de Loutherbourg and Edward Dayes belonging to Dr Monro, whose evening 'academy' he attended from 1793 or 1794 to study and copy drawings with other young artists. De Loutherbourg's small, detailed drawings record machinery like the water-returning Resolution engine designed by the engineers Boulton and Watt and installed to power blast-furnaces in 1781–2 (no.7). A watercolour by Dayes (Tate) shows the best-known of these, Bedlam, named for its baleful fire and smoke or after the hell-fire sermons of a local Methodist preacher. These drawings must have made an impression because Turner bought them at the Monro sale in 1833. He knew Coalbrookdale's iconic silhouette well enough by 1792/3 to introduce it in a watercolour alongside a ruined castle on a rocky coastline (no.18). Comparison with later views by de Loutherbourg (no.10) and Paul Sandby Munn (no.11) confirms the identification, but just because he can, Turner throws in a shipwreck. The ensemble looks like a variation on a painting by Joseph Wright of Derby – a scene from Shakespeare's *Winter's Tale* – that Turner may have seen in the Academy in 1790 or in a print published in 1794. Experimental, or simply playful, Turner's fantasy of a Coalbrookdale-on-Sea alerts us to modernity not just in literal topography, but imaginatively transformed.

A similar intervention occurs in an impressive finished watercolour probably dating from a year or two later (no.19). A large, new building with smoking chimneys like Richard Arkwright's cotton-spinning mills at Cromford, Derbyshire, is foregrounded in an imaginary panorama stretching from what looks like the Avon Gorge across southern England to Windsor Castle and the Thames valley. As impossible as this landscape is, its content of ships, wharf, cranes, road and fertile fields looks sufficiently convincing and connected to create a sense of modern prosperity underpinning feudal stability – all at a time when the state of the nation could hardly be more different. In the same spirit as Turner's

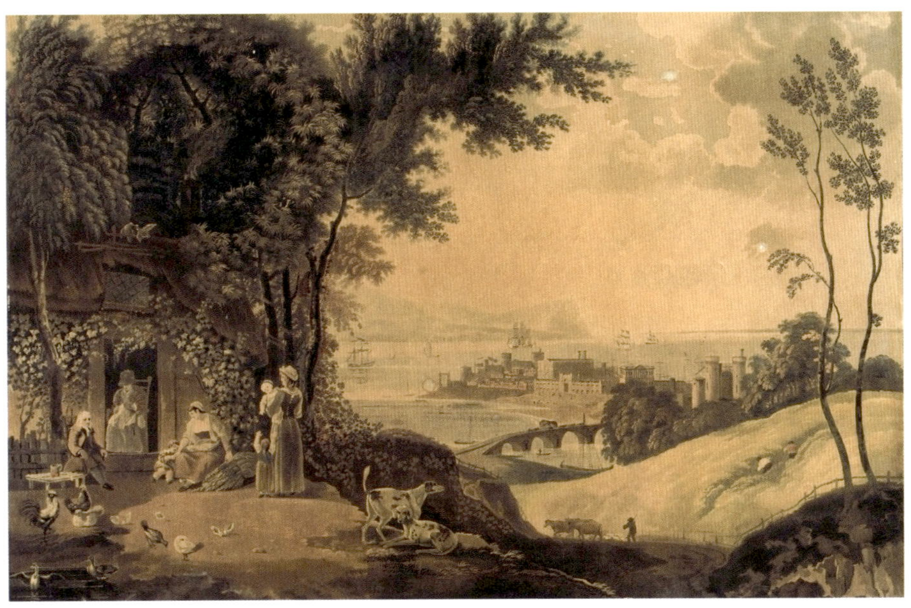

9
Thomas Medland after William Hodges, *The Effects of Peace, 22 April 1797.* Hand-coloured aquatint on paper, 67.3 × 89.6 National Maritime Museum, Greenwich, London

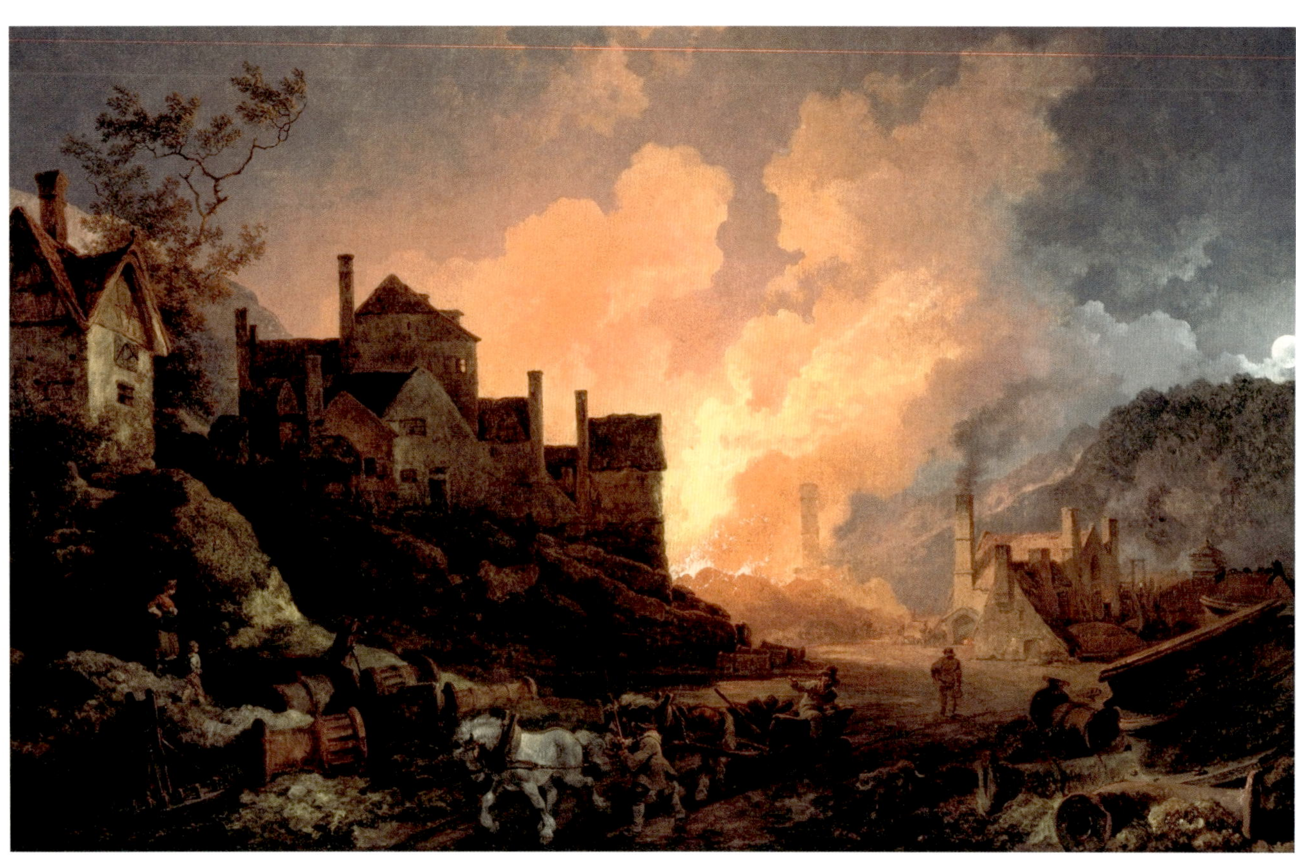

   10 Philip James de Loutherbourg, *Coalbrookdale by Night* 1801. Oil paint on canvas, 68 × 106.7, Science Museum Group Collection

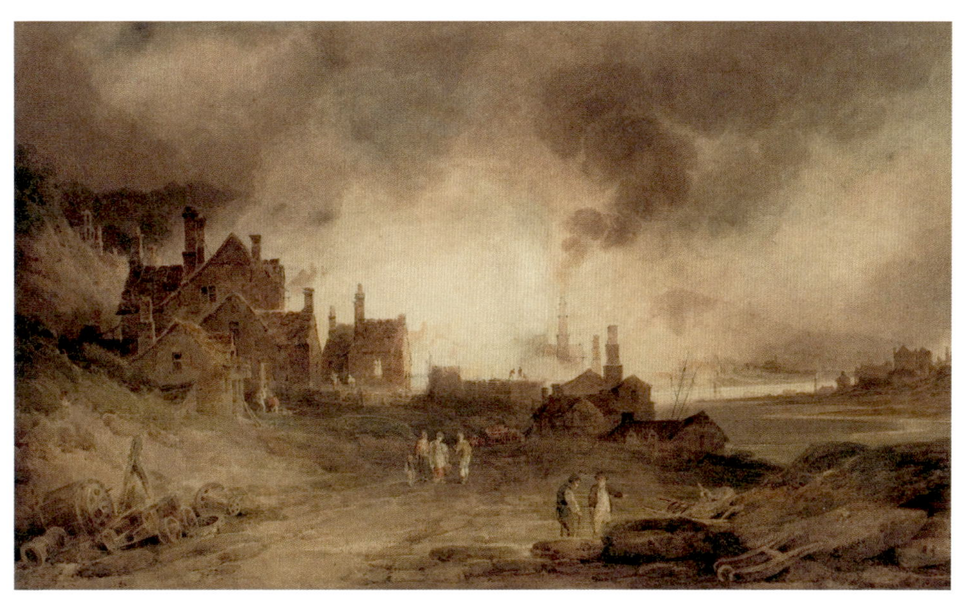

11 Paul Sandby Munn, *Bedlam Furnace, Madeley Dale, Shropshire* 1803. Watercolour on paper, 32.5 × 54.8, Tate

watercolour, in 1795 *The Times* published *The Way to Peace and Plenty*, a handbook for rich and poor in hard times.[37] Drought and bad harvests were causing bread riots. Despite individual wealth, the economy struggled to support the war, which was going badly, from a disastrous campaign in Flanders in 1794 to naval mutinies at Spithead and the Nore in 1797. Fearful of revolution and invasion, the government cracked down on political activism, with arrests for treason and sedition and restrictions on the press. Renamed 'Britain at Peace' and dated to just before the war began in 1793 by Turner's most recent biographer Eric Shanes,[38] the watercolour more likely belongs to the early war years, like a picture of the 'effects of peace' (no.9) exhibited with a 'consequences of war' by William Hodges in the winter of 1794–5. Having merely intended to encourage debate about national policy, Hodges was accused of 'democratic' ideas that undermined the war effort and had to withdraw his pictures.

Turner did not exhibit his 'Peace'. If it is any indication of his own political views, he soon turned to more coded ways of commenting on current affairs – through the lens of history. A watercolour of Caernarvon Castle exhibited in 1800 includes a Welsh bard and his audience (no.8). In his first original verse for the Academy catalogue Turner described the bard's 'song of pity' where 'jealous of the minstrel band / The tyrant drench'd with blood the land'. As the tyrant is the castle's builder, Edward I of England, whose subjugation of Wales crushed its indigenous culture, Turner may be showing his disdain for the current government's repressive 'Gagging Acts', but this would have been hard to prove when the most obvious modern oppressor was the French army overrunning swathes of Europe. Turner was not necessarily a Jacobin or a democrat and, even if he were, would have been unwise to advertise it. There is no evidence of involvement with dissident groups like the London Corresponding Society – anyway more moderate than its branches elsewhere – and plenty that he was a patriot. Writing about liberty and tyranny did not make him a revolutionary any more than imagining the benefits of peace made him anti-war.

Turner's reputation was rising fast by the later 1790s. He was elected Associate of the Royal Academy in 1799 and his clients and patrons included leading figures heavily invested in the national economy. Edward Lascelles and William Beckford had vast fortunes from plantations and slave-owning; Richard Colt Hoare from a family bank; the Duke of Bridgewater from coal and canal-building. Their commissions for views of their estates, antiquarian subjects or pictures to hang with their old master collections did not reflect their business interests. Turner's first commission for manufacturing subjects came from Anthony Bacon in 1798, for views of the Cyfarthfa iron-smelting works at Merthyr Tydfil that he had inherited from his father and leased to Richard Crawshay in 1786. Turner's preparatory drawings (no.20) are distant views of the buildings and no finished versions are known, but it cannot be a coincidence that he made detailed studies of ironworks, with machinery and workmen, around the same time. Cyfarthfa was famous for its cannon and may be the site of the cannon foundry in a vivid colour study (no.13) if it is not – as has also been suggested – one of those run by the Walker family in south Yorkshire and based on a drawing made in 1797. Sketchbooks contain drawings of forges with water-driven tilt hammers (no.15) or making anchors (no.14).

As records of working life sometimes directed towards the war effort, these drawings have the same immediacy and topicality as Turner's observations of fishermen using a windlass to haul their boat ashore (no.26) or small craft supplying a man-of-war (no.27). From *Fishermen at Sea* in 1796 to *The Battle of the Nile* in 1799, his first truly modern pictures were marines. Several years later, he began a picture of a forge. Could this have been intended for Bacon or for Crawshay, the current proprietor of Cyfarthfa? Evidently Turner was dissatisfied with it, as it languished in his studio until, eventually, he overpainted most of it with the casting of a statue of the Duke of Wellington and exhibited it as *The Hero of a Hundred Fights* (no.12). What remains of its earlier incarnation is a gloomy, barn-like interior, a great wheel and an ironmaster's wife or daughter, reminiscent of Wright's nativity-like

forges. Wright died in 1797 and Turner could
have known his *Iron Forge* (1772; Tate) in a print
by Richard Earlom (1773). He could not have
foreseen when he began his picture that industry
and war would define his lifetime and play such a
part in his art, nor that decades later steam power
would coalesce with his dynamic vision of nature
in definitive pictures of the machine age.

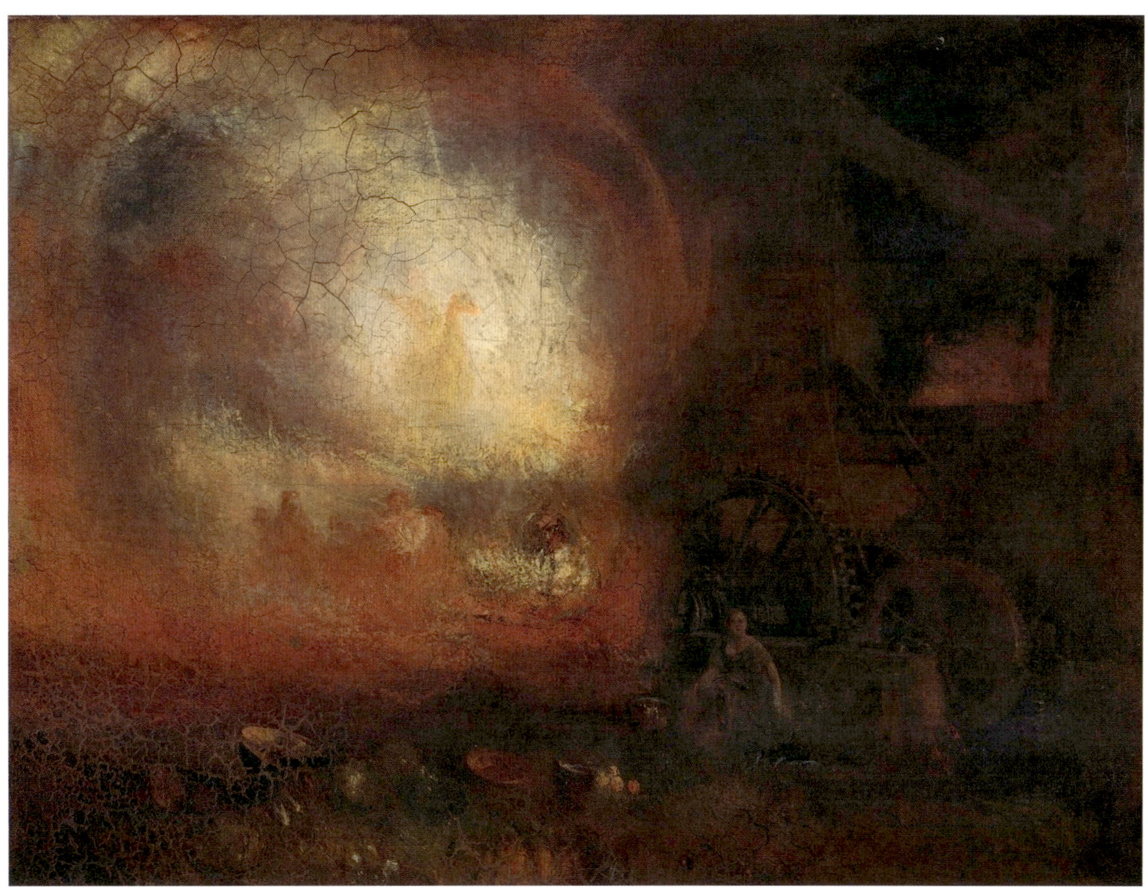

12 *The Hero of a Hundred Fights* c.1800–10, reworked and exhibited 1847. Oil paint on canvas, 90.8 × 121.3, Tate

Industrial Sublime

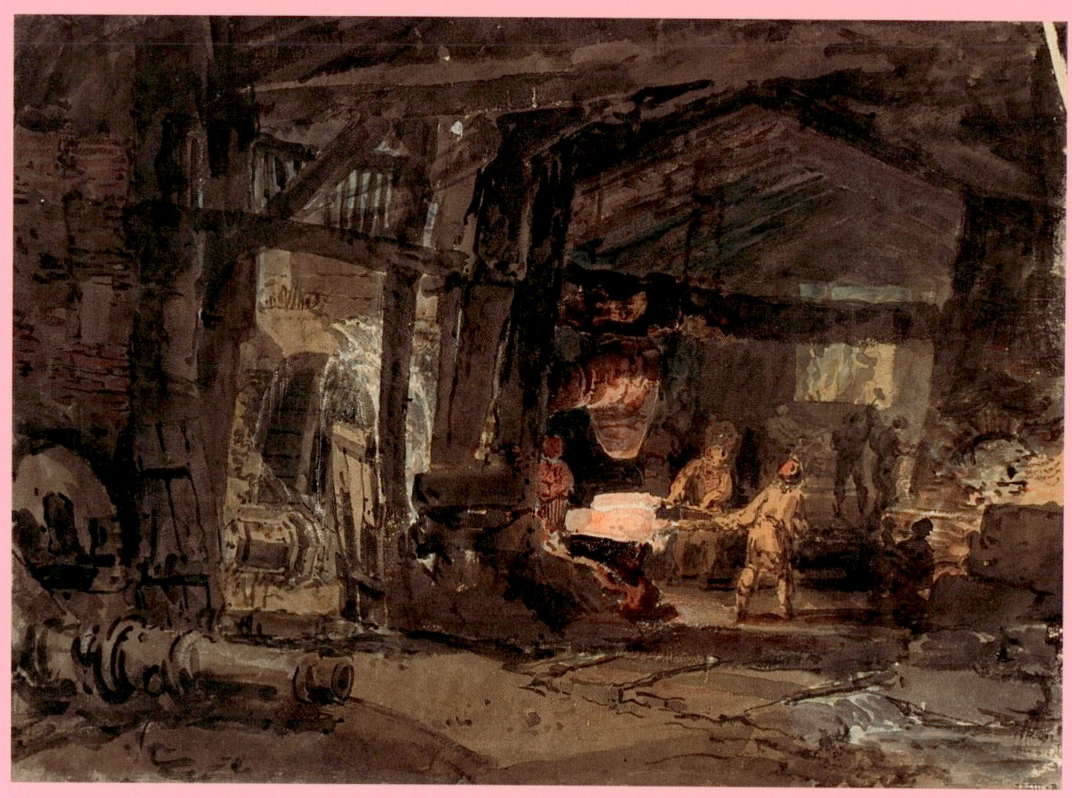

  13 *The Interior of a Cannon Foundry* 1797–8. Graphite and watercolour on paper, 24.7 × 34.7, Tate

Turner's tours of Britain brought him into proximity with sites in Wales and northern England where iron ore was mined and smelted, and a handful of early drawings and watercolours demonstrate the artist's fascination with industry.[39] These included foundries where cannons and anchors were produced: David Hill notes that Walker's iron foundries at Masborough and Burcroft, where Turner may have made his drawings of foundries producing anchors and cannons, specialised in munitions, supplying most of the guns for the *Victory*. Hill even hypothesises that the recently cast cannon in the foreground of *The Interior of a Cannon Foundry* (no.13) is 'waiting its turn on some gun carriage or perhaps on the decks of a man-of-war destined for Trafalgar'.[40] Cyfarthfa, another possible site for the works,[41] was also a prolific supplier of cannons and other weapons (Nelson visited it in 1802) and was depicted around this time by Julius Caesar Ibbetson.

Turner's main precursor as an artist of industry was Joseph Wright of Derby, who in the 1770s made paintings of iron forges and blacksmiths' shops. The industrial scenes of both artists can be viewed in relation to Edmund Burke's famous definition of the sublime as 'whatever is in any sort terrible, or is conversant about terrible objects, or operates in a manner analogous to terror'. Turner's drawings of dark, hot, noisy spaces with an implicit sense of danger (in *Making Anchors* [no.14] he uses gouache highlights to depict the molten metal) are clearly connected to this.

Whereas Wright's paintings could be traced back to a history of genre scenes focused on human activity, however, Turner in his drawings was above all observing industrial machinery: his drawing of a tilt forge (no.15), for instance, clearly documents its workings. Chiefly used to refine iron to make it malleable for the use of a blacksmith, the tilt forge worked by an external waterwheel powering progressively smaller wheels. These in turn tripped the tilt hammers, which fell upon the anvils and forged the metal. Turner's drawing demonstrates these stages with the clarity of a technical engraving.

These industrial scenes provide a counterpoint to the landscapes that were Turner's general focus during his sketching tours. In their attention to the production of cannons and anchors, they suggest that Turner was concerned with Britain's involvement in the French Revolutionary Wars (the years in which these drawings were made also saw the Battles of St Vincent and Camperdown in 1797 and the Battle of the Nile in 1798). As a result of these conflicts, Britain

required increased amounts of iron for military and naval purposes,
the more so because supplies from overseas sources (chiefly Sweden
and Russia) were interrupted. As so often in Turner's work, in these
drawings it is impossible to discern where the artist's sympathies
lie: does he sympathise with the conditions of the men carrying
out this work or the owners of the foundries? Are the cannons and
anchors intended to demonstrate patriotism or to critique the labour
underlying the war effort? Either way, they demonstrate that Turner
was already making clear connections between representations of the
specific landscapes he depicted and the broader geopolitical context.
JF

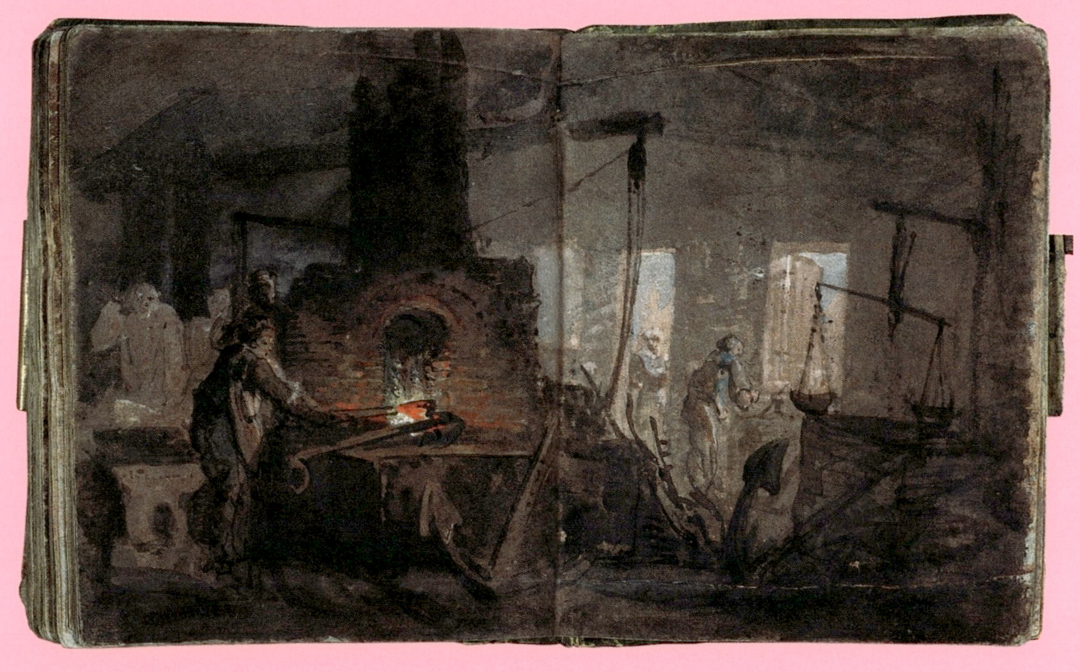

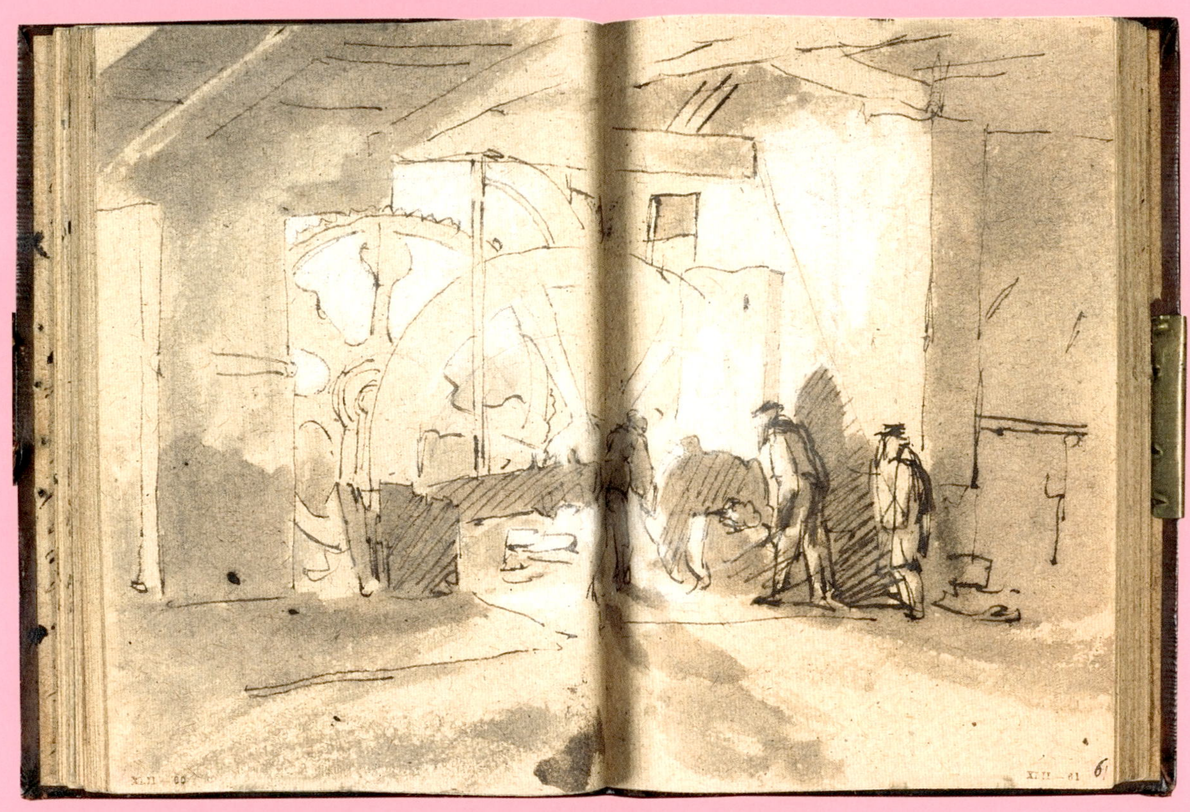

14 *Interior of a Forge: Making Anchors* 1796–7. Gouache, graphite and watercolour on paper, 11.3 × 18.6, Tate
15 *Interior of a Tilt Forge* c.1798. Graphite on paper, 17.4 × 25, Tate

Theatre of the Streets

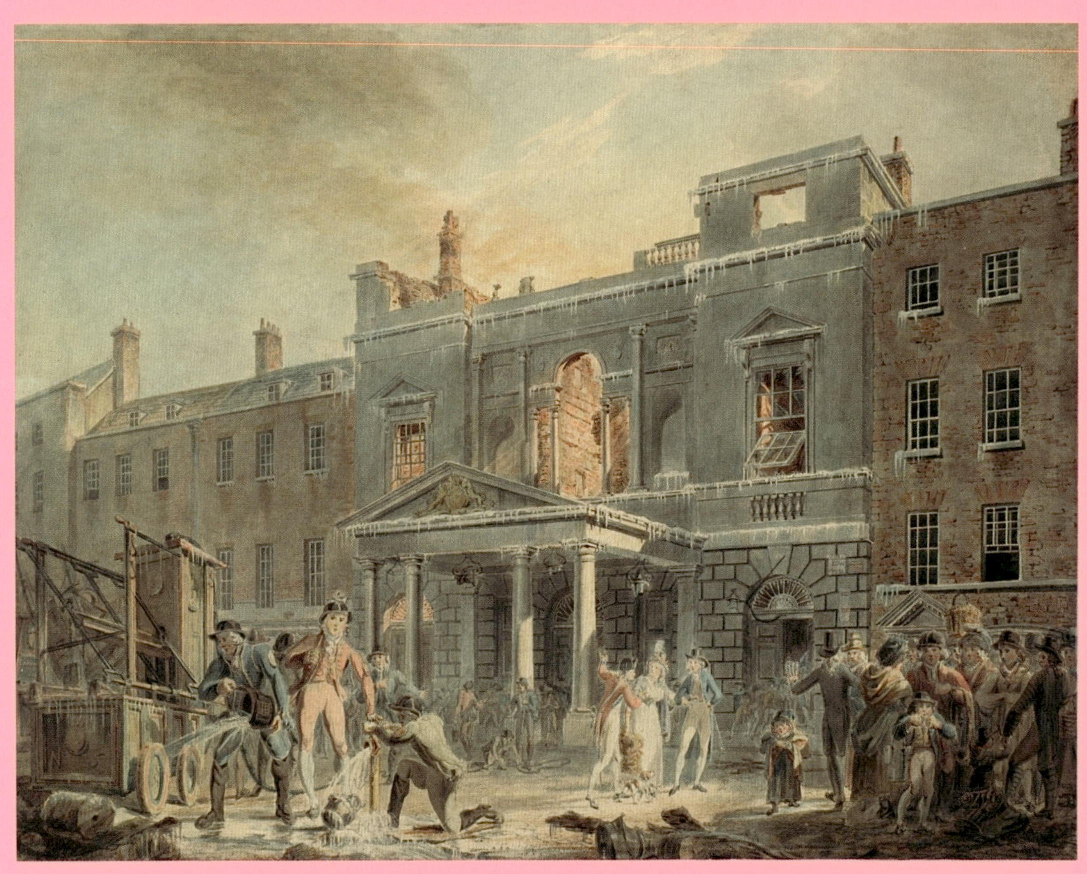

16 *The Pantheon, the Morning after the Fire* 1792. Graphite and watercolour on paper, 39.5 × 51.5, Tate

In the early hours of Saturday 14 January 1792, a few days after Turner resumed his studies in the plaster academy at the Royal Academy Schools,[42] the Pantheon Opera House on Oxford Street, London, burnt down. Turner documented the fire in two watercolours, including one, *The Pantheon, the Morning after the Fire* (no.16), depicting the main entrance of the building later that morning.

The building, originally a venue for concerts, masquerades and entertainments, and boasting a domed rotunda that was one of the largest rooms in England, had recently been converted into an opera house. Turner, who lived half an hour's walk from the Pantheon, witnessed this newsworthy event and produced his watercolour of the main entrance in time to exhibit it at the Royal Academy exhibition, which opened on 30 April.[43]

The watercolour is carefully constructed, even theatrical, presenting the scene as if it were a performance taking place against the backdrop of the Pantheon façade. We see signifiers of the time and place such as a fire truck, crowds and large icicles evoking the severe frost that night (Henry Angelo went even further, quoting a witness as describing 'vast clusters of icicles, twelve and fifteen feet in length, and as big as branches of trees, hanging from the north front parapet').[44] In truth it is unlikely that a fire truck would have been stationed at the entrance, since the fire started, and was extinguished, from the rear of the building (the billowing smoke and glow from behind the Ionic Venetian arch on the upper storey show that it is still burning in Turner's watercolour). It is behind the façade of James Wyatt's elegant building (which in fact was retained until Marks and Spencer acquired the property in 1937) that the work of extinguishing the fire would have been taking place.[45]

Turner's watercolour presents the event as popular entertainment – fittingly so, as the fire itself seems to have been planned. Shortly after the fire a rumour spread that it had been started deliberately, and while never proved, more recent archival discoveries reinforce the likelihood that this was the case. Following a secret agreement the previous year to return Italian opera to the Haymarket Theatre, it appears that the Pantheon's backers organised the fire to escape paying rent on the Pantheon and allow them to swiftly leave the opera business.[46]

Turner painted and exhibited his Pantheon watercolour soon after the fire. His view of High Green, Wolverhampton (no.17), however, was not exhibited until two years after he visited the town during a 1794 tour of the Midlands. The town's fair,[47] held every July, dated back to 1258 and was documented by Turner in the form of detailed drawings of buildings as well as (probably) related studies of figures at a fairground. In place of the stasis of the Pantheon watercolour *High Green, Wolverhampton* contains a dizzying abundance of incident that relates to the carnivalesque atmosphere of works such as Hogarth's *Southwark Fair* (1733; Cincinnati Art Museum) as well as those by Turner's contemporary Thomas Rowlandson. Exotic animals are exhibited, theatrical performances take place, waxworks are admired, and food and drink are sold. Perhaps most timely of all is a large 'King and Constitution' banner on the right: illustrating the counter-revolutionary nationalism that prevailed in the wake of the French Revolution, the banner is an early example of the references to contemporary politics that were to recur throughout Turner's work. JF

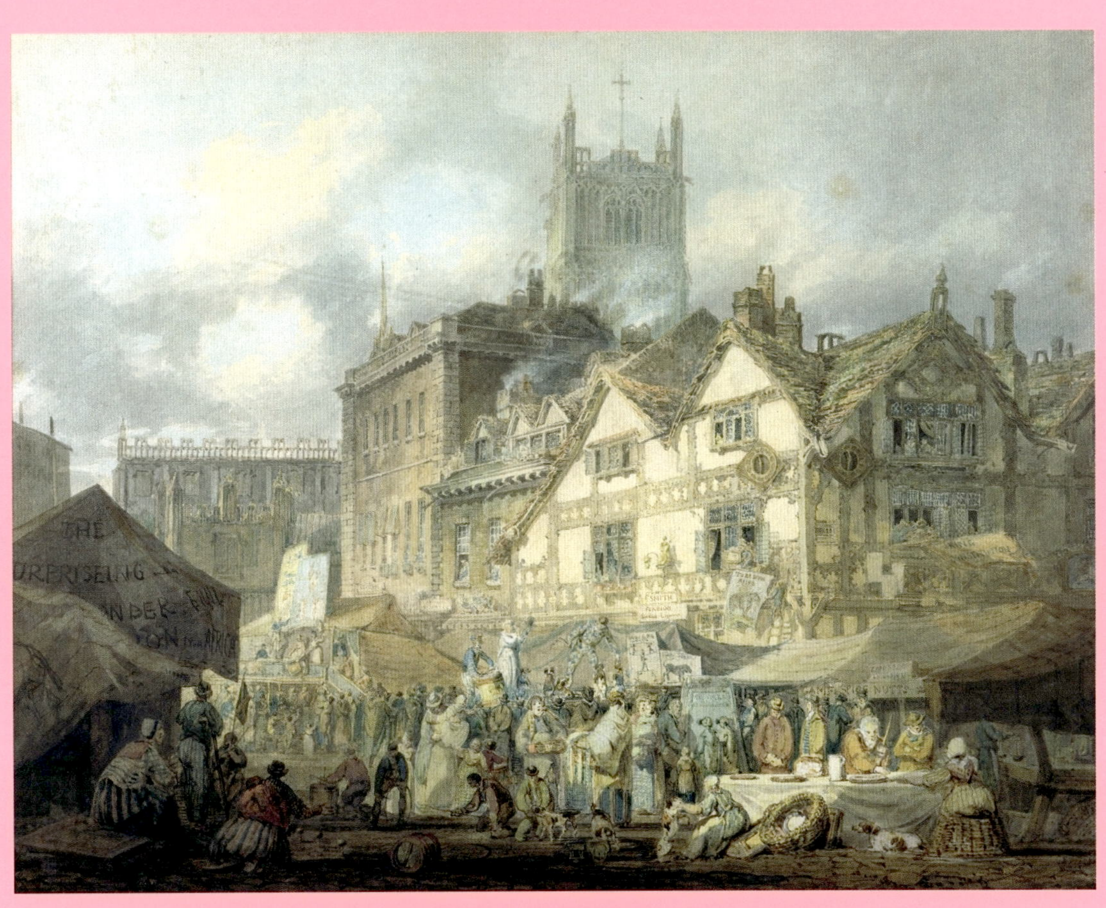

17 *High Green, Wolverhampton* 1796. Watercolour on paper, 31.8 × 41.9, Wolverhampton Arts & Culture

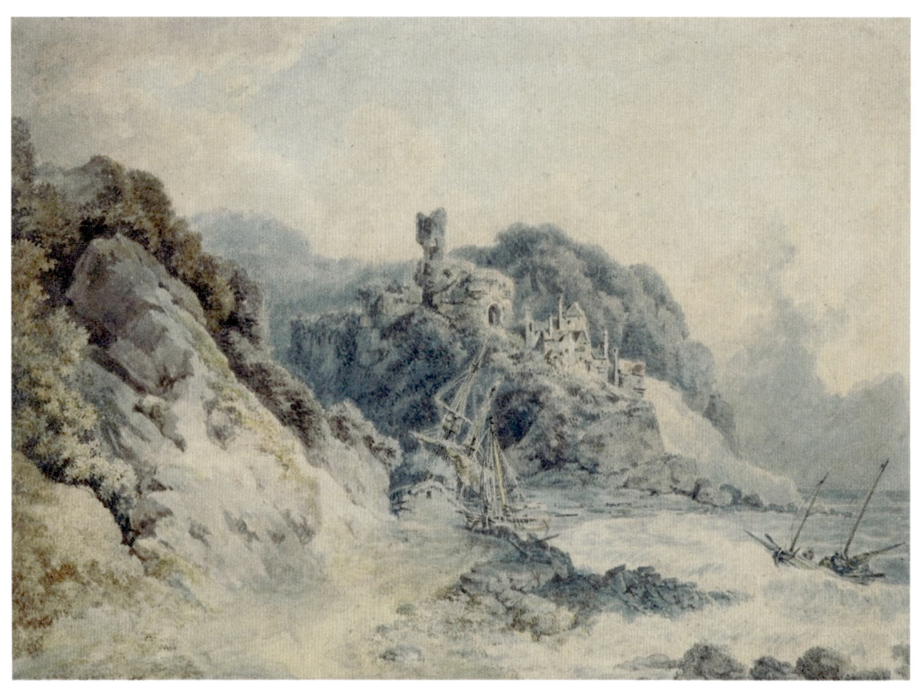

18 *Shipwreck on a Rocky Coastline with a Ruined Castle* 1792–3.
Watercolour and pencil on paper, 16.9 × 23.6, The Whitworth, The University of Manchester

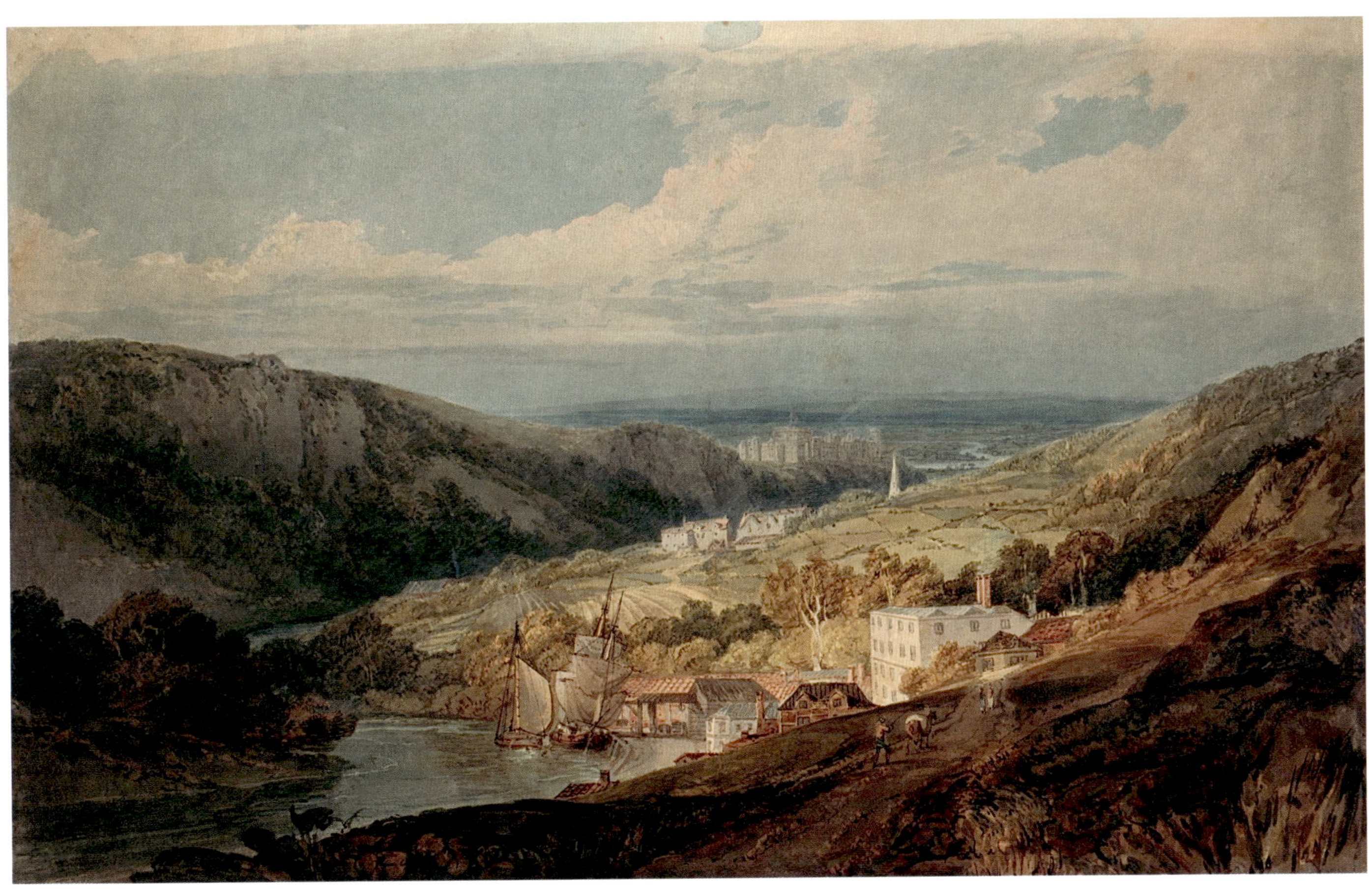

19 *Imaginary Landscape with Windsor Castle on a Cliff and a Distant Plain* 1794–5.
Gouache, graphite and watercolour on paper, 45.7 × 73.6, Tate

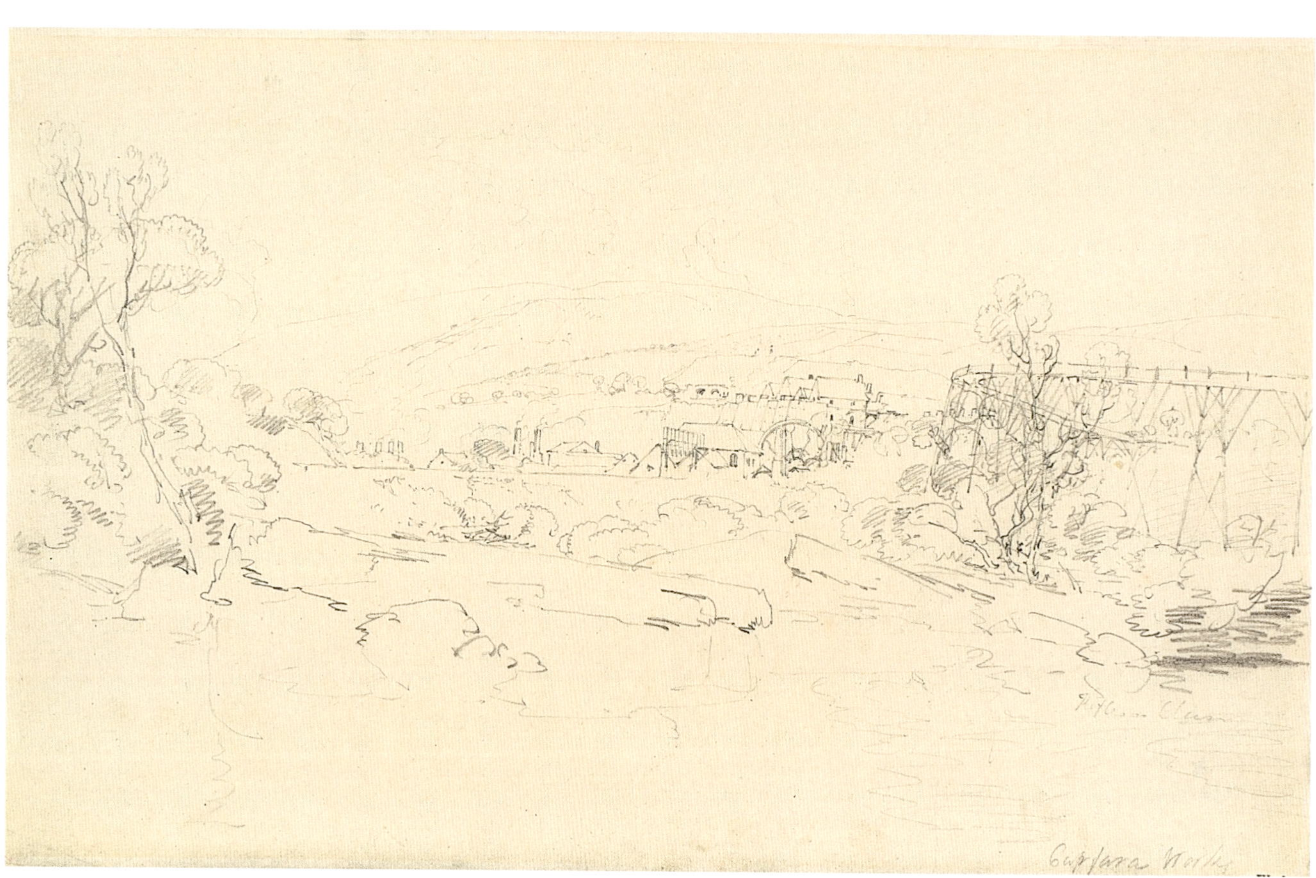

20 *View of Cyfarthfa Ironworks ?from the North-West* 1798. Graphite on paper, 28.8 × 45.7, Tate

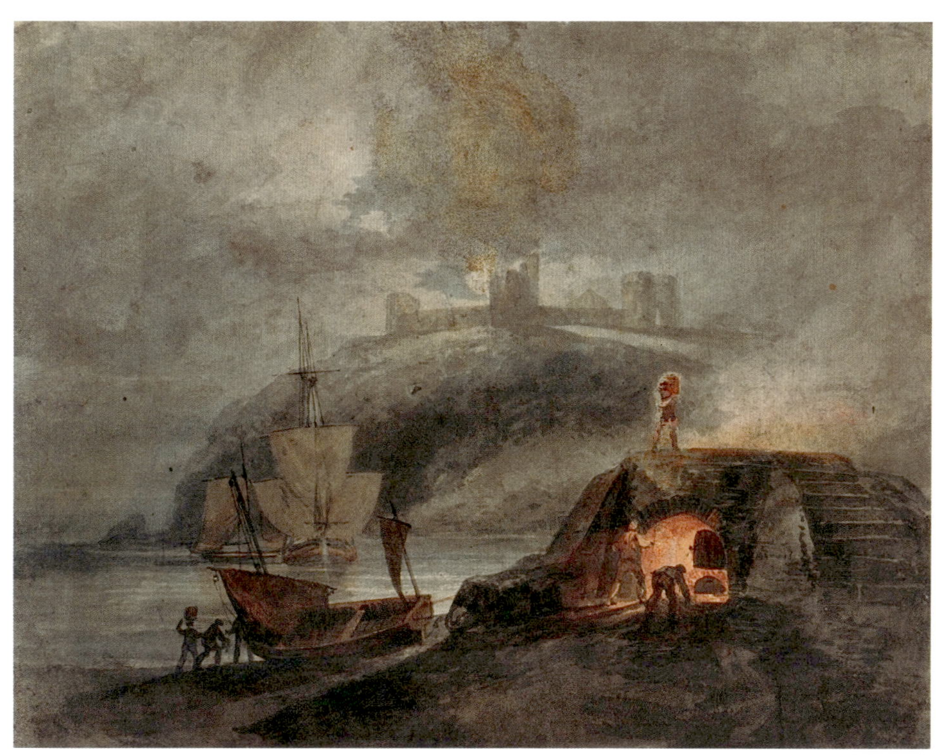

21 *Llanstephan Castle by Moonlight, with a Kiln in the Foreground* c.1795. Graphite and watercolour on paper, 21.3 × 28.1, Tate

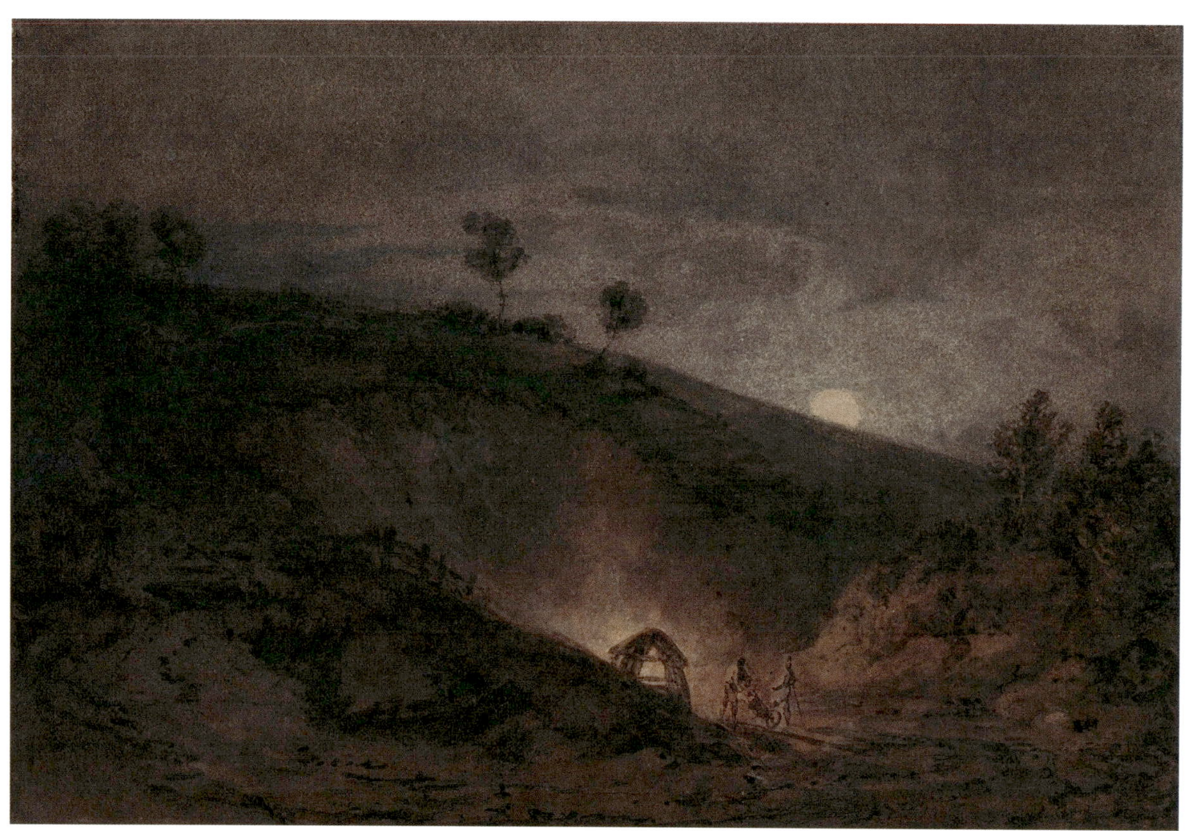

  22 *A Lime Kiln by Moonlight* c.1799. Watercolour on paper, 16.5 × 24, Herbert Art Gallery and Museum, Coventry

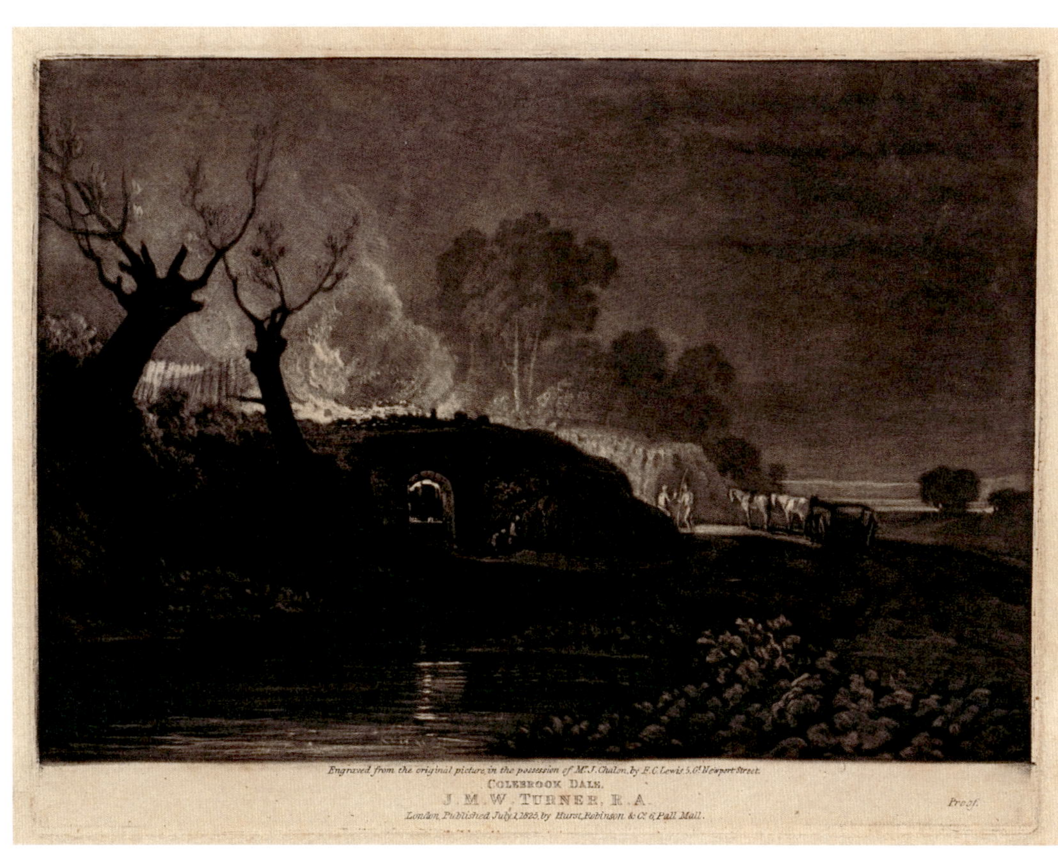

23 Frederick Christian Lewis after Joseph Mallord William Turner, *Colebrooke Dale* 1825. Mezzotint on paper, 13.6 × 19.8 (image), Tate

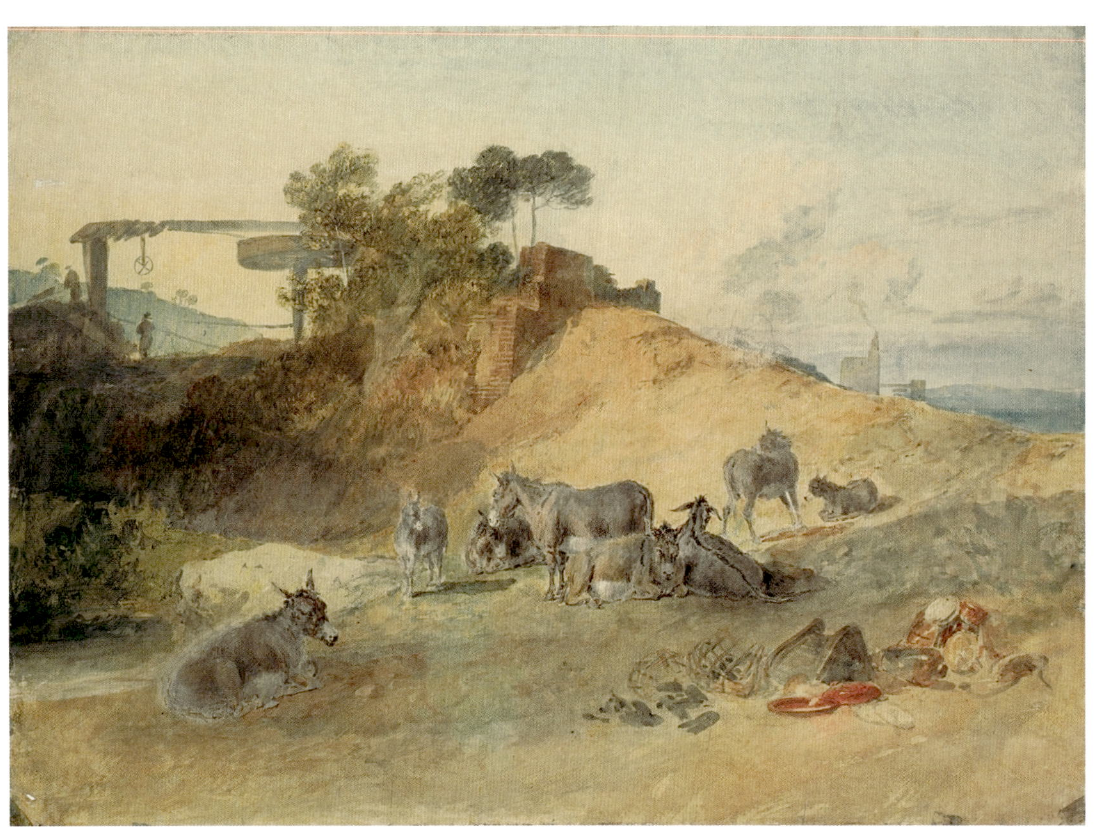

  24 *Donkeys beside a Mine Shaft* c.1805–7. Gouache, graphite and watercolour on paper, 57.7 × 78, Tate

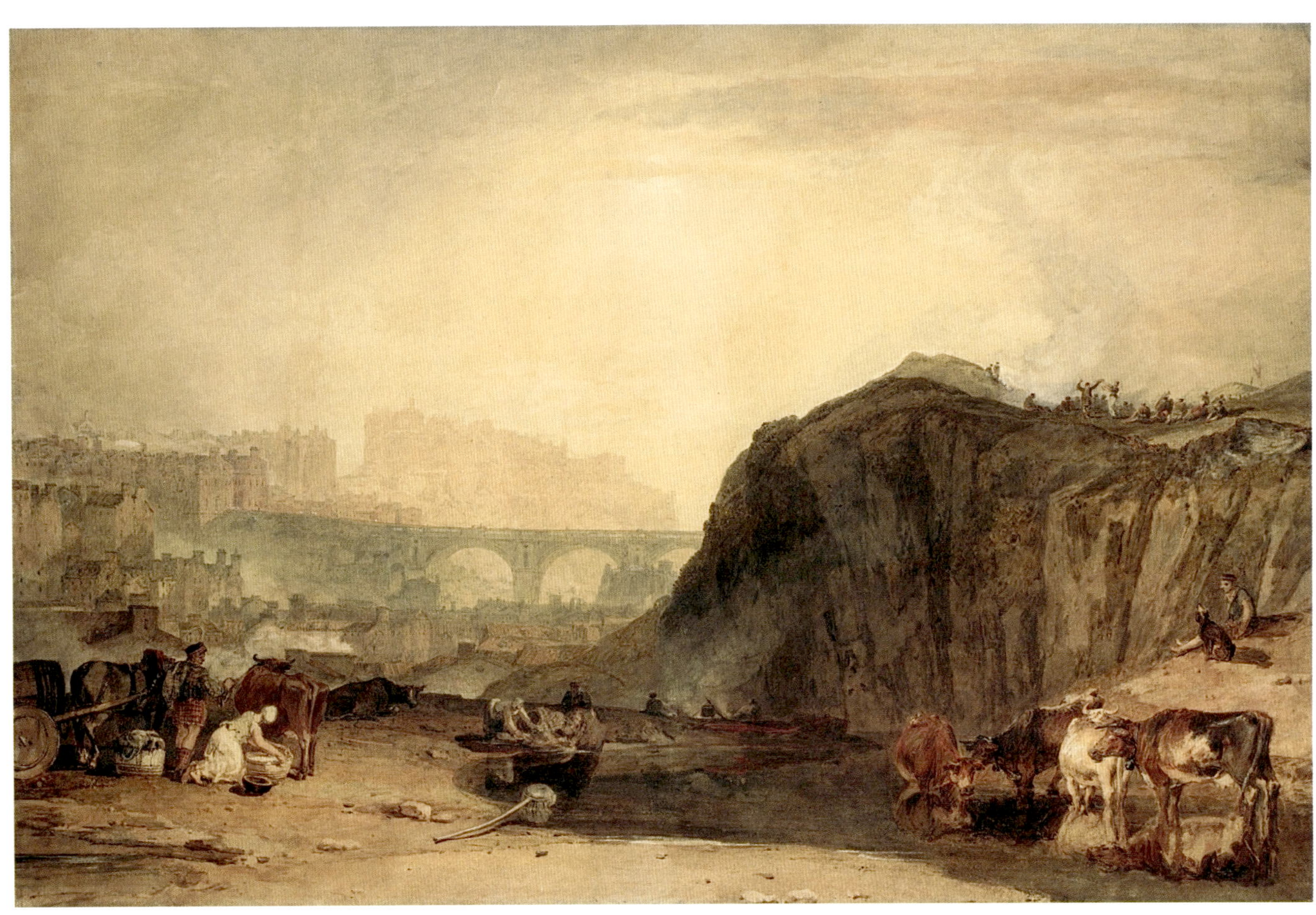

25 *Edinburgh, from Caulton-hill* exh. 1804. Graphite and watercolour on paper, 66 × 100, Tate

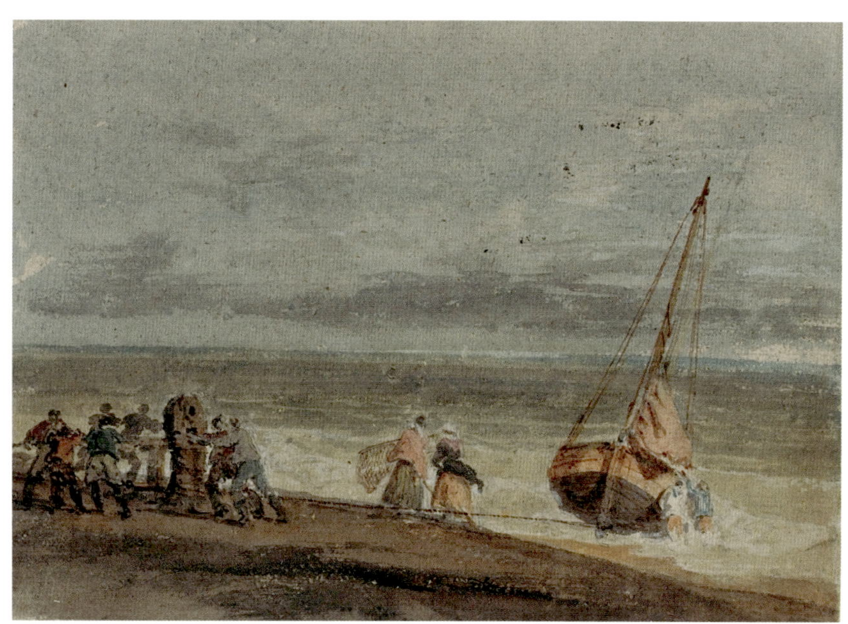

  26 *Fishermen Hauling a Boat through Surf on a Windlass* 1796–7. Watercolour and gouache on paper, 19.4 × 26.9. Tate

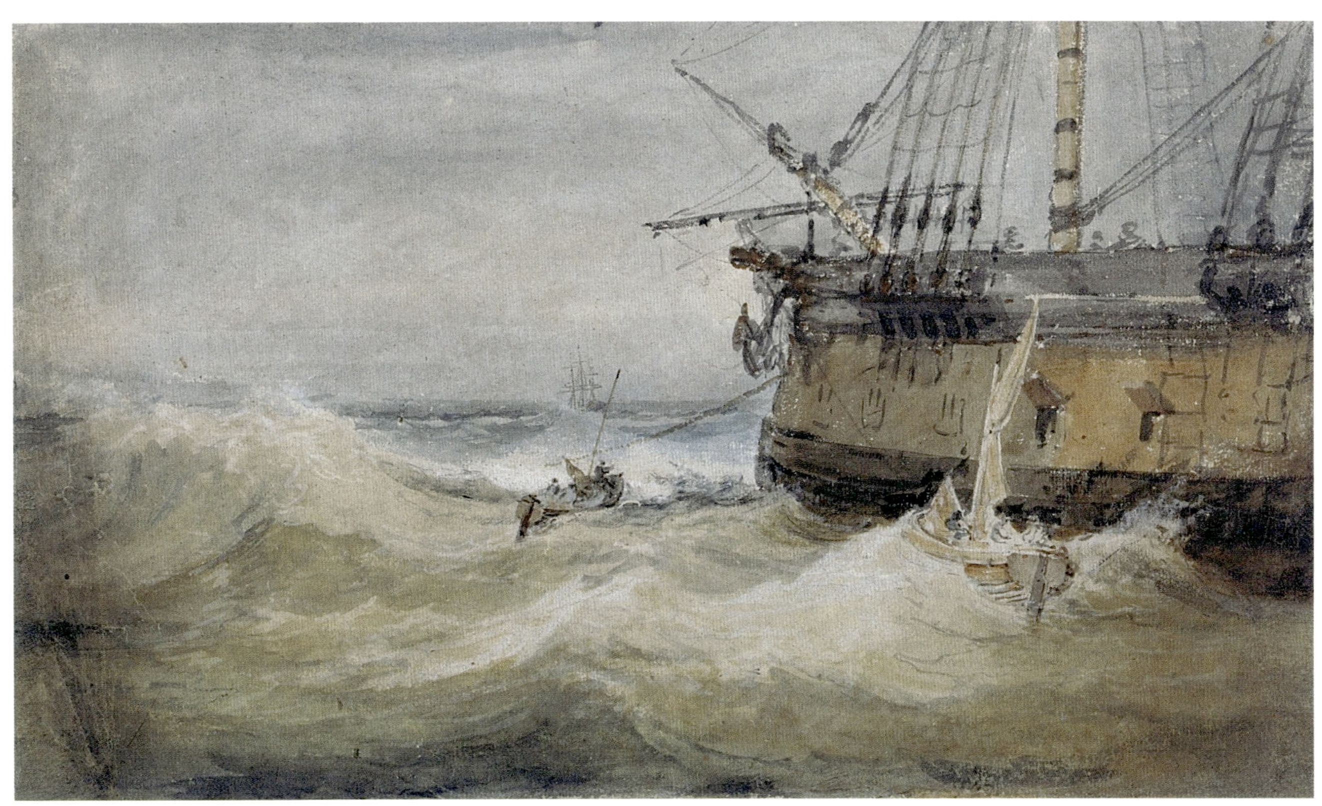

27 *Small Boats beside a Man-o'-War* 1796–7. Watercolour and gouache on paper, 35.4 × 61.7, Tate

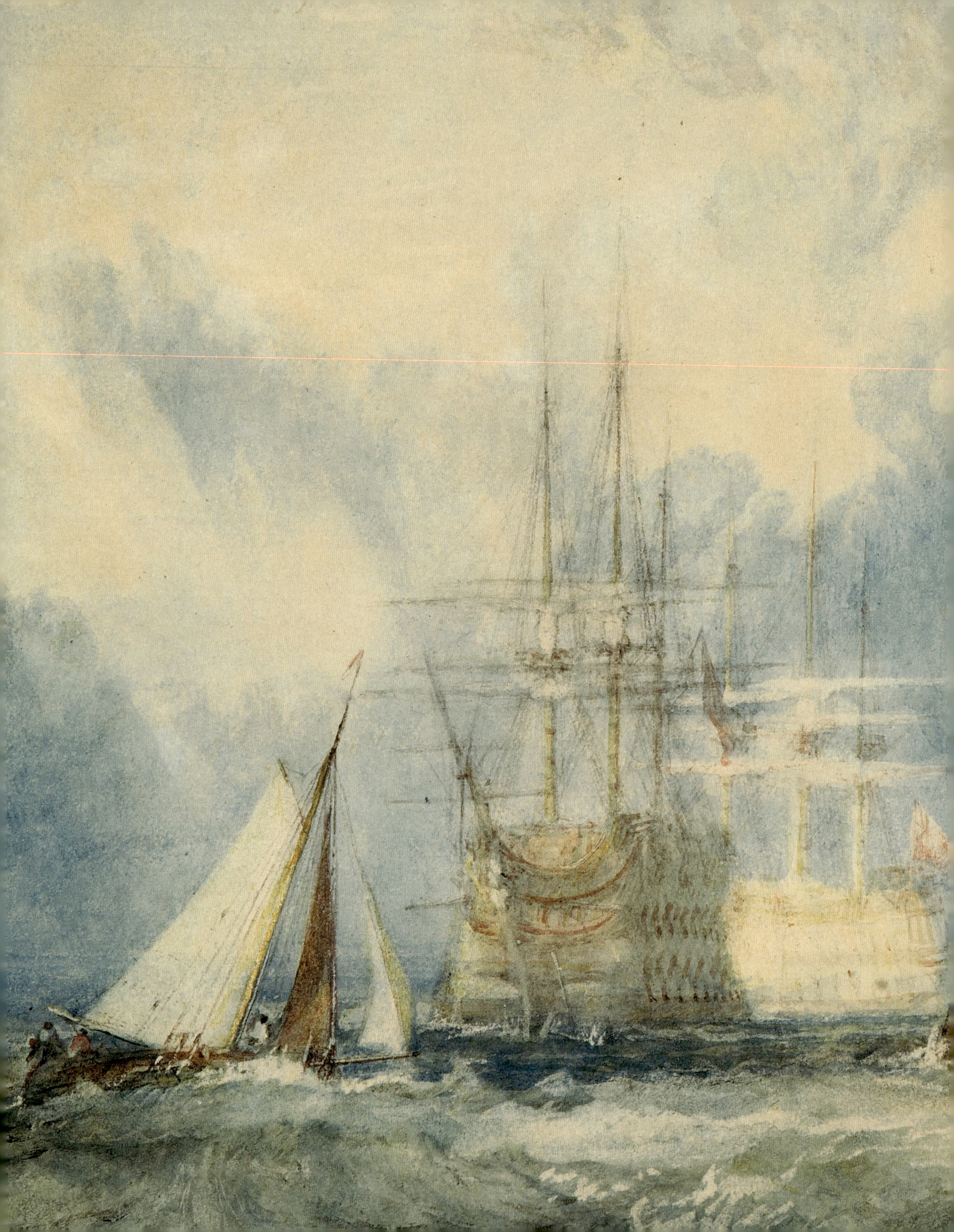

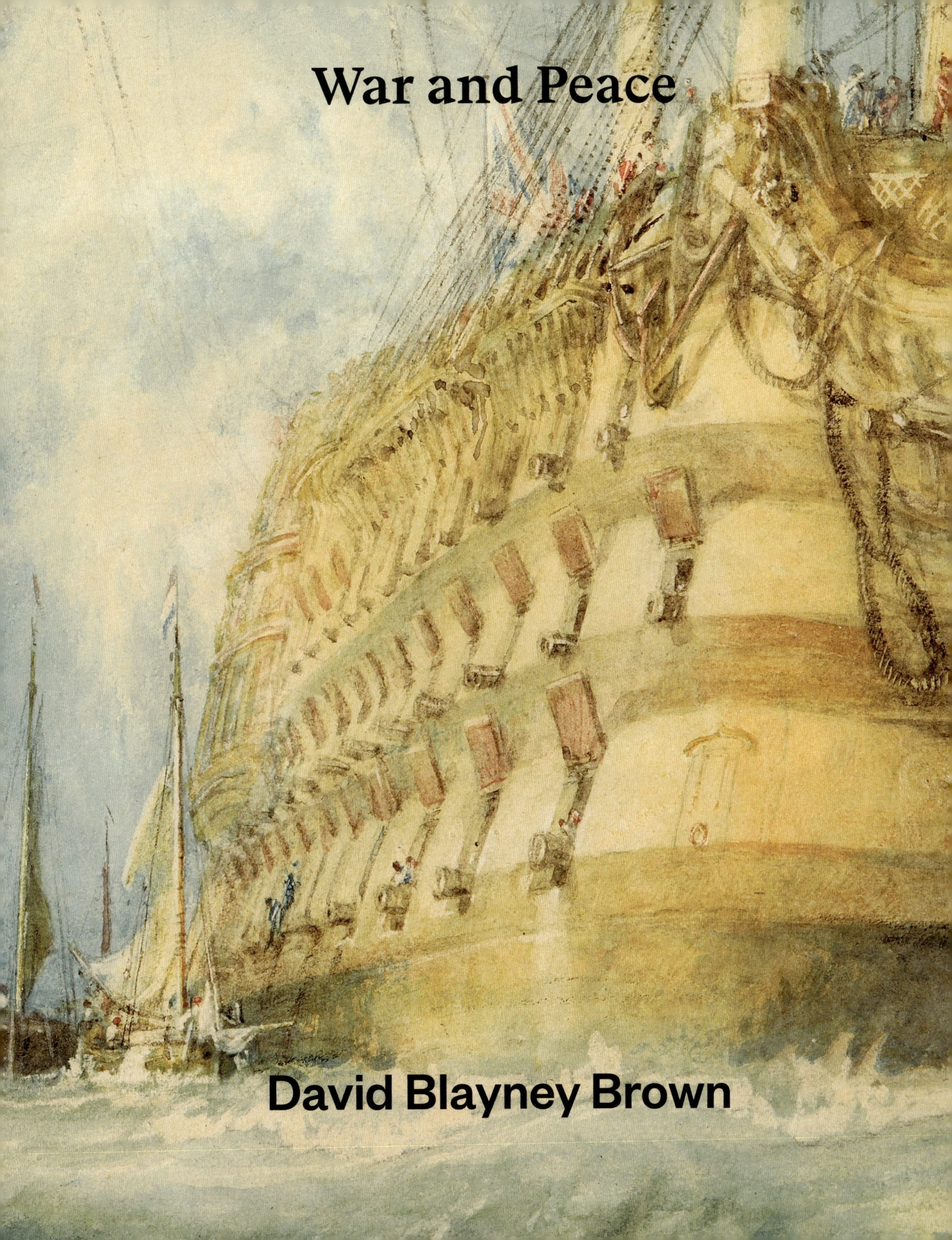

War and Peace
David Blayney Brown

Britain was at war somewhere in the world for most of Turner's life. The Revolutionary-Napoleonic War began in 1793, lasted with only short breaks until 1815 and haunted him for years afterwards. First declared on Britain and Holland by the new radical-republican government in Paris and expected to be short and contained, it became a clash of empires and ideologies fought on a global scale. Turner seized the opportunities it gave him as a painter of modern history, depicting events as far afield as Egypt and India and epochal British victories like Trafalgar. It featured in his poetry and literary illustrations. But he never attempted a comprehensive record and by the time he painted Waterloo in 1818, he had moved on from patriotic glorification to compassion for the suffering shared by all sides and ranks. Had his attitude to the war changed or become expressed more openly?

Britain had been drawn into the war reluctantly, divided as to whether it was just or merely unavoidable and without the unity of purpose that would be felt in 1914 or 1940. In opposition to an establishment terrified of a British uprising inspired by 'French principles', radicals, evangelicals, Whig politicians, artists, writers and clients of Turner such as William Beckford and Walter Fawkes sympathised with the Revolution's founding ideals or actively opposed war. Peace was a vanishing dream for the armed forces, the thousands of men conscripted and pressed into service and the families they left at home. Turner contrasted peace and war at various times and explicitly in a pair of pictures in 1842 (nos.160, 162). The possible impact of pictures of *The Effects of Peace* (no.9) and *Consequences of War*, exhibited by William Hodges in the winter of 1794–5 to engage with current debates, has already been noted. Protests by the king's sons the Dukes of York and Gloucester that works with a 'democratic' (by which they meant treasonous) tendency should not be exhibited may have deterred Turner from showing what looks like a similar 'peace' of his own. Perhaps he did not want others deciding for him if this watercolour (no.19) was an anti-war polemic, such as the royal dukes assumed Hodges's pictures to be, or (like 'Your England; Fight for it Now' posters during the Second World War) promoted what needed defending.

Turner's first picture of modern war, *The Battle of the Nile* (location unknown), was exhibited in 1799. Like a picture by Turner's mentor de Loutherbourg in the same exhibition (no.28), it depicted the explosion of the French flagship *L'Orient* when Nelson inflicted a crushing defeat on an enemy fleet in Aboukir Bay the previous year. Having occupied Ottoman Egypt as a bridgehead to India, Napoleon was now left exposed in the land of biblical plagues. Turner exhibited a *Fifth Plague of Egypt* in 1800 (see no.43) and a *Tenth* in 1802 (Tate), perhaps borrowing the biblical analogy from James Gillray's recent caricature *The Extirpation of the Plagues of Egypt* (no.29) – a memorable image even if the French, soon struck by plague themselves, could hardly be compared to ancient Egyptians punished for enslaving the Israelites. Meanwhile, Turner painted watercolours of the siege and capture of Seringapatam (Srirangapatna) in Mysore, whose ruler Tipu Sultan's conspiracy with Napoleon to rid India of Britain's East India Company had turned a fourth and last Mysore War into a proxy one with France (nos.45, 46). Based on drawings by British soldiers, they show the Company's soldiers and sepoys advancing across the River Kaveri and the spot where Tipu was killed but gloss over their slaughter and the looting that Arthur Wellesley, the future Duke of Wellington, only stopped by hanging and flogging. In Britain Tipu had been demonised as a bloodthirsty 'Tiger', and his defeat and death aroused popular jubilation. Like Nelson's victory at Aboukir, it curbed some of Napoleon's geopolitical ambitions and offset a run of failures on the European front.

Perhaps intended for engraving or for collectors like Beckford or John Soane who acquired plunder from Mysore, Turner's watercolours were more modest than the panorama of the conquest of Seringapatam by his Academy friend Robert Ker Porter, a hit at London's Lyceum Theatre in 1799 but too big for most British houses and unlikely to find a buyer when 'public patronage' was 'palsied' by the wartime economy.[48]

 Previous Page: *A First Rate Taking in Stores* 1818 (no.53)

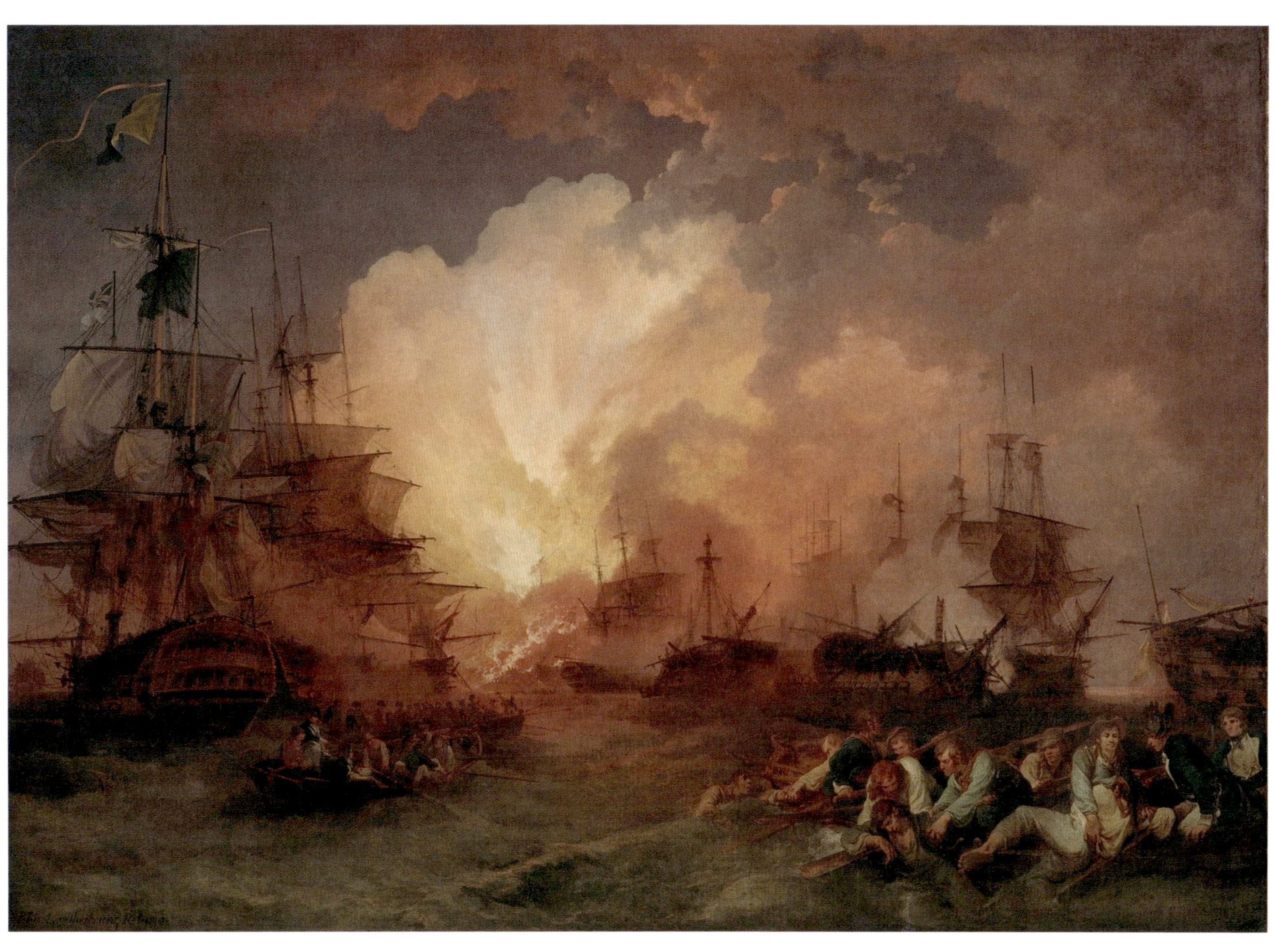

28 Philip James de Loutherbourg, *The Battle of the Nile* 1800. Oil paint on canvas, 152.4 × 214, Tate

Turner sold almost none of his large war pictures, succeeding better with smaller ones like a pair of contrasting soldiers and travellers on the St Gotthard Pass probably painted for John Allnutt around 1804 (no.48). Turner had visited the pass in 1802, during the ceasefire signed at Amiens that May, and seen the Devil's Bridge where in 1801 an Austro-Russian army under the Russian general Suvorov had broken through the French. Turner had presumably seen Ker Porter's panorama of this subject as well, but his troops, who seem to be Austrian, are advancing rather than fighting. Suvorov might have ended the war altogether if he had succeeded in liberating Switzerland and marched on Paris. Instead, the French regrouped and forced him to retreat.

Among those hoping for peace in the winter of 1801–2 were crewmen on the *Temeraire* – the heroic ship of Turner's 1839 picture (no.134) – who begged their commanders not to send her to the West Indies and a likely French attack but were hanged for mutiny, although they professed loyalty to king and country. For Turner his tour

of France and Switzerland in 1802 was his only sight of enemy or occupied territory. In Paris he visited Jacques-Louis David's studio and saw his vainglorious picture of Napoleon crossing the St Bernard astride a rearing charger like a modern Hannibal or Charlemagne (no.30). Rather than inventing such shameless propaganda (the First Consul had ridden a mule in the rear of his exhausted troops, led by a local guide), Turner at least tried to prepare himself with material evidence or eye-witness accounts. Presumably in case he should have to paint them, he obtained models of the special craft Napoleon had ordered for a cross-Channel invasion (no.32). When Nelson's flagship *Victory* returned to Sheerness for repairs after Trafalgar, he went aboard and interviewed survivors. Their contribution helped his *Battle of Trafalgar* (no.35) to unfold like a newsreel, panning across the ongoing battle and pausing at the French marksman and the *pietà* of Nelson's last moments. For his next wartime marine (no.41) Turner went to Portsmouth in 1807 to watch the arrival of the Danish naval fleet seized at Copenhagen to prevent it falling

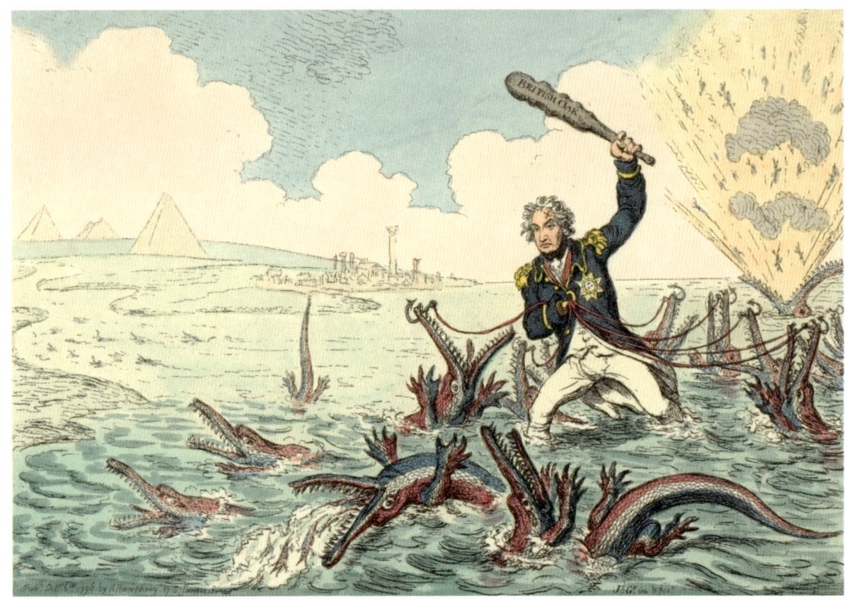

29
James Gillray, *Extirpation of the Plagues of Egypt* 1798. Hand-coloured etching on paper, 24.4 × 35.6, Yale Center for British Art, Paul Mellon Collection, New Haven

into French hands and being used to close the Baltic to British trade. His observations ensured that his picture contained accurate portraits of two of the ships but could not insure him against the backlash that followed Britain's assault on a neutral nation and bombardment of its capital.

Turner used a site visit and on-the-spot sketches for his painting of Waterloo (no.37), but visualised the carnage left on the field after the battle from the accounts of guides who led battlefield tours and took its emotional tone from Byron's poetry. Depictions of casualties such as Thomas Rowlandson drew being brought ashore at Yarmouth in 1797 (no.31) were rare even among artists' private sketches. Focusing on victims rather than victory and avoiding national feeling in an exhibition picture, as Turner did, was controversial, but not unprecedented. After Copenhagen Turner became wary of painting British successes and largely ignored the Peninsular War. His depictions of the home front, while broadly reassuring, showed his sceptical, questioning mind when noticing the impacts

of a wartime tax on pig iron (no.85), enclosure and crop rotation on the working poor of the Thames Valley (no.102) or Napoleon's Continental Blockade on Cornish fishermen, whose excess catches of pilchards, once exported, were instead sold from the beach as cheap manure (no.93). Representing the war metaphorically or covertly, he acknowledged its human costs more openly. Hardly a subject to boost morale, *The Wreck of a Transport Ship* (no.42) was not exhibited until 1851 and did not specify what if any incident it recorded. Shipwrecked infantry doomed to drown despite the efforts of fishermen to pull them from waves in which, according to Admiral Bowles, no ship could live – ordinary men overwhelmed by forces larger than themselves – they stand for everyone caught in the war but also point beyond it, to the drowning enslaved people (no.119), convicts (no.116) and much-needed lifesaving technologies (no.145) in Turner's later pictures.

Snow Storm: Hannibal and his Army Crossing the Alps (no.49) combined history and the elements to show how the war might end, dwarfing David's

30
Jacques-Louis David,
The First Consul Crossing the Alps at the Grand Saint-Bernard Pass 1800.
Oil paint on canvas,
259 × 221,
Château de Malmaison,
Rueil-Malmaison

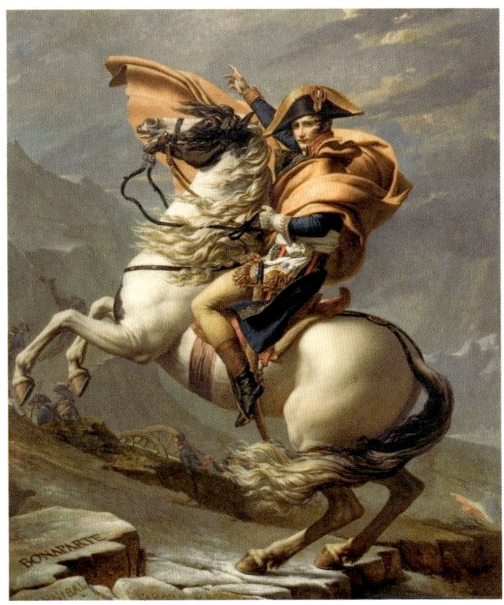

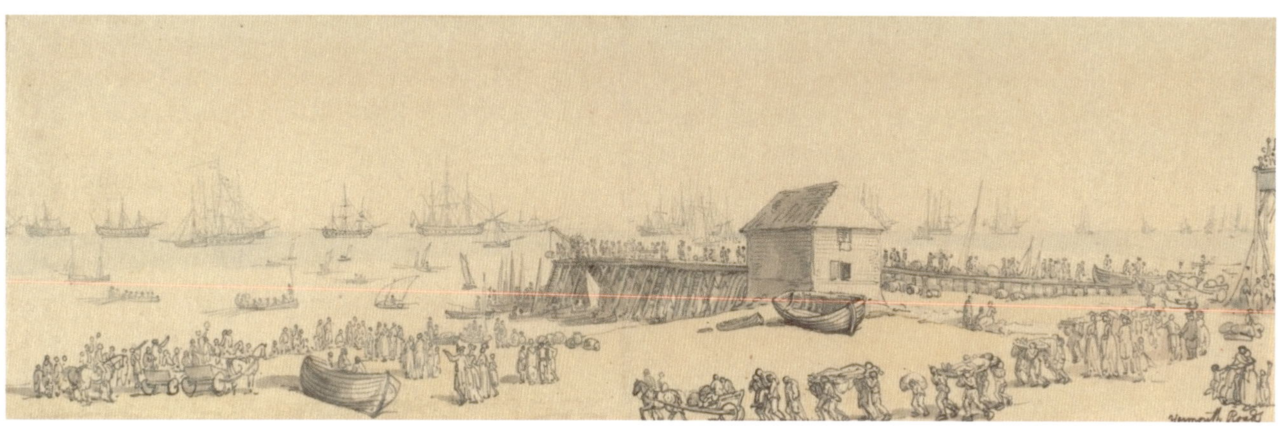

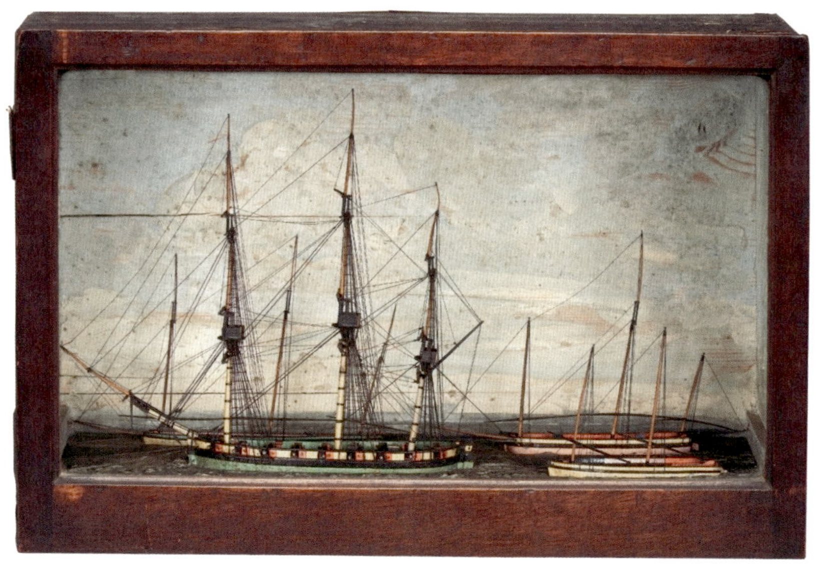

   31 Thomas Rowlandson, *Yarmouth Roads: Wounded Men Being Carried Ashore* 1797. Pen and watercolour on paper, 14.1 × 42.8, Tate
32 *Ship models including small craft for cross-Channel invasion, with the sea and background painted by Turner* c.1804.
Wood and mixed media, 45.9 × 29.8 × 21, Tate Archive

Hannibal-Napoleon with a blizzard that Turner had seen in Yorkshire, and proved an uncannily prophetic motif for later that year when the French retreated from Moscow, defeated by the Russian winter. Unable to recover from this debacle, Napoleon abdicated and went into exile on Elba in 1814. Preparing for the Academy exhibition in 1815, Turner thought the war was over. Returning to the ancient Punic wars between Rome and Carthage, he exhibited the first of two pictures of the rise and decline of Carthage (the latter followed in 1817). As warnings from the past against hubris and triumphalism, they were as relevant to victorious Britain as defeated France – not least because calling peace was premature in 1815 when Napoleon returned for the Hundred Days and was only decisively defeated at Waterloo in June. While Britain usually identified with Rome, a French contributor to the *Quarterly Review* – and by some accounts Turner himself – saw a new Carthage, a maritime empire bound eventually to collapse. Turner's 1815 exhibits included two watercolours, *The Battle of Fort Rock, Val d'Aouste, 1796* (no.51) and *The Lake of Lucerne, from the Landing*

Place at Fleulen (no.52), linked associatively by a woman who tends a dead or dying youth and is then seen weeping, mourning her loss or sensing grief to come. The 1815 watercolours were modest rehearsals for the more ambitious pairing of war and peace in *The Field of Waterloo* (no.37) and *Dort or Dordrecht: The Dort Packet-Boat from Rotterdam Becalmed* (no.33) – death and darkness contrasting with light and the freedom to travel Turner experienced again in Holland and the Rhineland in 1817.

In Britain the long war had driven technological advance and social change, made some rich and many poor and seeded demands for political reforms. Victory in 1815 prepared for a century of imperial hegemony but its immediate aftermath was an economic slump. Demobbed soldiers and sailors, wounded or maimed, were abandoned to fend for themselves, begging and dying on the streets. Others became radicalised. Dreadful weather in 1816, the 'year without a summer', compounded a sense of a continuing apocalypse. For continental Europe the fall of Napoleon meant

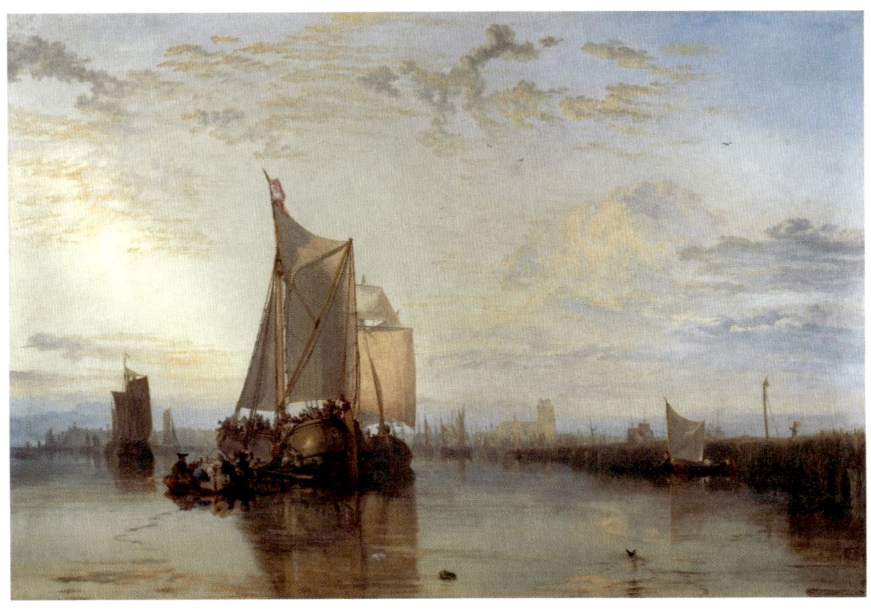

a return to reactionary dynastic monarchies. Peace did not allow Turner to forget the war. He reviewed it in pictures and illustrations to books like Walter Scott's *Life of Napoleon* (nos.61–4) and war poems by Thomas Campbell (no.65). George IV commissioned him to paint a vast *Battle of Trafalgar* (no.34; see also no.55). The last voyage of a Trafalgar veteran seen in Turner's 1806 picture became *The Fighting Temeraire* (no.134), an elegy for the heroic age of sail or for its victims – not forgetting the mutineers of 1801. Towed up the Thames to the breakers, she approaches a distant forest of masts, a ghost fleet assembled to say farewell, beneath a sunset as red as the blood that had drenched their decks. Another sanguine sky illuminates *Calais Sands*, where Fort Rouge, built by an earlier military ruler, Louis XIV, for coastal defence has survived a wartime British attempt to blow it up and assumed a peacetime role, signalling by light, flag or bell when the tide allows safe passage (no.56).

More than any British leader or soldier, Napoleon cast a long shadow – literally in *War. The Exile and*

the *Rock Limpet* (no.160) exhibited with *Peace – Burial at Sea* (no.162). Under British guard on St Helena the former emperor – heightened by his reflection – looms over a tiny shellfish that, unlike him, is free to join its 'comrades'. Illustrating Scott's *Life*, Turner tried to obtain a portrait of Napoleon but could have consulted those belonging to his friend Soane, who like Samuel Rogers and many other friends and patrons was fascinated by Napoleon. Picturing Napoleon at Marengo for Rogers's poem *Italy* (no.70), he reprised David's equestrian portrait in miniature. Arguably, Napoleon attracted more interest and admiration in Britain – even his nemesis the Duke of Wellington regretted not meeting him at Waterloo – than he did during the Bourbon restoration in France. Napoleon's reputation revived after the 1830 Revolution during the 'July monarchy' of Turner's acquaintance Louis-Philippe, alongside Anglo-French rapprochement. The king's embrace of 'all the glories of France' extended to repatriating Napoleon's remains for burial in Paris's Les Invalides, the likely inspiration for *War* and perhaps its companion *Peace*,

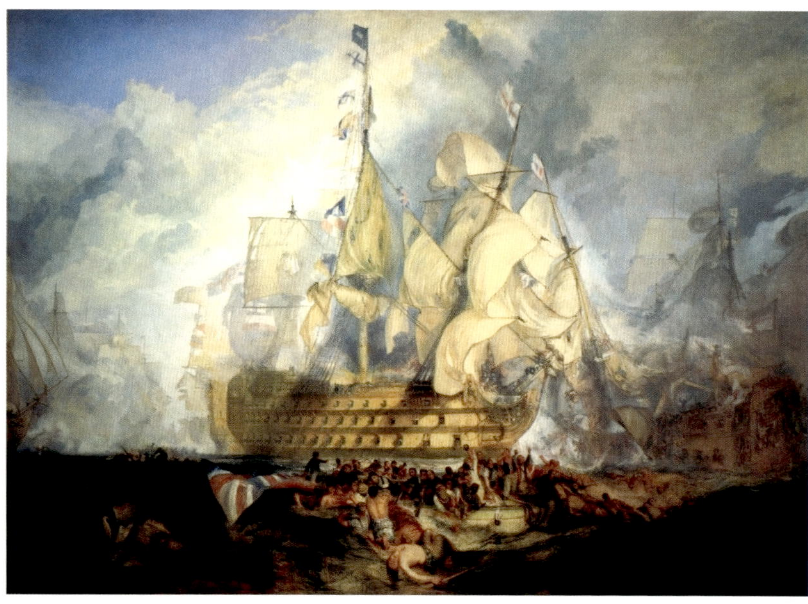

34
Battle of Trafalgar, 21 October 1805 1822–4. Oil paint on canvas, 261.5 × 368.5, National Maritime Museum, Greenwich

which, when completed, showed the burial of the
artist David Wilkie from the steamer *Oriental* off
Gibraltar but may have begun by depicting the
sailing frigate *La Belle Poule* sent to St Helena
to collect the late emperor. In the verse for *The
Opening of the Wallhalla, 1842* (no.81), celebrating
cultural revival in liberated, post-war Germany,
Turner recalled Napoleon's 'tide of war' before
'peace returns' with 'science, and the arts'.

Victories and Victims: Trafalgar and Waterloo

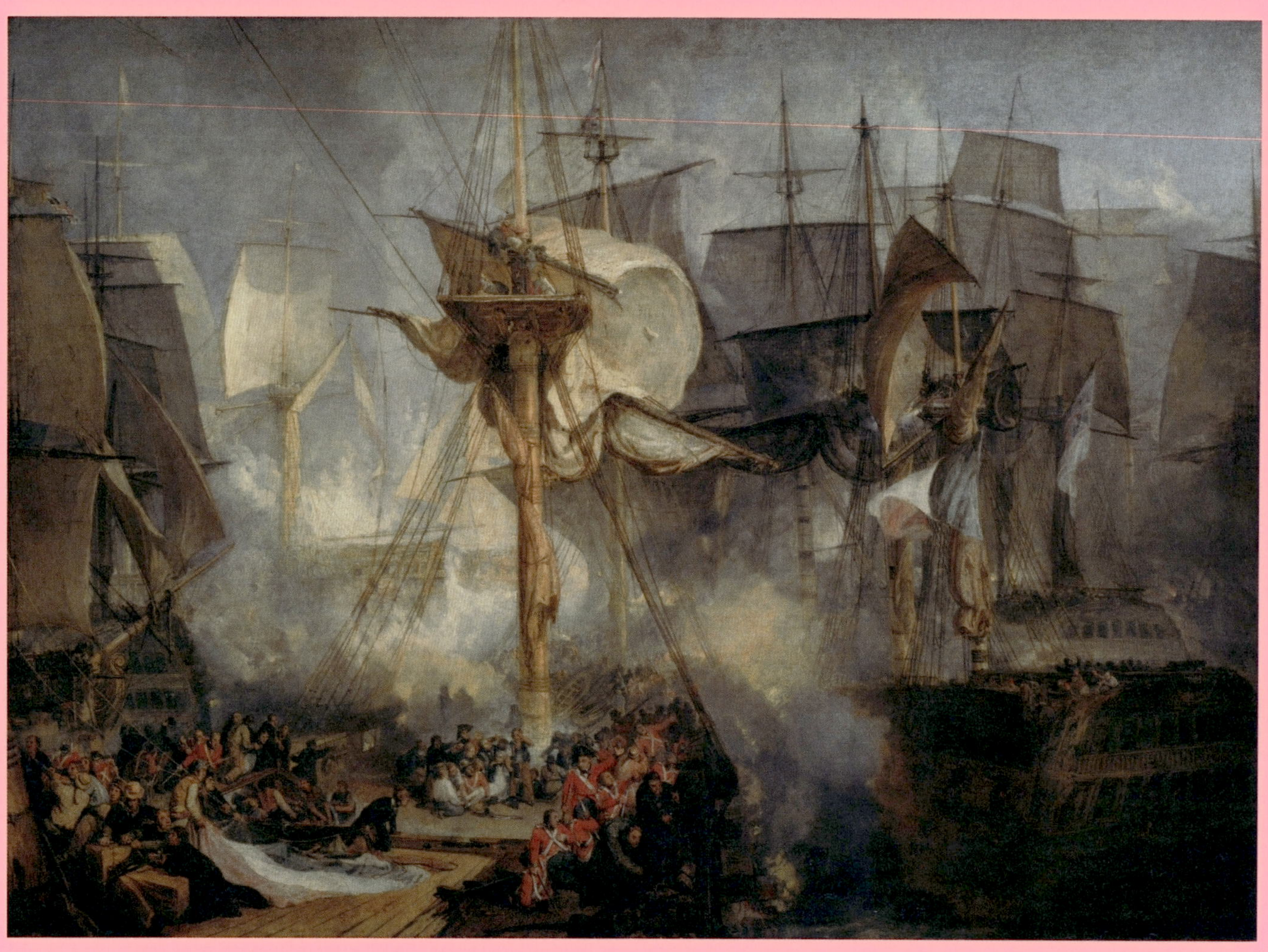

 35 *The Battle of Trafalgar, as Seen from the Mizen Starboard Shrouds of the Victory* 1806–8. Oil paint on canvas, 170.8 × 238.8, Tate

Nelson's defeat of the French and Spanish navies at Trafalgar on
21 October 1805 lifted the threat of a cross-Channel invasion and
inaugurated a century of British supremacy at sea. His death in
the battle and the estimated 1,587 men killed or wounded meant
the victory was also a national tragedy (French and Spanish losses
were never confirmed but have been estimated at about 16,000). The
exhibition at Turner's Gallery in 1806 was a tribute to Nelson and
Trafalgar. Turner visited Nelson's flagship *Victory* while she was
at Sheerness for repairs, met officers and crew, filled a sketchbook
with memoranda (no.39) – some probably contributed by the men
themselves – and made larger drawings including one of *Victory's*
quarterdeck, noting splintered timber, damaged rails and poundage
of guns (no.38).

These drawings and notes enabled him to give his *Battle of Trafalgar*
(no.35) a persuasive illusion of realism. In the press of ships engaged
at terrifyingly close range, *Victory* is sandwiched between the
Spanish *Santissima Trinidada* (left) and French *Redoutable* (right).
A French sniper's bullet strikes Nelson, who collapses just as the
French concede defeat by laying a tricolour on *Victory's* deck. Hardly
finished in 1806, the picture was reworked for the British Institution
in 1808 when John Landseer praised it as an '*epic*' combining a
'hero's' death with 'the whole of a great naval victory'.[49] It was shown
with a key to the narrative and protagonists and perhaps also a
picture known as 'The Victory returning from Trafalgar', a triple
'portrait' but not at the time described, as she is undamaged, sailing
in the wrong direction and not flying her ensign at half-mast as she
would if carrying Nelson's body (no.36).

Depicting Waterloo in 1818, three years after the battle on 16 June
1815, Turner moved from actions to their tragic aftermath. He
visited Waterloo in 1817, taking the usual clockwise tour, sketching
and making notes (no.40), and adapted words from Byron's *Childe
Harold's Pilgrimage* – 'Rider and horse – friend, foe, in one red burial
blent' – as the epigraph for his picture (no.37). Jan Piggott suggests
Turner had seen and borrowed the 'Discharge of rockets' from a
Waterloo Panorama exhibited by Henry Aston Barker in Leicester
Square in 1816.[50] That these are celebratory seems doubtful in a
picture so focused on death and loss. Non-partisan and democratic,
it does not privilege the allied victory or distinguish officers or
commanders from the general carnage. Allied losses were estimated
at 23,000, French at 25,000. As an indictment of the human cost of
war, and portrayal of women as mourners or comforters, it bears

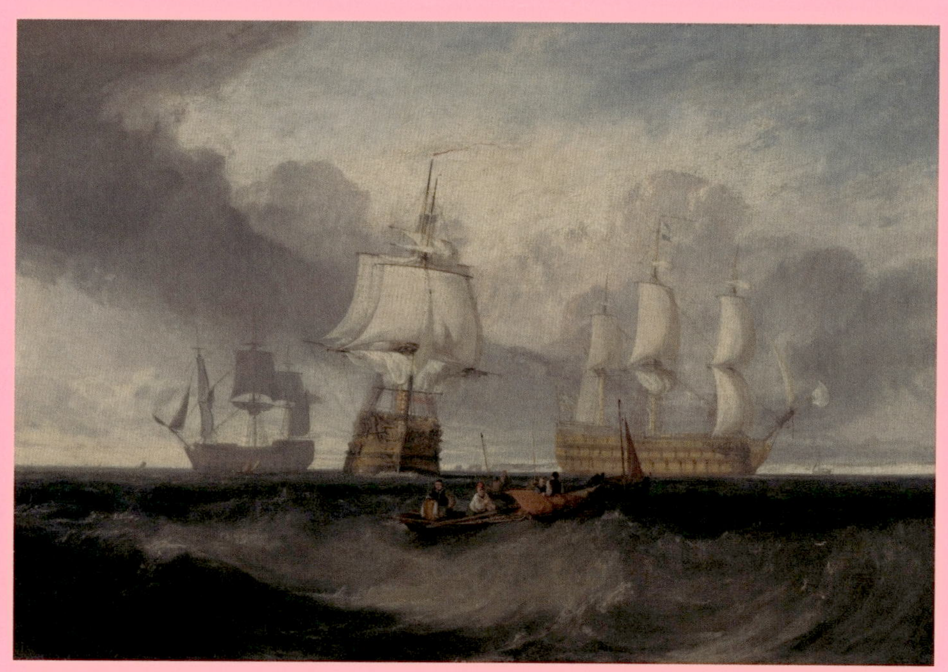

36 *The Victory Returning from Trafalgar, in Three Positions* c.1806.
Oil paint on canvas, 67 × 100.3, Yale Center for British Art, Paul Mellon Collection, New Haven

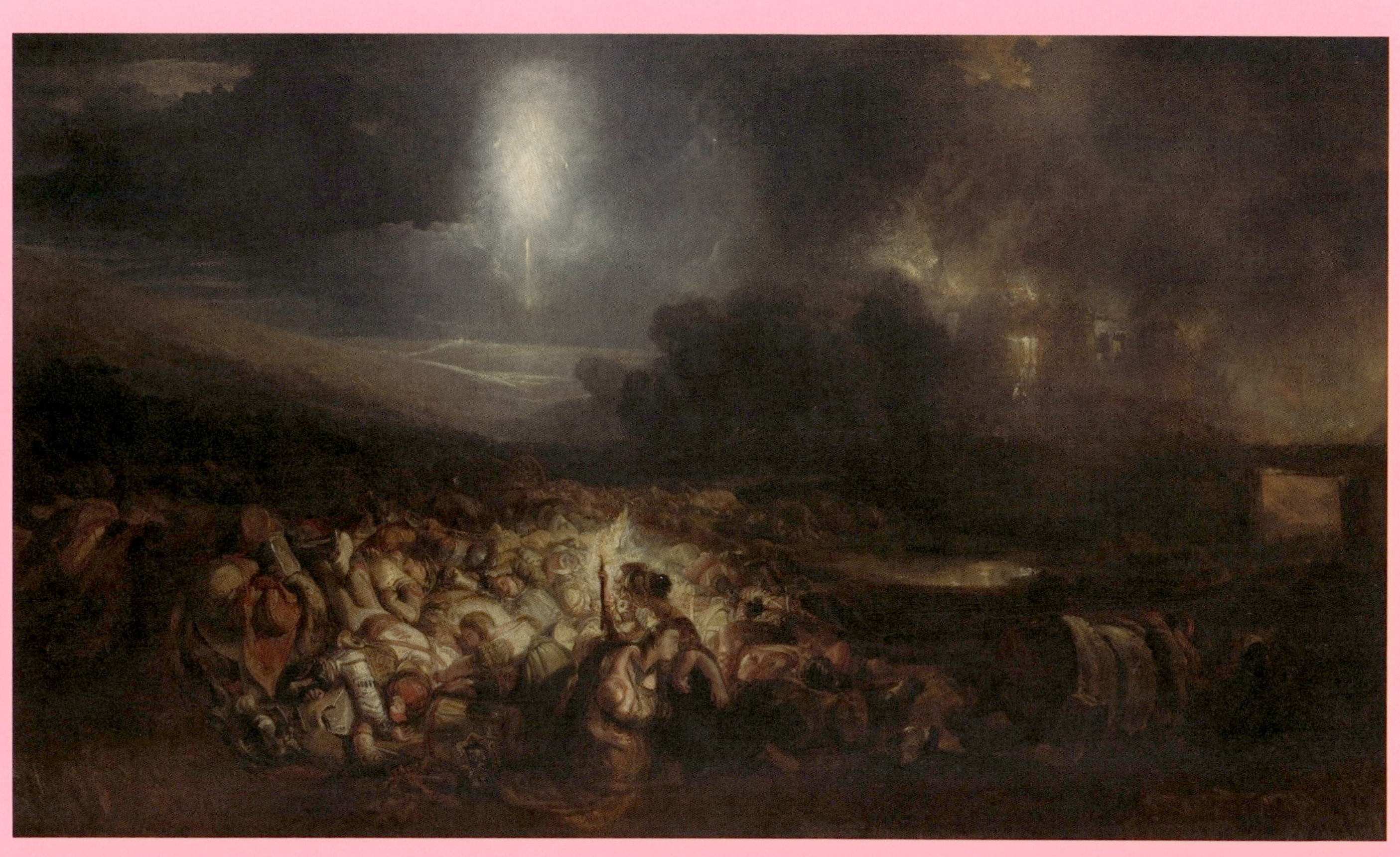

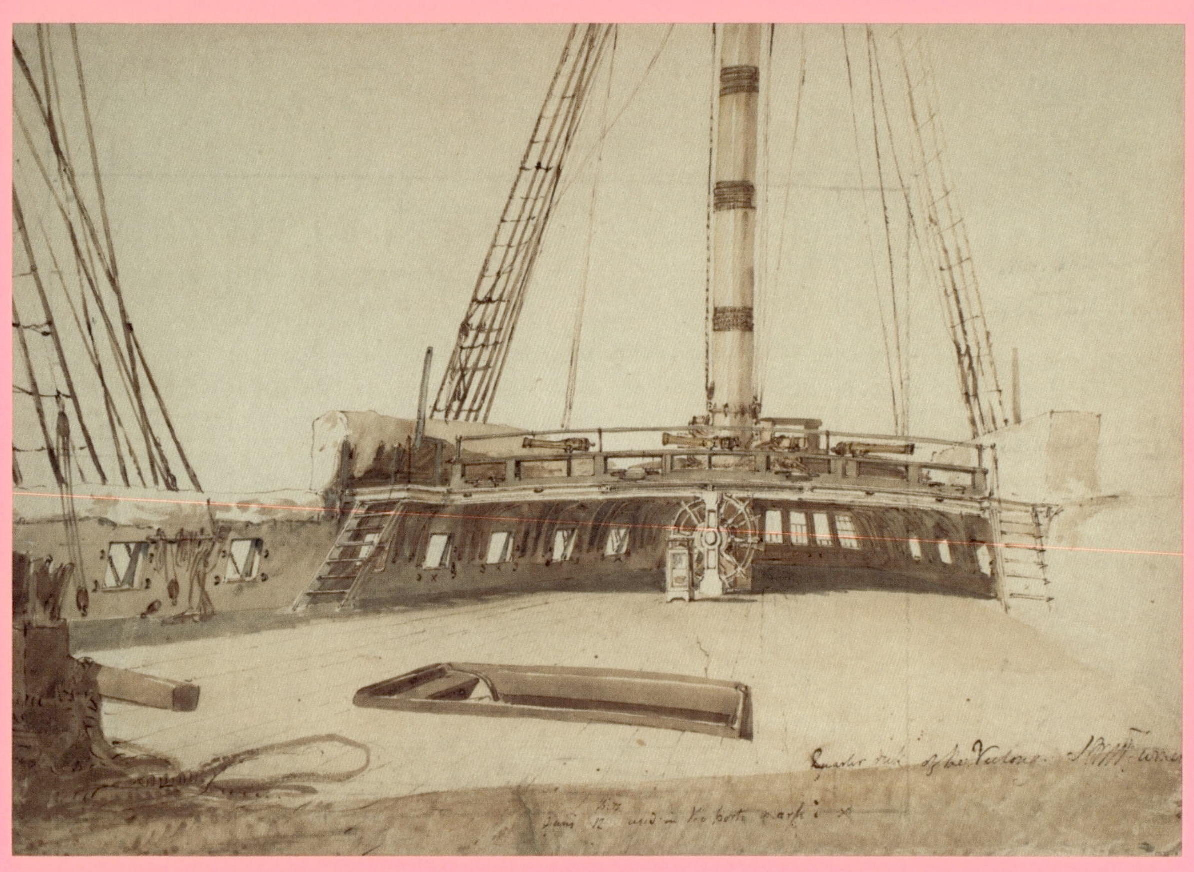

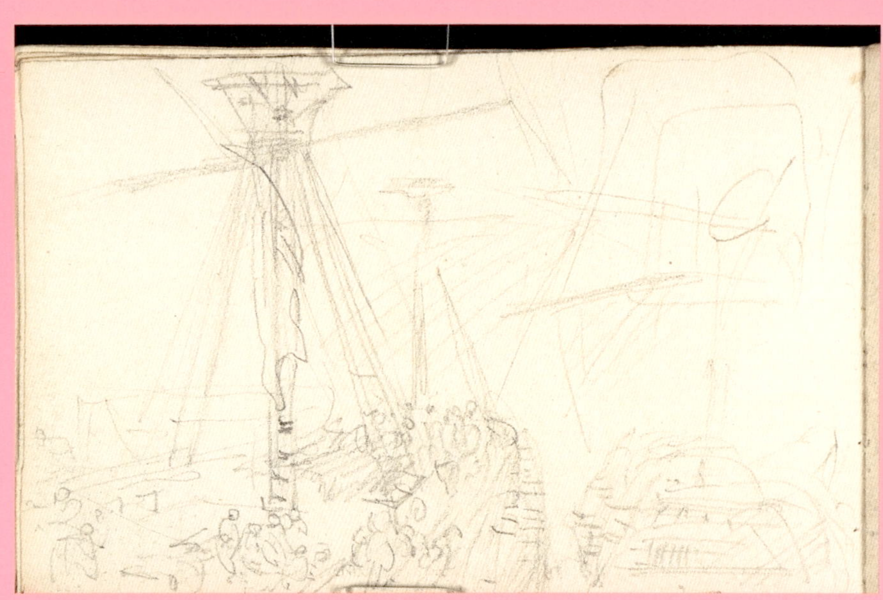

38 *The 'Victory': From Quarterdeck to Poop* 1805. Pen and ink, graphite and watercolour on paper, 42.4 × 56.5, Tate
39 *Study for* 'The Battle of Trafalgar, as Seen from the Mizen Starboard Shrouds of the Victory' 1805. Graphite on paper, 11.4 × 18.4, Tate

comparison with Goya's depictions of Peninsular horrors (also called 'Consequences') published long after his death,[51] modern war photography and – if Picasso saw it or F.C. Lewis's 1830 mezzotint – *Guernica* (1937; Museo Nacional Centro de Arte Reina Sofia, Madrid).[52]

Neither *Trafalgar* nor *Waterloo* found buyers although Walter Fawkes bought the smaller *Victory* and a watercolour of Waterloo (no.50) made around the same time as the picture, in which the mingling of the dead is emphasised by British, French and Scottish uniforms and the cyphers 'GR' (George III) and 'N' (Napoleon). Turner repeated Waterloo as illustrations to Byron (no.72) and Walter Scott, and – as his only royal commission – painted a larger, more conventional version of Trafalgar for George IV (no.34), working from oil sketches (no.55). DBB

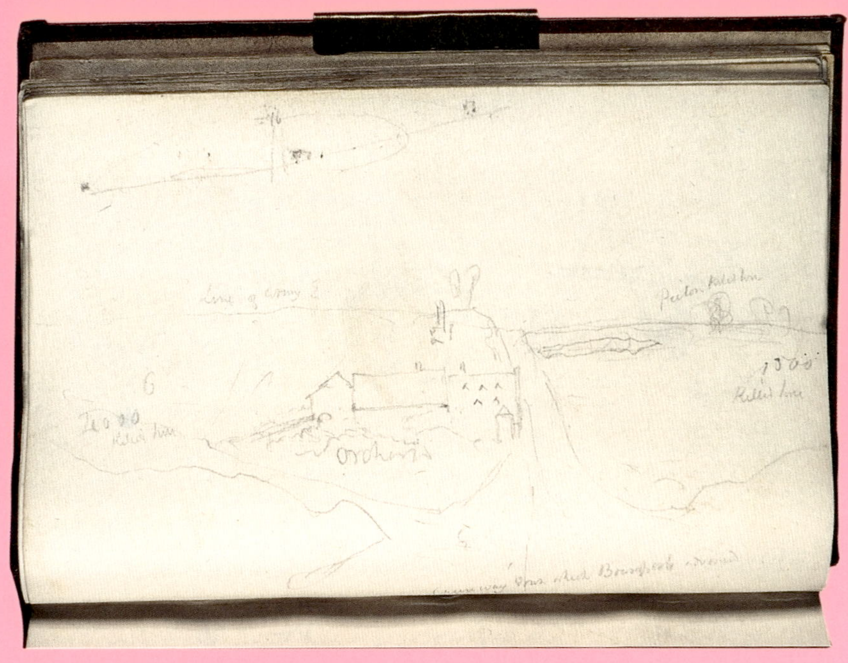

Hidden History: Seizure and Shipwreck

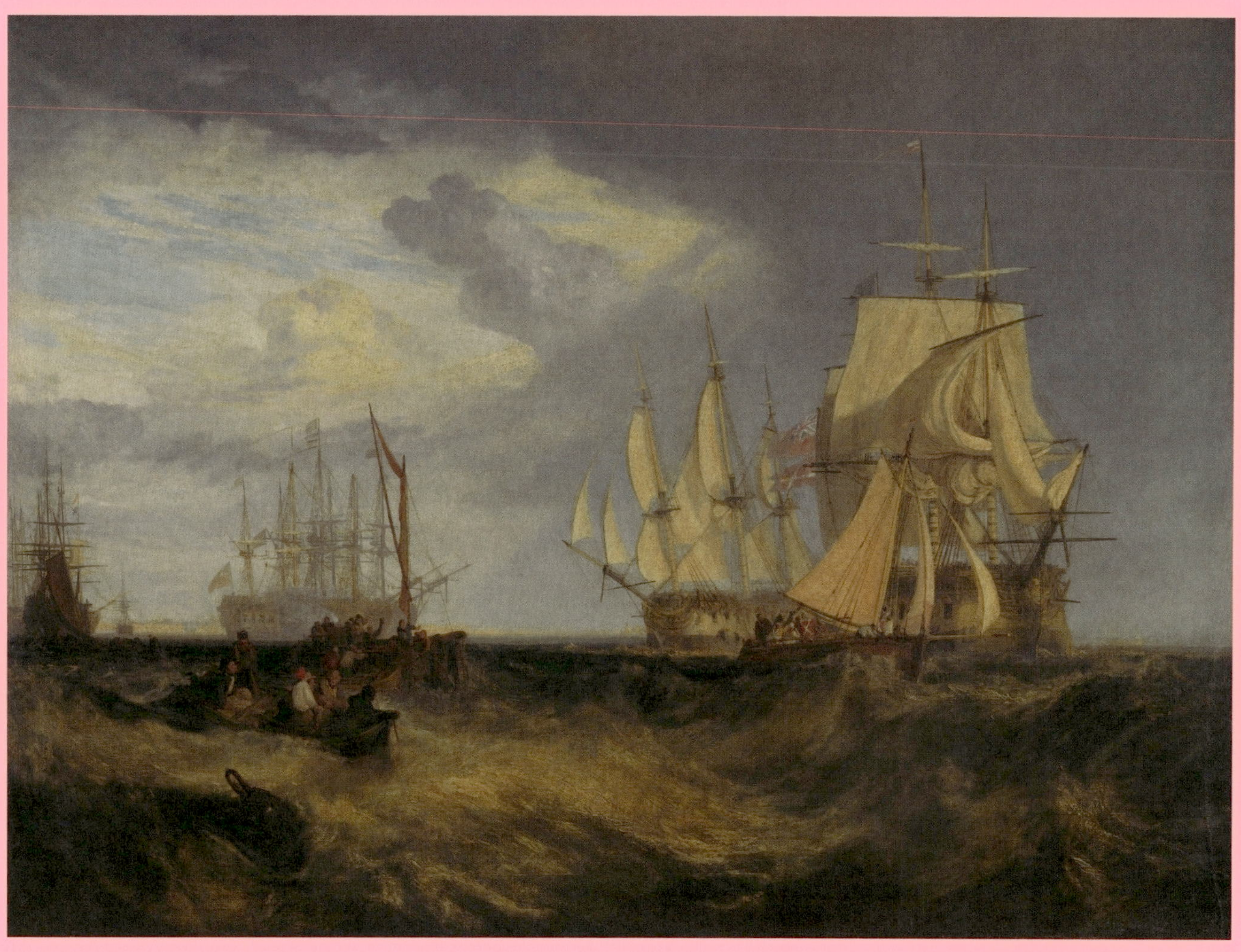

41 *Spithead: Boat's Crew Recovering an Anchor* 1807–9. Oil paint on canvas, 171.4 × 233.7, Tate

British assaults on the Danish fleet and capital in 1801 and 1807 were early examples of pre-emptive strikes. Turner depicted the first 'Battle of the Baltic' as an illustration to the poem by Thomas Campbell (no.71) and exhibited a picture in 1808 after watching captured Danish ships arrive off Spithead (no.41).

Denmark, with Sweden and Russia, was part of a League of Armed Neutrality, so not an enemy. But after Russia aligned with Napoleon at Tilsit in 1806, the British government feared the Danish navy would be co-opted into Napoleon's post-Trafalgar Continental Blockade and close the Baltic to British merchant shipping. An expeditionary force was despatched to persuade the Danes to surrender their fleet and, when they refused, seized it and bombarded Copenhagen, employing the incendiary Congreve rockets developed at Woolwich from prototypes originally used by Tipu Sultan at Seringapatam. Danish artists painted this 'most terrible night' but Turner reported its results from the British side. His picture shows two Danish ships, the *Three Crowns* and *Denmark*, arriving under British escort on 1 November 1807, having become separated from the larger squadron by bad weather.

Turner's subject was recorded by John Landseer as 'two of the DANISH SHIPS … seized at COPENHAGEN, entering Portsmouth Harbour', noting 'the grandeur of the lofty Danes'.[53] When shown again in 1809, the picture had been given its present title, *Spithead: Boat's Crew Recovering an Anchor*, although it is also known under its original title, *Spithead: Two Captured Danish Ships Entering Portsmouth Harbour*. Turning a neutral nation into an enemy, the British action had become toxic abroad and inflamed political conflict at home. While the Foreign Secretary, George Canning, argued Britain was already so 'hated throughout Europe' that it might as well launch 'all-out maritime war', the Lord Chancellor, Erskine, declared that if hell did not exist it should be created to punish ministers for their 'damnable measure'. If Turner thought it prudent to change his title, he nevertheless kept the Danish flags flying below the British to signal surrender. Although admired as a marine subject, the picture did not sell.

The Wreck of a Transport Ship (no.42) was not exhibited in 1810 when it was painted for Charles Anderson-Pelham, later Earl of Yarborough. With its towering seas, ship breaking up beneath terrified passengers, survivors clinging to wreckage and fishing boats trying and failing to rescue them, it is Turner's most spectacular picture of a maritime catastrophe. Two red-coated infantrymen among the struggling victims remind us that soldiers not only died fighting but in storms and wrecks on their way overseas. Turner did not name the ship or locate this disaster. They may be imaginary or suggested by events either too common or terrible to identify. The wreck of the *Minotaur* off Holland, with which Lord Yarborough seems to have come to associate it, occurred some months after he commissioned the picture. A keen sailor and founder, and first Commodore of the Royal Yacht Squadron, Yarborough is remembered on his monument on the Isle of Wight for his dedication to Britain's 'maritime interests' and improving 'naval architecture'. That these were clearly failing, leaving an island nation vulnerable, was perhaps the point for painter and patron. DBB

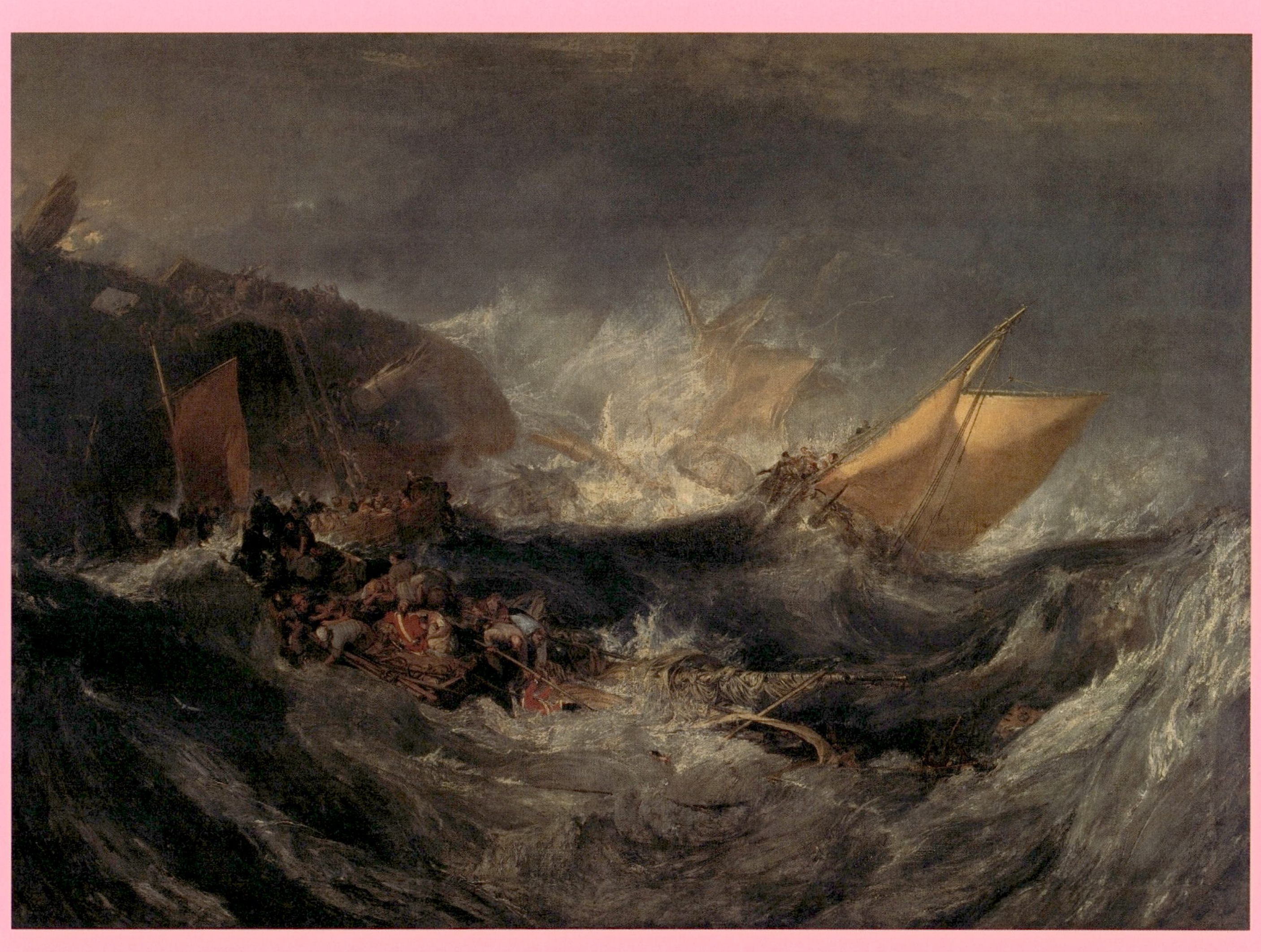

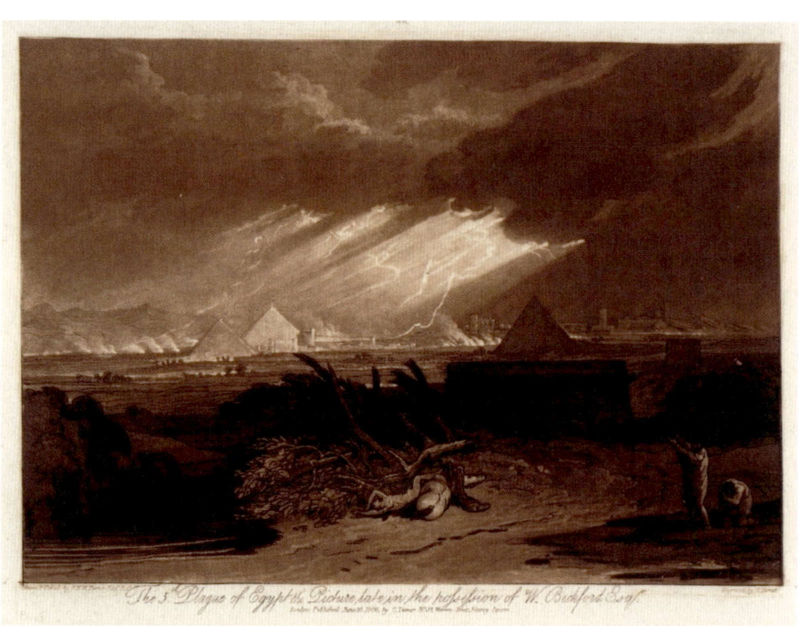

 43 Charles Turner after Joseph Mallord William Turner, *The Fifth Plague of Egypt* 1808. Etching and mezzotint on paper, 18 × 26 (image), Tate

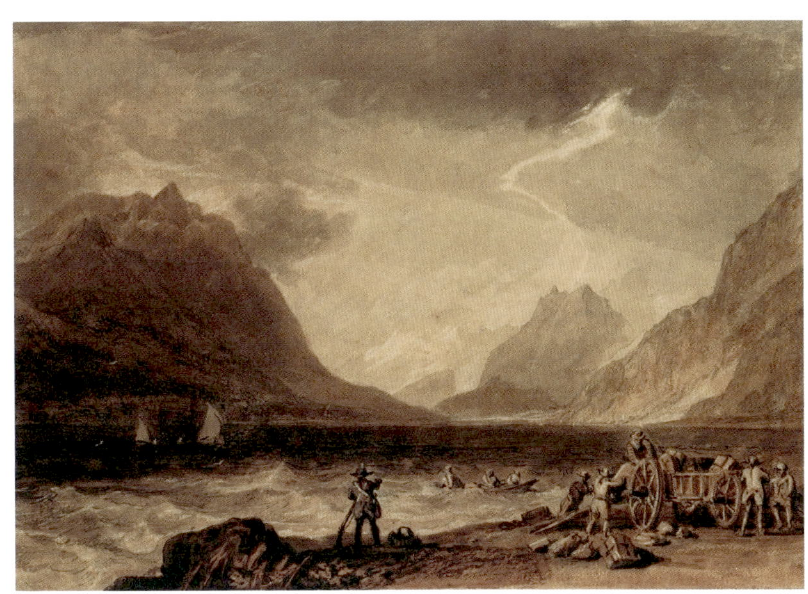

44 *Lake of Thun* c.1806–7. Graphite and watercolour on paper, 18.5 × 26.4, Tate

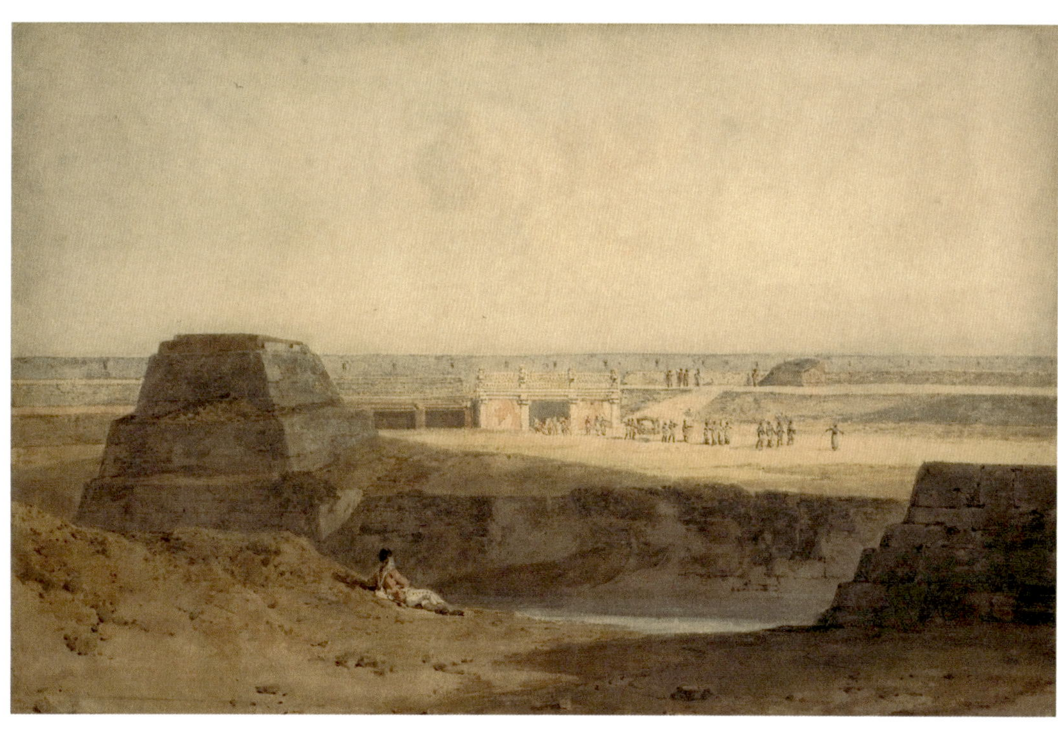

45 *The Fortress of Seringapatam, from the Cullaly Deedy Gate* 1800.
Graphite and watercolour on paper, 47.5 × 67.7, Nirmalya Kumar Collection

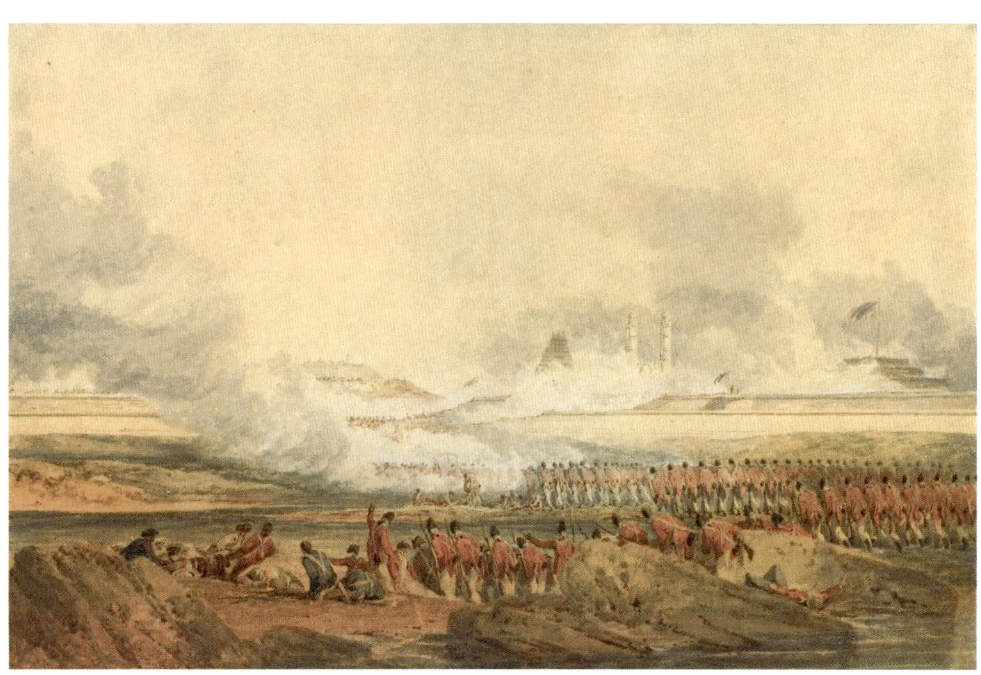

46 *The Siege of Seringapatam* c.1800. Graphite, watercolour and gouache on paper, 42.1 × 64.7, Tate

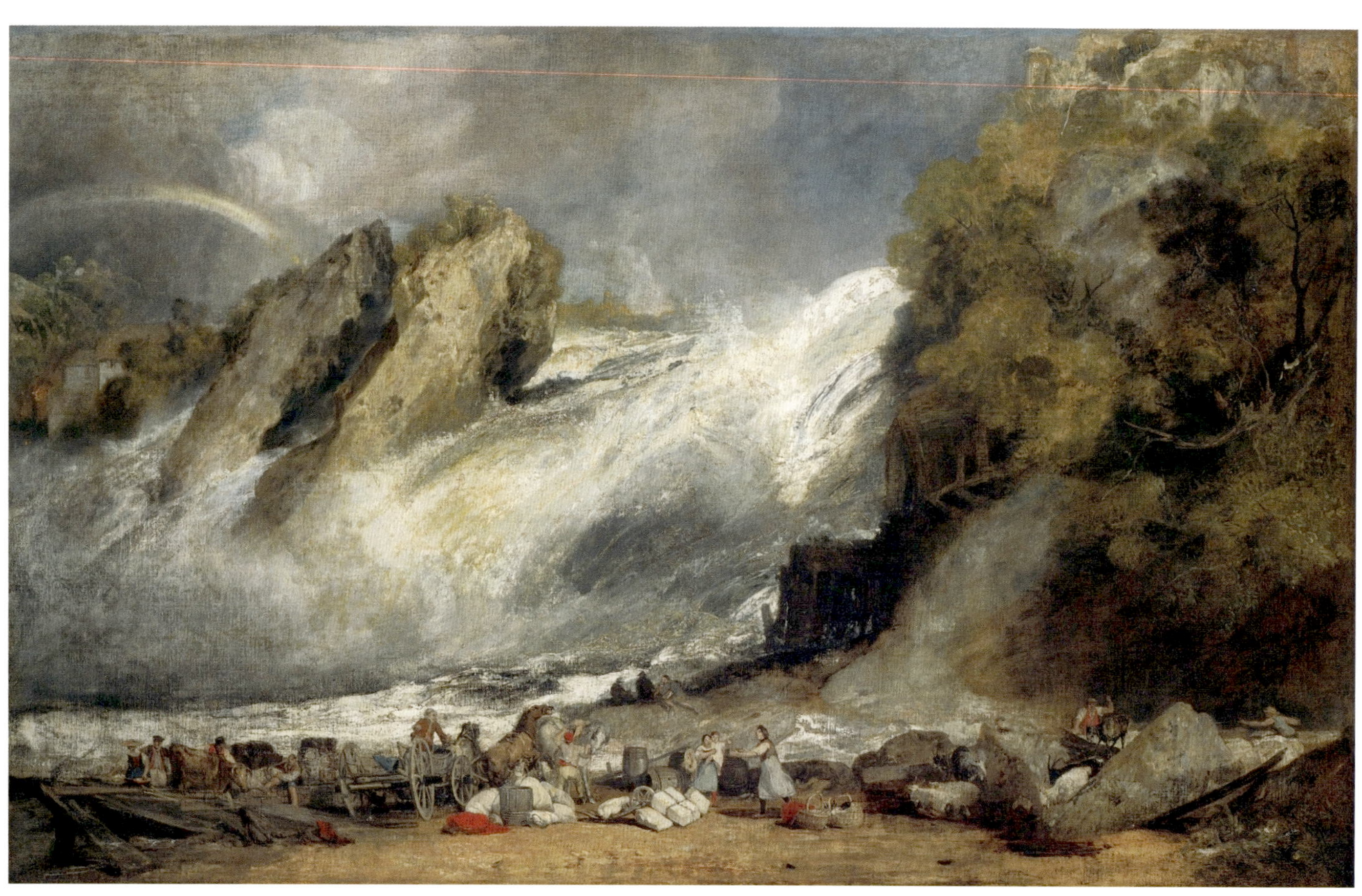

 47 *Fall of the Rhine at Schaffhausen* c.1805–6. Oil paint on canvas, 148.6 × 239.7, Museum of Fine Arts, Boston

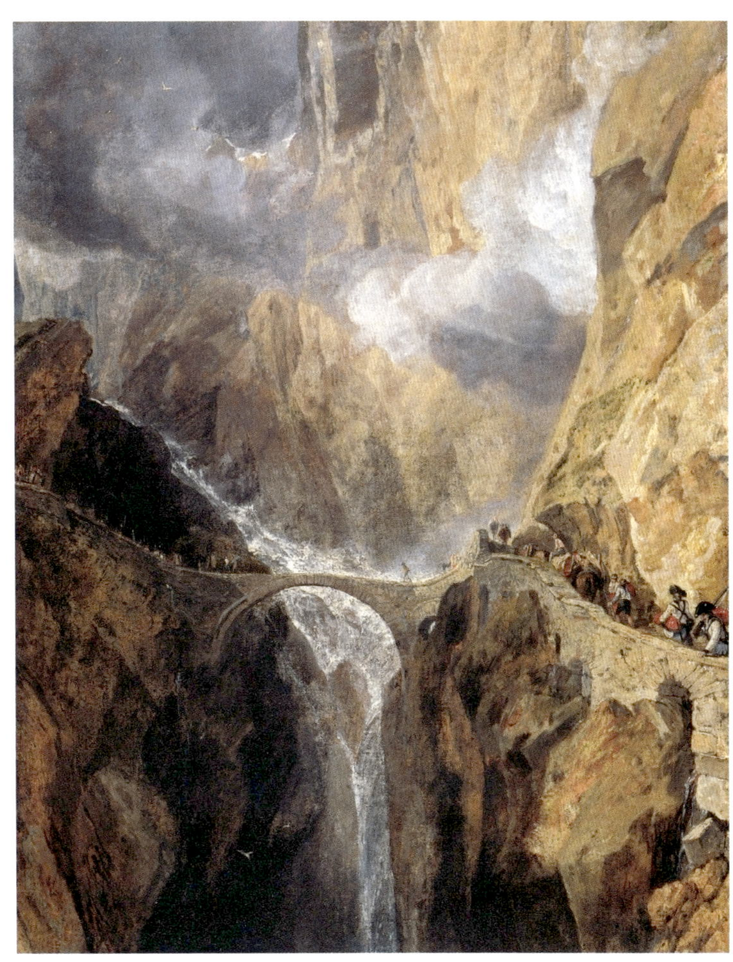

48 *The Devil's Bridge, St Gotthard* 1803. Oil paint on canvas, 76.8 × 62.8, Schorr Collection

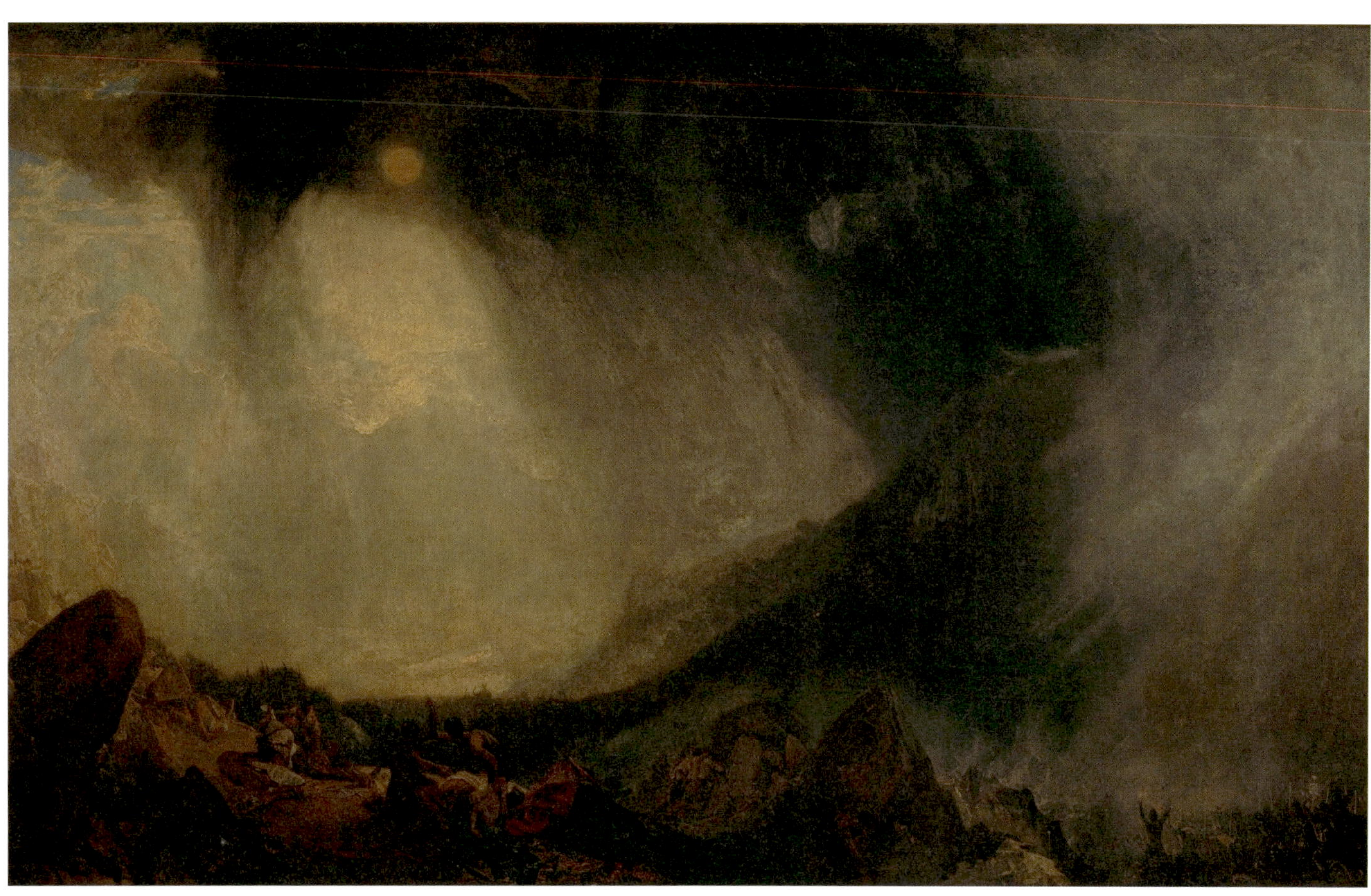

   49 *Snow Storm: Hannibal and his Army Crossing the Alps* exh. 1812. Oil paint on canvas, 146 × 237.5, Tate

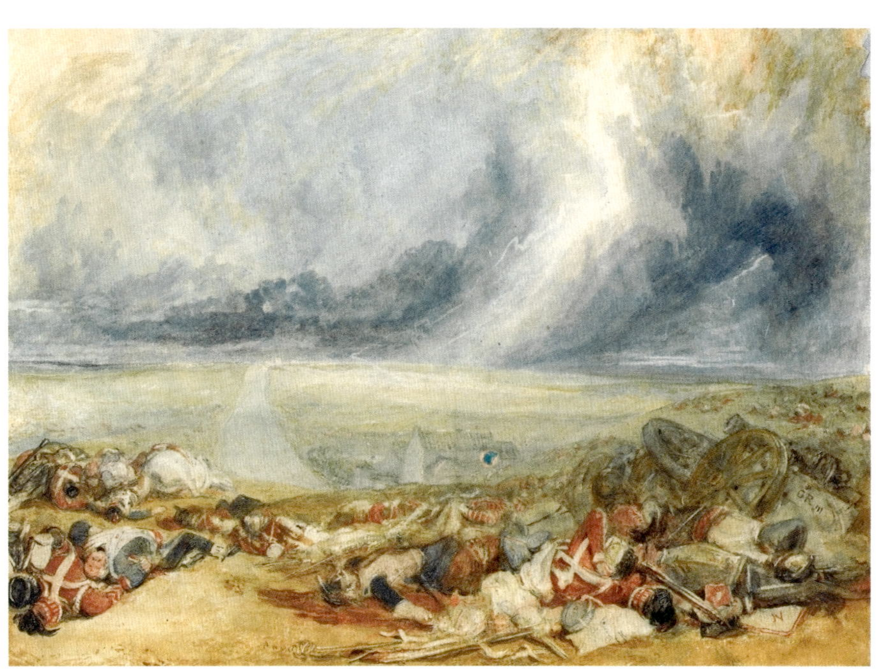

50 *The Field of Waterloo* 1817. Watercolour and graphite on paper, 28.8 × 40.5, Fitzwilliam Museum, Cambridge

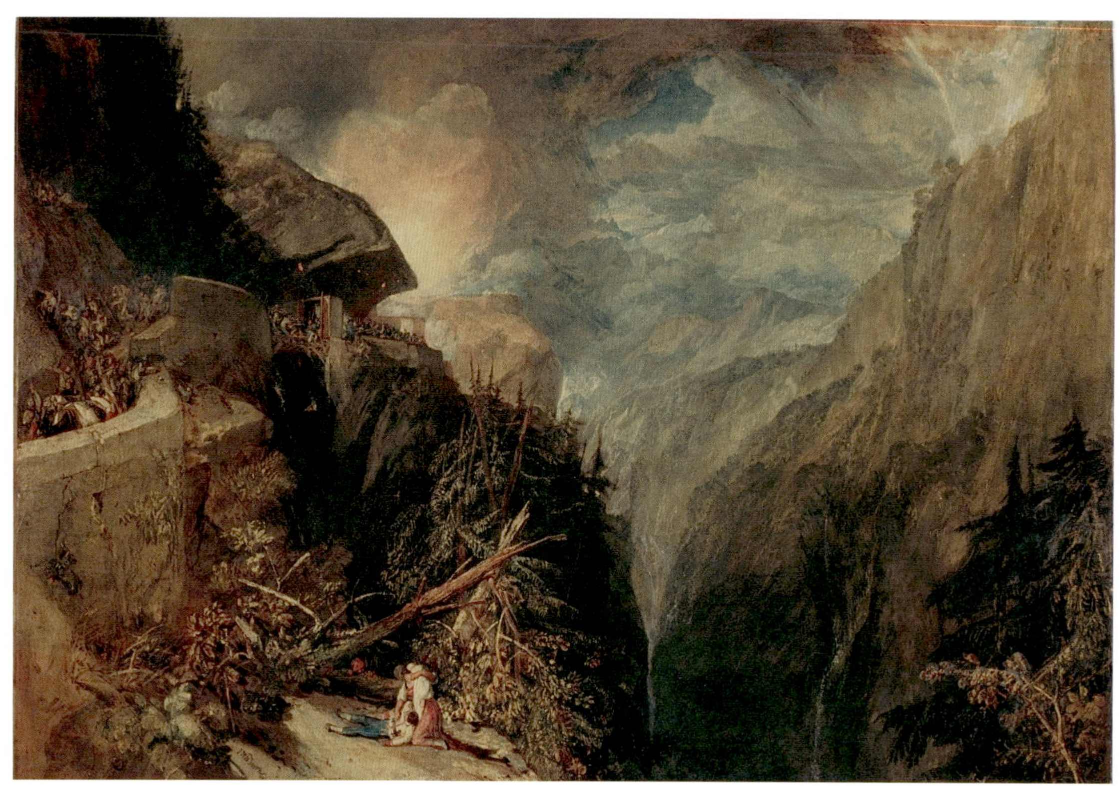

 51 *The Battle of Fort Rock, Val d'Aouste, Piedmont, 1796* exh. 1815. Gouache and watercolour on paper, 69.6 × 101.5, Tate

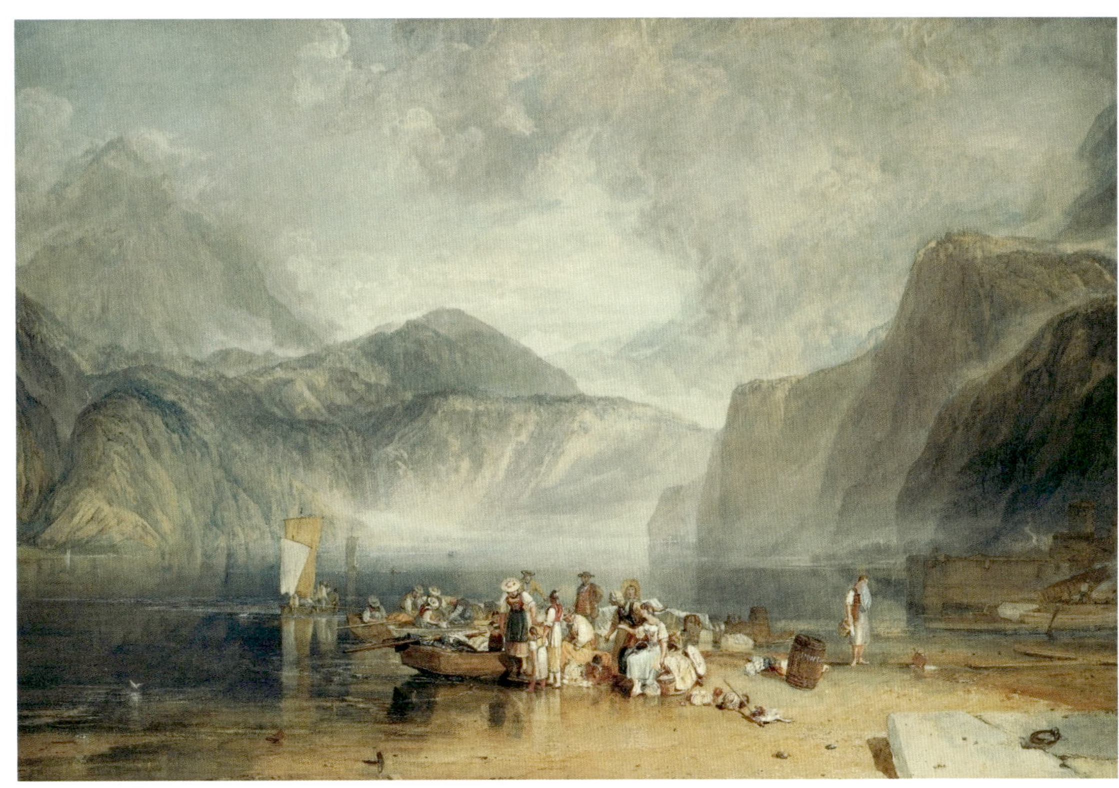

52 *Lake of Lucerne, from the Landing Place at Fleulen, Looking towards Bauen and Tell's Chapel, Switzerland* 1815.
Watercolour, gouache and gum arabic on paper, 66 × 100, Clode Collection

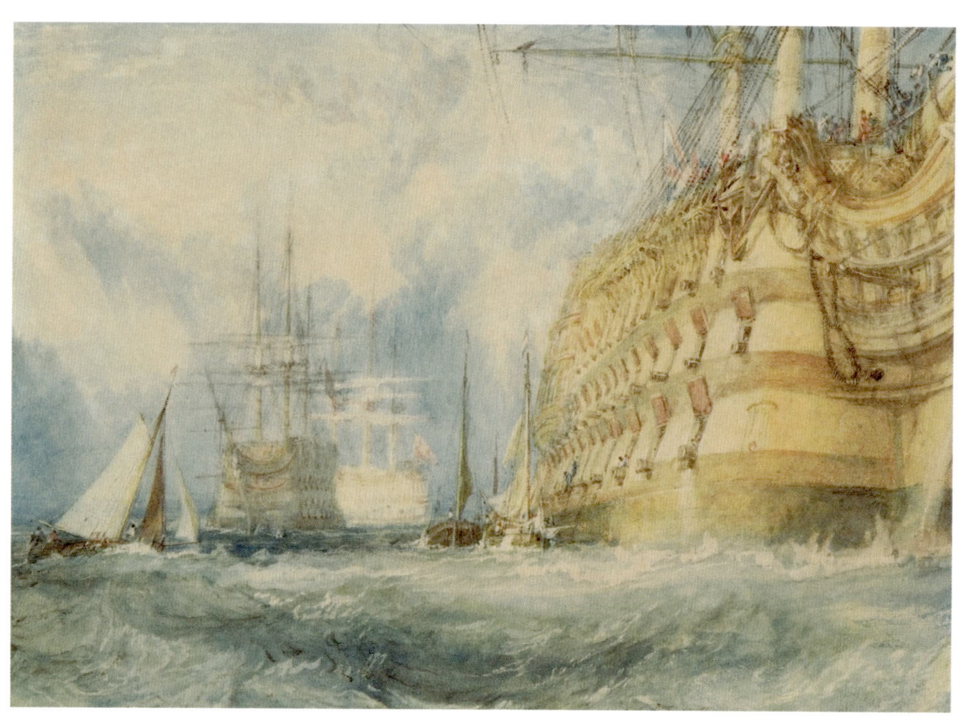

  53 *A First Rate Taking in Stores* 1818. Watercolour and graphite on paper 28.6 × 39.7, The Higgins Bedford

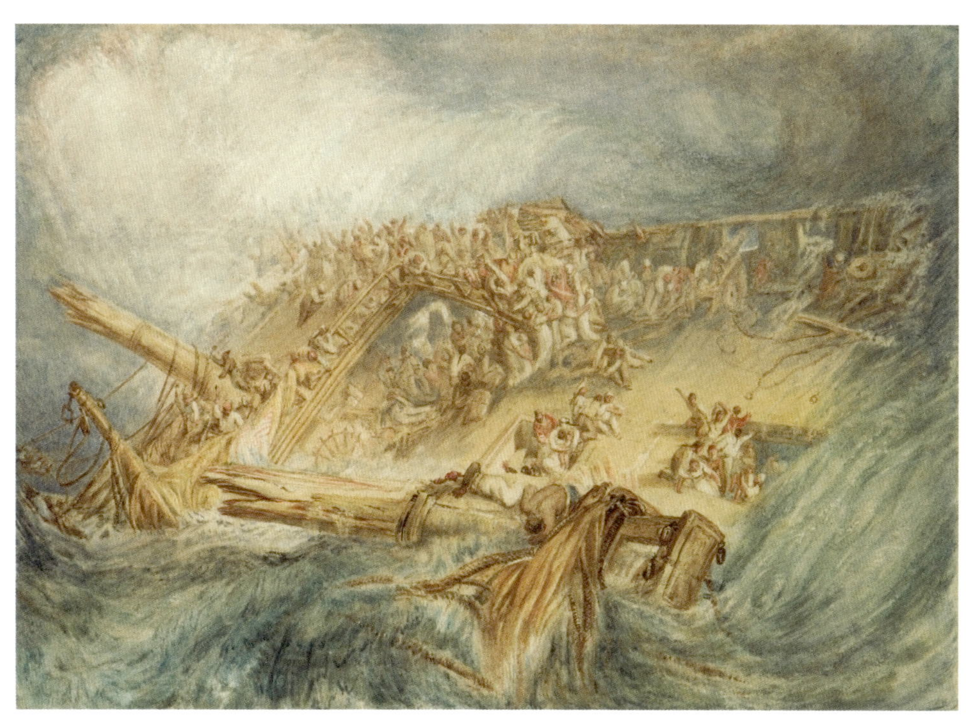

54 *The Loss of an East Indiaman* c.1818. Watercolour on paper 28 × 39.5, The Higgins Bedford

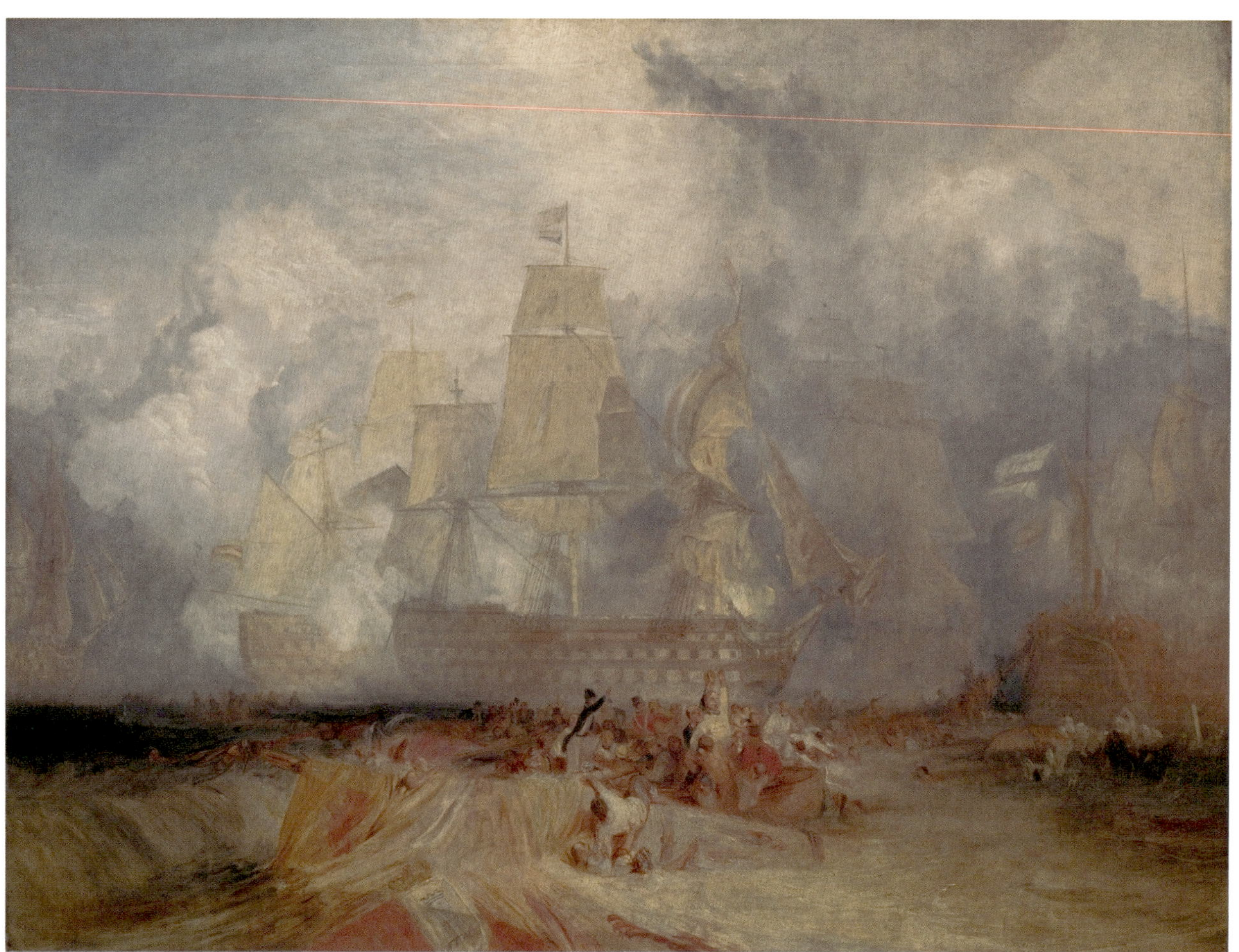

  55 *Second Sketch for* 'The Battle of Trafalgar' c.1823. Oil paint on canvas, 90.2 × 121.3, Tate

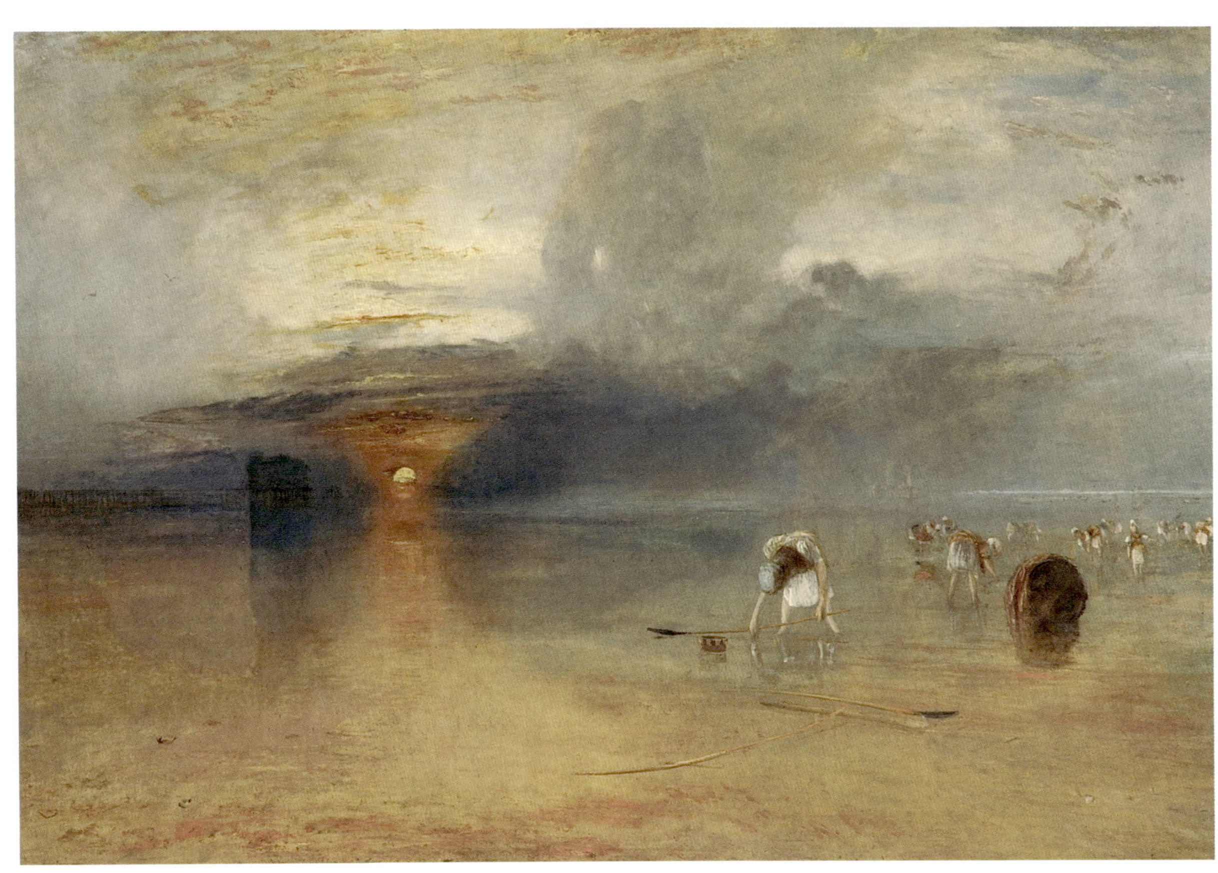

56 *Calais Sands at Low Water: Poissards Collecting Bait* 1830. Oil paint on canvas, 68.8 × 103.8, Bury Art Museum, Greater Manchester

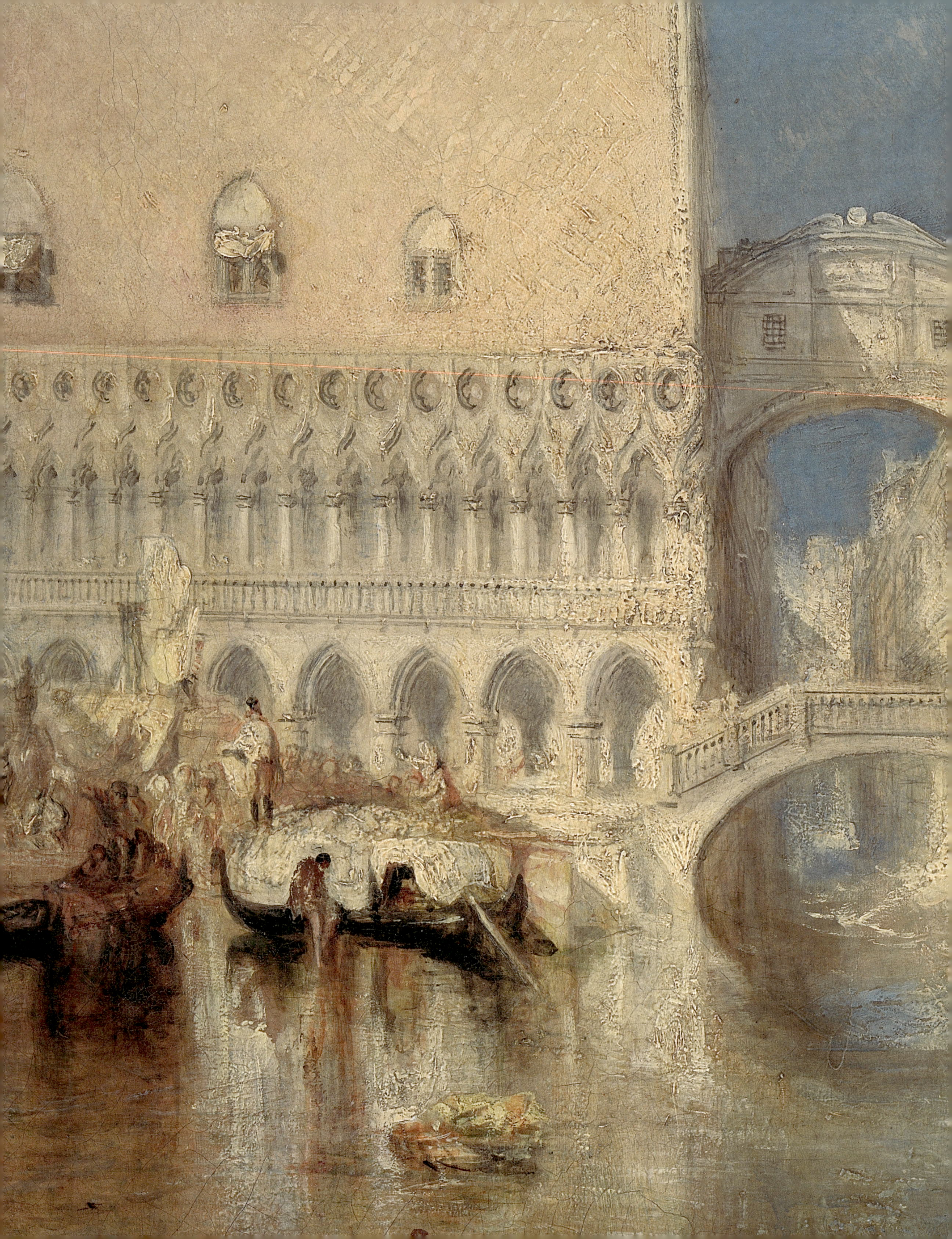

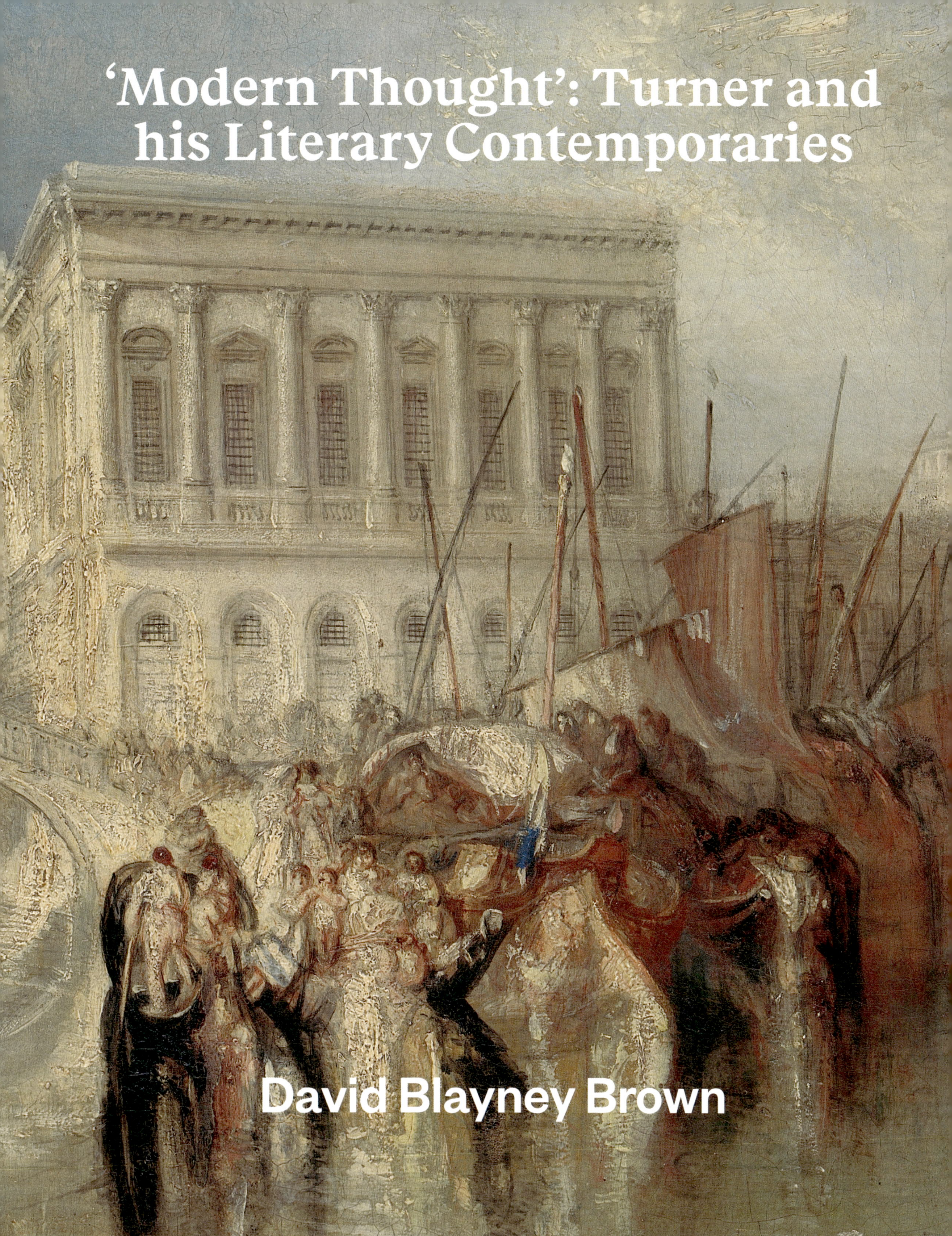

'Modern Thought': Turner and his Literary Contemporaries
David Blayney Brown

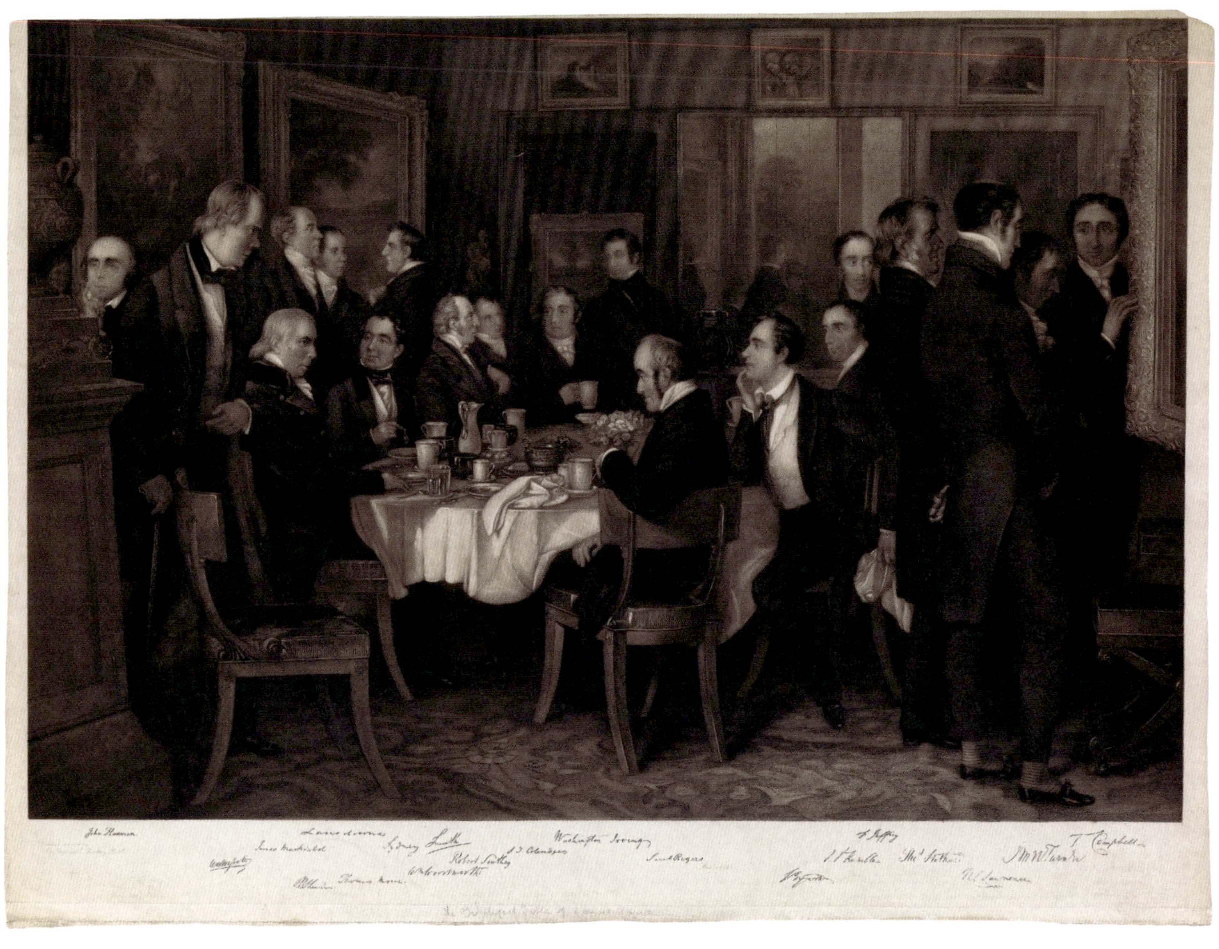

Previous page: *Venice, the Bridge of Sighs* exh. 1840 (no.80)
57 Charles Mottram after John Doyle, *Samuel Rogers at his Breakfast Table* c.1823.
Engraving and mezzotint on paper, 58 × 86.6 (image), Tate

Turner's reading, poetry, book illustrations and work with authors, publishers and editors reflected his modern interests. He illustrated Byron, Thomas Campbell, Samuel Rogers, Walter Scott and Thomas Moore but not – at least directly – William Wordsworth or S.T. Coleridge. He believed painting could not thrive without 'poesy' and was often described as a poetic artist. We should not infer from this an absolute retreat from the real world into a timeless, imaginary one. The writers he knew and worked with were among the most modern of their day.

For Ruskin, Rogers was the first poet to introduce Turner to 'modern thought', followed by Byron and Scott. While this says more about Ruskin, whose parents gave him the 1830 edition of Rogers's verse travelogue *Italy* illustrated by Turner for his thirteenth birthday, Rogers worked closely with Turner, collected his work including a drawing of the *Victory* (no.38) and hosted writers and artists at legendary breakfasts in St James's Place. A print imagines Turner (second from the right, his hand raised) at one in 1815 with Byron, then at the height of his fame (no.57). Rogers had mentored Byron since 1811 when he introduced him to Moore, his future biographer. Although no certain meeting between them is recorded, Turner and Byron had many mutual contacts. Turner's friend George Jones began illustrating Byron's best-selling *Childe Harold's Pilgrimage* when it first appeared in 1812. Another, Thomas Phillips, painted Byron (as an unnamed 'nobleman' in Albanian dress) in 1813. In 1816 Turner visited Byron's Cambridge contemporary Henry Gally Knight, whose *Phrosyne; A Grecian Tale* (1813, published 1817), inspired by Greek passages in the second canto of *Childe Harold* (1812), described a dance recalling 'ancient Greece and Liberty' that probably suggested the folkloric Romaika in Turner's picture of the Temple of Aphaia ('Jupiter Panellenius') on Aegina (no.121).

If Byron became Turner's favourite modern poet, it was not because he was a celebrity but for the love of travel and humanitarian conscience he expressed in enviably fluent rhymes. Turner supplied views of places associated with Byron for John Murray's edition of Byron's *Life and*

Works (1832–4) and on his own initiative, as he did for no other contemporary author, painted six pictures referencing *Childe Harold*. The first, *The Field of Waterloo* (no.37), appeared with verse adapted from the 'Waterloo stanzas' in the poem's third canto (1816). Whether or not Turner shared Byron's loathing of 'the victors – & the victory', he responded to his compassion for the fallen regardless of which side they had fought on. Byron's tribute to 'our enemy ... freedom's champion', the French general Marceau killed early in the Revolutionary war, prompted another picture 'from Byron's "Childe Harold"' in 1835, and his 'palace and a prison' in his lament for the downfall of Venice during the Austrian occupation became *Venice, the Bridge of Sighs* (no.80).

In 1822, a year after the Greeks rose against the Ottoman empire, Turner referred to Byron's *Giaour* (1813) for a watercolour (no.58) commissioned (with subjects from Scott and Moore) by Walter Fawkes for his library at Farnley. Turner's shackled Greek women prefigure Delacroix's *Greece on the Ruins of Missolonghi* (no.59) probably shown in London in 1828 in aid of Greek relief. In 1823 John Cam Hobhouse, a friend of Fawkes and Byron, helped found the London Philhellenic (Greek) Committee and Byron returned to Greece to join the rebels. Byron's death there in 1824 and Hobhouse's involvement in recommending subjects made the Greek cause a dominant theme in Turner's later Byron illustrations. Vignettes in *Life and Works* included *Scio (Fontana di Melek Mehmet, Pasha)* (no.67) with Greeks and Turks near the site of a Turkish massacre in 1822, and a view of the Parthenon with Turkish horsemen brandishing scimitars and raising clouds of dust (no.73) incorporated from Byronic 'landscape illustrations' originally made for Edward Finden. As a symbolic memorial to Byron, perhaps for engraving as a companion to *Lord Byron's Dream* (1827; Tate) by his friend Charles Eastlake, Turner made a watercolour (no.120) of the Temple of Poseidon at Sounion, where Byron had carved his name on a column and whose 'marbled steep' he recalled in *Don Juan* (1819–23) with his political credo, 'A land of slaves shall ne'er be mine'. A distressed ship in the background recalls William Falconer's poem *The*

Shipwreck (1764) mentioned in Byron's notes to *Childe Harold* and, as Sam Smiles suggests in this book, ancient and modern battles off the Greek coast.

For 'bloody and most bootless Waterloo!' in Byron's *Age of Bronze* Murray used Turner's vignette *The Field of Waterloo. From Hougoumont* showing Frenchmen slain near their eagle standard (no.72). While Byron despaired that the allied victory would inaugurate an authoritarian dark age in Europe, Scott saw it as ending a long storm. Calm after cosmic conflict is an underlying theme of Scott's nine-volume *Life of Napoleon* in which his text and Turner's images follow the emperor's rise and fall (nos.61–4). From his conservative standpoint Scott admires Napoleon for rescuing France from revolution before telling how his 'mingled character' succumbs to hubris and divine justice. Scott's radical contemporaries could agree that Napoleon was a fallen angel but could not bring themselves to celebrate his defeat. Scott praised Byron's Waterloo verses as poetry but lamented

that his politics prevented him from sounding the proper 'note of triumph ... over a field of glory such as Britain never reaped before'.

Just as a vignette of the British ship *Bellerophon* carrying the captive Napoleon part-concluded Scott's *Life* (no.64), one of George IV's yacht *Royal George* fronted the second volume of Scott's *Provincial Antiquities* (no.103). Bringing the king to Scotland in 1822 on a state visit stage-managed by Scott to support the Union and discourage a Scottish rebellion, she appears with George's emblem, a white horse, and a handshake between Scotland and England. Like the historical novels that made Scott's name when he was revealed as their author, his direction of the royal visit showcasing the rediscovered regalia of the Scottish kings and Highland kilts and tartan sought to reconcile patriotic unionism with respect for ancient national traditions. Turner planned a suite of pictures of the ceremonies, including an Edinburgh dinner with Scott among the guests (no.104). That Turner responded as sympathetically to this

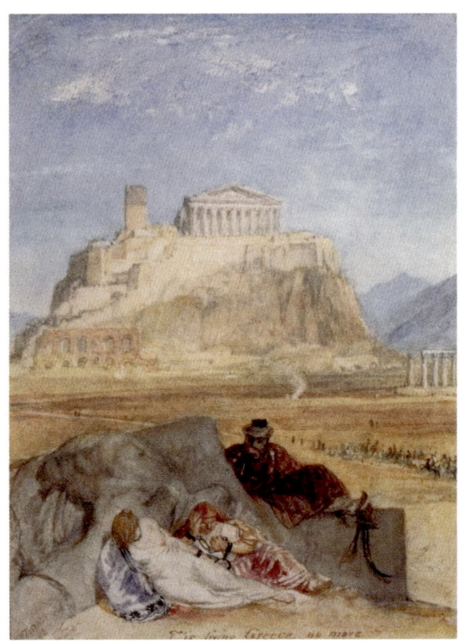

58
Acropolis, Athens, ''Tis Living Greece no More' 1822,
Watercolour on paper.
18.7 × 13.7,
Museum of the
City of Athens, Athens
Vouros-Eutaxias

establishment Tory as to the libertarian Byron and Campbell shows how adroitly he navigated the politics of 'modern thought'.

A champion of liberty and independence across Europe and of reform in Britain, Byron did not acknowledge himself as radical, disingenuously telling Hobhouse in 1820, '*radical* is a new word since my time … and I don't know what it means – is it uprooting?'[54] Tories had begun to conflate radicals and liberals but Scott was not too doctrinaire to encourage his fellow Scot Campbell, who was accused of spying or even treason, to publish *Hohenlinden* when Campbell read it to him in a stagecoach, and to welcome the first draft of *The Battle of the Baltic.* Turner illustrated both lyrics for Campbell's *Poetical Works* (1837). Campbell was suspect in reactionary circles because, while in Germany in 1801, he had got to know the French general Jean-Victor Moreau, and his once famous poem *The Pleasures of Hope* (1799) invoked the French Revolution, Polish partition, British maladministration during famine in Bengal and

the horrors of slavery to urge a better future. But he shared Scott's disgust at revolutionary anarchy and his wartime poems are unequivocally patriotic. *Ode to the Germans* calls Britain to their aid against the French, and Campbell's support for Polish resistance to Russian occupation in 1794 (and again in 1831) was as heartfelt as Byron's for the Greeks. One of Turner's finest vignettes, *Kosciusko* (no.66), depicts the rebellion led by that archetypal Romantic hero. *The Battle of the Baltic* (no.71), celebrating Nelson's assault on the Danish and Swedish fleets in 1801 to prevent their 'armed neutrality' being exploited by France, may have been a more troubling subject for Turner, who had painted the controversial seizure of the Danish navy in 1807 before it became a national embarrassment (no.41).

Injecting some fatalism into Campbell's optimism, Turner adapted the title of Campbell's *Pleasures* for his own 'MS' *Fallacies of Hope*, cited as the source for most of the verses he wrote for his pictures and, printed in the Royal Academy catalogues, his claim to be a published poet.

59
Eugène Delacroix,
*Greece on the Ruins
of Missolonghi* 1836.
Oil paint on canvas
213 × 142,
Musée des Beaux-Arts,
Bordeaux

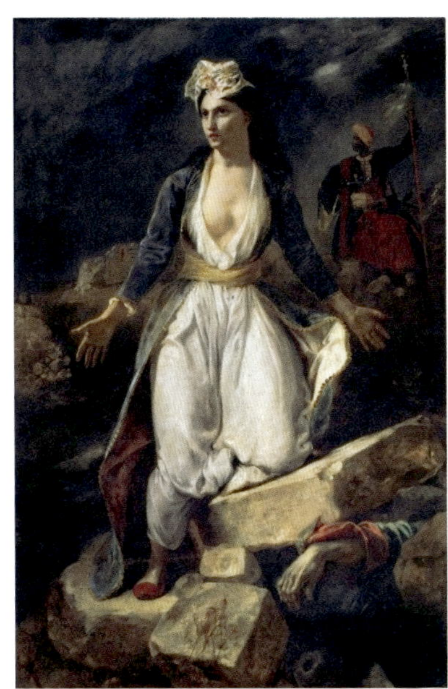

He paraphrased words from Campbell's *Ye Mariners of England* ('the flag which braved the battle and the breeze') for *The Fighting Temeraire* (no.134). This picture that Turner called his 'darling' had been conceived poetically in a 'first sketch' (no.141) inscribed with verse describing how light 'blushes red' at the disgrace of a noble ship destroyed for the price of her timber, and was greeted by the critic Michael Angelo Titmarsh (aka the novelist Thackeray) as a 'national ode'. As the 'Bard of Hope', Campbell might seem more progressive than Rogers, the 'Bard of Memory' after his *Pleasures of Memory* (1792). This would be unfair to Rogers, for whose *Italy* (1830) Turner made vignettes contrasting republican freedom with invasive tyranny (no.70), and illustrated his *Poems* (1834) using the poet's recollections of his radical friends Charles James Fox and John Horne Tooke (nos.68–9), and earlier political campaigners. The 'love of our country' Rogers expresses in *Pleasures* is not just scenic: it is humane, associative and trans-historical as it was for Turner, who used *To an Old Oak* to picture a new ship being built from its timber (no.60).

Recalling the Napoleonic Wars, these simple yet profound images touched hearts.

Turner's illustrations made Rogers's *Italy*, previously published anonymously, a best-seller. Collaborating closely with Rogers and personally commissioned by Campbell, he seems not to have had the same rapport with Scott despite visiting him in Scotland and picturing them together in Scott's favourite scenery – Scott was the only writer he portrayed in this way. Ruskin thought Turner and Scott were 'the principal types … of the age' because they were '*seers* rather than thinkers', but Scott's son-in-law J.G. Lockhart urged his publisher Cadell to trust Turner's discretion in illustrating the *Life of Napoleon*, without 'fear for his tact' as 'he will judge best'.[55] Turner's illustrations to Moore's original poetry were not modern subjects, but Moore's biography of Byron – which did much to restore the poet's reputation after his death – was the 'life' Turner visualised scenically in Murray's *Life and Works*. While Byron never lived to see Turner's empathy with his work, Ruskin claimed 'sympathy' between

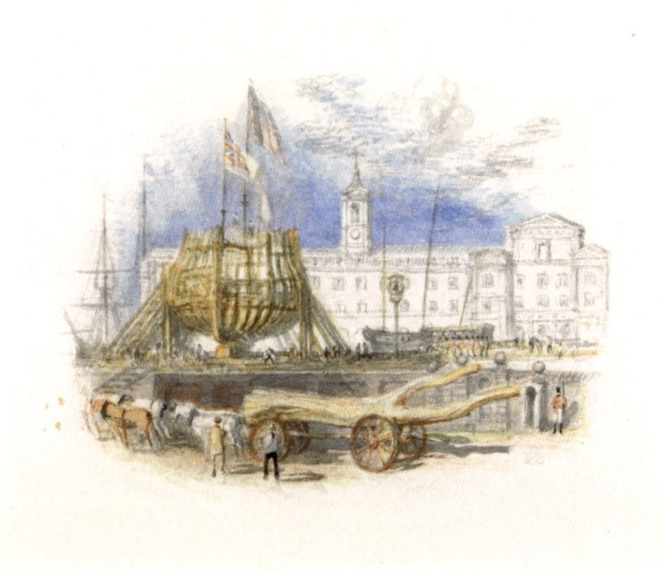

60
Ship-building (An Old Oak Dead), for Rogers's 'Poems' c.1830–2, Graphite and watercolour on paper, 19.1 × 24.8, Tate

Turner and John Keats because, like P.B. Shelley, they confronted 'terror and power'.[56] Although Turner never named Shelley with an exhibited picture, Sam Smiles connects an oil sketch (no.124) with Shelley's post-Peterloo protest poem *The Masque of Anarchy*.[57] The horror expressed by Turner's friend Fawkes about the 1819 massacre – declaring he would rather perish in a 'temple of liberty than see it converted into a barracks' – was reported by the same Tory minister that Shelley targets in the poem ('I met Murder on the way – He had a mask like Castlereagh').

Absent from Turner's literary associations during their years of fame were Wordsworth and Coleridge. Turner's verses for *London from Greenwich Park* (no.90), which were his earliest for a modern subject and describe City churches rising above 'a world of care', recycle words from James Thomson's *Seasons* (1726–30, 1746) with what sounds like an ambivalent echo of 'Earth has not anything to show more fair' in Wordsworth's sonnet *Composed upon Westminster Bridge* (1802, published 1807). Turner and Coleridge had a mutual friend in John Soane. But the *Lyrical Ballads* by Wordsworth and Coleridge (1798) seem to have passed him by and Wordsworth's *Prelude* (published posthumously 1850) came too late to challenge Byron's *Childe Harold* as a creative self-portrait. Retrospectively 'illustrating' Turner in *Modern Painters* with passages from Wordsworth's *Excursion* (1814), Ruskin assumed a pastoral nostalgia the artist did not share with a poet who had outgrown youthful radicalism, detested many aspects of modern life and probably turned the imagery of *Rain, Steam, and Speed* (no.135) into a diatribe against the Kendal and Windermere Railway:

> ... As her long-linked Train
> Swept onwards, did the vision
> cross your view?
> Yes, ye were startled...[58]

From Wordsworth's late reactionary phase this was more hostile than his sonnet *Steamboats, Viaducts and Railways* (1834) with its 'prophetic sense of future change'.[59]

Modern subjects by Turner also embellished the illustrated annuals that became fashionable in the 1820s. Charles Heath's *Keepsake* reproduced them alongside celebrity contributors like Mary Shelley, Caroline Norton and Laetitia Landon, the 'female Byron'. Heath often obtained images separately and paired them with text afterwards – a haphazard method that may explain the mismatch between Turner's view of Ehrenbreitstein being blown up by the Prussians prior to reconstruction in 1815 (no.76) and Ralph Bernal's recent 'Tale of Ehrenbreitstein' in the *Keepsake for 1833*, but often showed artist and authors thinking alike. In the 1836 edition, now edited by Mrs Norton, *The Sea! The Sea!* (no.78) accompanied a naval story by Lord Nugent; *The Wreck* (no.77), a poem by F. Howard about a mother and child saved by a lifeboat; and *Fire at Sea* (no.79), an account by Captain Frederic Chamier of women escaping from a burning Indiaman, *Orontes*. Although his women are free agents, travelling east to find husbands, and were rescued, Chamier's story may have been partly inspired by reports of drowning women and children from the convict ship *Amphitrite*, which Turner also seems to have painted (no.116). Painter and author probably knew each other through Soane, whose grand-daughter Chamier married in 1832.[60] Bespoke or not, these marines are among Turner's most powerful vignettes. Similarly, the landscape view of steamboats alongside the Tower of London (no.92), published in Alaric Watts's *Literary Souvenir* in 1831 with an article on the Tower's history, was one of his 'happiest efforts'. Overlooking the steamers, the text relates remarks made at the Tower's Small Armoury by the Russian Tsar in 1814. Astonished that Britain still had 'exhaustless resources' of weaponry after a long war, he pronounced it 'worse than folly to think of subjugating such a country'.[61] Ten years later, Turner saw all this destroyed by fire.

The Life of Napoleon

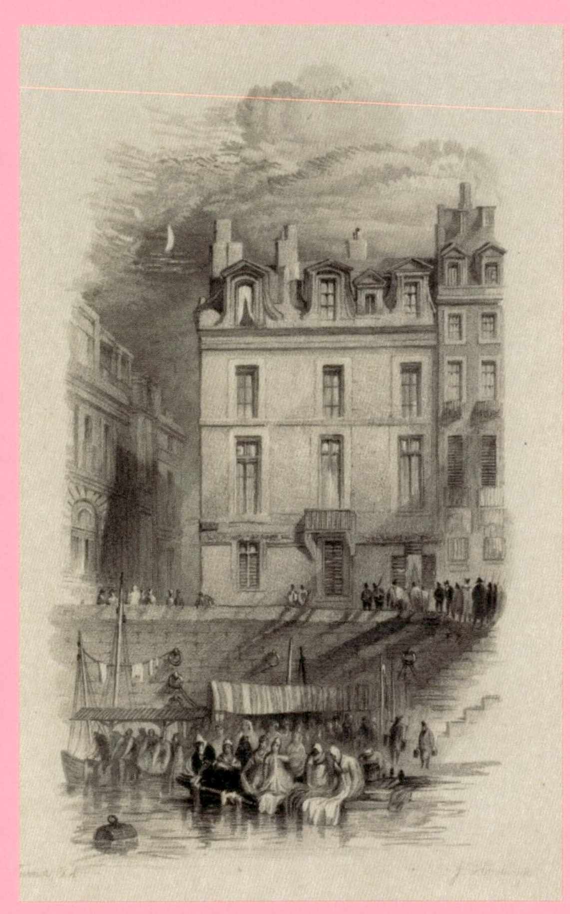

 61 John Horsburgh after Joseph Mallord William Turner, *Napoleon's Logement, Quai Conti* 1834–6. Line engraving on paper, 11.5 × 7 (image), Tate

Despot, tyrant, fallen angel, radical reformer, political visionary, military genius, historical phenomenon, Romantic hero – Napoleon was whatever people wanted him to be. His rise and fall fascinated his contemporaries and provided object lessons and cautionary tales for the future. Literary tributes and critiques included Byron's 'Odes', first published anonymously as if 'from the French' of one of Napoleon's soldiers (1815); Hazlitt's four-volume *Life of Napoleon Buonaparte*, his final 'epic' work (1828); and Alfred Tennyson's *Buonaparte* (1832). Turner's epigraphs for pictures, drawn from his *Fallacies of Hope*, also reflect on Napoleon. 'Who rode on thy relentless car, fallacious Hope?', Turner asks in lines for *The Opening of the Wallhalla, 1842* (no.81), perhaps echoing Byron's question in *The Age of Bronze*: 'But where is he, the modern, mightier far, / Who, born no king, made monarchs draw his car?' Addressing the tiny crustacean at Napoleon's feet in *War. The Exile and the Rock Limpet* (no.160), Turner compares its shell to a soldier's tent amidst 'a sea of blood', adding that, unlike the captive ex-emperor, 'you can join your comrades'.

Walter Scott's *Life of Napoleon* (1827) occupied nine of the twenty-eight volumes of his *Miscellaneous Prose* (1834–6). The publisher Robert Cadell planned the illustrations for this likely 'best seller' with the editor, Scott's son-in-law J.G. Lockhart. Instead of portraits and battles, Lockhart recommended more evocative subjects including some Turner had coincidentally drawn in France in 1832. Complementary landscape frontispieces and title- vignettes form a critical commentary on Scott's text and his subject's character and career in peace and war. Portentous events take place in appropriate settings with contrasted natural effects seemingly enacting divine justice. The crescent moon above Quai Conti, where Napoleon arrived in Paris as a young soldier, denotes his impending rise and the parted curtains of his attic window, the beginning of an epic drama (no.61). His exploits in Italy, the Alps and Rhineland are brightly lit but later scenes turn darker and apocalyptic with stormy skies, waning moons and sunsets.

The execution of the Bourbon Duc d'Enghien at Vincennes in 1804 – which sent shock waves across Europe and Scott saw as a turning point in Napoleon's moral decline – takes place beneath a gloomy prison with Napoleon's sinister Chief of Police watching from a rampart (no.62). At the palace of Fontainebleau after his first fall in 1814, Napoleon bids farewell to his Imperial Guard in a blaze of torchlight, a dark carriage waits to take him into exile and clouds obscure the moon (no.63); Turner wanted the engraver, William Miller, to emphasise the 'Falling Star' he marked in the margin of a proof.[62] In Turner's closing vignette Napoleon stands captive on the deck of the British ship *Bellerophon* in 1815. At sunset small boats filled with curious sightseers crowd around to see him before he leaves for St Helena (no.64). DBB

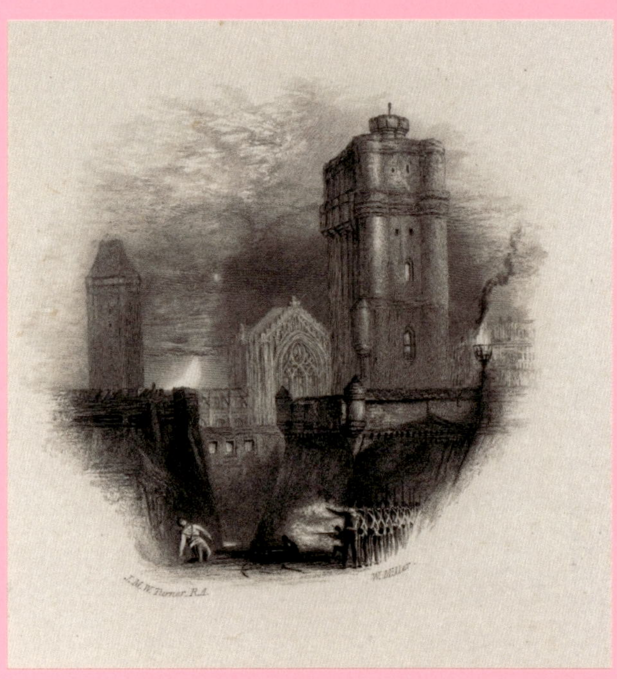

 62 William Miller after Joseph Mallord William Turner, *Vincennes* 1835. Line engraving on paper, 7.7 × 8, Tate

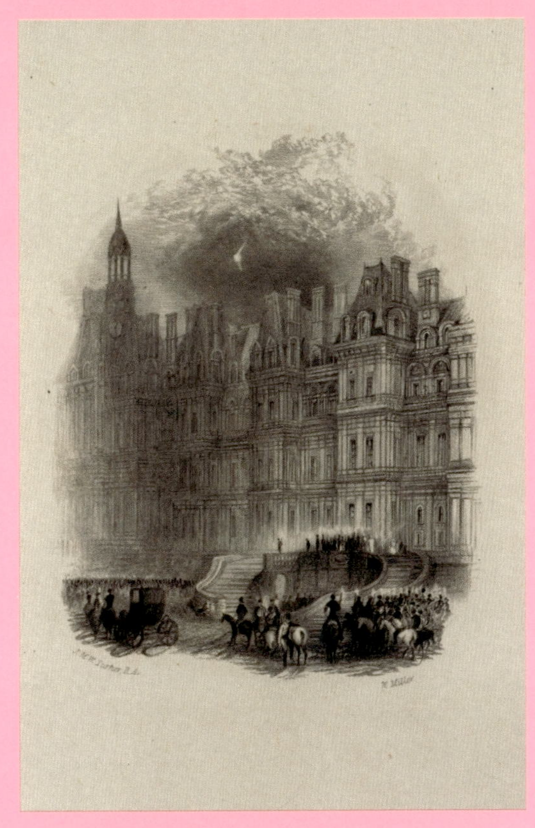

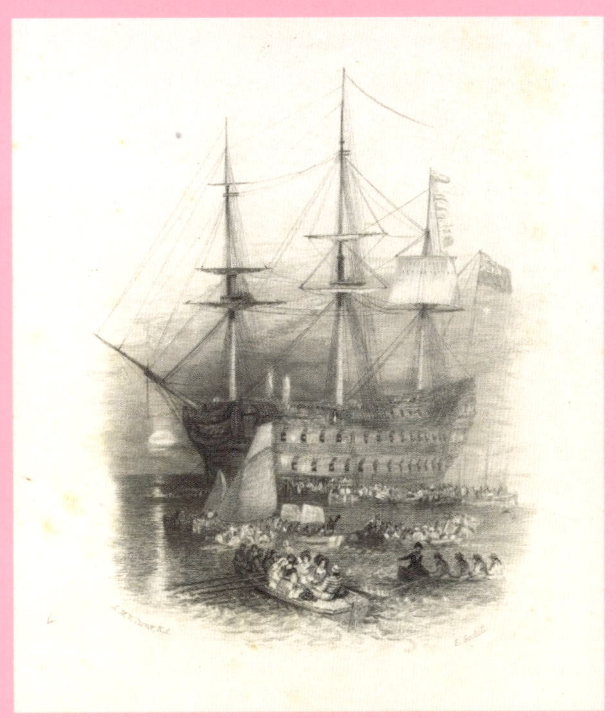

63 William Miller after Joseph Mallord William Turner, *Fontainebleau* 1834–6. Line engraving on paper, 9.5 × 7.5 (image), Tate
64 Edward Goodall after Joseph Mallord William Turner, *The Bellerophon, Plymouth Sound* 1836. Line engraving on paper, 11 × 8.5 (image), Tate

Liberty and Tyranny:
Campbell, Byron, Rogers

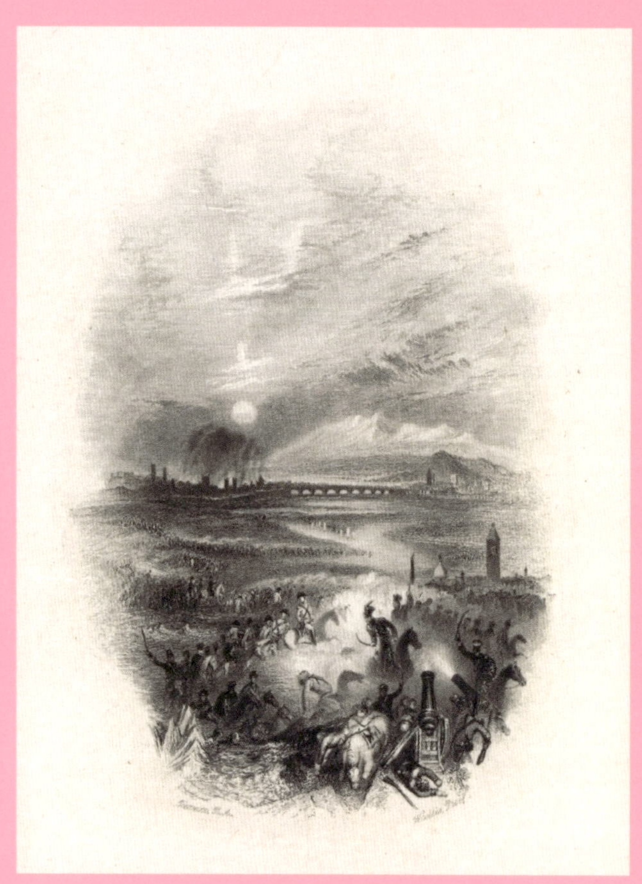

 65 Robert Wallis after Joseph Mallord William Turner, *Hohenlinden* 1837. Line engraving on paper, 10.4 × 7.4 (image), Tate

Writers with liberal or radical inclinations took up humanitarian causes, championed freedom and civil rights, and espoused nationalist movements.

During travels in Germany Thomas Campbell witnessed the French occupation and wrote poems supporting German freedom. *Ode to the Germans* calling on Britannia to aid 'her sister Allemania / To burst the Tyrant's chain' was illustrated by Turner for Campbell's *Poetical Works* (1837) with the Prussian fortress of Ehrenbreitstein reduced by French occupation to a 'camp of slaves'. For *Hohenlinden* he pictured the poet's description of snow turning red as General Moreau defeated the Austrians in 1800 (no.65). Campbell was particularly affected by the plight of Poland, where in 1794 Catherine the Great's Russian army had crushed the rebellion led by Thaddeus Kosciusko with a massacre and burning of Warsaw that shocked liberal Britons. Turner's vignette *Kosciusko* (no.66, preparatory study no.74) shows this 'bloodiest picture in the book of Time' and honours a hero previously associated with American independence. Perhaps witnessed by Turner who was in London at the time, a Polish patriot scattered earth from Kosciusko's grave on Campbell's tomb during the poet's funeral at Westminster Abbey in 1844. The Literary Association of the Friends of Poland founded by Campbell with a German lawyer, Adolphus Bach, in 1832 was reborn as the Anglo-Polish Society during the Second World War for exiles serving with the allies.

Byron took up the cause of Greek independence from Ottoman rule and died in Greece in 1824. Greek subjects – Scio (no.67), Athens (no.73) – appear among the vignettes and landscapes that Turner supplied to the publishers John Murray and Edward Finden and were reproduced in Murray's edition of Byron's *Life and Works* (1832–4) with a biography by his fellow poet Thomas Moore. Byron's mentor Samuel Rogers, who had inherited a banking fortune, might seem an unlikely radical to modern readers, but his verse travelogue *Italy* celebrates William Tell's historical struggle for Swiss liberty in contrast to Napoleon's victory at Marengo (no.70) that put north Italy under French control and laid foundations for his military dictatorship. Like many of his friends, Rogers admired Napoleon for modernising France and regretted the necessity of war. For Rogers's *Poems* (1834) Turner illustrated *Human Life*, with its fond recollections of Charles James Fox – twice Foreign Secretary, campaigner for peace and against the slave trade, and lover of reading – at his beloved house at St Anne's Hill (no.69) and John

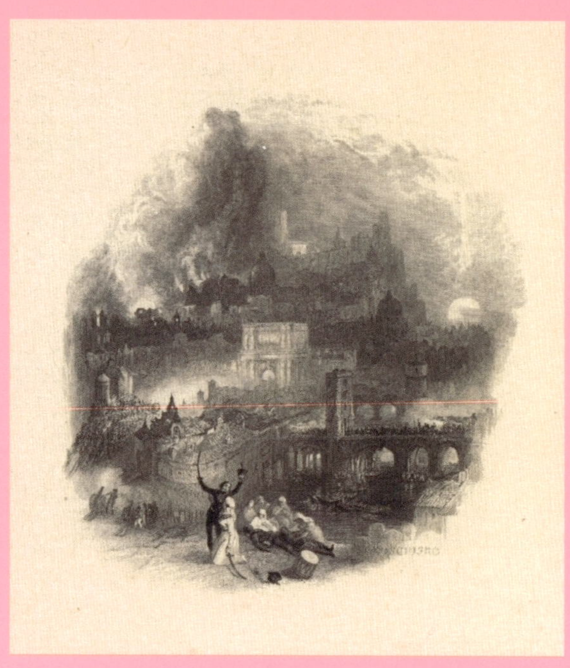

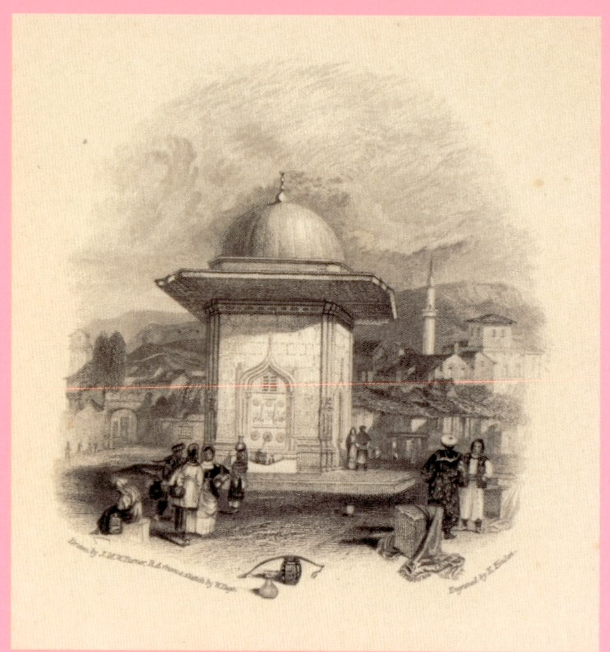

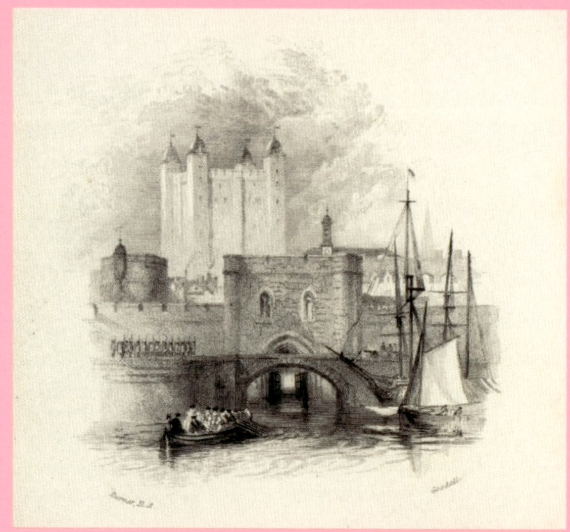

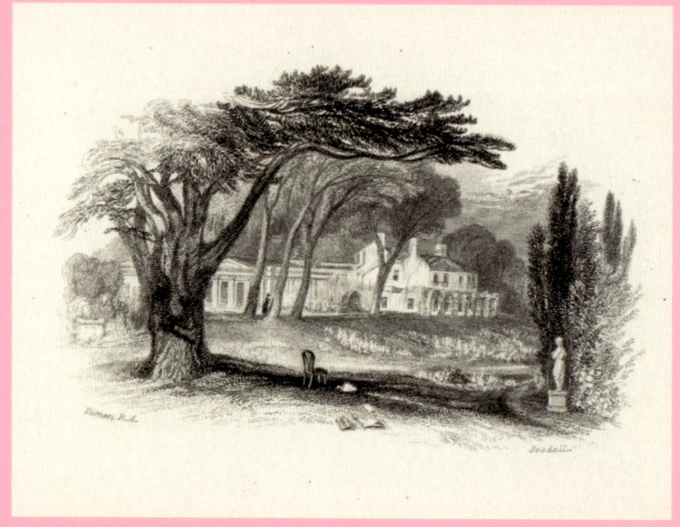

66 Edward Goodall after Joseph Mallord William Turner, *Prague – Kosciusko* 1837. Line engraving on paper, 84 × 80 (image), Tate

67 Edward Finden after Joseph Mallord William Turner, *Scio (Fontana di Melek Mehmet, Pasha)* 1833. Line engraving on paper, 23.3. × 17.6 (platemark), Tate

68 Edward Goodall after Joseph Mallord William Turner, *Traitor's Gate, Tower of London* 1834. Line engraving on paper, 9 × 8.7 (image), Tate

69 Edward Goodall after Joseph Mallord William Turner, *St Anne's Hill* (I) 1834. Line engraving on paper, 29.2 × 15 (sheet), Tate

Horne Tooke, a more radical friend whom Rogers supported at his trial on a charge of high treason in 1794 and who was imprisoned in the Tower. At the end of the poem Tooke is the unnamed politician who reviews his career and remembers earlier martyrs 'for the general good' like Thomas More – seen with modern redcoats in Turner's *Traitor's Gate, Tower of London* (no.68). DBB

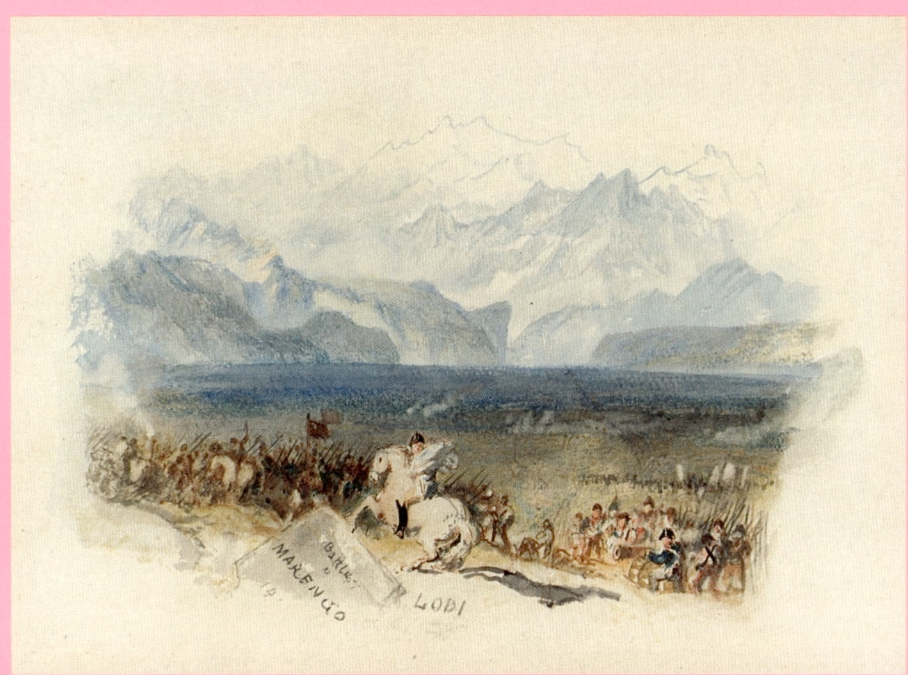

70 *Marengo, for Rogers's 'Italy'* c.1826–7. Graphite, watercolour and gouache on paper, 21.4 × 29.8, Tate

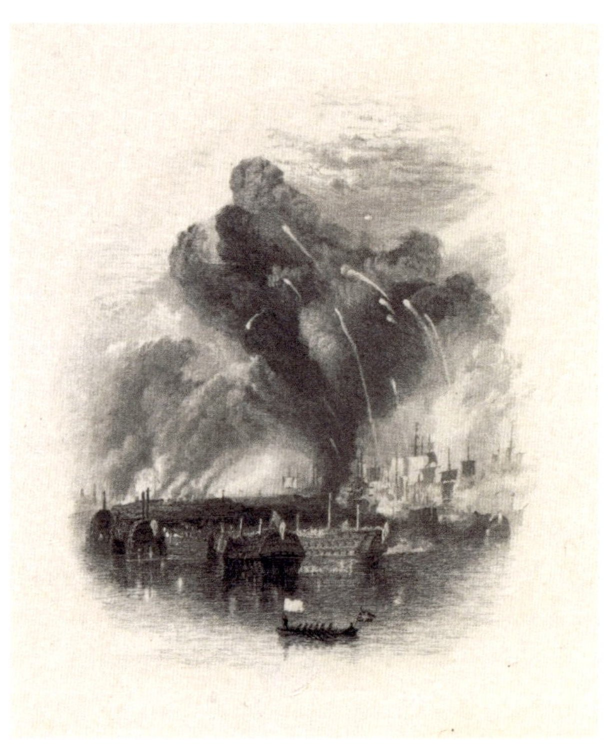

71 Edward Goodall after Joseph Mallord William Turner, *Battle of the Baltic* 1837.
Line engraving on paper, 8.3 × 7 (image), Tate

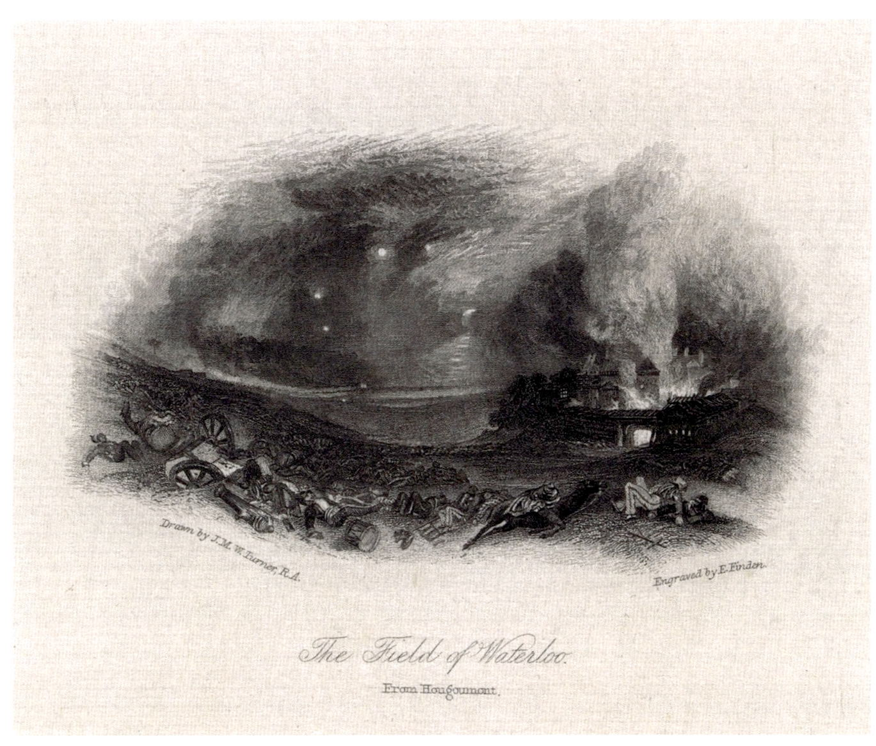

72 Edward Finden after Joseph Mallord William Turner, *The Field of Waterloo. From Hougoumont* 1833. Line engraving on paper, 5 × 9 (image), Tate

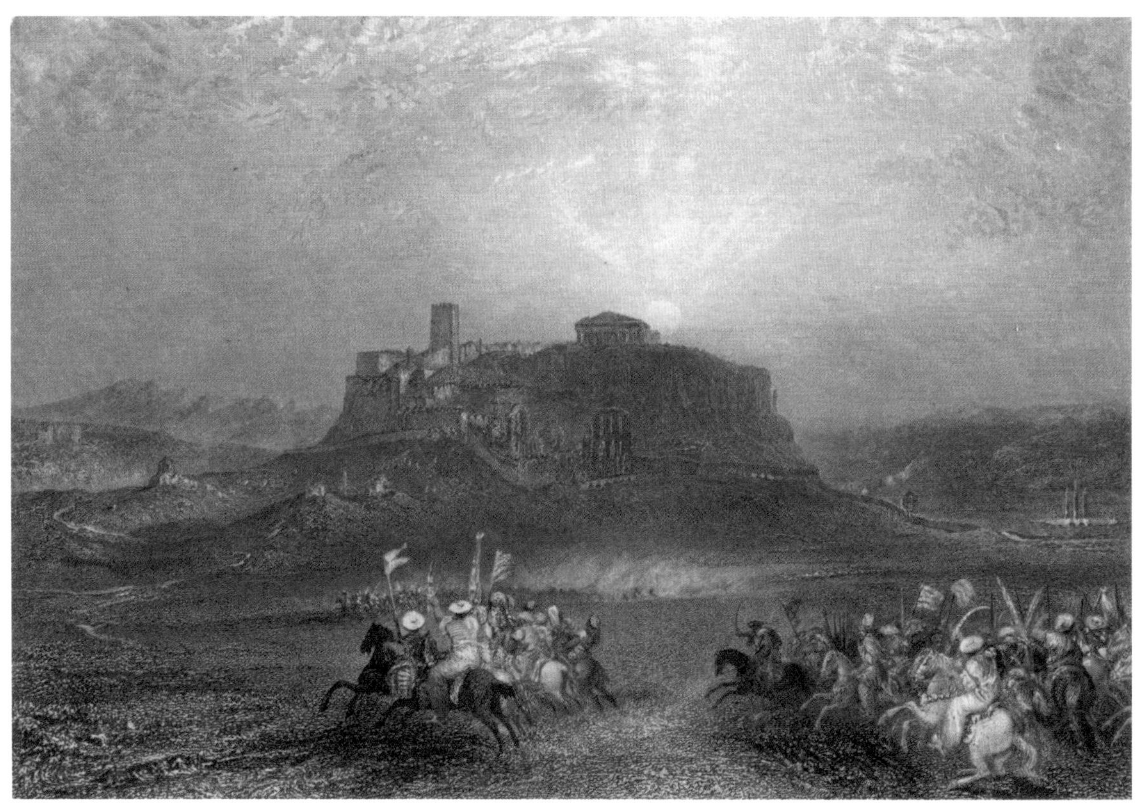

73 John Cousen after Joseph Mallord William Turner, *The Acropolis, Athens* 1832.
Line engraving on paper, 18.2 × 25 (image), Tate

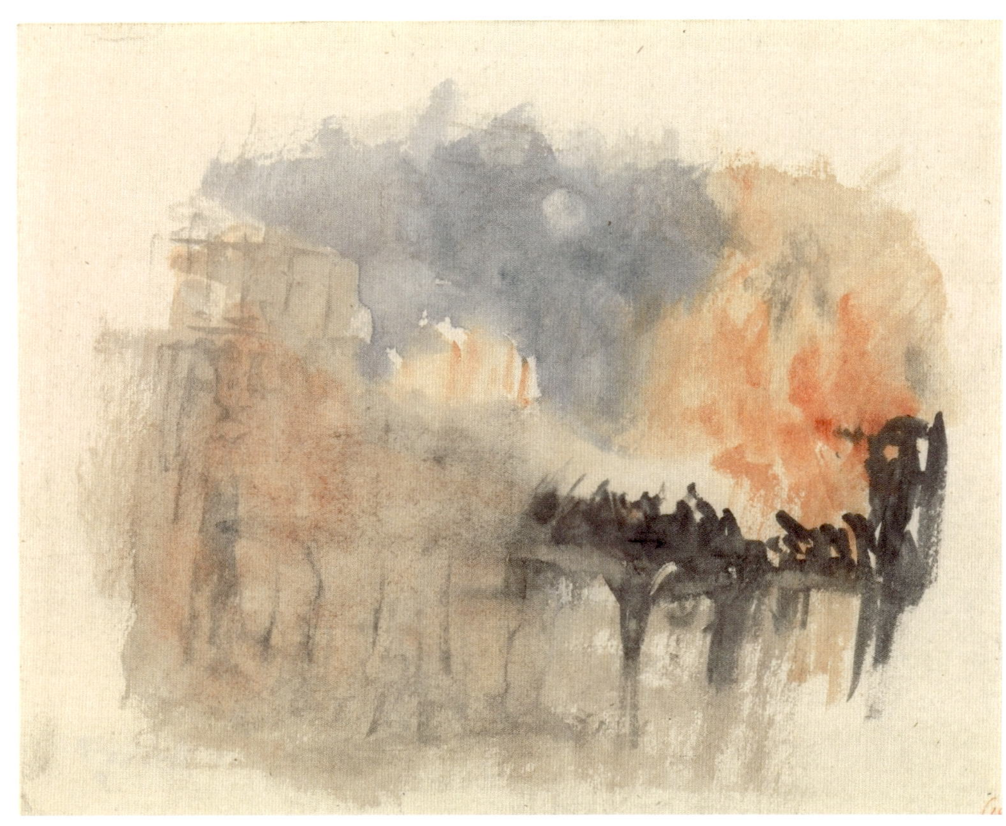

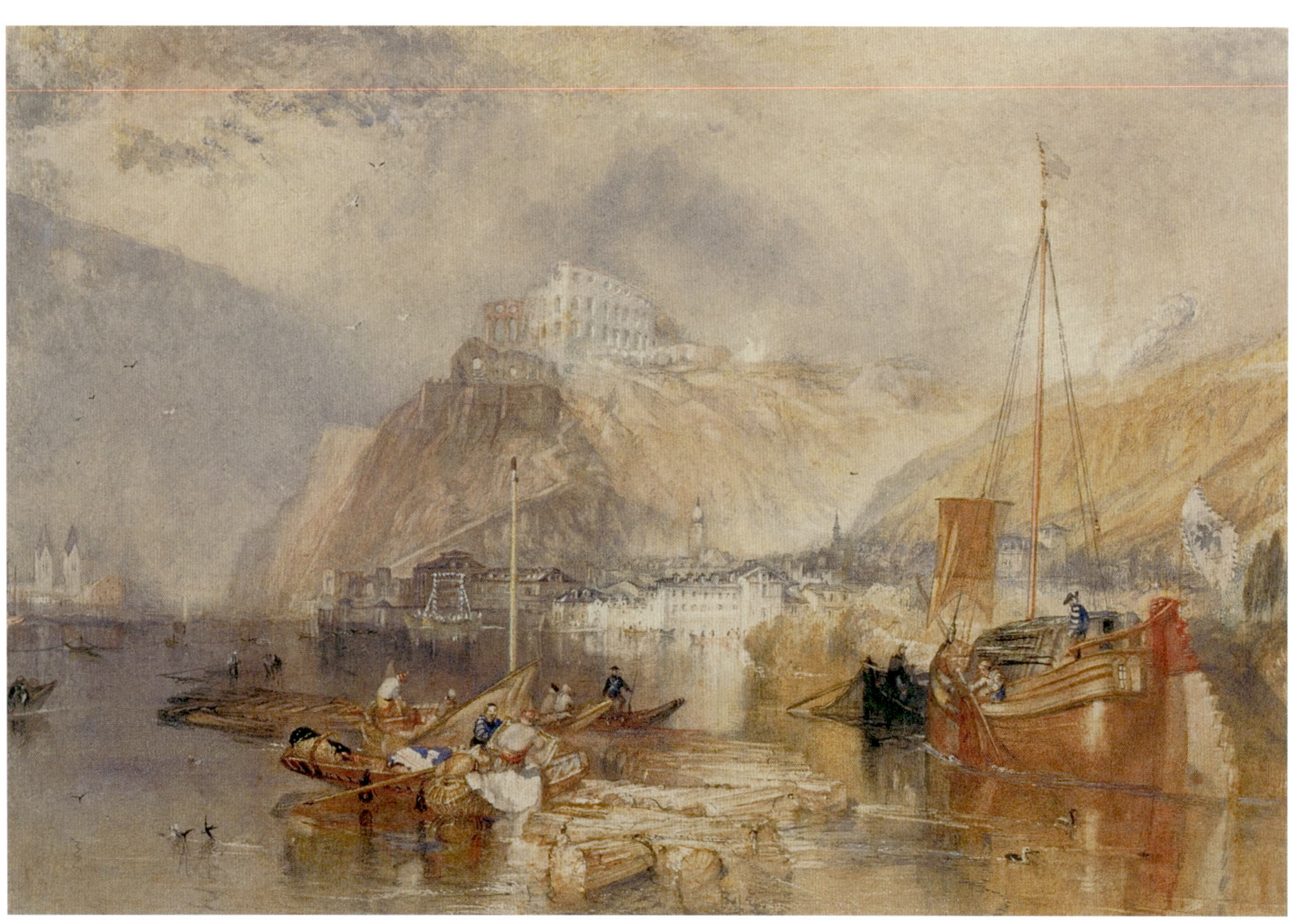

75 *Ehrenbreitstein* c.1832. Watercolour on paper, 29.5 × 43.5, Bury Art Museum, Greater Manchester

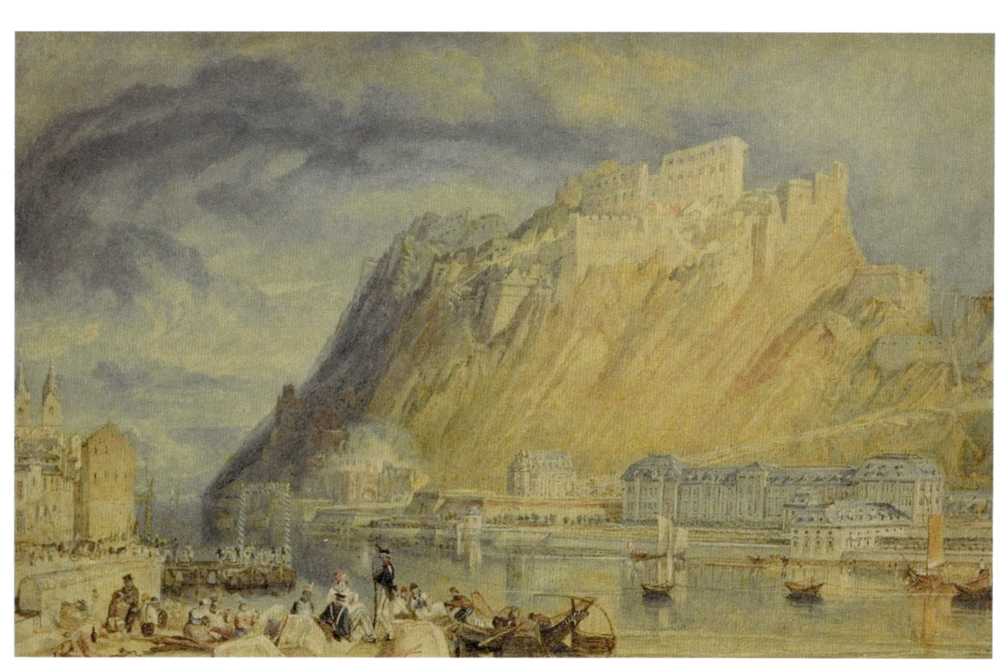

76 *Ehrenbreitstein, During the Demolition of the Fortress* 1819–20. Watercolour on paper, 17.5 × 28.4, Bury Art Museum, Greater Manchester   **107**

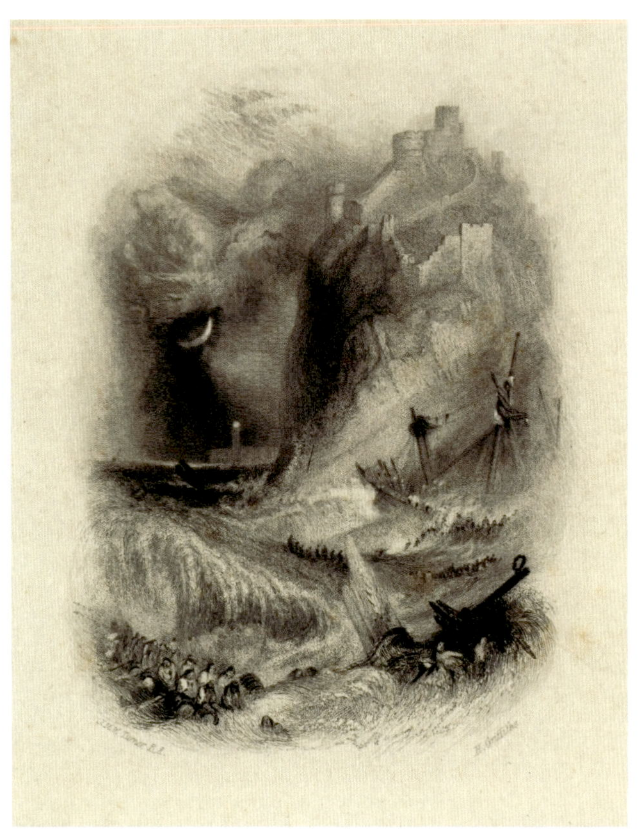 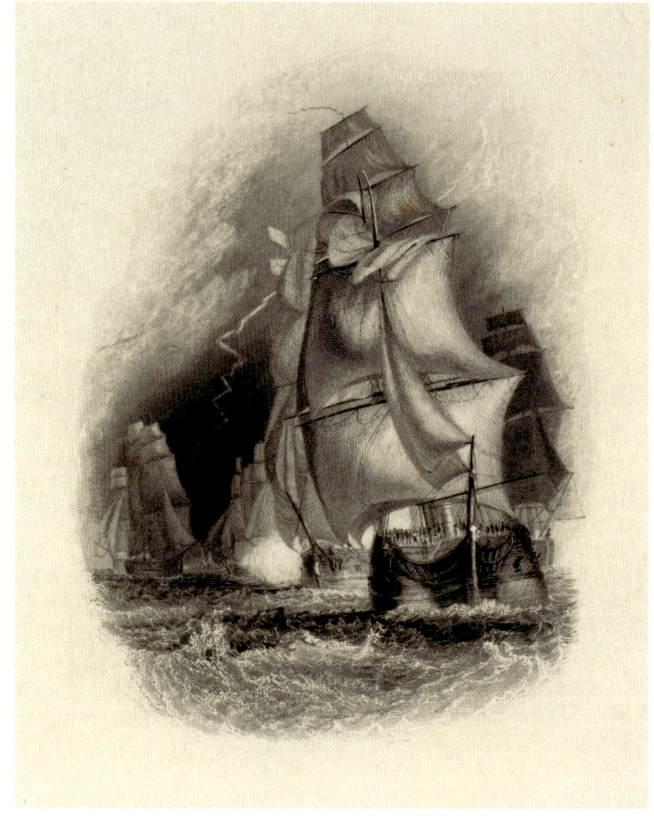

 77 Henry Griffiths after Joseph Mallord William Turner, *The Wreck* 1836. Line engraving on paper, 11 × 8 (image), Tate
78 James Tibbitts Willmore after Joseph Mallord William Turner, *The Sea! The Sea!* 1837. Line engraving on paper, 12.5 × 9.6 (image), Tate

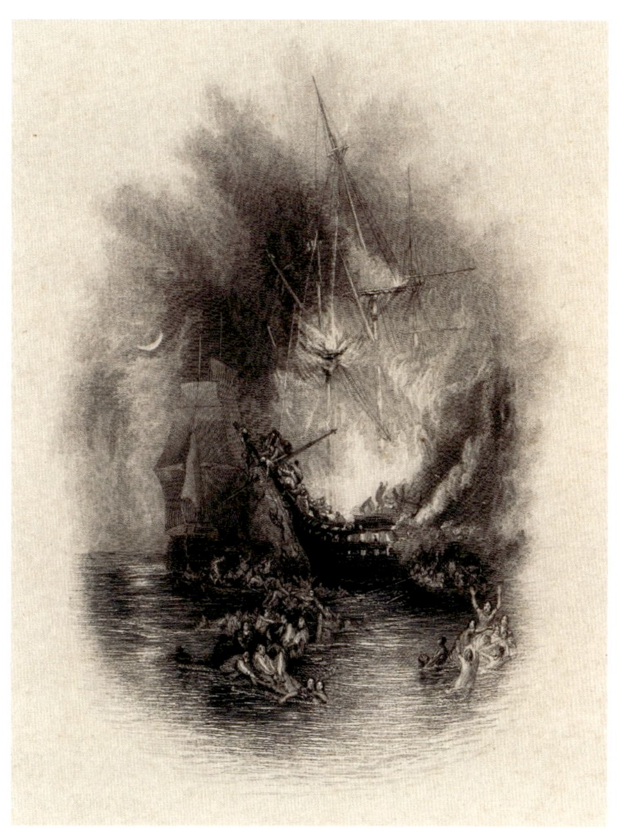

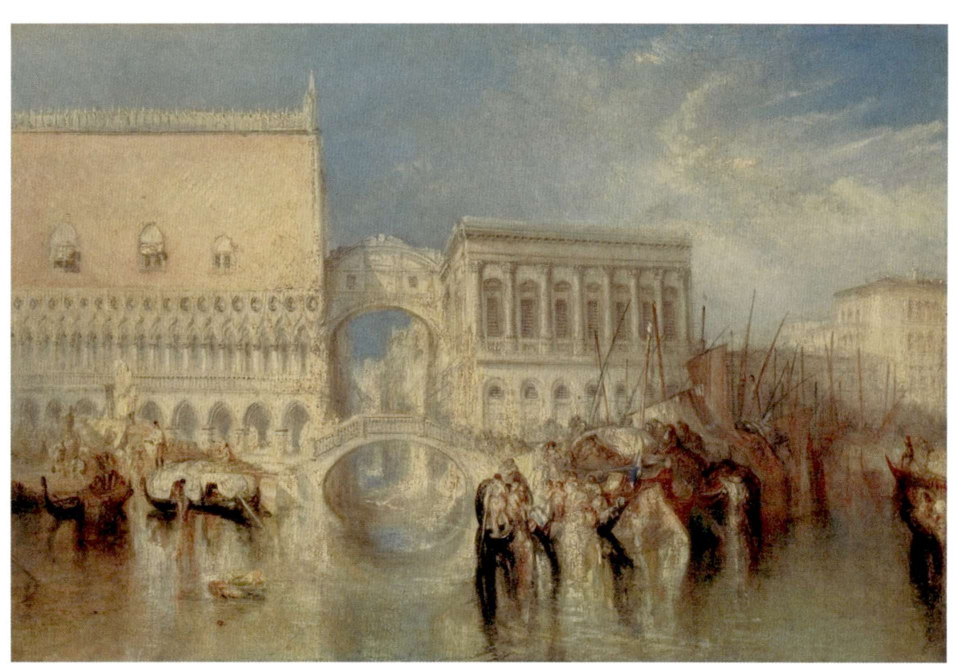

   80 *Venice, the Bridge of Sighs* exh. 1840. Oil paint on canvas, 68.6 × 91.4, Tate

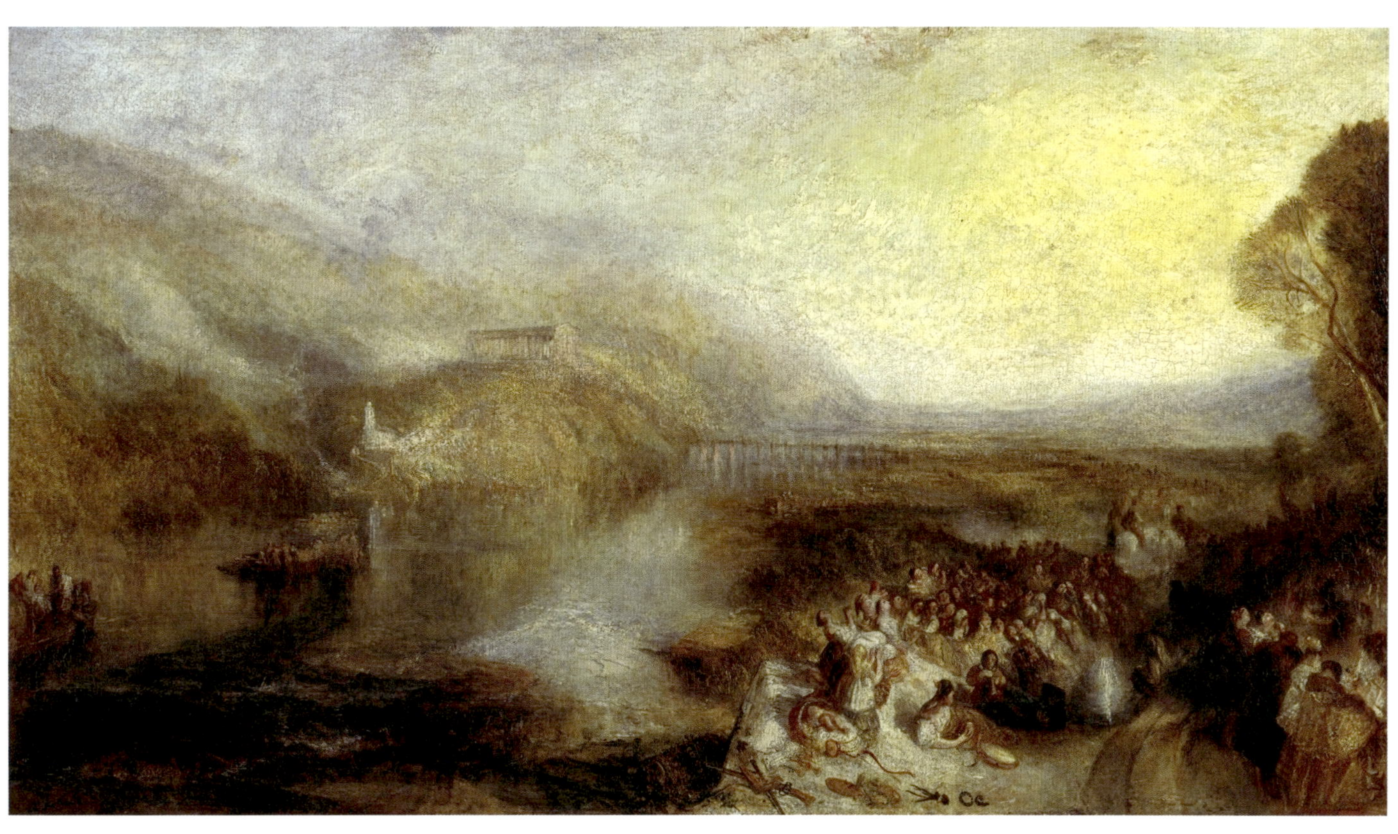

81 *The Opening of the Wallhalla, 1842* exh. 1843. Oil paint on mahogany, 112.7 × 200.7, Tate

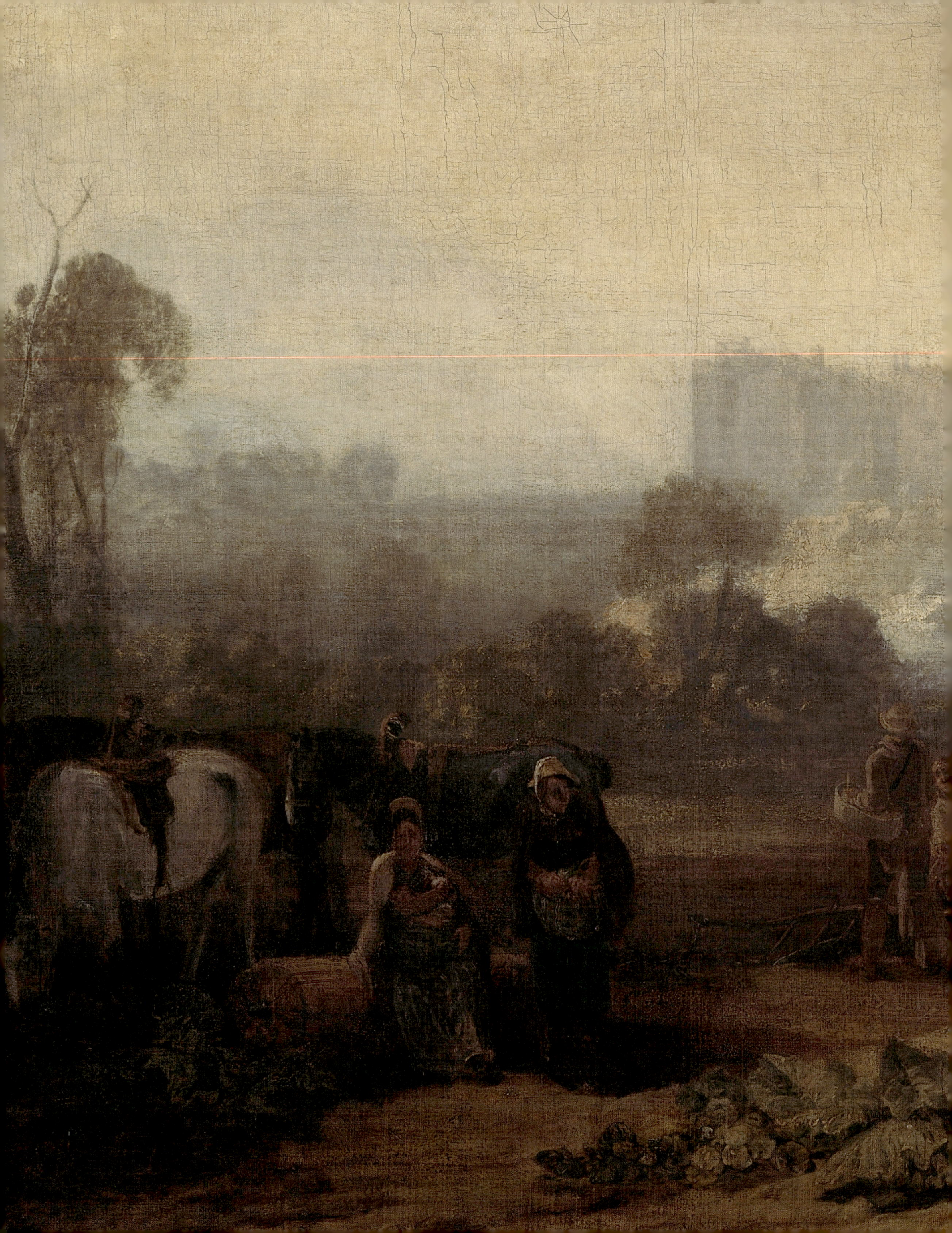

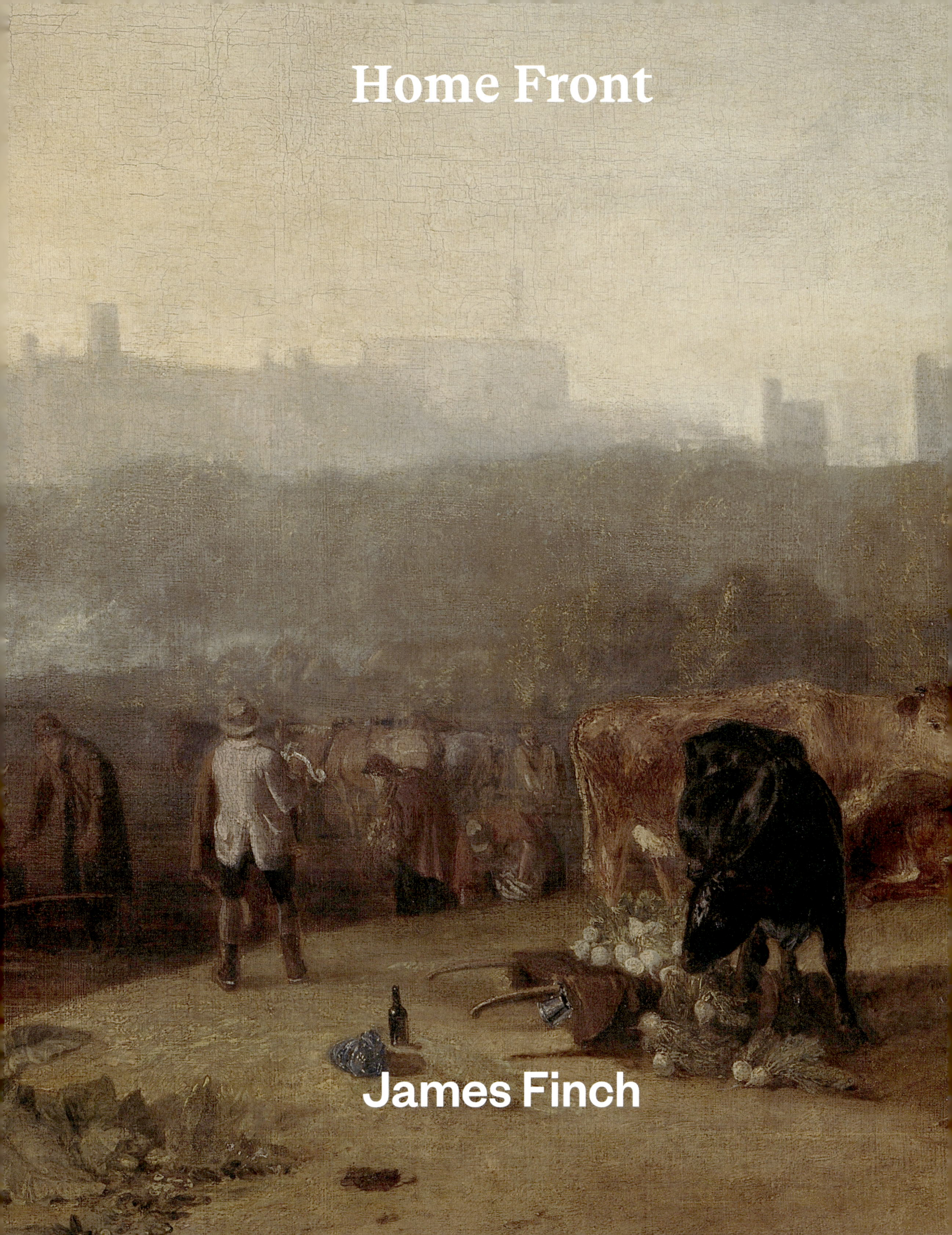
Home Front
James Finch

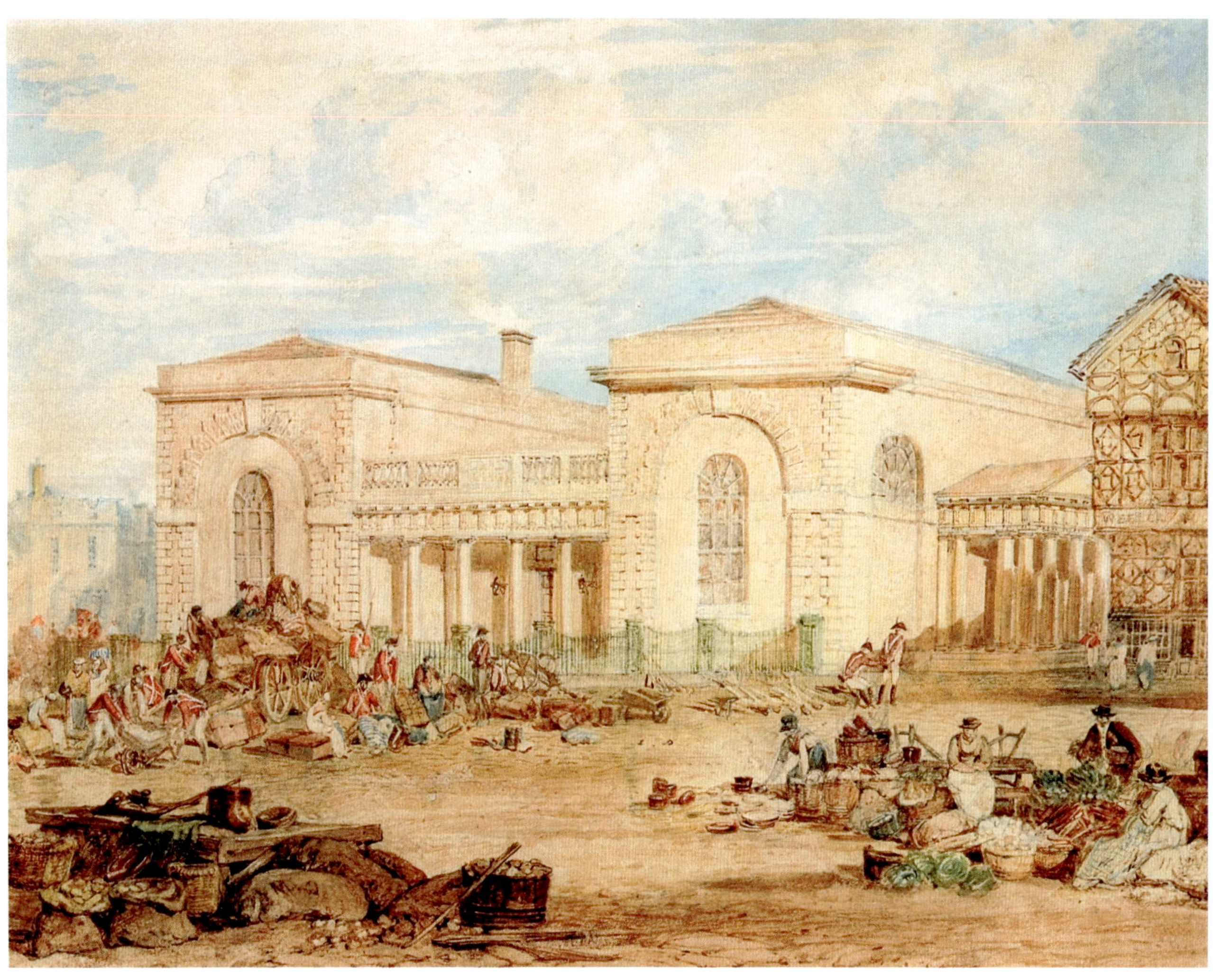

Previous Page: *Ploughing Up Turnips, near Slough ('Windsor')* exh. 1809 (no.83)

82 *The New Council Room, Salisbury* 1805. Watercolour on paper 30 × 39, Courtesy of the Trustees of the Cooper Gallery, Barnsley

England: Richmond Hill on the Prince Regent's Birthday (no.84) exhibited in the 1819 Royal Academy Exhibition at Somerset House, was Turner's largest painting yet. More than three metres wide, the painting depicted a garden party held in the Prince Regent's honour in the manner of an Arcadian idyll.[63] The true subject of the work, however, was no less than England itself, as Eric Shanes has shown.[64] The date is 23 April, the Prince Regent's official birthday, which coincided with St George's Day and celebrations of Shakespeare's birthday – two potent symbols of national pride.[65] The landscape is magnificent, celebrating Richmond's natural splendour and the grandeur of the Thames (on which the Lord Mayor's barge can be seen).[66] The mood is relaxed and joyous, with plentiful military signifiers (guns, a large flag, soldiers recruiting for the army, a large flag) making the argument that a well-run military enabled national peace and security.[67] The artist is also present in spirit: his home, Sandycombe Lodge, is slyly indicated where a cypress tree meets the horizon, while he too laid claim to an April 23rd birthday.[68] In sum, this was a portrait of England as a prosperous and untroubled land – a calculated bid to attract the Prince Regent's attention.

Turner's plan failed: *England: Richmond Hill* remained unsold. Nonetheless in 1822 he envisaged an even more ambitious royal subject: a 'Royal progress' of nineteen scenes celebrating George IV's visit to Edinburgh that year.[69] The trip marked the first formal visit of a British monarch to Scotland since the 1707 Act of Union (and indeed since Charles I in 1633) and was coordinated by Sir Walter Scott (whose *Provincial Antiquities and Picturesque Scenery of Scotland* Turner had illustrated in 1818).[70] Turner, one of several artists present (including David Wilkie), filled sketchbooks with drawings, including thumbnail sketches of the full series, although only four pictures were ever started.[71] These include scenes of George IV leaving his ship the *Royal George* aboard the royal barge (no.103), at a banquet held in his honour (receiving a silver basin of rose water 'for the purification of the royal hands'; no.104) and at the church of St Giles.[72] Aborted the series may have been, but it

is a tantalising glimpse of Turner's aspirations as a painter of recent history and his sense of the national significance of the occasion.

It is not only through such explicit statements that we see Turner reflecting on the 'state of the nation'. Rather, this was accomplished through the totality of his landscape and topography. From the beginning of his career Turner travelled widely, making sketching tours and fulfilling commissions such as a set of Salisbury views for Sir Richard Colt Hoare (c.1795–1805). *The New Council Room, Salisbury* (no.82) was ostensibly a statement about the architectural merits of the new building, in contrast with another watercolour in the series showing the remains of the Old Council House (which burnt down in 1780). More arresting, however, are the groups of soldiers unloading packages and laying out rifles, absent from preparatory works and only introduced in the final watercolour.[73] The identity and role of these soldiers remain uncertain, although one possibility is that they represent the 62nd Regiment, a 2nd Battalion of which was recruited in the area in 1804.[74] Their prominence surely reflects increased military presence throughout Britain following the outbreak of war with France in 1803, while the easy conversation taking place between soldiers and local women visualises the way in which the scene was at once incongruous and commonplace.

Wartime conditions were also the context for the 1807 painting *A Country Blacksmith Disputing upon the Price of Iron, and the Price Charged to the Butcher for Shoeing his Poney* (no.85). Turner's audience would have understood this picture, with its long title, as a response to the Pig Iron Duty Bill, introduced to service government debts incurred in financing the war with France.[75] The argument it depicts is a demonstration of the knock-on effects of the war for working-class civilians. Turner's decision to paint the work was surely influenced by the success of Wilkie's *Village Politicians* at the Royal Academy the previous year. In 1807 *A Country Blacksmith* was exhibited at the Royal Academy near Wilkie's second genre painting, *The Blind Fiddler.* Here Wilkie retreated from the potentially contentious subject matter of *Village Politicians,* in contrast to Turner's topical and socially engaged picture.

In *Ploughing Up Turnips, near Slough* (no.83) of 1809 Turner turned his attention to rural agriculture. The picture has been read both as a patriotic statement about self-sufficiency[76] and an indictment of the dispossession of agricultural workers resulting from land enclosure, which tied them to subsistence wages rather than enabling them to raise their own food on common land.[77] Windsor Castle looms in the distance, setting up a relationship between Windsor and the 'near Slough' of the title, and the vast inequalities this implied.[78] Windsor Castle also inevitably evokes George III, known popularly as 'Farmer George' for his interest in progressive agriculture.[79] Indeed, the turnip in particular was closely identified with the king, partly because the vegetable could only be grown effectively within a crop rotation system dependent upon the enclosures that proliferated during his reign.[80] John Barrell has shown that Turner's resting, tired workers are exceptions to the traditional landscape dichotomy of figures in repose (pastoral) and those tirelessly working (georgic), and in both *A Country Blacksmith* and *Ploughing Up Turnips* he produced complex, nuanced scenes of labour that situated individual working lives within broader networks of social and economic power.[81]

The threat of invasion by France provided a new context for depictions of the British coastline, as sites either of security and resilience or of vulnerability. Between 1807 and 1810 Turner exhibited a series of marine paintings of the Thames estuary, an expanse of water lacking picturesque appeal but loaded with historical resonance.[82] The estuary had been vulnerable to attack, for example in the raid on the Medway during the Second Anglo-Dutch War of 1667, but was at this time considered secure. In *Sheerness as Seen from the Nore* (no.87) fishermen catch herring on a choppy sea in the presence of a guardship. Even so, for viewers in 1808 the very mention of the Nore may have triggered discomforting associations with the Nore Mutiny of 1797, in which sailors demanded better pay and conditions, and other concessions. The *Sandwich*

was the ship on which the flag of mutiny had been run up and from whose yardarm the leader of the mutiny Richard Parker was hanged two weeks later. The ship was decommissioned and repurposed as a prison ship in Chatham later that year, but even so Turner wrote that his related painting from 1809, *Guardship at the Great Nore, Sheerness*, depicted 'Old Sandwich'.[83] What, then, are we to make of the guardship in Sheerness? There is no evidence that Turner here depicted the *Sandwich,* but his awareness of the mutiny lends the guardship a spectral potential – a sense of multiple, shifting temporalities often found in his work.

From the late 1790s England's south coast was transformed by a new wave of defensive architecture, most notably the 'Martello towers' or defensive forts built at regular intervals.[84] Perhaps Turner's most explicit depiction of this phenomenon, the print *Martello Towers near Bexhill, Sussex* (no.97) from his *Liber Studiorum* series, depicted the wartime coastline with bleak clarity, showing two cavalrymen galloping along the shore against a coastline marked by several towers between Bexhill and Pevensey.[85] Shortly after this print was published, Turner began work on a group of watercolours commissioned by the brothers George and William Bernard Cooke to be engraved for their publication *Picturesque Views on the Southern Coast of England* (1811–26). Perhaps belying the title of the publication, many of Turner's contributions included military subject matter, such as the barracks and military canal depicted in his view of Hythe (no.95). The coherence of Turner's project and the depth of his engagement with the locations he depicted are confirmed by the long poetic text he wrote to accompany his images.[86] He submitted this for publication, and while it was rejected by the Cookes as largely unintelligible, this does not diminish its value as an aid in interpreting Turner's images.[87] One example can be found in Turner's watercolour *Plymouth with Mount Batten* (no.98), in which resting seamen seem to watch female reapers or gleaners at work nearby; John Gage, who sees wartime effort and industry (particularly in women's work) as a central theme of Turner's

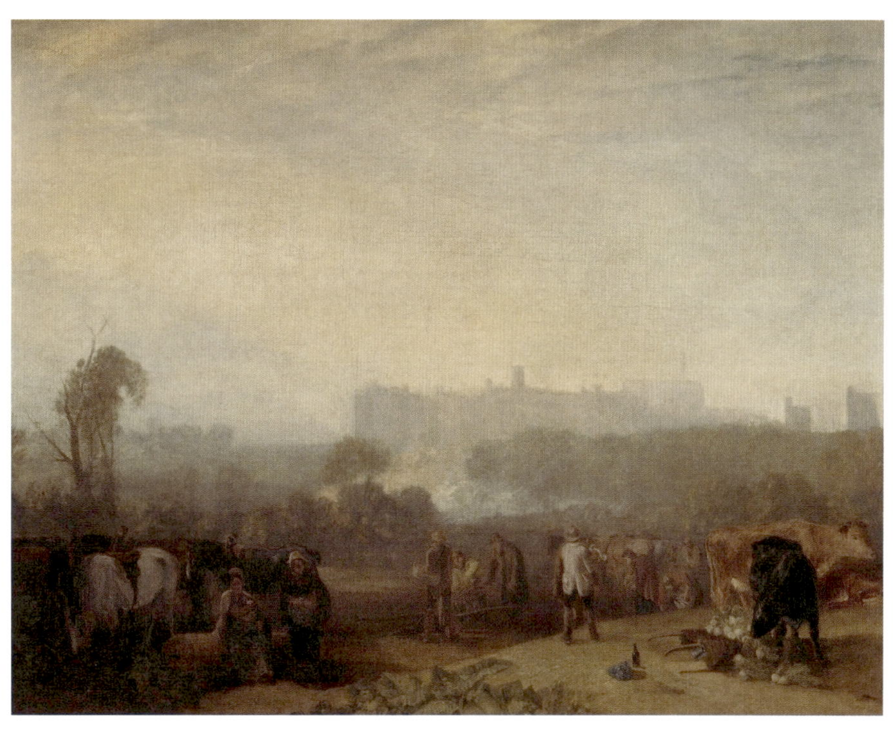

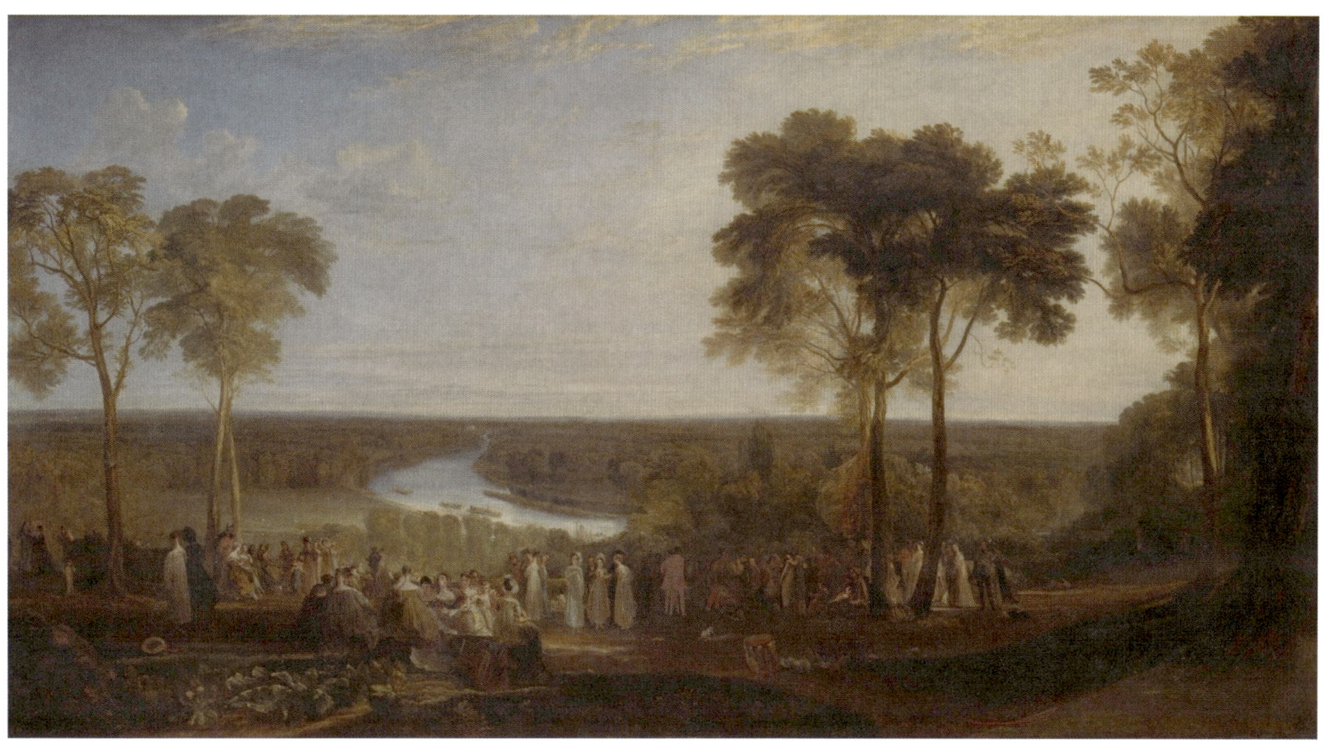

83 *Ploughing Up Turnips, near Slough ('Windsor')* exh. 1809. Oil paint on canvas, 101.9 × 130.2, Tate
84 *England: Richmond Hill, on the Prince Regent's Birthday* exh. 1819. Oil paint on canvas, 180 × 334.6, Tate

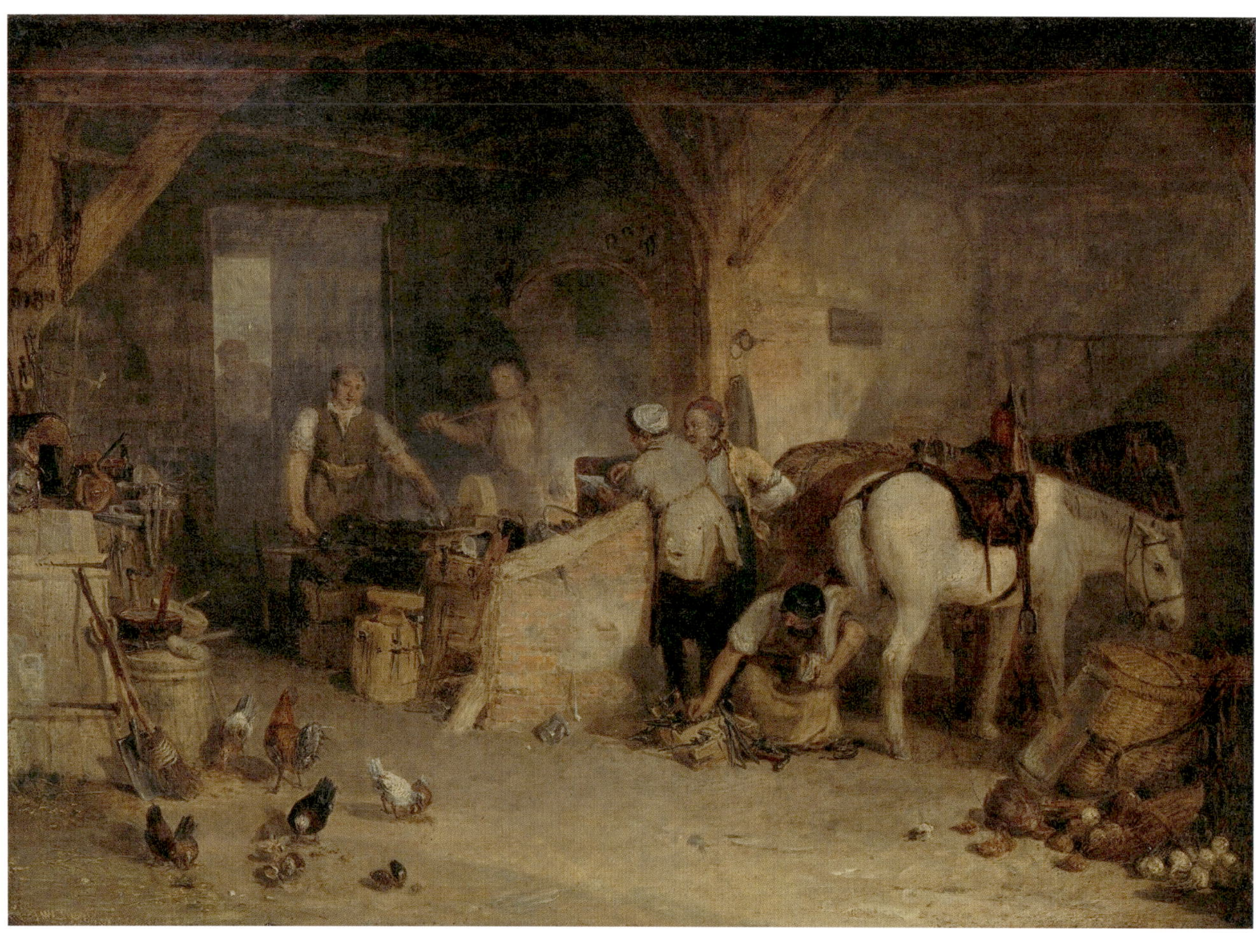

  85 *A Country Blacksmith Disputing upon the Price of Iron, and the Price Charged to the Butcher for Shoeing his Poney* exh. 1807.
Oil paint on mahogany, 54.9 × 77.8, Tate

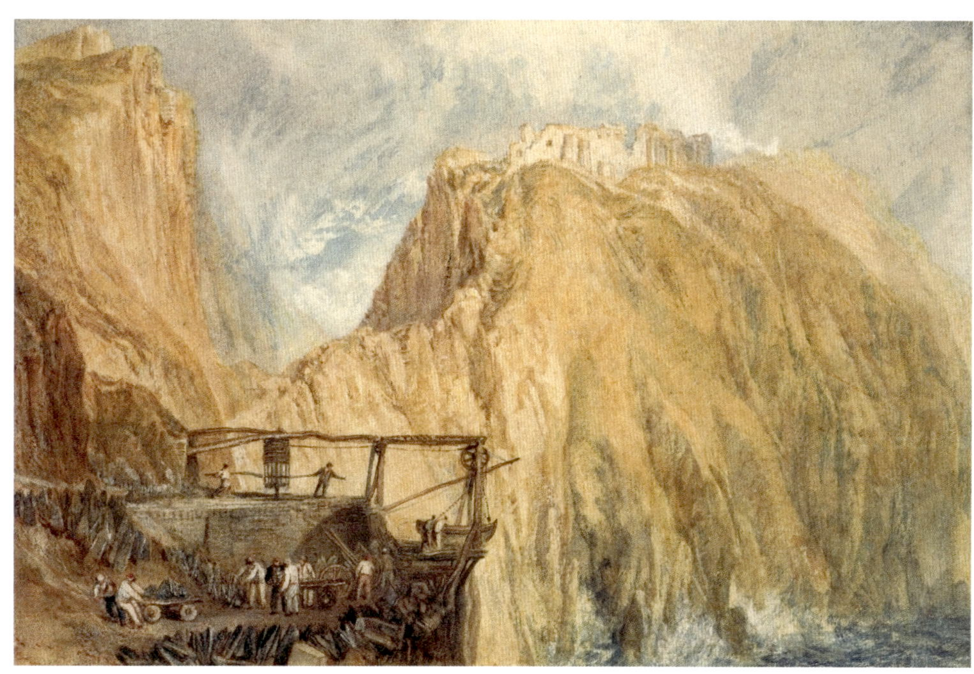

86 *Tintagel Castle, Cornwall* 1815. Transparent and opaque watercolour over graphite, 15.7 × 23.8, Museum of Fine Arts, Boston

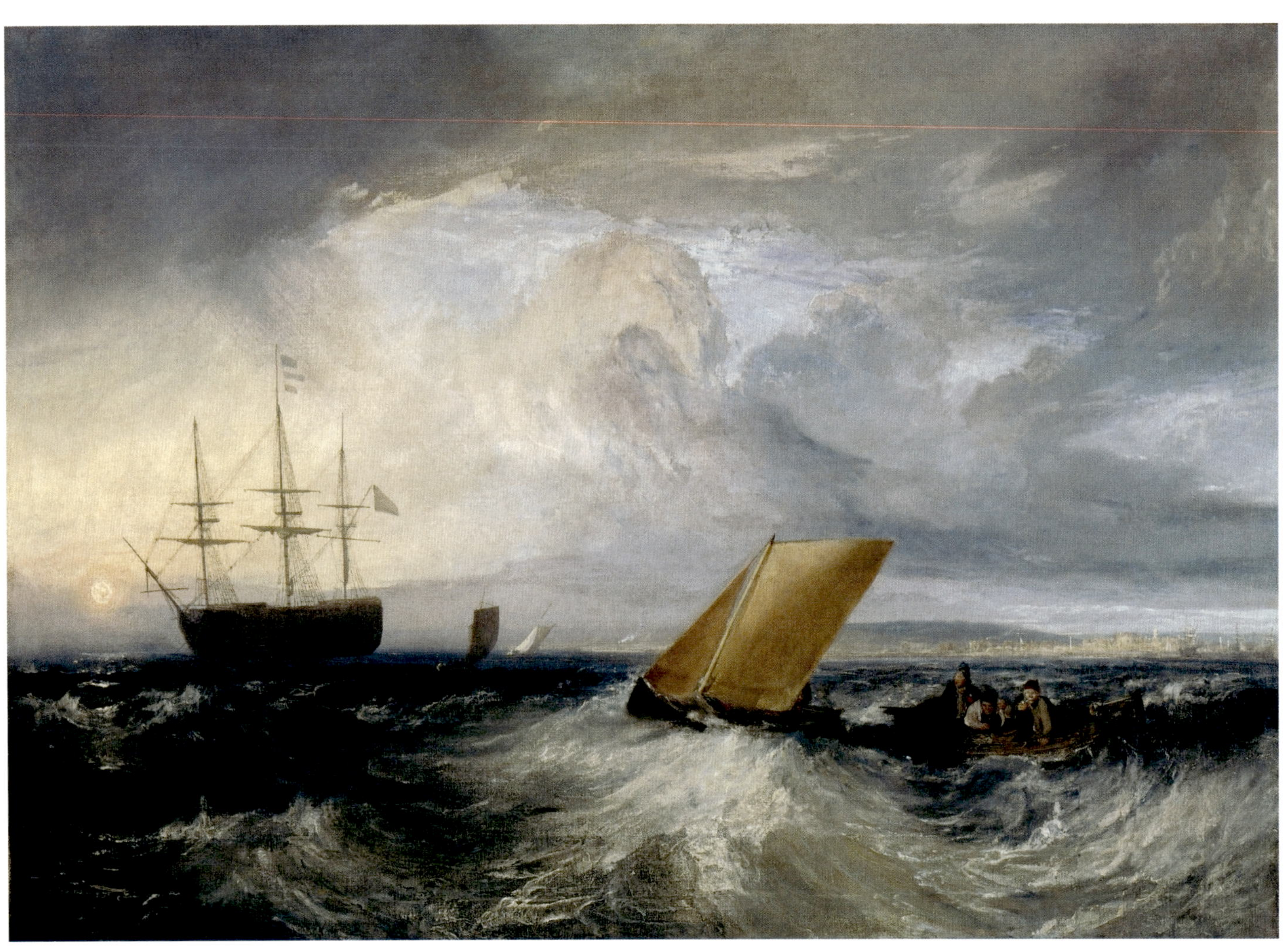

  87 *Sheerness as Seen from the Nore* 1808. Oil paint on canvas, 104.5 × 149.6, Museum of Fine Arts, Houston

poem, suggests that a passage in it may relate to this scene.[88]

Turner was a keen sailor who acquired a boat after renting a riverside house in 1805, and his passion for the waterways connecting Britain is evident in many of his watercolours and prints. He grew up during the canal-building boom of the late eighteenth century, when the likes of writer and picturesque theorist William Gilpin complained that the canals 'disfigured' the landscape and 'cut it in pieces'.[89] By the nineteenth century, however, they were considered legitimate subject matter for painters: Turner's 1811 *Liber Studiorum* print *Windmill and Lock* (no.99), for instance, celebrates the recently opened Grand Union canal,[90] while his 1825 view of Lancaster (no.100) is framed by the majestic Lune Aqueduct carrying the Lancaster Canal over the river Lune.

In the mid-nineteenth century much of the traffic and investment that had sustained the canal network was diverted to the railways, whose dynamism Turner captured so effectively in *Rain, Steam, and Speed* (no.135). Long before this, though, Turner had meditated on the absorption of the canals into tranquil rural landscapes. A watercolour of *More Park, near Watford, on the River Colne* (no.102), for instance, foregrounds Lot Mead Lock on the Grand Union Canal. More Park was landscaped by 'Capability' Brown in the eighteenth century, and in bringing together the grounds and canal, Turner shows the assimilation of the canal into the landscape – no longer 'disfiguring' it but intrinsic to it. A painting of Chichester Canal (no.3), meanwhile, shows the sun setting on the canal, empty but for a stationary collier and rowing boat. Chichester Canal was intended to be part of a network of canals linking the south coast and London, allowing vessels to avoid encountering hostile ships on the coast, but the scheme fell apart with few sections completed. The canal was a disastrous investment for its supporters, including Turner's patron Lord Egremont (who nevertheless commissioned this painting for Petworth House). *Chichester Canal* seems to both lament a commercial failure and to delight in the tranquil new landscape that the venture produced.

Another canal scene, *Kirkstall Lock, on the River Aire* (no.101), focuses on an inconvenient spot on the Leeds and Liverpool canal. A low double-arch bridge forces barges to lower their sails and untie their horses in order to pass, causing a bottleneck of canal traffic that contrasts with the stagecoach speeding along the Leeds to Bradford road.[91] Coach travel shaped the development of towns like Stamford in Lincolnshire, which, as Turner showed in an 1828 watercolour (no.88), became a popular resting place on journeys between London and York.[92] Turner vividly captures the travellers and pedestrians sheltering from a sudden storm, but again there may be more to this image than verisimilitude: it could be seen as a response to contemporary criticism of the Church of England for its active opposition to parliamentary reform. A clergyman traverses the road in the rain towards the Bull and Swan Inn, with two dogs barking at his feet. Behind, meanwhile, a bolt of lightning ominously strikes at the tower of St Martin's Church down the high street.[93] In a view of Coventry made some years later for the same series (no.89), on the other hand, the sun shining down on the town's churches may allude to the survival of the Church after the 1832 Reform act.[94] In this way effects of weather and lighting, empty signifiers in the hands of many artists, were repurposed by Turner to shine a light on contemporary affairs of national significance and woven into his nuanced and wide-ranging picture of early nineteenth-century Britain.

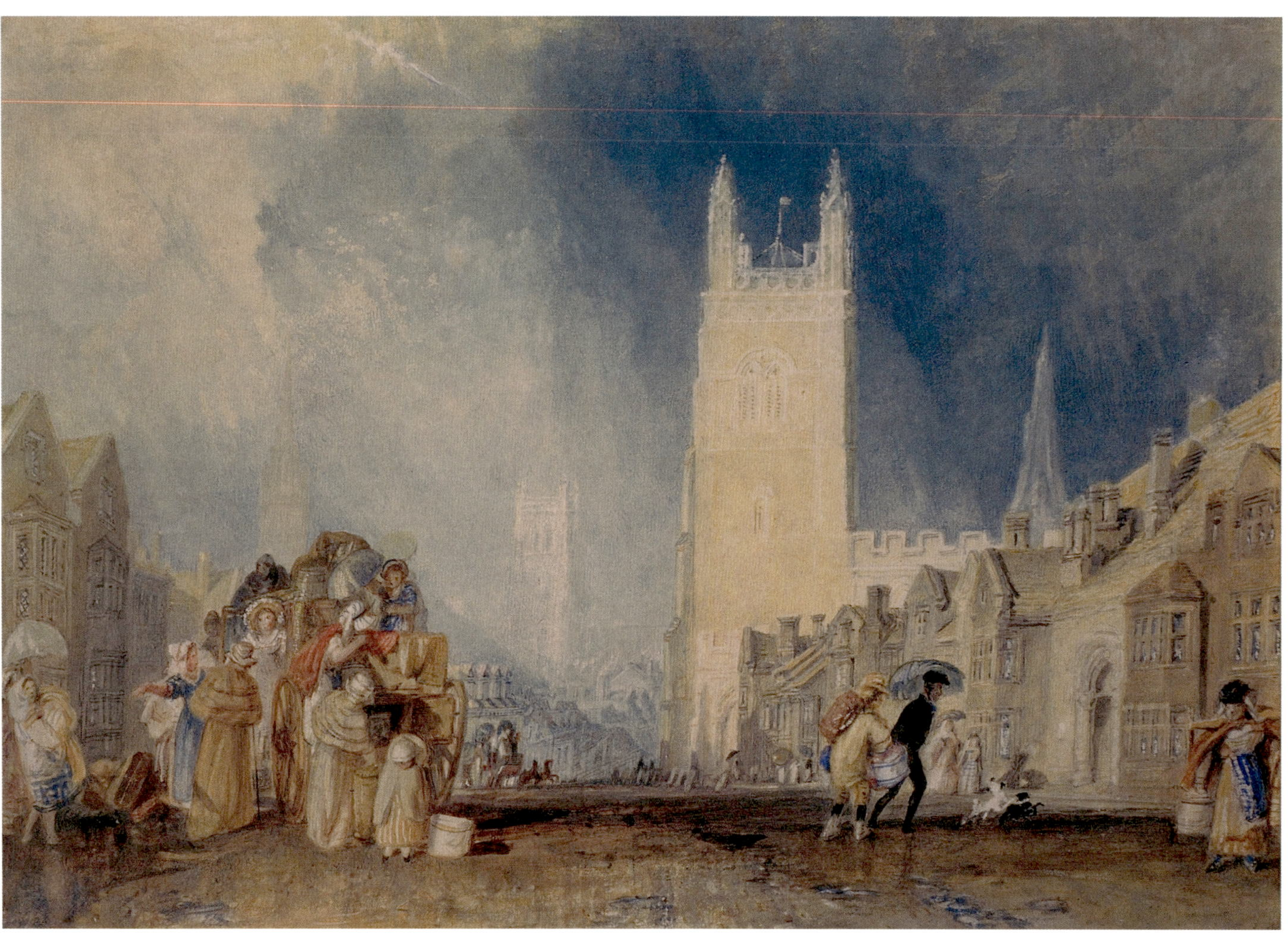

 88 *Stamford, Lincolnshire* c. 1828. Watercolour on paper, 23.9 × 42, Usher Gallery, Lincoln

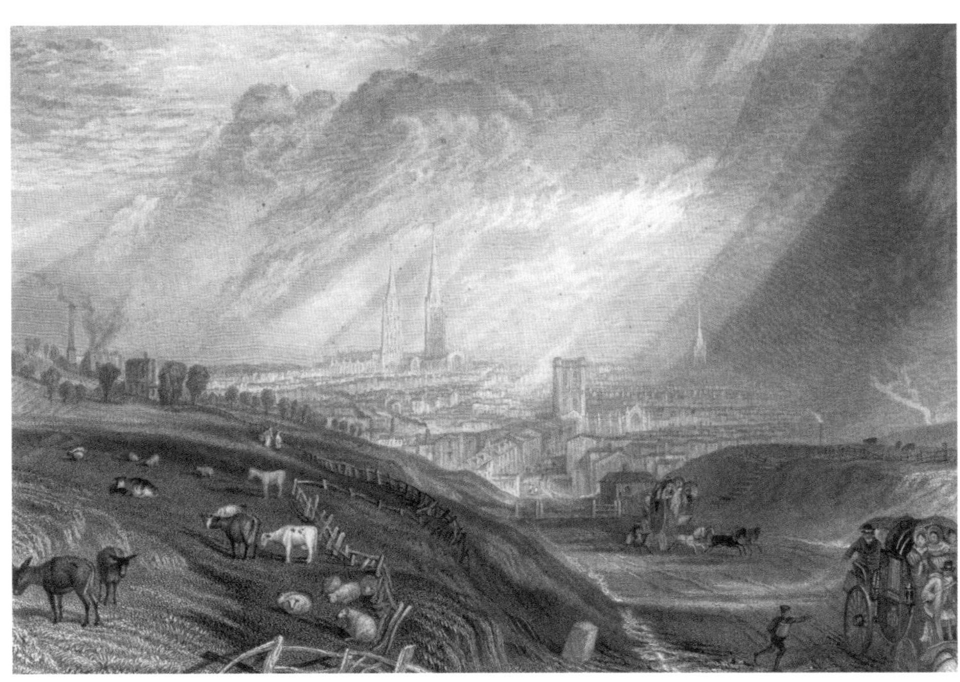

89 Samuel Fisher after Joseph Mallord William Turner, *Coventry, Warwickshire* 1833. Line engraving on paper, 9.4 × 14.7 (image), Tate

London

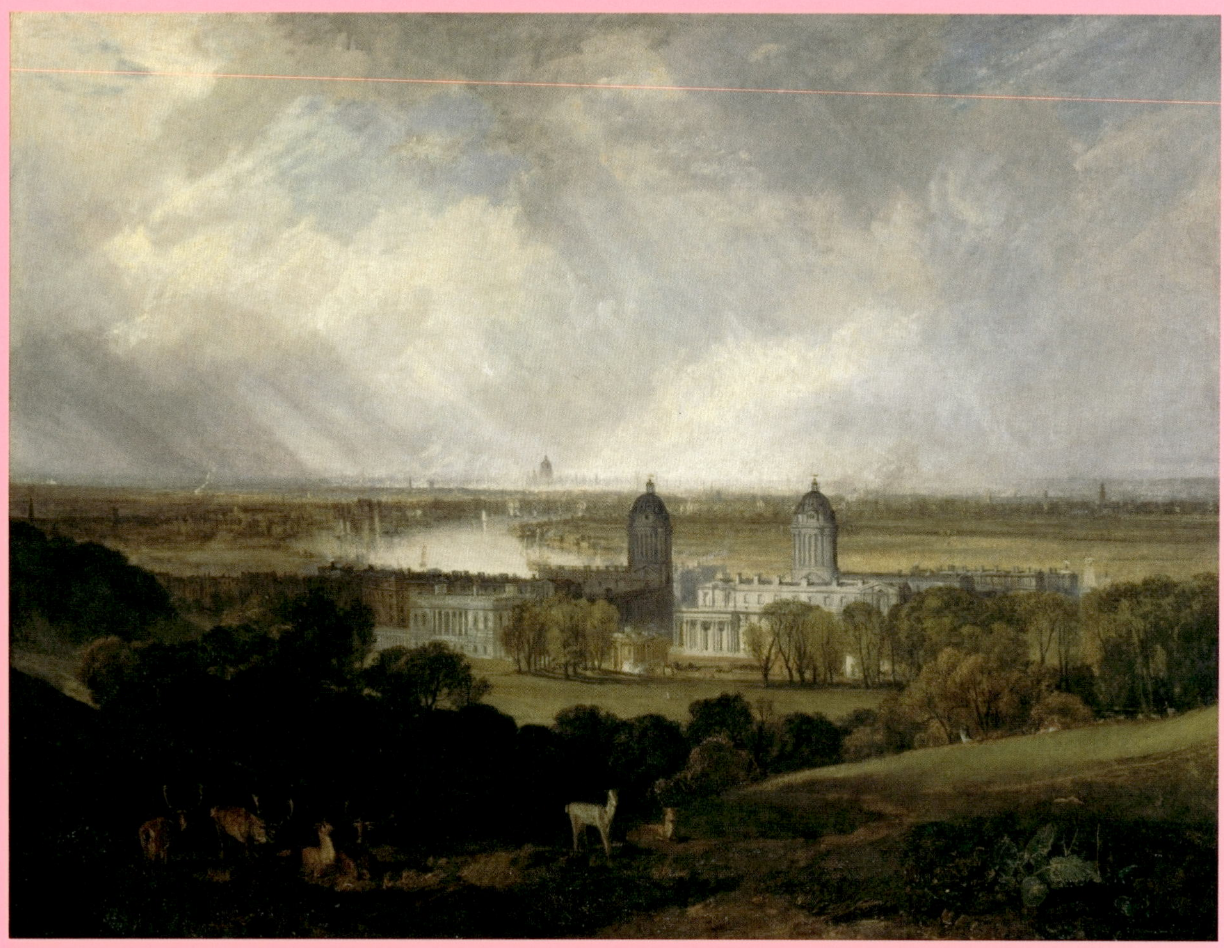

 90 *London from Greenwich Park* exh. 1809. Oil paint on canvas, 90.2 × 120, Tate

Artists depicting London in the nineteenth century often took as their viewpoint one of two spots in Greenwich Park. Turner, who rarely painted his native city, did so once from each of these positions.

In 1809 he exhibited a view taken from One Tree Hill (no.90), a low viewpoint in the deer park common with eighteenth-century topographical artists. This provided a verdant, pastoral frame for the grand architecture of Greenwich Hospital and the Queen's House.[95] The image appears peaceful and harmonious, but as in so many cases this impression is complicated by the verses Turner chose to accompany the painting when it was exhibited.[96] These verses, Turner's own, establish a fundamental tension between the oppressive city and the grandeur of its architecture:

> Where burthen'd Thames reflect the crowded sail,
> Commercial care and busy toil prevail,
> Whose murky veil, aspiring to the skies,
> Obscures thy beauty, and thy form denies,
> Save where thy spires pierce the doubtful air,
> As gleams of hope amidst a world of care[97]

An 1825 watercolour (no.91), possibly produced as a design for an unrealised series of prints,[98] surveys the city from a more elevated and panoramic viewpoint. This is Observatory Hill, site of the Royal Observatory, and in selecting that perspective, Turner shifts attention from the grand architecture of the hospital buildings (which are brusquely cropped from the image) to the Thames as a commercial artery. In contrast to the earlier painting, the river in this scene is densely populated, both by large steamers heading downstream towards the coast and innumerable ships assembled around the city docks. The teeming activity of the Pool of London can be best appreciated in a group of related watercolours, subsequently engraved, that Turner made around this time. A view of the Tower of London from across the Thames (no.92), for instance, takes in two steam packets (possibly being loaded for subsequent continental travel) and a prison hulk – emblems, perhaps, of the best and worst of recent marine technologies.

In the foreground of the 1825 *London from Greenwich* stands a group of figures whose prominence, unusual in a Turner watercolour, lends credence to the idea of the work as a title-page or frontispiece design. As Stephen Daniels and John Bonehill have argued, these figures, assembled around a group of globes, maps and plans of London and its buildings, may depict two men who had unsuccessfully launched attempts at major interventions into the London landscape.[99] The politician and would-be urban planner Frederick William Trench (arms raised, in a top hat) devised an ambitious scheme for a new colonnaded riverside way linking Whitehall and the City. This scheme was abandoned in 1825, the year of Turner's watercolour, and Trench frames with his hands the area it would have occupied. The sculptor John Flaxman, meanwhile, gestures to the land around Greenwich Observatory, the site of his most ambitious unrealised project, a 230ft-high statue of *Britain by Divine Providence Triumphant* that he proposed for the site in 1799.

This scene, somewhat satirical, uses maps (dated 1526 and 1825) to highlight the growth of the city since the Tudor period, and foregrounds the commercial and economic power of the capital. Everything about the scene, from the viewpoint to the accumulation of objects and the barely legible overpainted maps and plans in the foreground, disrupts the way of picturing the city offered in Turner's earlier painting. Fundamentally, perhaps, the two works make contrasting points about London's civic architecture. In the painting Turner posits Wren's architecture as a salve for the cares of urban life. In the later watercolour, however, the artist seems to take aim at Trench, Flaxman and, by extension, any number of those who would make 'improvements' to the city. JF

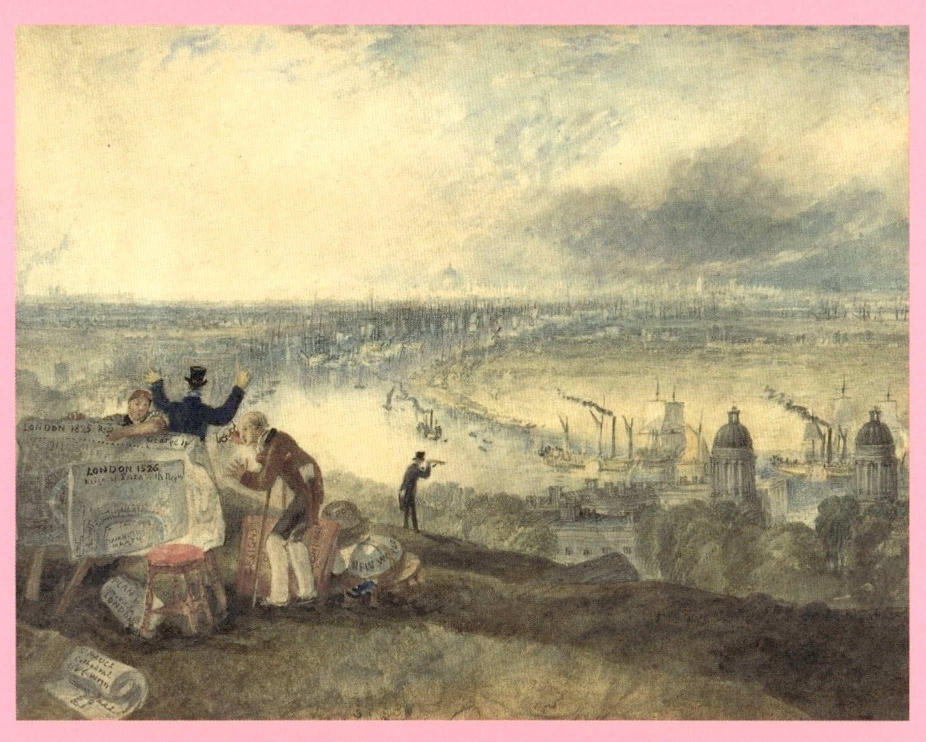

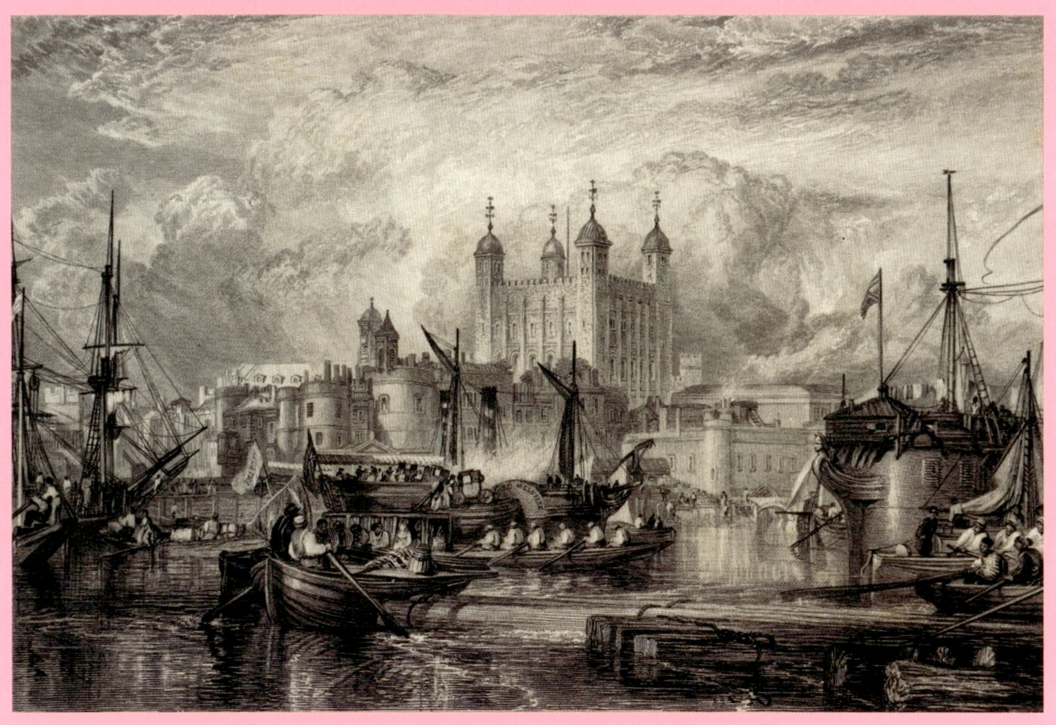

91 *View of London from Greenwich* 1825. Watercolour, graphite, pen and ink on paper, 21.3 × 28, Metropolitan Museum, New York
92 William Miller after Joseph Mallord William Turner, *The Tower of London* 1831. Line engraving on paper, 9.4 × 14.7 (image), Tate

Defence

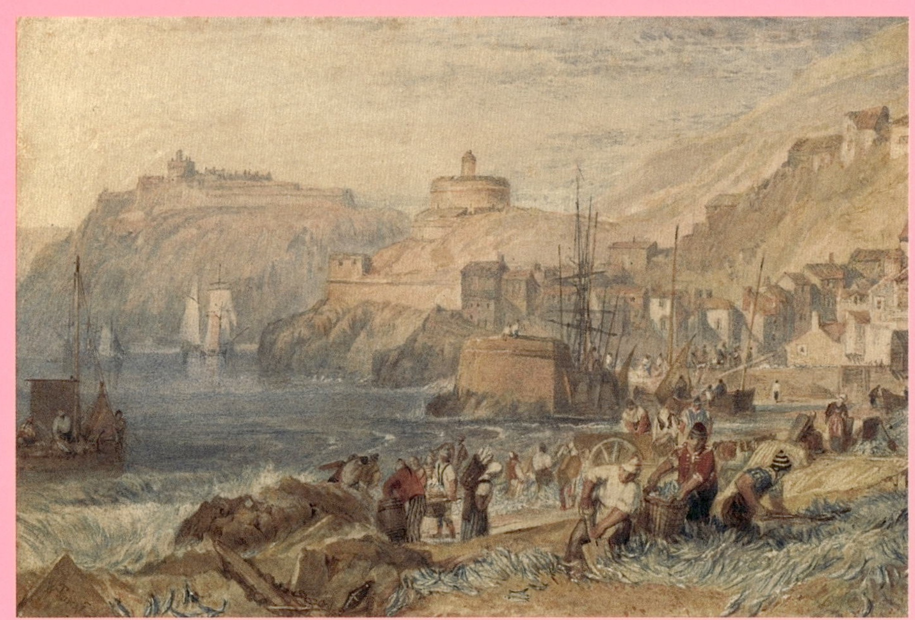

 93 *St Mawes, Cornwall* c.1823. Watercolour on paper, 14.2 × 21.7, Yale Center for British Art, Paul Mellon Collection, New Haven

In 1811 Turner reached an agreement with the engraver brothers George and William Cooke to produce topographical watercolours for the publication *Picturesque Views on the Southern Coast of England*, which was issued in instalments between 1814 and 1826. That year he spent two months in Dorset, Devon and Cornwall making sketches that served as the basis for many of the watercolours reproduced in the series.

Coastal defences, whether contemporary or historic, are prominent in many of these watercolours. The main subject of Turner's view of the Cornish town of St Mawes (no.93) is pilchard fishing, which by the early 1820s had recovered from blockades that interrupted access to continental markets during the war. Beyond the town, however, the imposing castles of Pendennis and St Mawes (both built during the 1540s to counter the invasion threat from France and Spain) loom large, like earlier counterparts to the Martello towers that were erected at regular intervals along the south coast during the Napoleonic Wars.

Turner chose to depict Rye (no.94) from the Royal Military Road, built across marshland between 1804 and 1809 to connect the town with nearby Winchelsea. The sea has burst through a temporary dam, forcing workers and a horse and cart to flee from the onrushing water. Turner visited Rye more than once, including while the road was under construction, but has taken significant licence with topography in his watercolour (particularly in the placement of the River Brede, and Camber Castle on the right). These changes help to create a sense of powerful natural forces threatening to overwhelm human endeavour.

Nearby Hythe (no.95) changed visibly during the wars: it was the only town that the Royal Military Canal passed through, and the Royal Staff Corps barracks (completed in 1810) housed soldiers for many years after the war. Both can be seen in Turner's watercolour, painted around the time of the radical MP William Cobbett's 1823 visit to the town. Cobbett poured scorn on the canal and the barracks, saying they were 'most expensive, most squandering', and one wonders whether Turner intended to pay tribute to British readiness, or to highlight the unnecessary effort and expense that Cobbett saw.[100]

Even within the restraints of small-scale topography Turner's approach varied widely. His meticulous rendering of St Mawes, in which even distant details are clearly legible, is very different to

Hythe, in which sharply defined military figures in the foreground give way to a more fluid background (a proof impression of George Cooke's print of *Hythe* in the Tate collection carries extensive remarks by Turner, including criticism that the distant marshland is 'all a swamp'[101]). At the same time techniques and motifs are repeated. The scene of Rye, in which turbulent waves and a stormy sky create a powerful sense of foreboding, nonetheless shares certain details with the tranquil St Mawes view: foreground figures wearing blue and white stripes, and agitated flicks of blue equally suited to rendering rolling waves or pilchards heaped on the beach.

Picturesque Views on the Southern Coast of England was followed by another ambitious (and similarly abandoned) project, *Picturesque Views in England and Wales* (1825–38). In this series Turner revisited the south coast, again reflecting on the wars and their aftermath in several of his views. The warships in *Devonport and Dockyard* (no.96) are being 'paid off' (decommissioned and retired from the navy), while carefree figures in the foreground display 'general relations of Jack ashore' according to John Ruskin, an early owner of the watercolour.[102] Dark storm clouds are passing and the docks are bathed in sunlight, possibly symbolising post-war peace. JF

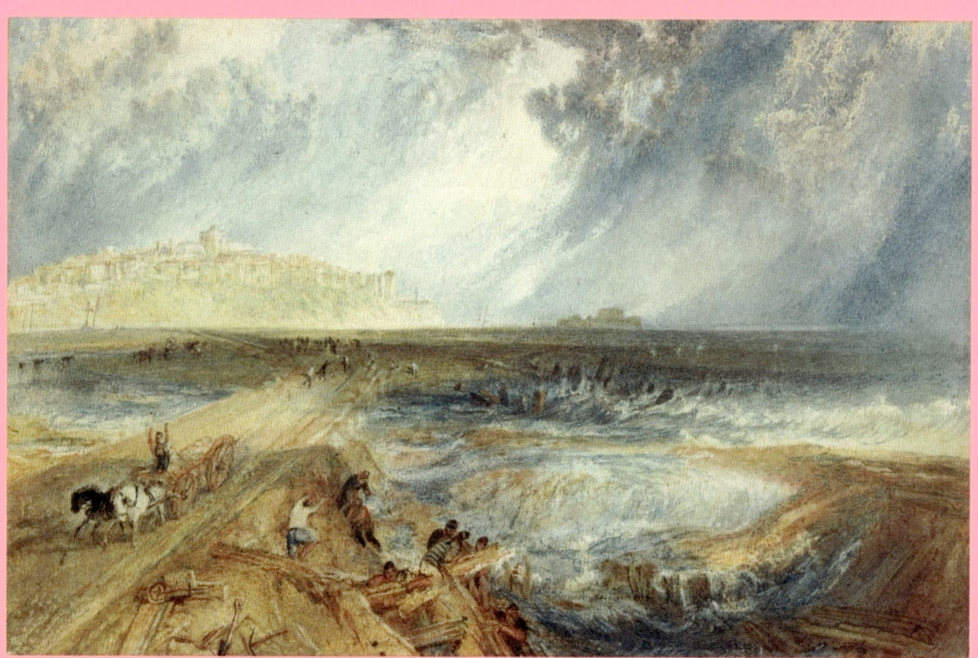

94 *Rye, Sussex* c.1823. Watercolour on paper, 14.7 × 23.1, National Museum of Wales, Cardiff

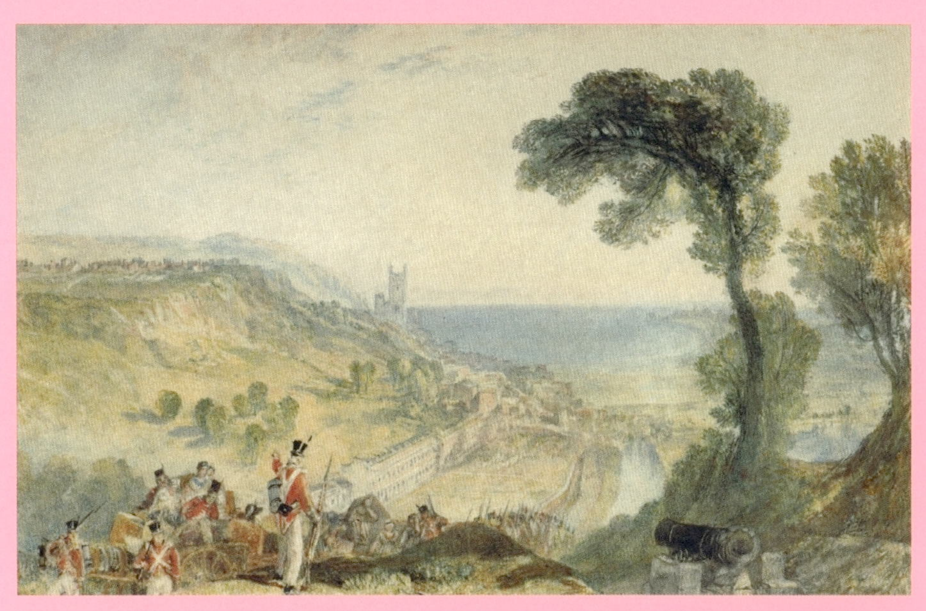

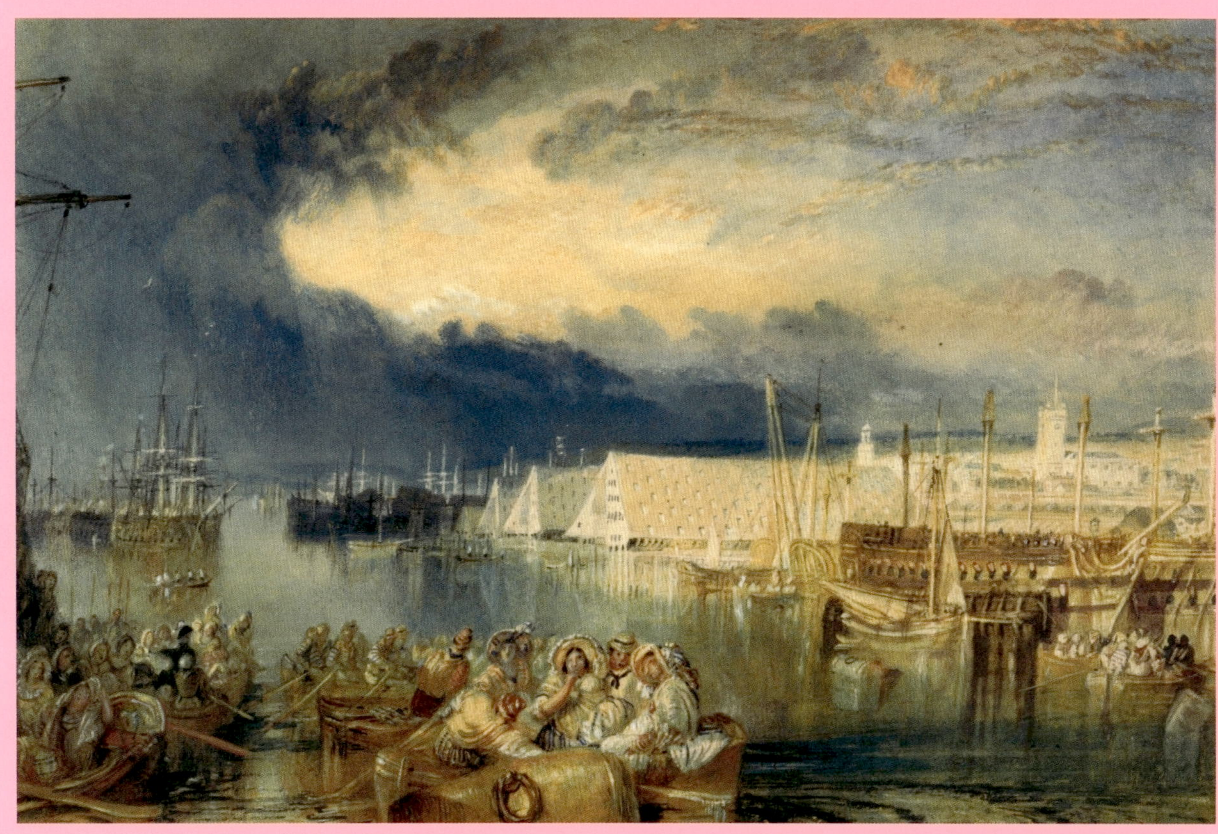

95 *Hythe, Kent* 1824. Watercolour on paper, 14 × 22.9, Guildhall Art Gallery, City of London
96 *Devonport and Dockyard, Devonshire* 1825–9. Watercolour and gouache on paper, 29.8 × 44,
Fogg Art Museum, Harvard Art Museums, Cambridge, Massachusetts, USA

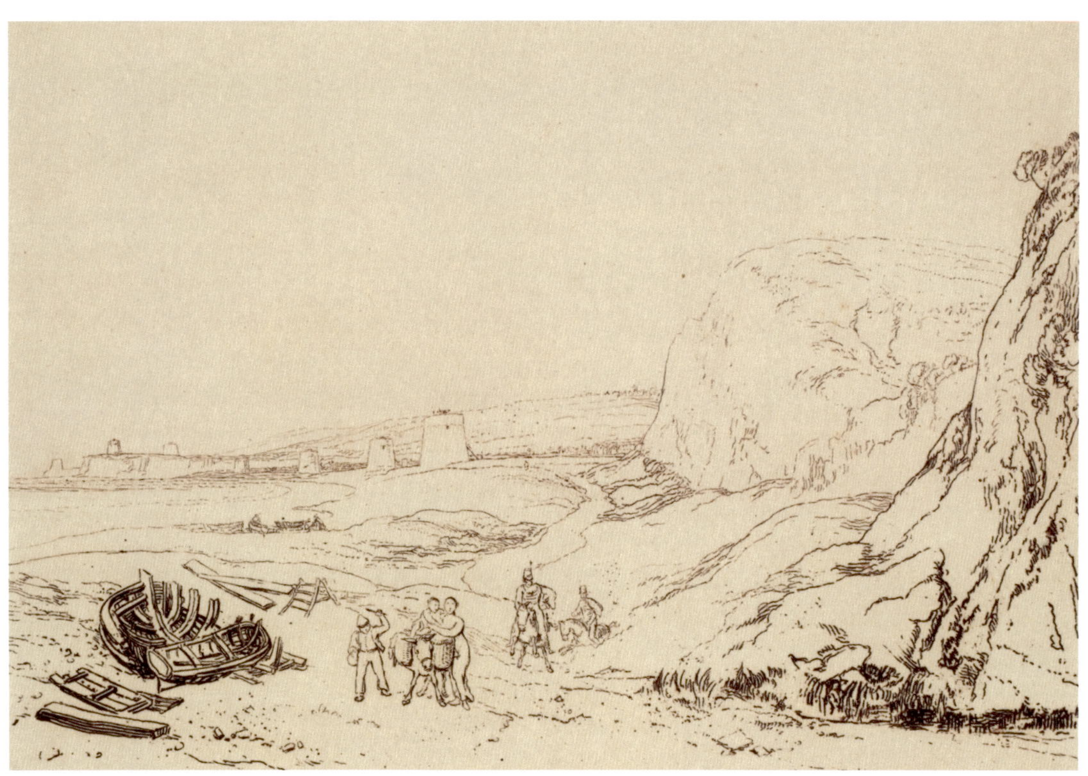

97 *Martello Towers, near Bexhill, Sussex* 1811. Etching on paper, 17.6 × 25.7 (image), Tate

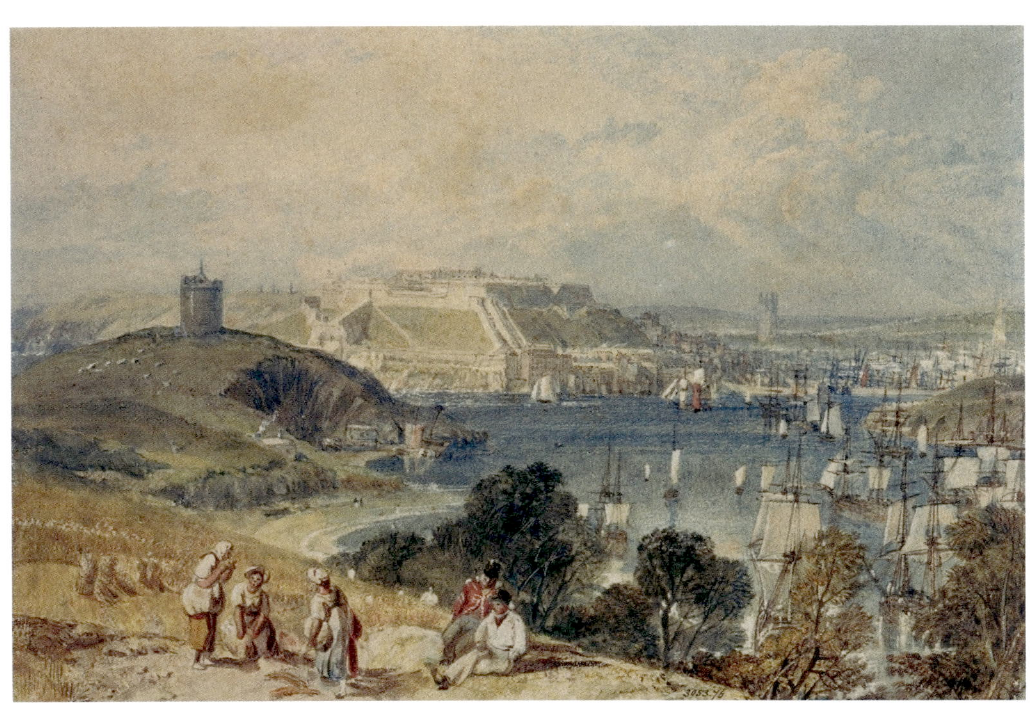

98 *Plymouth with Mount Batten* c.1816. Watercolour on paper, 14.6 × 23.5, Victoria and Albert Museum, London

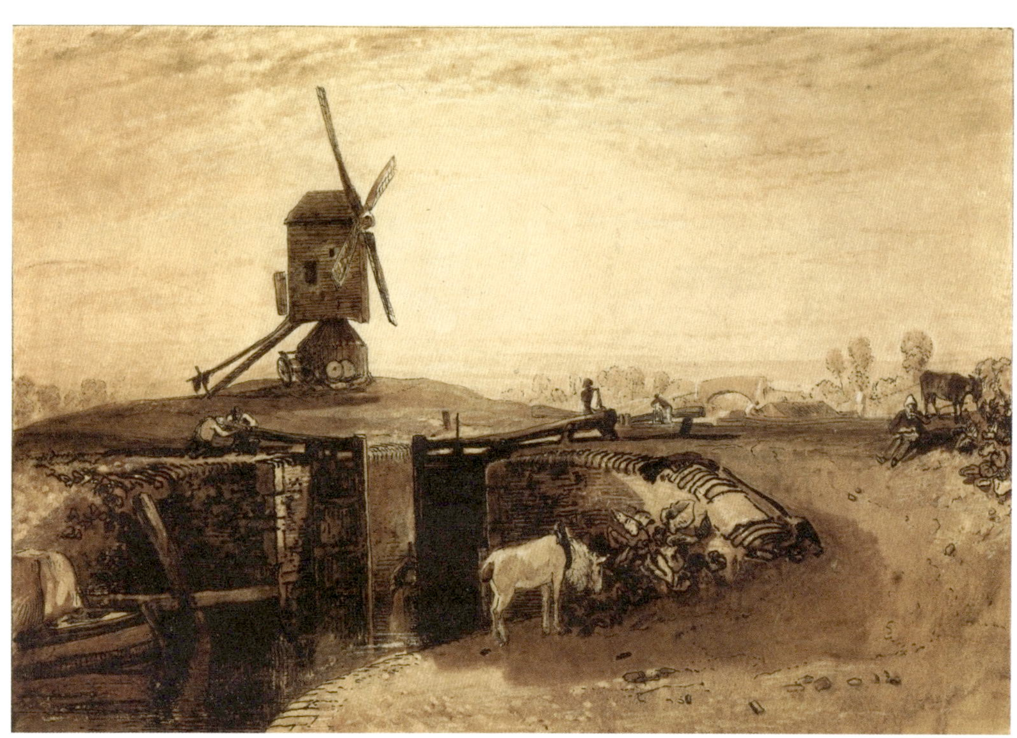

   99 *Windmill and Lock* 1811. Etching and watercolour on paper, 17.7 × 25.8 (image), Tate

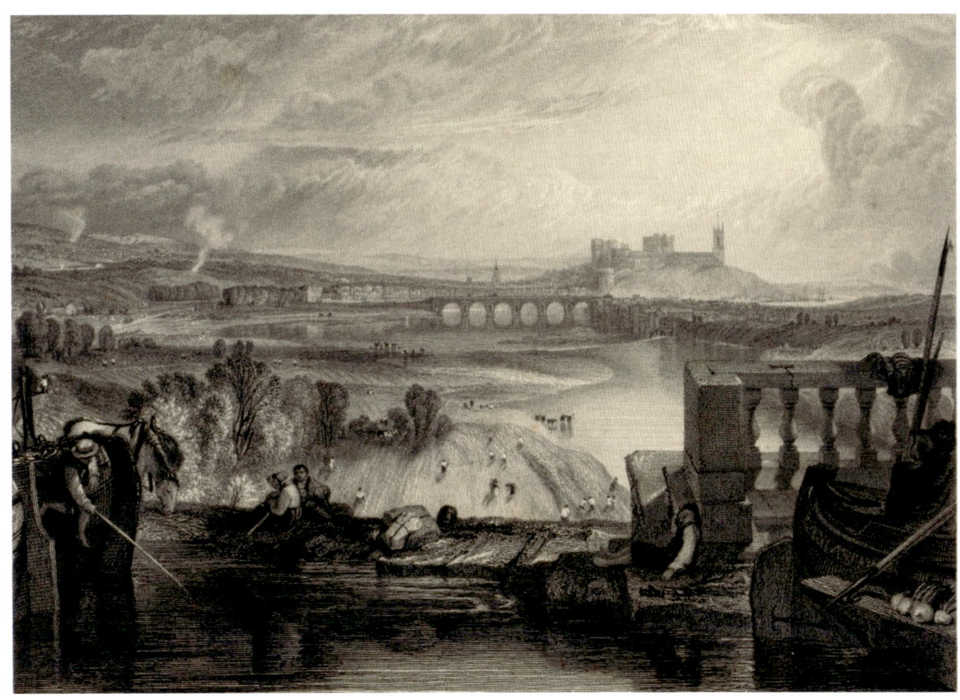

100 Robert Wallis after Joseph Mallord William Turner, *Lancaster from the Aqueduct Bridge* 1827.
Line engraving on paper, 16.5 × 23.2 (image), Tate

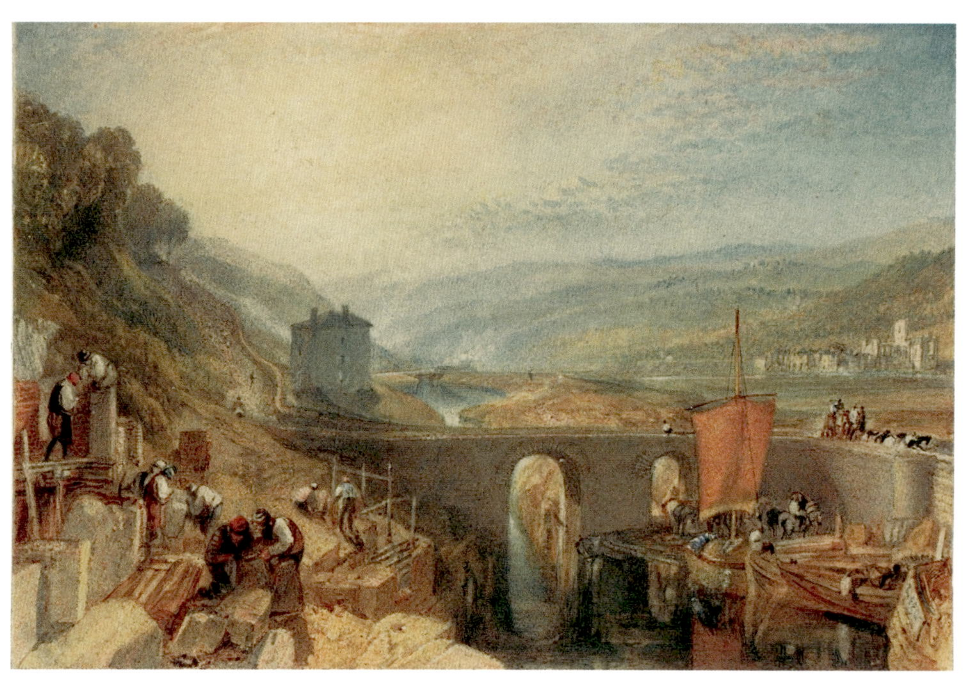

  101 *Kirkstall Lock, on the River Aire* 1824–5. Watercolour on paper, 15.9 × 23.5, Tate

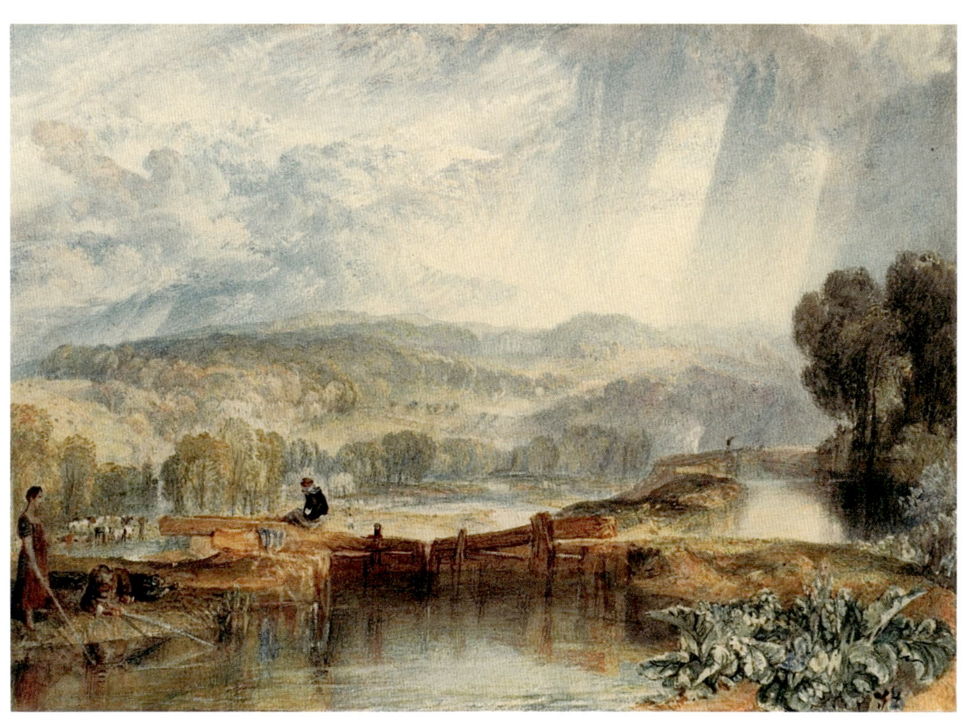

102 *More Park, near Watford, on the River Colne* c.1823. Watercolour and gouache on paper, 15.8 × 22.1, Tate

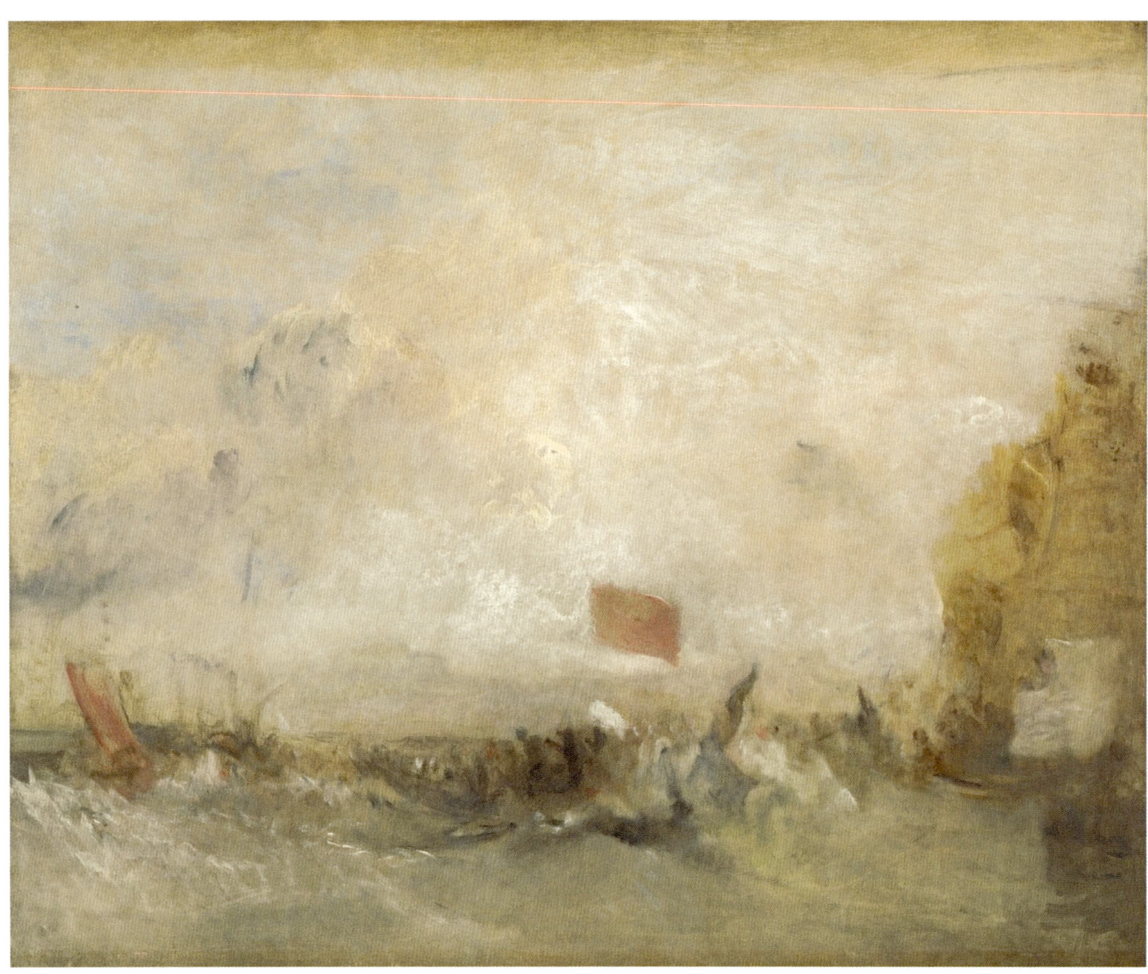

 103 *George IV's Departure from the 'Royal George'* 1822. Oil paint on mahogany, 75.2 × 92.1, Tate

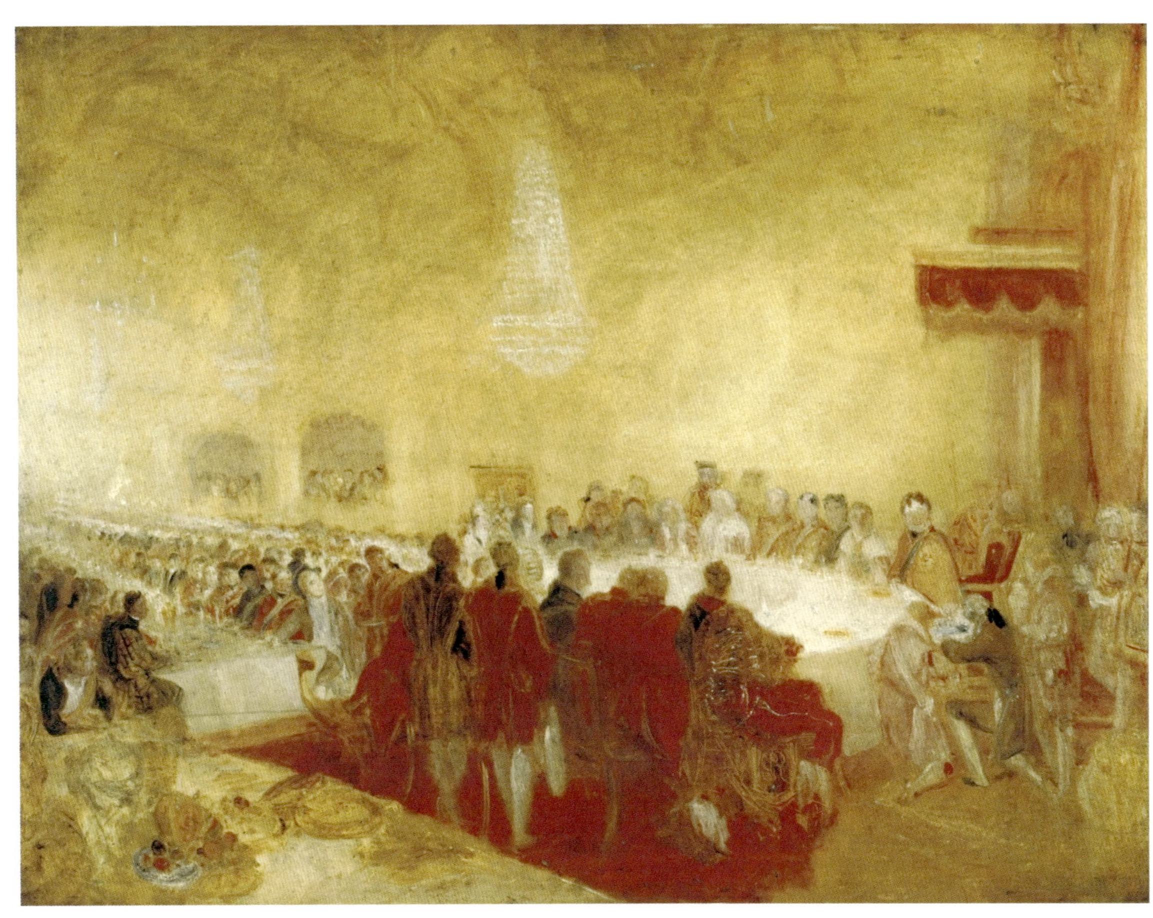

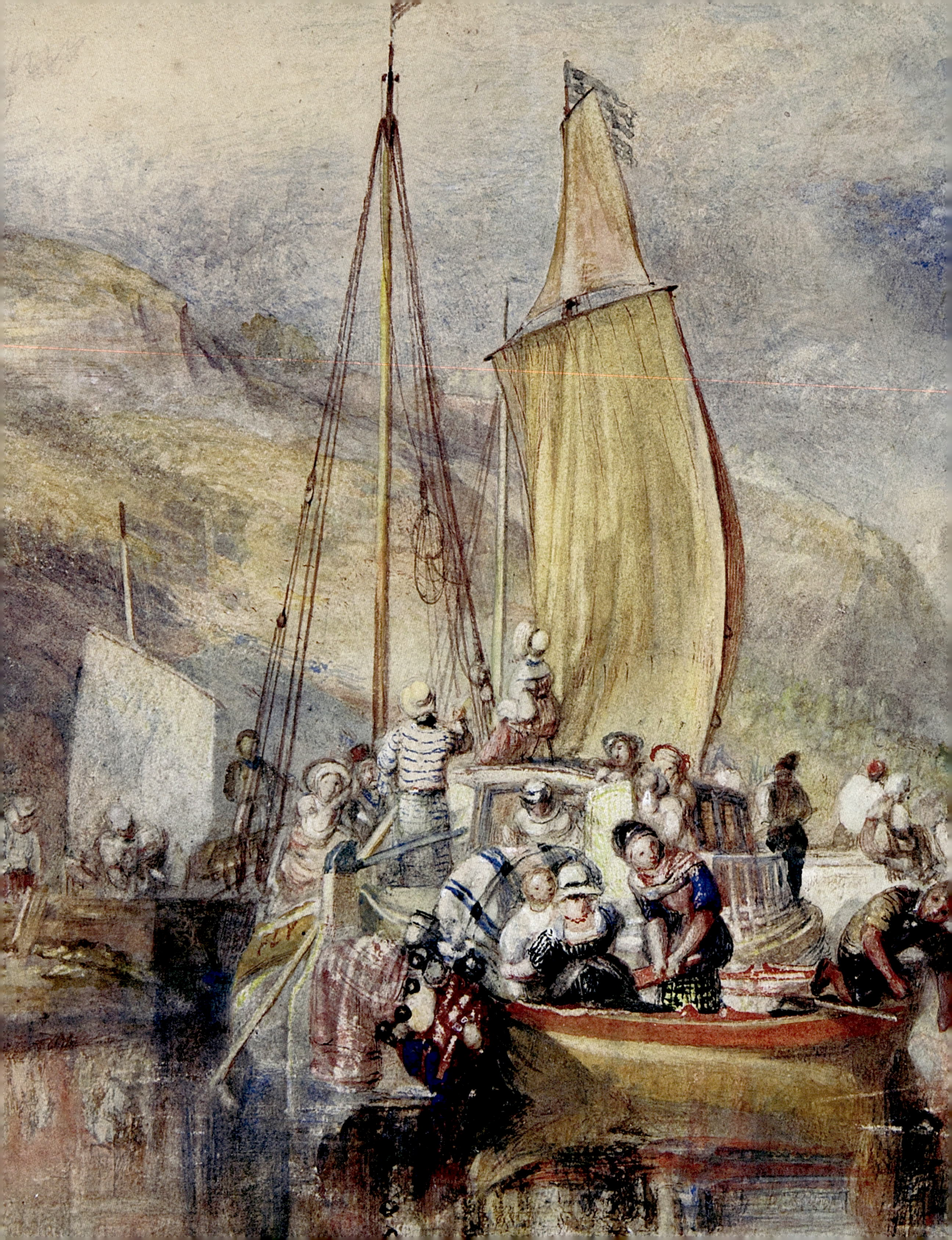

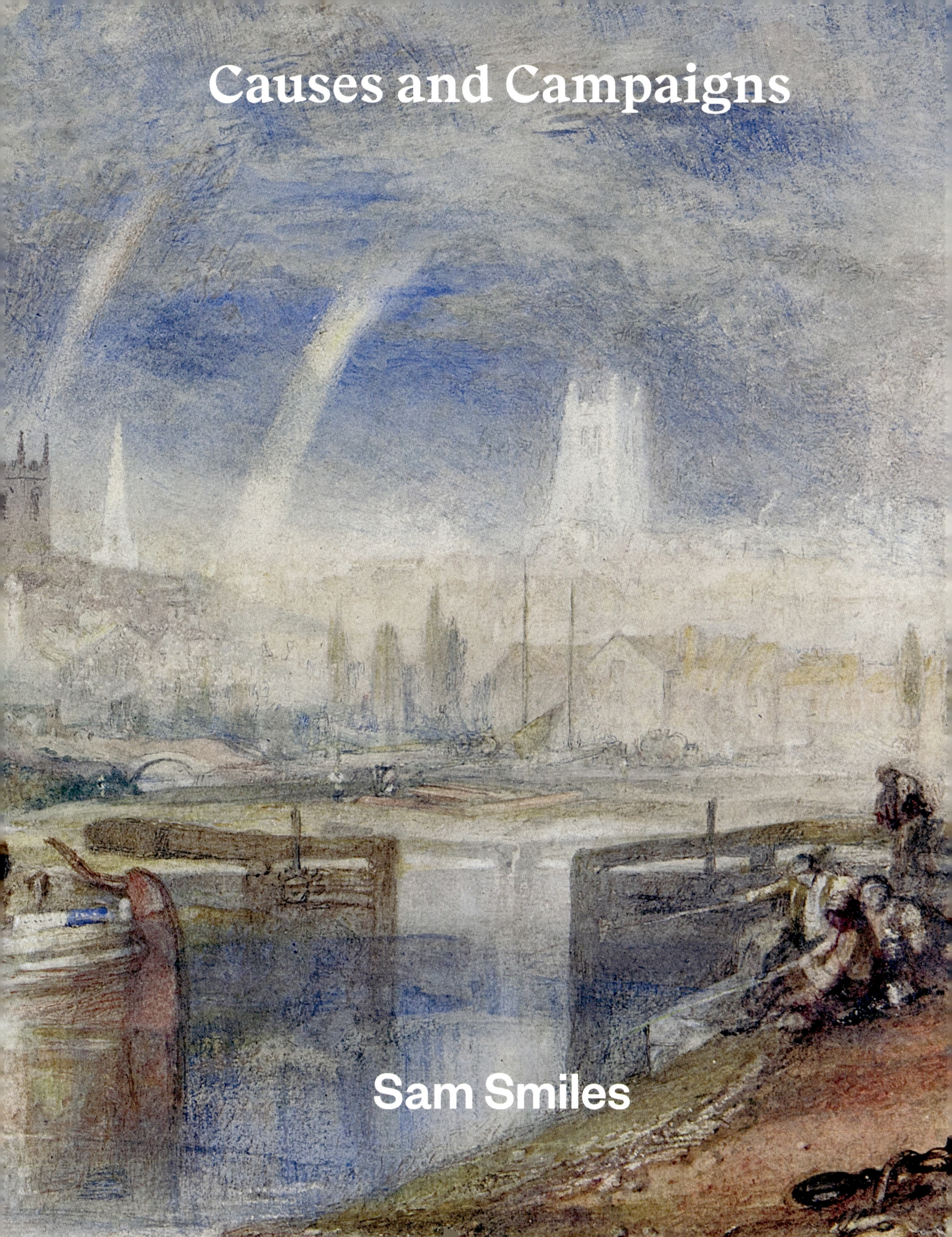

Causes and Campaigns
Sam Smiles

Turner's practice as a painter is marked by the number and variety of contemporary issues with which he engaged. Today, when we almost expect creative talent to be aligned with humanitarian and left-wing causes, an artist whose career demonstrates a consistent interest in progressive tendencies is unexceptional, but in Turner's England it was most unusual. Few other artists of the time were more assiduous in registering the political complexion of the contemporary world. Of all his contemporaries, William Blake is perhaps the closest comparison, although Blake's enthusiasm for radical, even revolutionary social ideals exceeded Turner's more measured support for liberal and humanitarian concerns. However, Blake's work circulated principally among a narrow circle of admirers, his ideological leanings were bound up with metaphysical ideas and few comprehended his world view; Turner, in contrast, was very much a public artist, showing regularly at the Royal Academy and widely disseminating many of his works through engravings.

The causes Turner referred to over his career include parliamentary reform, freedom of expression, religious toleration, Greek independence from Ottoman rule and the abolition of slavery. However, trying to work back from these instances to establish Turner's personal politics is no easy matter. Whatever modern scholars have concluded about his allegiances, he was not a propagandist and it would be wrong to consider his allusions to these issues as the pictorial equivalent of pamphleteering. Admittedly, some of these subjects were declared unambiguously in his pictures and accordingly it is relatively straightforward to interpret what may have been the intended message; but others were only hinted at, often quite cryptically and sometimes heavily disguised. Given that many of those who encountered his work, as patrons or viewers, may have felt very differently about the causes he supported, Turner had good reason to tread carefully.

Moreover, for all our understanding of his interest in these subjects, we need to remember that his

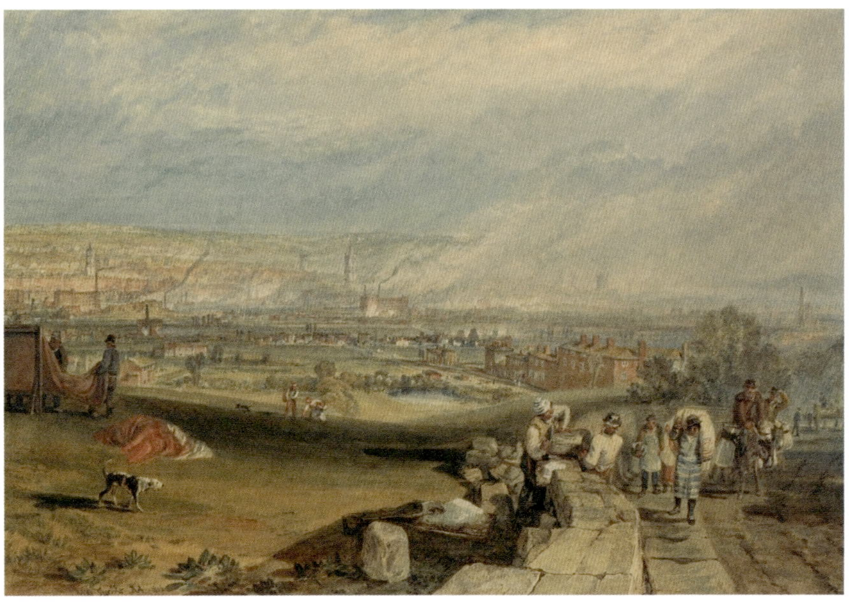

105
Leeds 1816.
Watercolour and pen
and ink on paper,
29.2 × 43.2.
Yale Center for British Art,
Paul Mellon Collection,
New Haven

Previous page: *Nottingham* 1831 (no.115)

commitment to landscape and, more generally, to painting as an art was paramount. Necessarily, therefore, his treatment of topical issues and concerns was integrated in a wider presentation of the contemporary world and was couched in his distinctive stylistic idiom. That strategy almost certainly resulted in many viewers gliding over the details that give the key to the social or political reference of a particular image. But those willing to attend to it fully would be shown something significant, namely how contemporary causes are not the province of politics alone, and therefore removed from everyday concerns, but detectable in places and situations at first sight quite remote from them.

As a preliminary example, we might consider the role of foreground figures (staffage) in Turner's paintings, especially his watercolours. Traditionally, they would be introduced to populate the image with enlivening detail, to add incident and enrich its pictorial interest. They are, to that extent at least, usually seen as generic figures adding relatively little to understanding the depicted location. Turner's staffage, in contrast, has been seen by some commentators as transgressive, especially in the nineteenth-century circumstances of agitation for political change, insofar as his emphasis on placing working-class activity in full and detailed view not only recognises its importance for that particular place but also hints at the new circumstances of the age in which such figures can no longer be taken for granted.[103] His insistence on this is echoed in the (unused) text he wrote to accompany his watercolours for *Picturesque Views on the Southern Coast of England*, where he took pains to look in detail at the contemporary livelihoods of those who worked in the locations he depicted.[104] It also seems clear that his determination to bear witness to a changing world was not welcomed by those who held fast to the hierarchical Britain of previous generations. It has been plausibly argued, for example, that Turner's watercolour of *Leeds* (no.105), with its careful depiction of cloth-workers and factories, was originally designed as the frontispiece for the Revd Thomas Dunham Whitaker's antiquarian

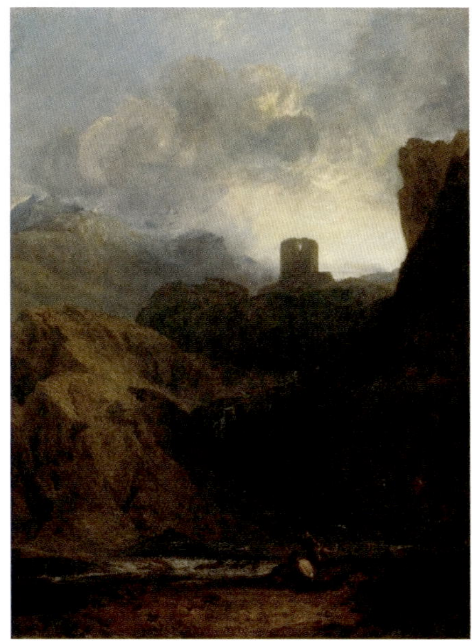

106
*Dolbadern Castle,
North Wales* 1800.
Oil on canvas,
119.4 × 90.2
Royal Academy of Arts

publication *Loidis and Elmete*, but was rejected by Whitaker because it showed aspects of the new Yorkshire he so detested.[105]

So where did Turner stand on the major social and political debates of his time? One indication of his underlying sympathies is provided by his reaction to the French Revolution and its aftermath. Turner did not go as far as his friend Thomas Girtin, who by 1798 had his hair cropped in sympathy with republican ideals, but in 1803 he sided with the 'democratic' faction at the Royal Academy, including John Hoppner, Robert Smirke, Thomas Stothard, Martin Archer Shee, Henry Fuseli and Thomas Banks, all of whom had welcomed at least the early phases of the revolution. Moreover, three works exhibited in 1800 show Turner's willingness to champion liberty and oppose repression: *Dolbadern Castle* (no.106) specifies the loss of individual freedom in the person of the medieval Welsh prince Owain Goch, part of the context of *The Fifth Plague of Egypt* (see no.43) is the enslavement of the Israelites as a people, while *Caernarvon Castle,*

North Wales (no.8) recalls the suppression of a whole culture in Edward I's destruction of the Bardic order. By dint of their historical parallels these subjects could be said to throw a critical light on the recent assault on civil liberties by William Pitt's government as it attempted to combat the influence of the French Revolution: the trial of Thomas Paine in 1792, the Treason Trials of 1794, the suspension of Habeas Corpus (1794–5) and the so-called 'Gagging Acts' (1795) that restricted freedom of speech and assembly.[106]

It is probable that Turner's political sympathies were encouraged, perhaps even developed, by his friendship with the Yorkshire landowner Walter Fawkes. Having probably first met Turner in the 1790s, Fawkes was Turner's most important patron from 1802 until his death in 1825 and became a very close friend. From at least 1808 Turner stayed regularly at Farnley Hall, Fawkes's country seat in Yorkshire, and there painted *Fairfaxiana* (c.1815–20), a series of watercolours depicting the history of political reform in

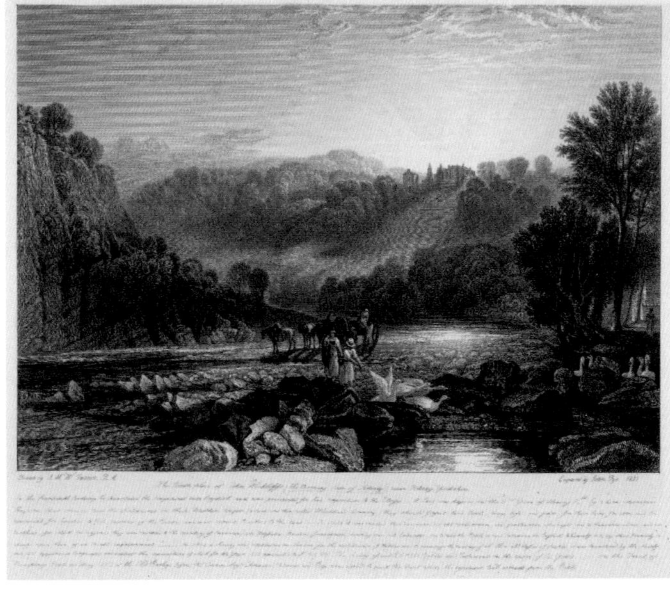

107
John Pye, the younger, after Joseph Mallord William Turner, *Wycliffe, near Rokeby* 1823.
Etching and engraving, printed on Chine Collé, 27.9 × 43.1,
Trustees of the British Museum

144

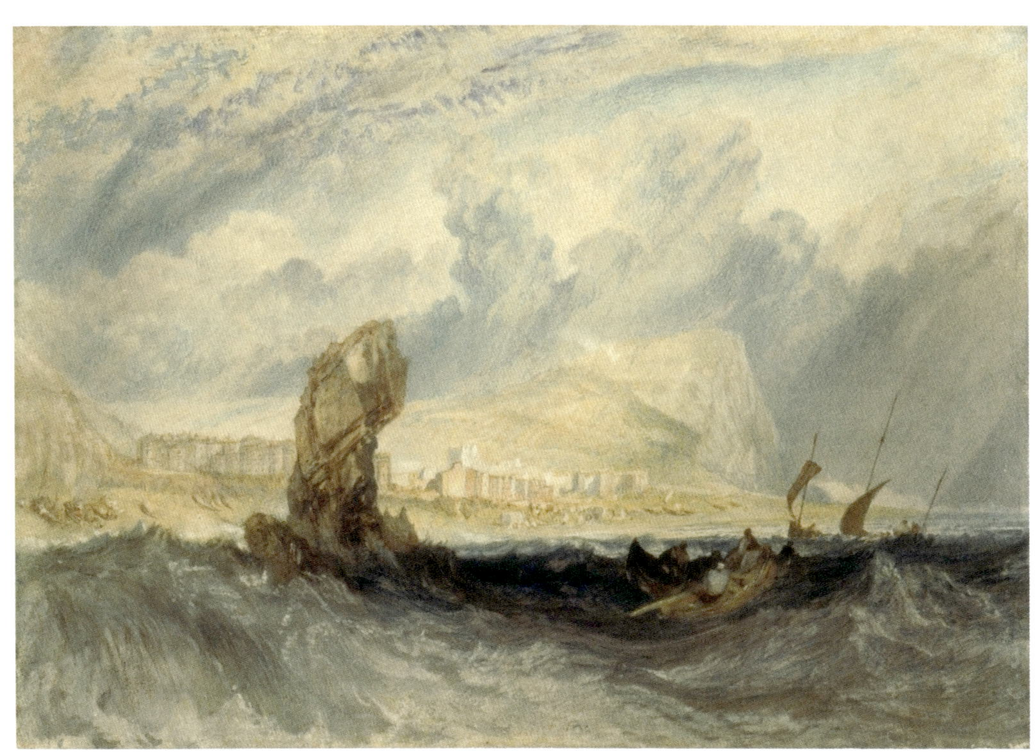

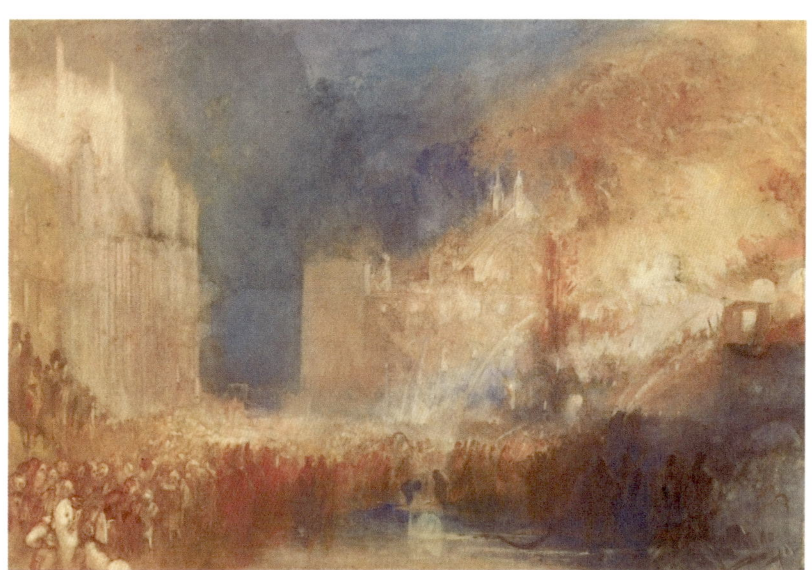

109 *The Burning of the Houses of Parliament*, c.1834–5. Watercolour and gouache on paper, 30.2 × 44.4, Tate

England and honouring Fawkes's ancestor, the Parliamentarian military commander Thomas Fairfax. Fawkes was nominally a Whig, but his politics were radical. Although he was only briefly MP for Yorkshire (1806–7), he supported his old school friend, the radical reformer Francis Burdett, and was actively involved in Westminster and local politics. Throughout his career he championed parliamentary reform and the extension of the franchise and repeatedly spoke against political, religious and social repression. He was particularly angered by Peterloo, the violent suppression of the reform meeting held at St Peter's Field, Manchester, on 16 August 1819, which resulted in the deaths of over a dozen spectators and serious injuries to some 400–700 others.

Turner's endorsement of Fawkes's political beliefs explains the addition of a lengthy inscription to a handful of presentation proofs of the engraving *Wycliffe, near Rokeby* (no.107). Starting with a more politically explicit title, *The Birthplace of John Wicliffe ('The Morning Star of Liberty'), near Rokeby, Yorkshire*, the text relates the struggle for freedom of expression from John Wycliffe's time to the present and ends with a reference to 'the Trial of Humphrey Boyle before Mr Common Serjt. Denman[.] Women and Boys were ordered to quit the court while the defendant read extracts from the Bible.' A working-class shopman, Boyle was working for the radical publisher Richard Carlile –in prison for blasphemy and seditious libel at the time – when he was arrested in December 1821 at Carlile's shop in Fleet Street, 'The Temple of Reason'. Boyle had published a pamphlet that attacked religion as idolatry, criticised the constitution and supported reform. Accused of blasphemy and seditious libel, at his trial he read explicit passages from the Bible to demonstrate its inclusion of obscene material and the court was cleared when he did so. The text added to Turner's *Wycliffe* plate was presumably for circulation only among three or four of Fawkes's closest friends and allies but shows Turner's willingness to support radical causes via the most outspoken dissenting voices in the 1820s.

It has been argued that a seemingly innocuous watercolour of *Sidmouth* (no.108) is marked by similar concerns. Under Lord Liverpool's Tory administration legislation was drafted to quell the civil unrest that had arisen as a result of the economic hardship following the Napoleonic Wars. Habeas Corpus was suspended in January 1817 and the notorious Six Acts were passed in December 1819 to make sure that large meetings, such as the 60,000 or more who had attended St Peter's Field, became impossible. As Home Secretary, Henry Addington, Lord Sidmouth, was behind this legislation and in progressive circles he was blamed for the Peterloo Massacre as well. As Eric Shanes has pointed out, in 1823 Sidmouth remarried, to a considerably younger woman, which attracted some bawdy comment. By transforming a sandstone rock stack into a priapic feature emerging from the sea Turner seems to have intended the same lewd association with a man many considered an enemy of liberty.[107]

Turner's enduring commitment to reform can be found in a mysterious unfinished painting formerly catalogued as *Death on a Pale Horse (?)* but now identified as *The Fall of Anarchy* (no.124). Recent research has shown that it was begun around 1833 and probably depicts the climactic episode in Shelley's *The Masque of Anarchy*. Shelley had written the poem in immediate response to the Peterloo debacle, but it was considered too contentious to publish and did not appear in print until 1832, after the Great Reform Act had become law, widening the electoral franchise. Shelley describes Anarchy, one of the oppressors of the people along with Hypocrisy, Murder and Fraud, as 'Anarchy the Skeleton', who rode

> On a white horse, splashed with blood;
> He was pale even to the lips,
> Like Death in the Apocalypse.

Turner's depiction of this crowned skeletal figure falling off a rearing mount corresponds to the moment when Anarchy is vanquished by a mysterious light-filled mist that takes on bodily form and awakens thoughts of resistance in the people. Anarchy falls dead from his horse, which tramples his murderous followers to dust, freeing the world of tyranny. Nevertheless, the fact that the painting is unfinished is significant. Even in the circumstances of the mid-1830s, with a newly reformed Parliament, such a subject might have proved too contentious for public display.[108]

Turner's watercolour of Stoneyhurst College (no.111) addresses another key object of reformist campaigning, Catholic emancipation. Catholics and nonconformists had been barred from public office including the armed forces, Parliament and the judiciary for some 150 years, until the repeal of the Test and Corporation Acts in 1828 and the passing of the Roman Catholic Relief Act in 1829 removed these obstacles. Religious toleration was achieved because of public pressure and because George IV and his ministers, fearful of armed conflict in Ireland, hastily abandoned their opposition to emancipation. This victory for the proponents of reform not only undermined the centrality of the Anglican Church in England, it also paved the way for the Great Reform Act of 1832. Turner's watercolour depicts the Roman

Catholic public school established in 1794 and in the foreground shows a rider turning in his saddle to quieten the vociferous crowd of children on the left, while on the right other children collect the toy boat that has successfully completed its journey across the water. Read allegorically, the mounted figure may be understood as standing for the king and his ministers' U-turn, the gesticulating crowd on the left the Protestant ultras who opposed emancipation, and those on the right the Catholics and their supporters welcoming the passage of the legislation. In the background storm clouds are passing away, leaving the college bathed in light and blessed with a rainbow's symbol of hope.[109]

In terms of Turner's whole career, these and other instances of a direct reference to contemporary social and political issues are not a major part of his vast oeuvre, perhaps two dozen examples or so all told, but together they constitute a reckonable body of work. In these paintings Turner aligned himself with the cause of progress and freedom, but he could not be meaningfully

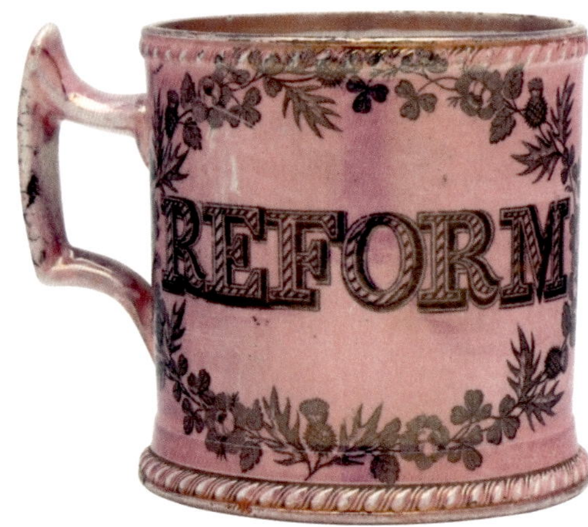

110
Chetham & Robinson/
Chesworth & Robinson,
Reform Mug c.1832. Pink
lusterware with transfer
print, 8.2 × 10.8,
Fitzwilliam Museum,
Cambridge

described as a political artist, perhaps especially because he often chose subtle, perhaps over-subtle, means to refer to these concerns. Nevertheless, it seems fair to say that even if his allusions and use of symbolism were too obscure to reach a wide audience, he was declaring a personal stake in these issues and their ethical implications, and siding with the people when a demonstrable wrong was being called to account.

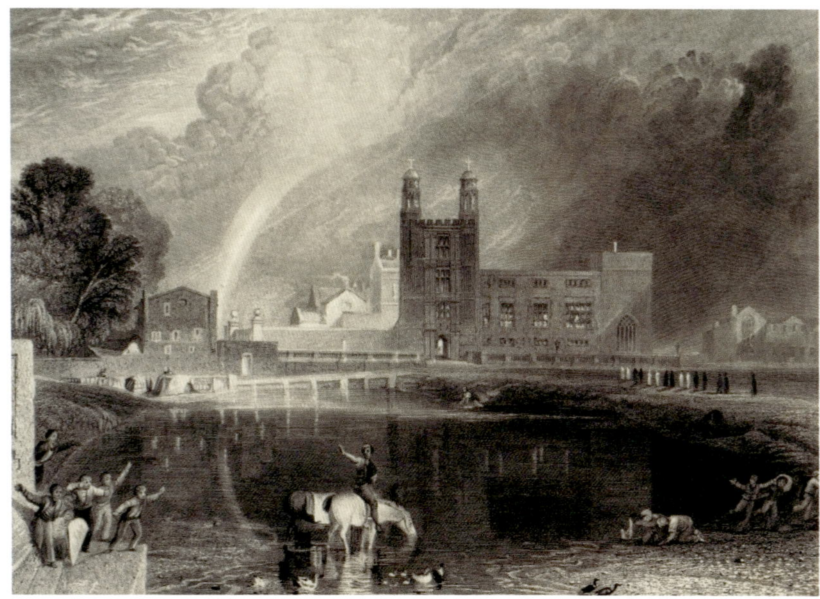

111
James Baylis Allen after Joseph Mallord William Turner, *Stoneyhurst, Lancashire* 1830. Line engraving on paper, 16.1 × 23.5 (image), Tate

Reform

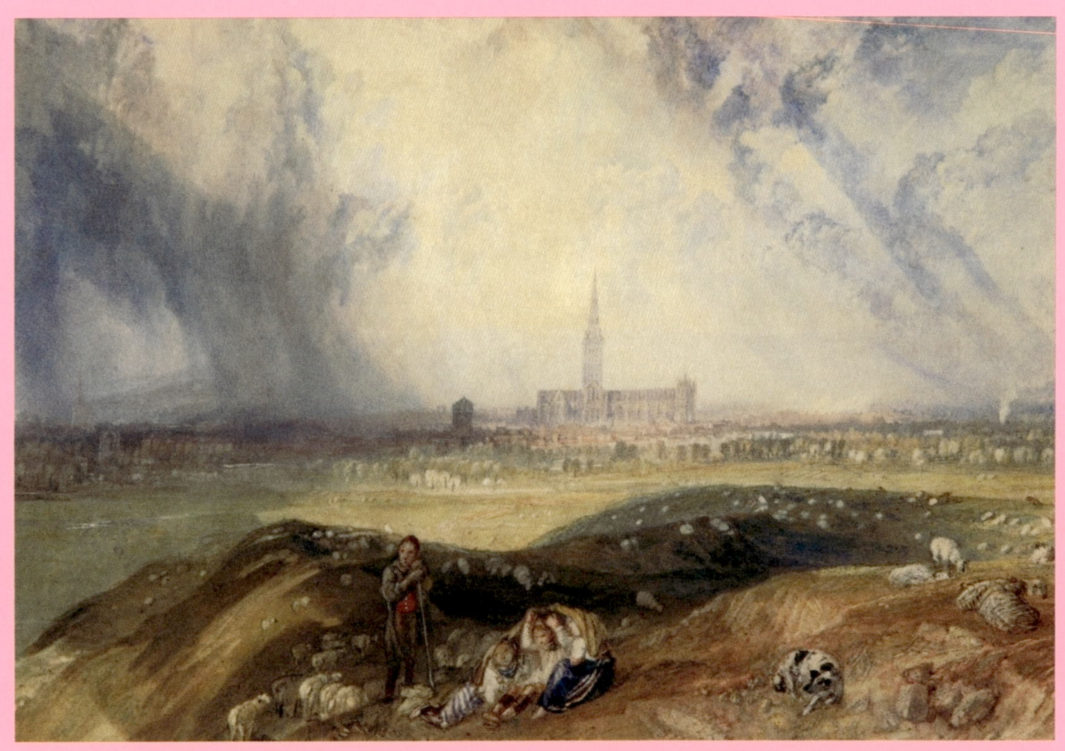

    112 *Salisbury, from Old Sarum* c.1827–8. Watercolour on paper, 27.2 × 41, The Salisbury Museum

The traditional security of the Anglican Church and the political establishment were both under threat in the later 1820s, as demands for Catholic emancipation and electoral reform became more insistent. In *Ely Cathedral, Cambridgeshire* (no.113) children throwing stones personify popular anger at the bishops' resistance to change. In *Salisbury from Old Sarum* (no.112) Turner's vantage point is the notorious constituency of that name, the former location of a castle and cathedral, whose eleven absentee electors sent two MPs to Parliament to represent this uninhabited site. Choosing to paint the epitome of a rotten borough in the late 1820s was not an innocent decision and the storm breaking over Salisbury Cathedral is perhaps intended to suggest current tensions.

More obviously tied to contemporary politics, *The Northampton Election, 6 December 1830* (no.114) shows the reformist Whig MP Lord Althorp being carried through the streets after winning his seat. The image is strewn with inscribed banners, one at bottom centre reading 'The Purity of Elections and Triumph of Law'. On the balcony is a seated man wearing an old-fashioned tricorne hat and resting his gouty foot on a stool. This emblem of reaction is being tapped on his shoulder by the figure of Marianne, the personification of France,

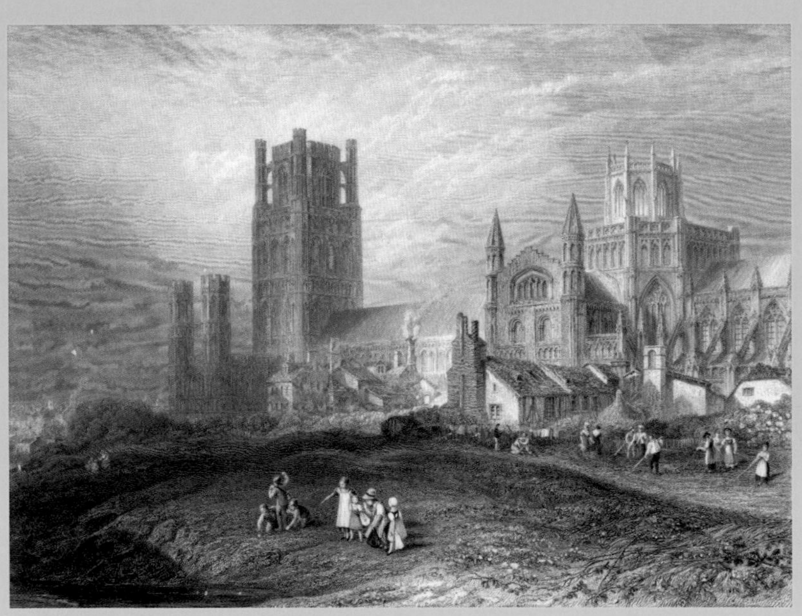

whose 1830 Revolution could be seen as a warning if reform in Britain were to be frustrated. The watercolour was probably intended for the series *Picturesque Views in England and Wales*, as were Turner's images of Old Sarum and Nottingham, but the publisher, Charles Heath, may have felt it was too contentious to be engraved.

The oil painting *The Prince of Orange, William III, Embarked from Holland, and Landed at Torbay, November 4th, 1688, after a Stormy Passage* (no.126) was exhibited at the Royal Academy in 1832 and so coincided with the Great Reform Bill's final passage through Parliament. Its celebration of the Glorious Revolution was a declaration of support for a political settlement that had limited the rights of the monarch, but the 'stormy passage' in its title refers not simply to the fleet's voyage in 1688 but also to the protracted attempts to extend representative democracy in the 1830s.

Nottingham (no.115) was painted after the Great Reform Act had passed into law but recalls one of its key opponents. Nottingham Castle, on the left, was owned by the Duke of Newcastle who controlled a number of pocket boroughs and evicted tenants who voted for reform candidates in the general elections of 1829 and 1830. When the second Reform Bill was defeated in the House of Lords in October 1831 the people of Nottingham set fire to the castle, which Turner alludes to in the stubble-burning below it. On the right more allegorical elements are included. Lock gates open, allowing progress to begin towards the town bathed in light under a double rainbow.[110] The Greek flag on the barge's mast is surely intended to link reform with the birthplace of democracy. By a train of association the flag might also remind a viewer of Byron's agitation for Greek liberty and from that to his maiden speech in the House of Lords in 1812 opposing the death penalty for Nottingham stocking makers, who tried to sabotage the mechanisation of their industry. SS

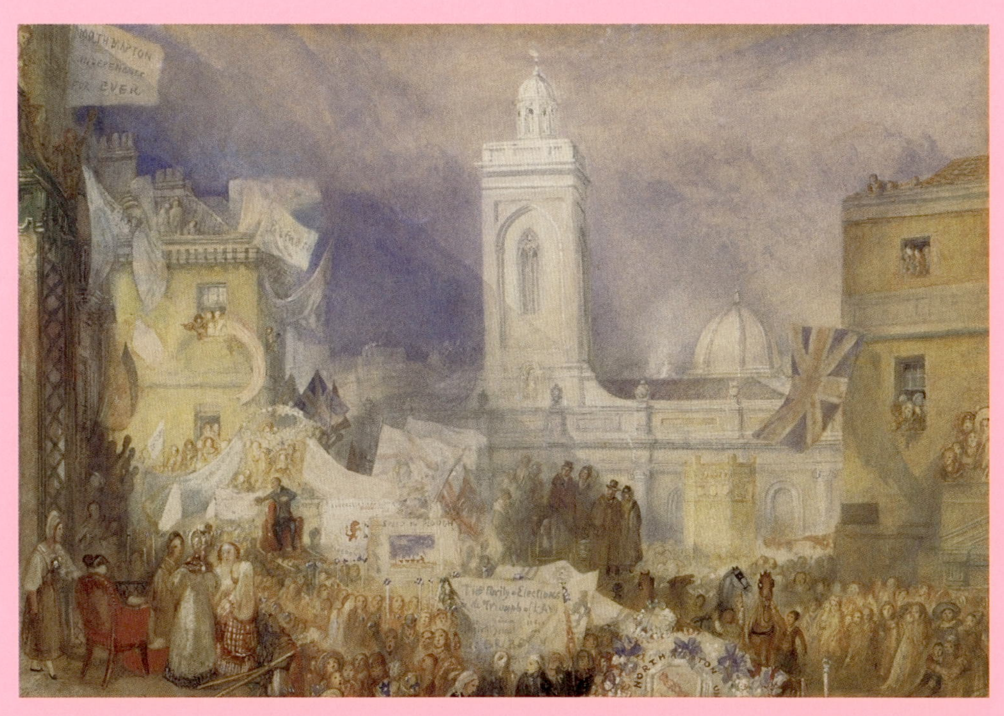

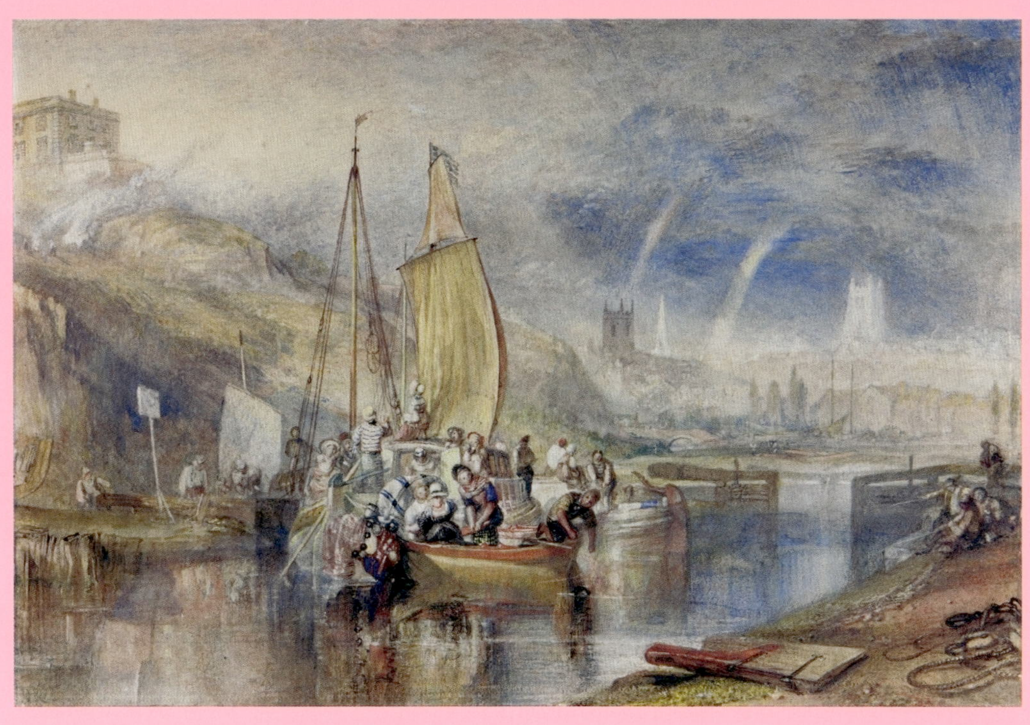

114 *The Northampton Election, 6 December 1830* c.1830–1. Watercolour, gouache and ink on paper, 29.2 × 43.8, Tate
115 *Nottingham* 1831. Watercolour on paper 30.5 × 46.3, Nottingham City Museums

Humanitarian Sympathies

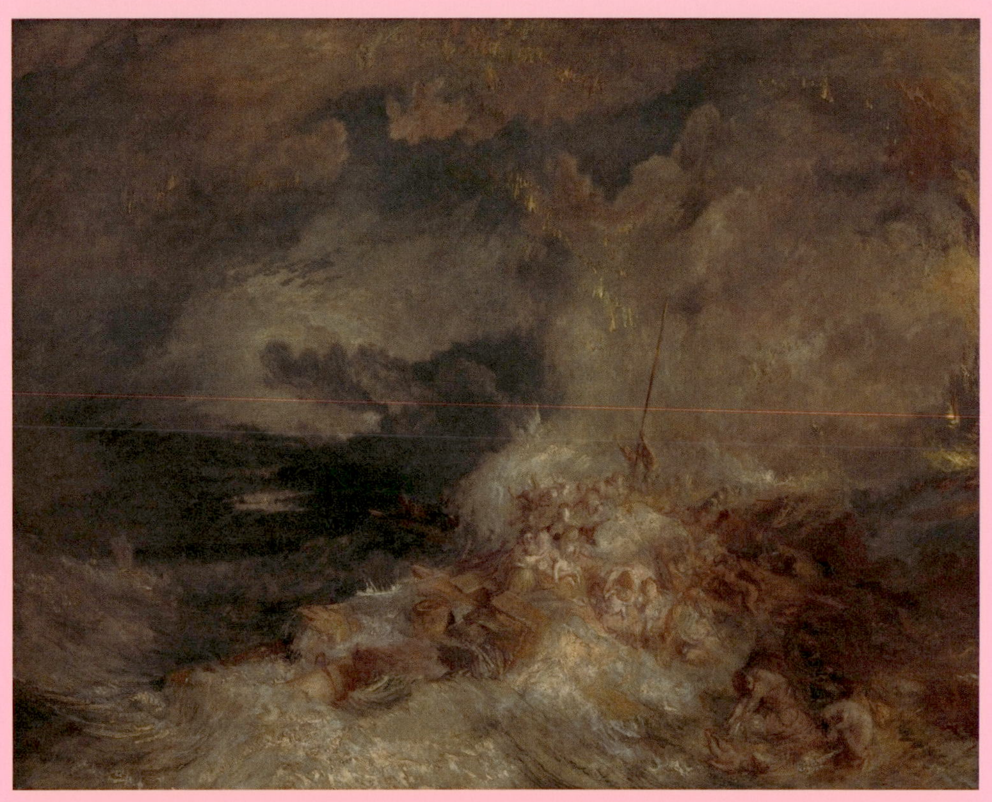

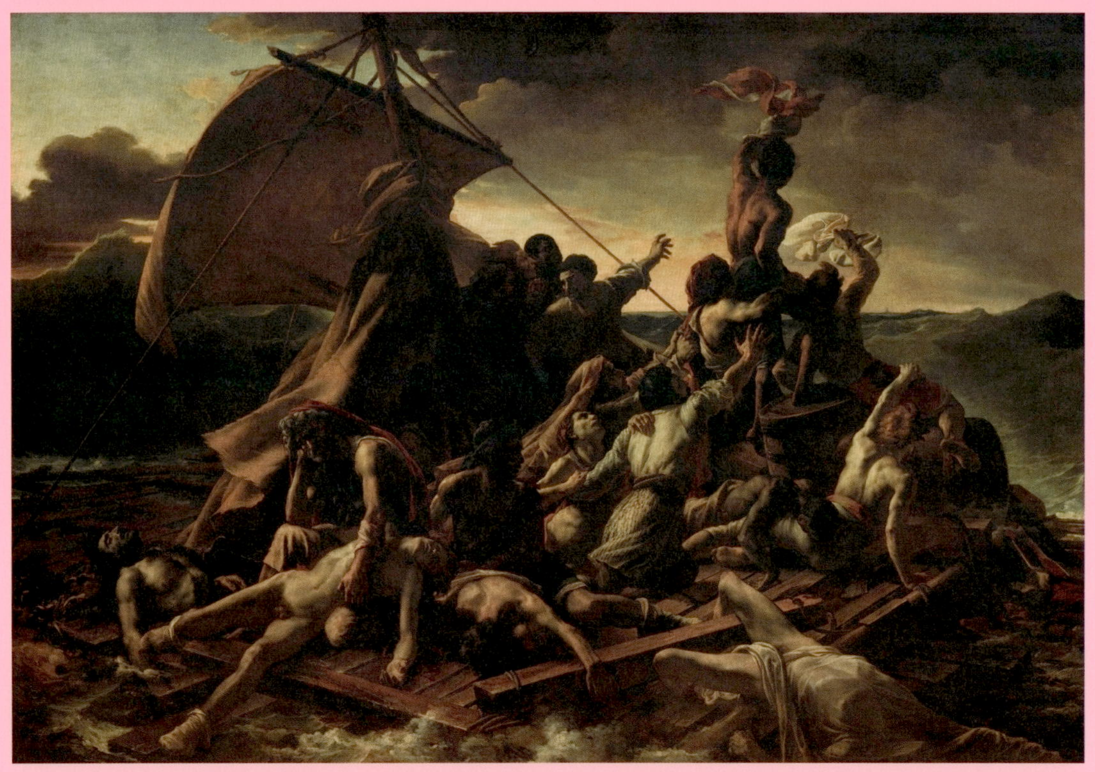

116 *A Disaster at Sea* ?c.1835. Oil paint on canvas, 171.4 × 220.3, Tate
117 Théodore Géricault, *The Raft of the Medusa* 1819. Oil paint on canvas, 491 × 716, Musée du Louvre, Paris

Turner had painted ships in distress from early in his career, most
notably the oil painting *The Wreck of a Transport Ship* (no.42) and
the watercolours *The Loss of an East Indiaman* (no.54) and *A Storm
(Shipwreck)* (1823; British Museum). Together with his depiction
of sailors struggling in the water in *Battle of Trafalgar* (no.34) and
drowning slaves in *Slave Ship (Slavers Throwing Overboard the Dead
and Dying – Typhon Coming On)* (no.119), they constitute a tragic
gallery of human suffering. The unfinished painting now known as
A Disaster at Sea (no.116) is another treatment of the theme and was
probably based on a real incident, the loss of the *Amphitrite* on 1
September 1833.[111] Dispatched for New South Wales and carrying 108
female convicts and 12 children, the ship grounded off Boulogne at
low tide. Fearful that his cargo would abscond if taken to dry land the
captain refused all offers of rescue. The *Amphitrite* broke up, all the
women and children drowned and only three members of the crew
survived.[112] Turner had probably seen Théodore Géricault's *Raft of the
Medusa* (no.117) when it was exhibited in London in 1820, and used
a similar pyramidal arrangement of the figures on the raft. Beyond
its topical interest and horrifying subject, he may have intended the
picture to reflect on the tragic consequences of an inflexible regime
and its uncaring attitude to the lower orders. However, the fact that
he left it unfinished suggests that he considered it too outspoken to
be exhibited publicly.

From at least the 1820s Turner's position on slavery appears to have
shared common ground with the majority of public opinion. In 1828
he dedicated J.P. Quilley's mezzotint (no.123) of his painting *The
Deluge* (c.1805; Tate) to the recently deceased Whig politician, John
Joshua Proby, first Earl of Carysfort, an active opponent of the slave
trade who may have commissioned the original picture in which
a Black man appears in a heroic role, rescuing drowning women.
The print's publication coincided with the campaign of the Anti-
Slavery Society whose activities influenced the passing of the Slavery
Abolition Act in 1833.[113]

The World Anti-Slavery Convention met in London in June 1840,
while Turner's *Slave Ship* was on view at the Royal Academy. An
impassioned visual polemic, the picture draws on contemporary
accounts of slavers jettisoning their human cargoes to escape arrest
by British ships patrolling the slave ports[114] and perhaps also refers
back to a notorious incident in 1781 when the master of the disease-
ridden *Zong* forced 133 African victims overboard to capitalise on the
terms of his insurance, which compensated for enslaved people lost

at sea but not for those dead from disease.[115] Turner accompanied his painting with lines from his *Fallacies of Hope* attacking the heartless commercialism of the slave trade. Having once been prepared to condone and profit from chattel slavery when in 1805 he had invested (unsuccessfully as it turned out) in a Jamaican estate to be run by African slave labour, he now renounced it in terms that can perhaps be viewed and read as a personal apology as well as a public call to action.[116] SS

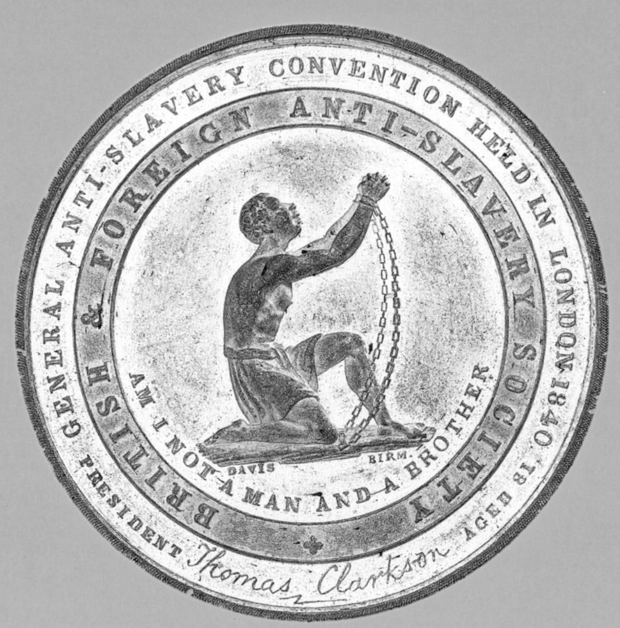

  118 Joseph Davis, *British & Foreign Anti-Slavery Society Medal* 1840. White metal, 5.2 × 5.2, National Maritime Museum, Greenwich, London

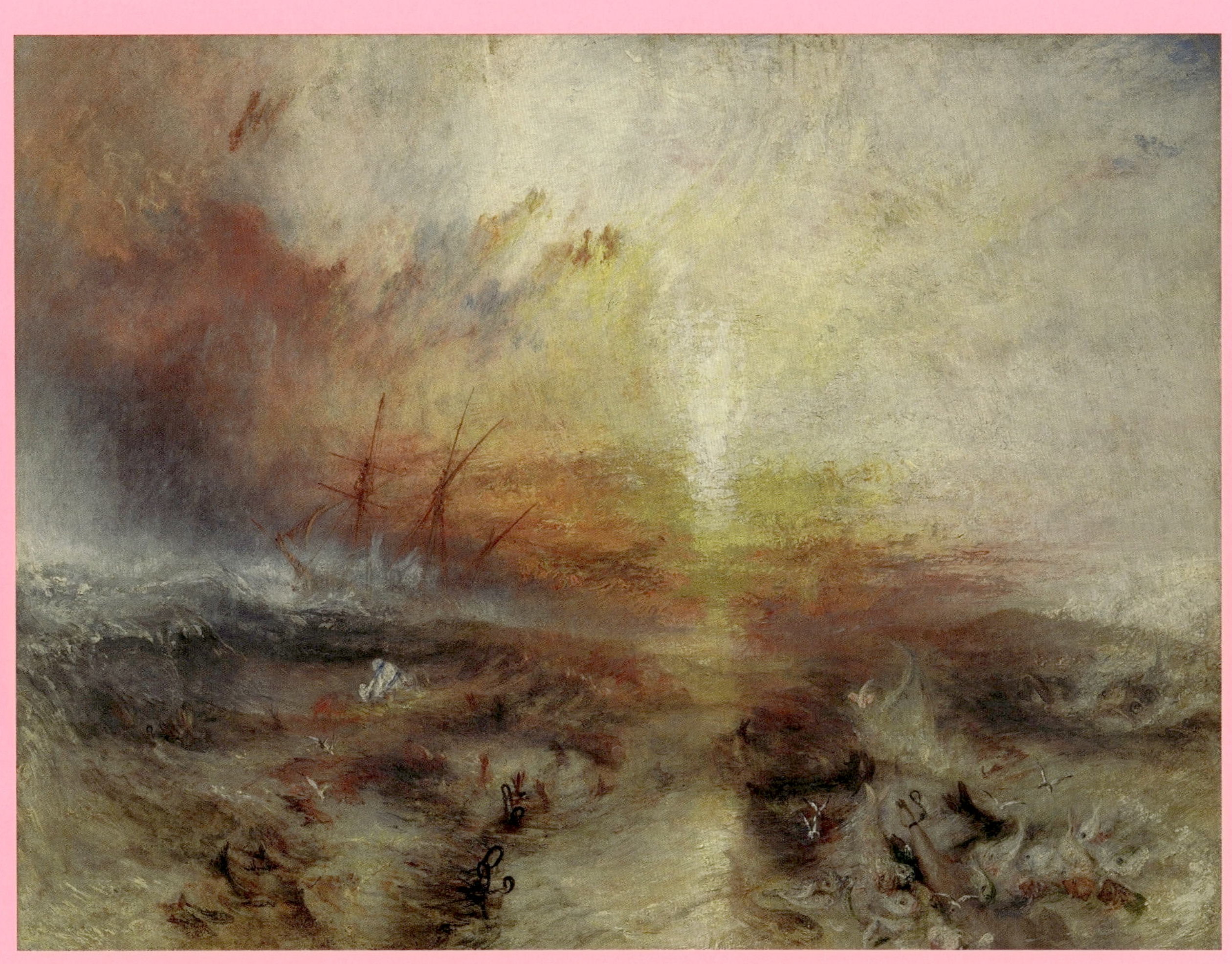

119 *Slave Ship (Slavers Throwing Overboard the Dead and Dying – Typhon Coming On)* 1840. Oil on canvas, 90.8 × 122.6, Museum of Fine Arts, Boston

Greek Independence

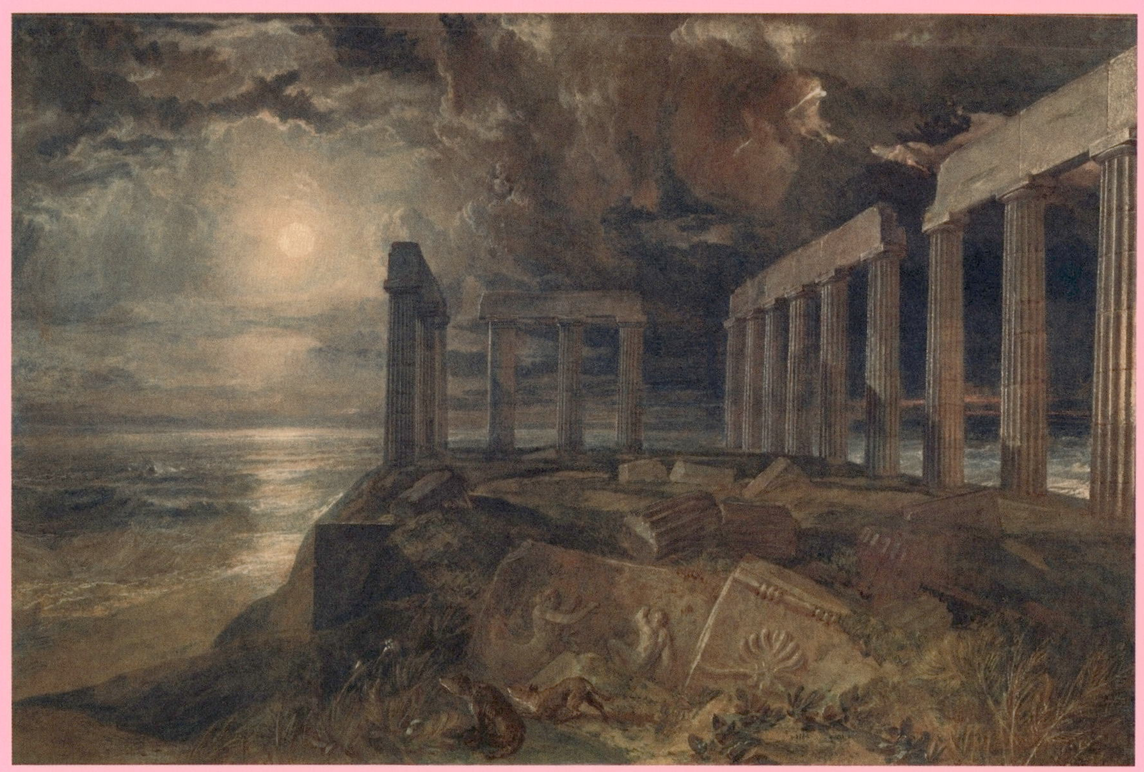

 120 *The Temple of Poseidon at Sounion (Cape Colonna)* c.1834. Graphite, watercolour and gouache on paper, 38.2 × 58.8, Tate

The Greek War of Independence broke out in 1821 and concluded
with an armistice in 1828 and the formal establishment of Greece
as an independent, sovereign state in 1830. A lightning rod for
liberal sentiment across Europe, it attracted high-profile supporters
like Byron. Turner's love of Byron's poetry and illustrations of his
Greek passages – initially prompted by Walter Fawkes – is discussed
elsewhere in this book (pp.89–90, 99).

Turner's sympathy for the Greeks' plight under Ottoman rule
preceded the war. In 1816 he showed two large paintings at the Royal
Academy, *The Temple of Jupiter Panellenius Restored* (private
collection) and *View of the Temple of Jupiter Panellenius, in the
Island of Ægina, with the Greek National Dance of the Romaika:
The Acropolis of Athens in the Distance* (no.121). Based on drawings
by the antiquarian and poet Henry Gally Knight, the first was a
reconstruction of the temple, some 20 miles south-west of Athens,
in its original state at dawn with a wedding procession. The second
showed the temple in ruins at sunset, underlining the collapse of
classical Greek civilisation. Yet the performance of the national dance
showed that culture can survive subjugation.

Turner's watercolour *Fishmarket at Hastings* (no.122) includes two
men in Greek dress, one crouching with his arm in a sling, the other
standing and attempting to catch the attention of a fisherman and
some middle-class women who have come to buy his catch. Painted
in 1824 when the London Philhellenic Committee was raising
funds for the Greek war and Byron joined the cause, the watercolour
seems designed to bring the Greek situation into everyday public
consciousness. David Blayney Brown suggests that Turner chose
Hastings for this encounter in punning reference to Frank Abney
Hastings, a former Royal Navy captain who fought in Greece in 1822,
returned to England in 1824 to raise funds to build a steam warship,
Karteria, for the Greek fleet and commanded it when it entered
service in 1826.

Another watercolour *The Temple of Poseidon at Sounion (Cape
Colonna)* (no.120) is one of two Turner made of the site that Byron
had hymned in the 'Isles of Greece' passage in Canto III of *Don Juan*
as his ideal final resting place, where he had 'dream'd that Greece
might yet be free'. A distant ship founders in the waves, watched
by wolves or jackals in front of a relief depicting Triton, Poseidon's
son. Byron's poem had recalled the sinking of the Persian fleet at
Salamis and this must surely be Turner's reference point too, together

perhaps with the much more recent and equally decisive Battle of Navarino (1827) when the Ottoman fleet was defeated by allied forces. Unlike Byron, who died before the war was over, Turner could link the Greeks' victory over Persia in 480 BCE with their successful battle for independence in his own age. SS

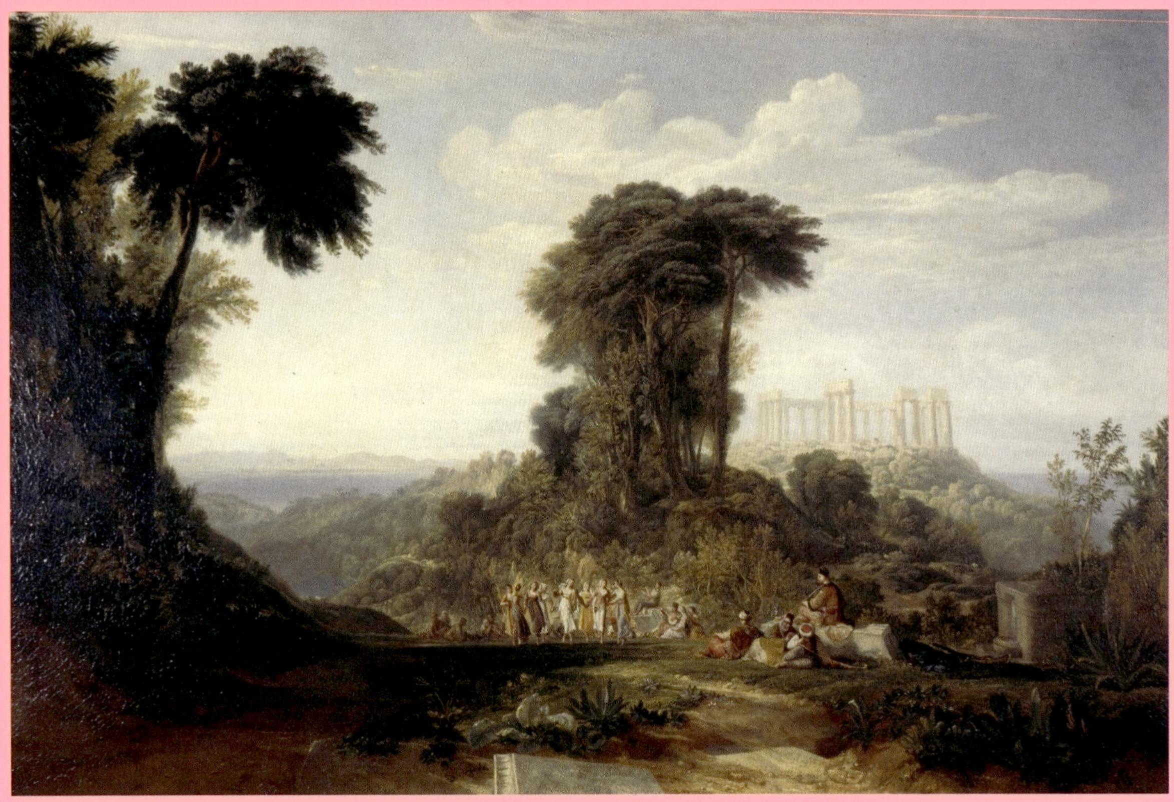

121 *View of the Temple of Jupiter Panellenius, in the island of Ægina, with the Greek National Dance of the Romaika: The Acropolis of Athens in the Distance* 1816. Oil paint on canvas, 118.2 × 178.1, private collection

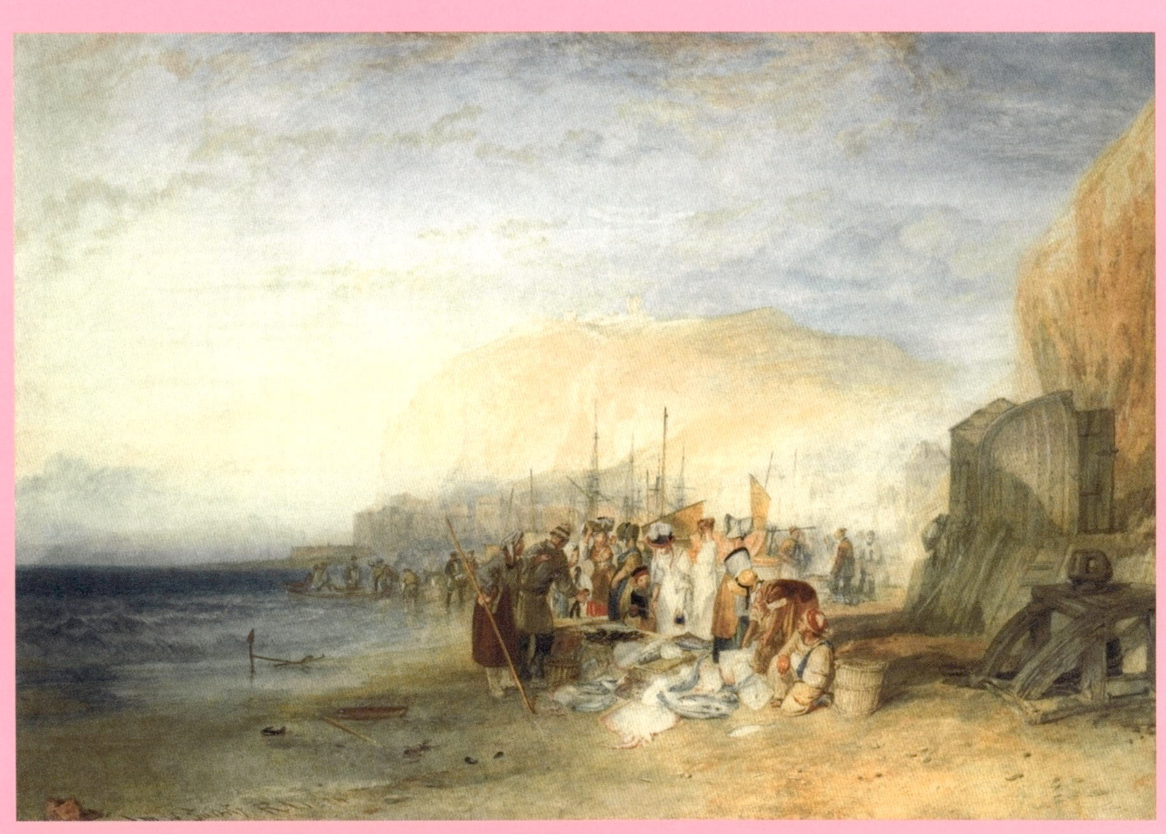

122 *Fishmarket at Hastings* 1824. Watercolour on paper, 44.3 × 66.3, Hastings Museum and Art Gallery

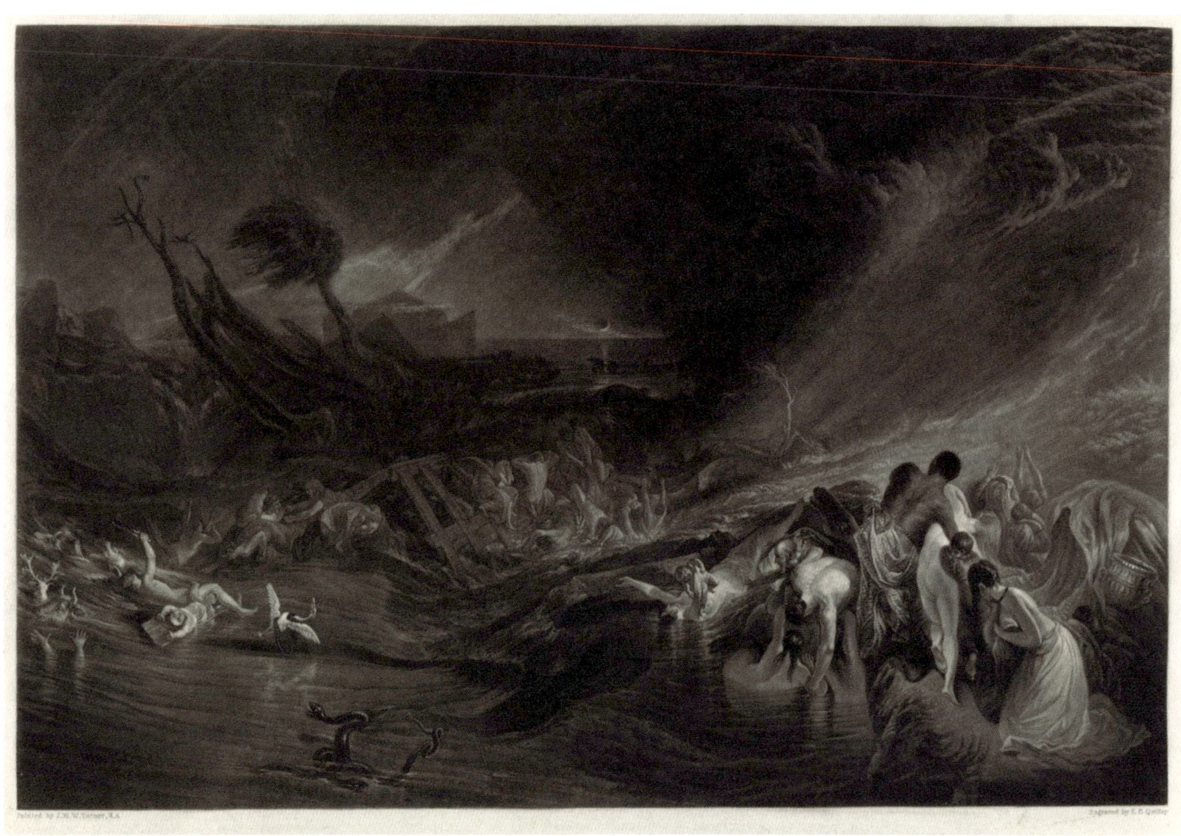

  123 John P. Quilley after Joseph Mallord William Turner, *The Deluge* 1828. Mezzotint on paper, 37.9 × 57.7, Tate

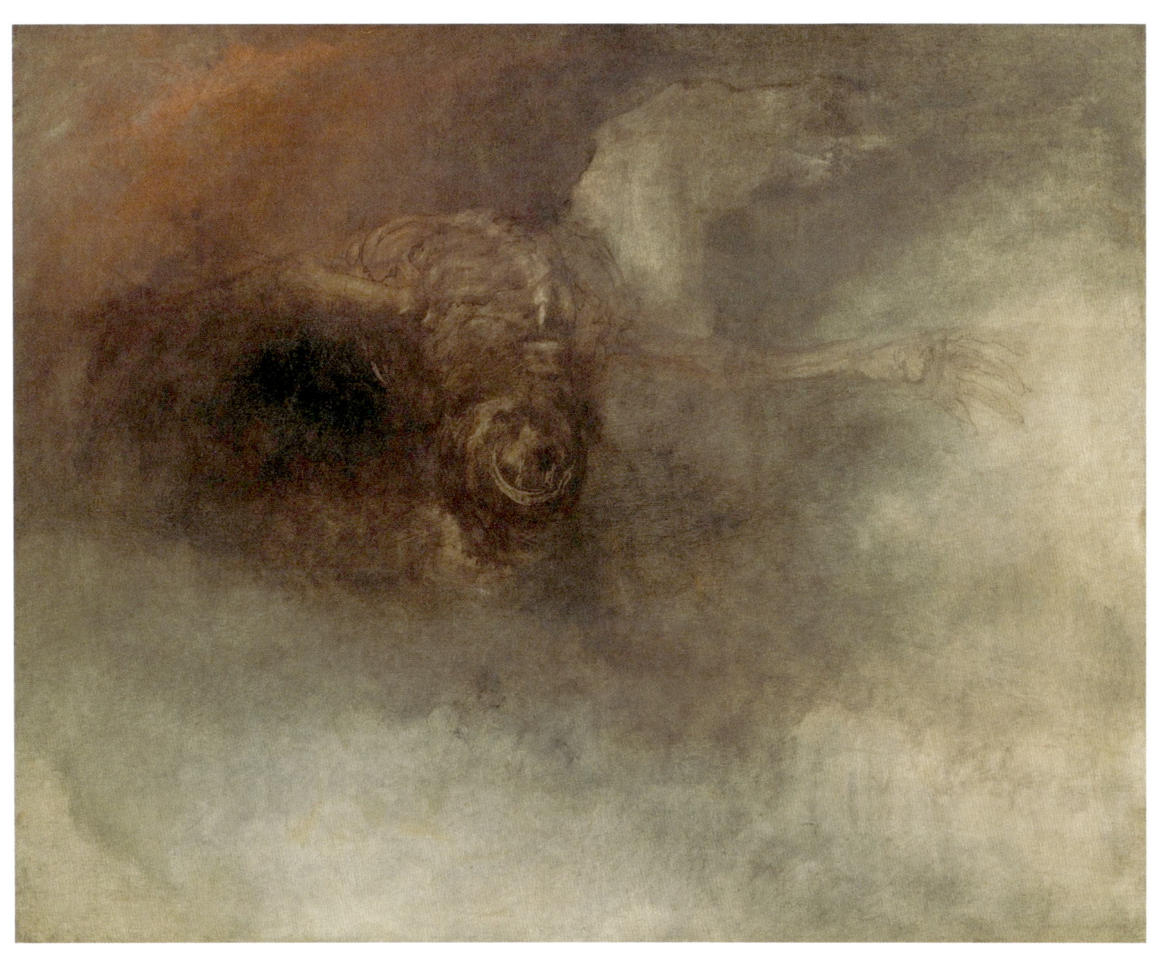

124 *The Fall of Anarchy* (?) c.1833–4. Oil paint on canvas, 59.7 × 75.6, Tate

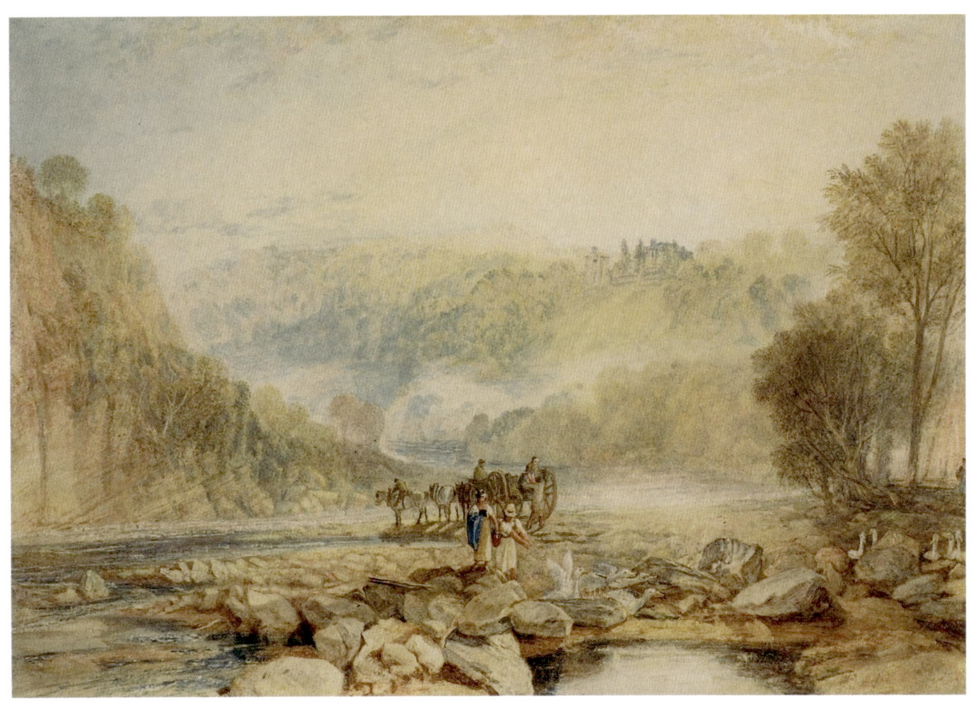

125 *Wycliffe, near Rokeby* c.1816. Watercolour and bodycolour on paper, 29.2 × 43,
Walker Art Gallery, National Museums Liverpool, Liverpool

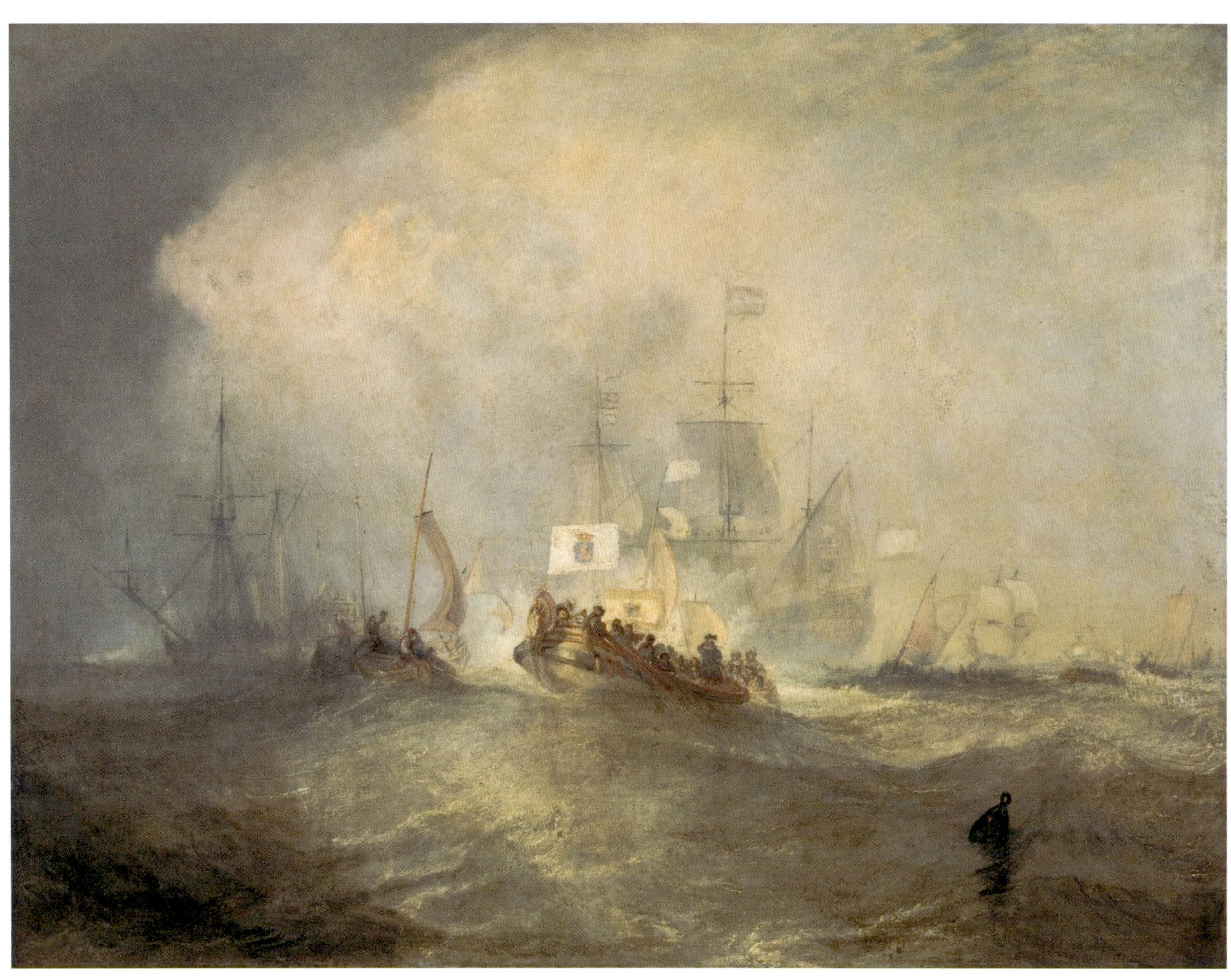

126 *The Prince of Orange, William III, Embarked from Holland, and Landed at Torbay, November 4th, 1688, after a Stormy Passage* exh. 1832. Oil paint on canvas, 90.2 × 120, Tate

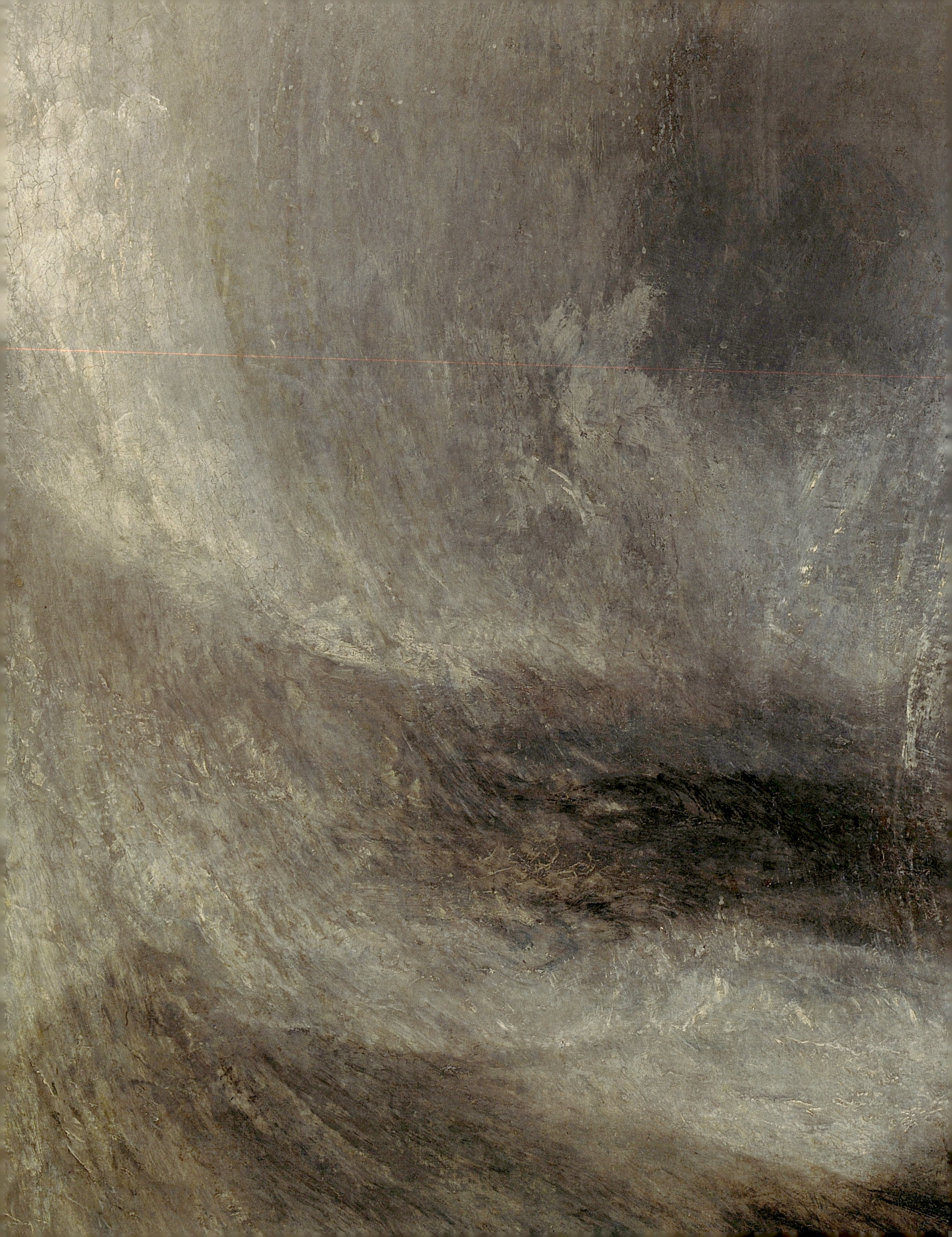

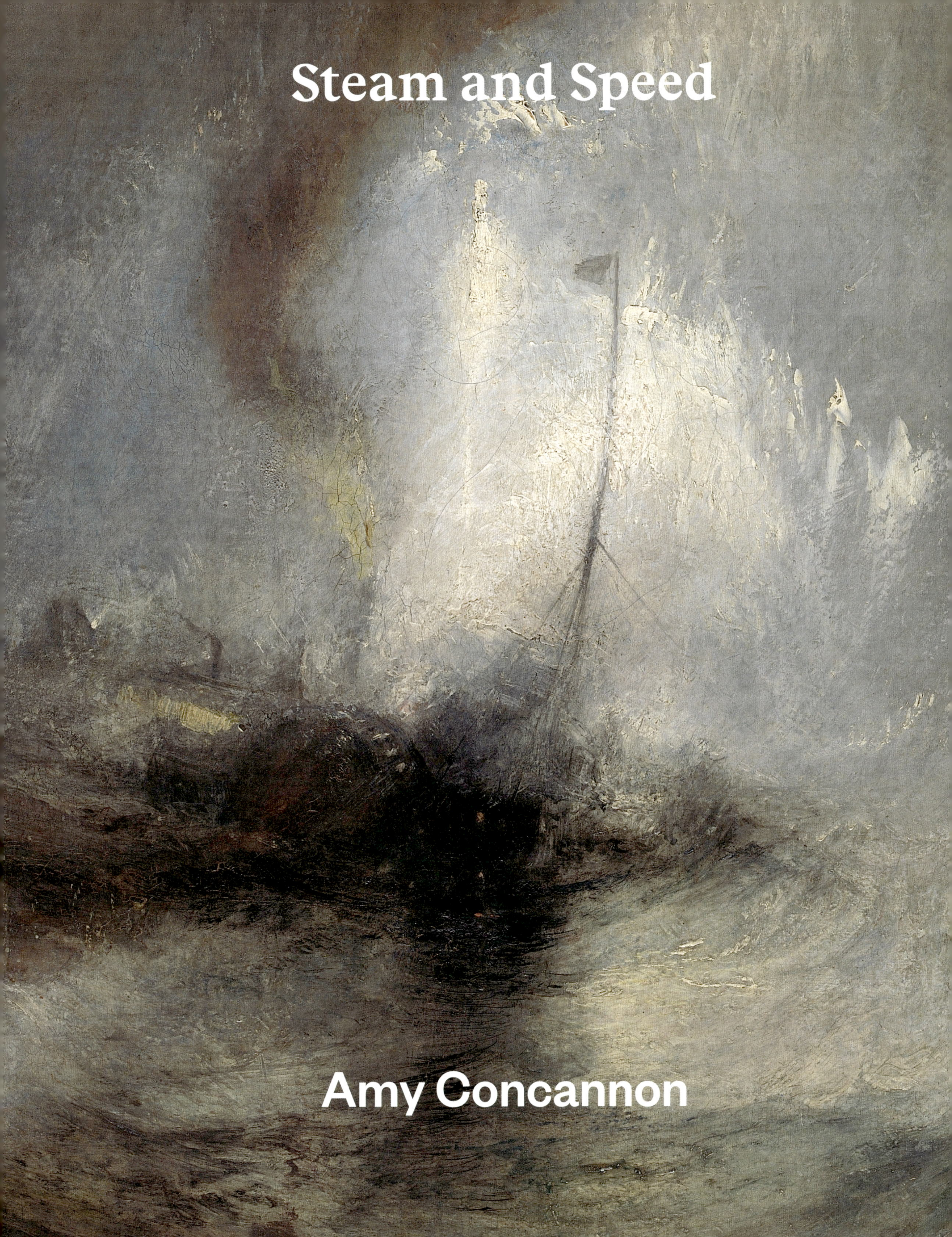
Steam and Speed
Amy Concannon

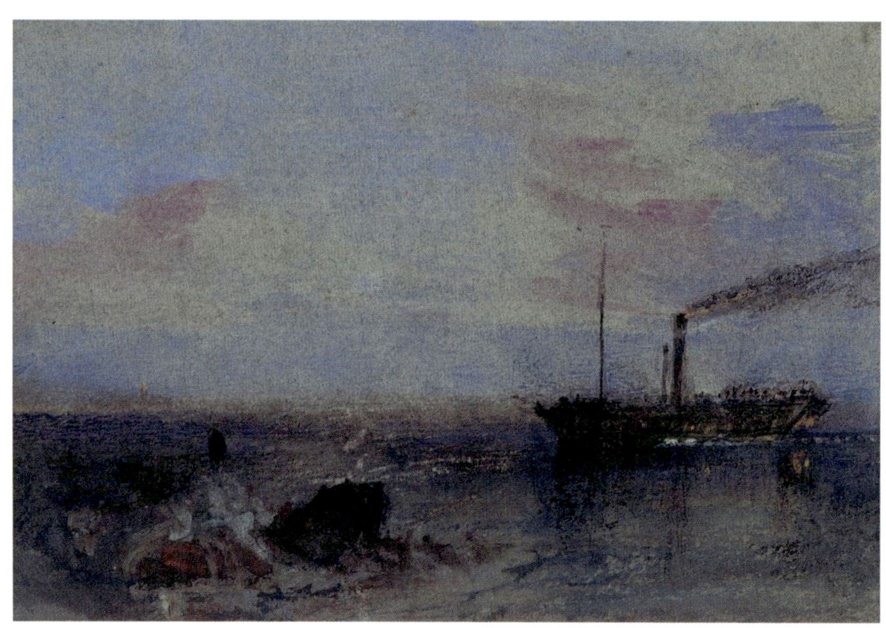

Previous page: *Snow Storm – Steam-Boat off a Harbour's Mouth* exh. 1842 (no.136)

127 *Seascape with a Boat* 1835. Watercolour, bodycolour and chalk on paper, 14.2 × 19.3, Museums Sheffield

Steam power and its by-product, speed, were among the defining phenomena of the modern world. Steam was considered the 'arm of Britain's power', the means by which the nation could expand its influence and might.[117] According to the scientist Mary Somerville, an associate of Turner's, the 'history of former ages exhibits nothing to be compared with the … activity of the present. Steam, which annihilates time and space, fills mankind with schemes for advantage or defence.'[118] This 'annihilation of time and space' is most powerfully emblematised through railways and steamboats, new technologies that completely revolutionised perceptions of distance, speed and time. Laying a new iron network across Britain's landscape, railways drew conurbations and their hinterlands together and, like steamboats, made it possible to travel at previously unimaginable speeds, a simultaneously thrilling and alarming prospect. Regional time zones were gradually eliminated as Greenwich Mean Time was rolled out across the nation to facilitate railway timetabling. Bringing fundamental changes to the way that life was lived – whether you used them or not – railways and steamships were thus lead icons for this new, fast-paced world and Turner's depictions of them have become symbols of nineteenth-century modernity. But these were not the only transformations wrought by steam technology. A snapshot of its myriad uses appeared in 1833:

> Most of the London presses are worked by steam; logs and marble are sawed … money is coined, whiskey distilled, water is pumped, bullets are driven, gun-barrels bored … ships' cables twisted, linen is bleached, sugar refined … and houses warmed, by steam; in short, there is scarcely an object of human necessity, comfort or luxury, in the production of which some use is not made of this universal and most accommodating of all agents.[119]

There is a cumulative rhythm to this list that conjures a sense of a new, all-pervading reality – of life sped up, and driven by mechanised processes. It also evokes the new sensory landscape created by steam-powered technology: smoke, soot, high-pitched whistles and the drumming of machinery. Steam power changed the face of Britain and beyond, on land, at sea and in places both urban and rural. It aided Turner's own life, allowing him to travel faster down the Thames to Margate on new steam packets and take his work in bold new directions.

If industrial works and processes came to Turner's attention during his early visits to Wales and the Midlands (see 'Signs of the Time', pp.25–37), over time the artist found ways to invest his depictions of steam-powered industry with a greater profundity, as an aspect of modern society to be both celebrated and questioned. Befitting the city's description as 'the great emporium of the coal-trade', Turner's watercolour of *Newcastle-on-Tyne* (no.138) is a patriotic scene of productivity, presided over by a Union Jack, in which medieval buildings and new industrial architecture alike are swathed in steam and smoke.[120] Turner amplified the drama of old and new beneath a heavy atmosphere in his depiction of Dudley, a medieval town that in 1712 had hosted the first operation of a steam engine and where in 1821 the first iron steamship was built (no.132). Other explorations of the haze arising from steam-powered industry would remain unfinished, the most significant example being *The Thames above Waterloo Bridge* (no.133). The year 1832 saw the launch of the first Thames-built steamship, constructed by Waterloo Bridge, but that year also saw another potential spur for Turner's picture, John Constable's depiction of the same view (no.128), which showcases the contrast between the banks of the Thames in this location – one side grand and green, the other an agglomeration of towers and smoke. Turner took this latter characteristic further by obscuring the geographical markers of this famous stretch of river such that atmosphere becomes the primary subject. This played into debate around the aesthetic and environmental impacts of steam power and coal consumption in urban places. The tower that Turner includes on the right-hand side of his unfinished painting had been criticised as 'a specimen of the anti-picturesque', and the area around it as 'a profusion of gawky chimnies [sic], and clouds of annoying smoke, fætid smells, and stunning or creaking noises'.[121] While patriotic rhetoric might see towers and smoke as indicators of progress and Britain's commercial prowess, the very real threat that their 'poisonous' effluvia posed was increasingly recognised. Indeed, Turner may have also been inspired to paint *The Thames above Waterloo Bridge* by the launch in 1829 of a government investigation into smoke pollution.[122]

Bringing both gains and losses, steam power therefore presented the ideal modern paradigm for an artist so adept in revealing poignancy in subjects both mundane and monumental. The tension between gain and loss is the essence of two of Turner's most memorable reflections on the phenomena of steam power, *Keelmen Heaving in Coals by Moonlight* (no.6) and *The Fighting Temeraire* (no.134). In the former, labourers shovel Newcastle coal from barges into ships ready for export. It was supposedly executed for Manchester cotton manufacturer Henry McConnell and intended as a pair to a painting he already owned, the brightly sunlit *Venice: The Dogana and San Maggiore* (1834; National Gallery of Art, Washington). At this time Venice's mercantile star was waning; the moonlight in *Keelmen* might thus be said to celebrate the round-the-clock productivity of Britain's flourishing industrial economy. This moon, however, is key to the work's duality. In the same year that Turner completed *Keelmen*, it was reported that the 'hardy, laborious race of keelmen' were being 'deprived of their ancient occupation ... by means of new appliances' – railways that ran directly from coal fields to the port, which negated the need for coal barges.[123] Seen by moonlight in Turner's painting, the sun had already set on the keelmen's traditional occupation. Similarly, in *The Fighting Temeraire* the sun sets not only on a vessel imbued with national pride and memory – the ship having played a vital part in Nelson's victory at Trafalgar – but also on the age of sail. Steam is the dynamic force here, as the diminutive, fire-fuelled steamer tows a great hulk from a by-gone age to its final berth for breaking up, a symbolic sight personified by the

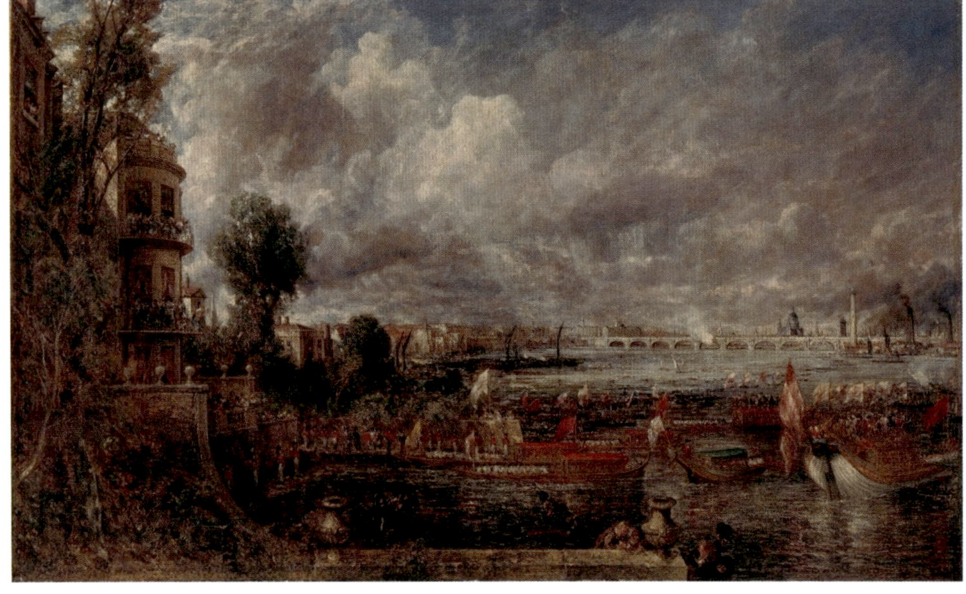

128
John Constable, *The Opening of Waterloo Bridge* ('*Whitehall Stairs June 18, 1817*') exh. 1832. Oil paint on canvas, 130.8 × 210, Tate

Spectator as 'a superannuated veteran led by a sprightly boy'.[124]

The steam tug's prominence in *The Fighting Temeraire* was the culmination of several decades' study and assimilation of steamboats into Turner's work. Perhaps predictably for an artist drawn to maritime subjects, they became his most frequently depicted manifestations of modern steam power. Having sketched them since their first appearance on British waters in the 1810s, they became a more established feature of his watercolours in the 1820s, reflecting their increasing ubiquity on the Thames and off the coast. In his two watercolours of the Channel port of Dover (nos.139, 140) steamships are a relatively inconspicuous but crucial presence, registering the present within a setting layered with time, from the ancient chalk cliffs to the medieval castle and Napoleonic defences. Even in sketches made for Turner's own purposes, steamboats are often discernible by faint calligraphic squiggles of smoke emanating from a funnel.

Turner's commitment to the motif of the steamboat was crystallised in the print series *Turner's Annual Tour: Wanderings by the Seine, from Embouchre to Rouen*. Published in 1833, half the images contain steamboats.[125] In two drawings for the series (nos.143, 144) the steamboat is the central subject, emphasised by the contrast of deep black gouache and pastel-toned surroundings. The vessels take on additional patriotic significance here. Not only did they advertise British engineering abroad (British engineers were often employed aboard continental steamships, and one tourist noted that only the meals were French) but also signalled a new sense of post-war freedom and optimism.[126] Steamships unleashed British tourists on the continent, creating new itineraries that promised to take them further and faster than ever before. Affluent tourists – many of whom had made their fortunes from the expansion of modern capitalism and industry – were a target audience for *Turner's Annual Tour*, a fashionable commodity issued in time for the Christmas market that traded on collectability

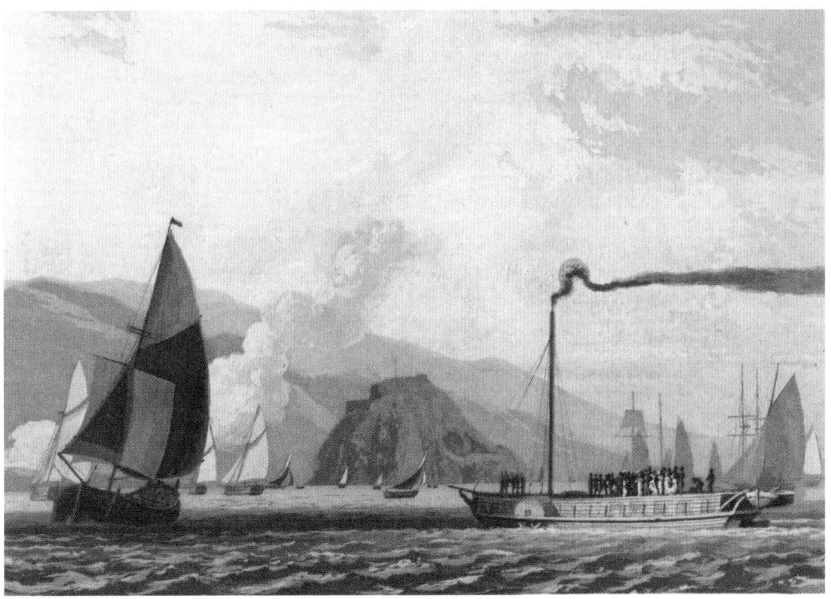

129
William Daniell, *Steam Boat on the Clyde near Dumbarton* 1817. Aquatint on paper, 16.2 × 24.1, Tate

and advanced Turner's celebrity as a household name. From concept to imagery, these were thoroughly modern productions; should the paper on which the images were printed have been steam-pressed, they would also have been physical manifestations of steam power.

While enthusiasts claimed steamboats were a 'new object of admiration, a new instance of the beautiful', the reviewer of the print series in which *Between Quilleboeuf and Villequier* appeared could not bring themself 'to admire masses of smoke, or consider steamboats as instances of the picturesque'.[127] Any risk arising from Turner's decision to centre the steamship in *Quilleboeuf* was, however, offset by the medium of its circulation. Steam power was most often depicted in prints, typically in technical diagrams or in topographical scenes like Turner's own *Ports of England* series (see, for example, *Dover*). Souvenir prints of the popular tourist resort of Brighton, for instance, regularly featured steamboats, since a major attraction there was the Chain Pier, built to dock the cross-channel steam packet. Yet in Turner's painting of this subject, made for one of its investors, Lord Egremont (no.4), a paddle steamer is almost obscured by a traditional sail vessel, while the modern structure is carefully assimilated into an atmospheric marine landscape. Turner's sensitivity towards convention while pushing its boundaries insulated him from criticism of the kind his contemporaries faced. That 'poor objects [occupied] the greater space' was the charge levelled against an 1837 depiction of a smoke-belching steamer in Bristol's harbour by James Baker Pyne, while in 1848 James John Wilson Carmichael came under fire for exhibiting a painting of a steam train that was 'rather more an engineering water colour subject, than suitable for an oil picture'.[128] Conversely, Turner's *Rain, Steam, and Speed* (no.135) had been generally well received in 1844, although Ruskin – who passionately protested the spread of railways – later retorted that Turner had merely painted it 'to show what he could do with an ugly subject'.[129]

In Turner's hands these 'poor', 'ugly' subjects became versatile narrative devices in oil

paintings that explored, as was expected of this medium, themes of grand profundity. The bittersweet relationship between steam and sail in *The Fighting Temeraire* is a prime example of this, as is his investment of the ocean-going steamship *Oriental* with an intense pathos in *Peace – Burial at Sea* (no.162). Elsewhere, he wove modern marine technology into one of his long-favoured themes, nature's threat to man. In *Lifeboat and Manby Apparatus* (no.145) and *Wreckers – Coast of Northumberland* (no.146) hope rests on modern invention. The former shows a mortar-fired rope, the celebrated invention of Captain Manby for saving mariners in peril, while in the latter, as Turner's extended title tells us, a steamboat comes to the aid of a foundering sailing vessel. But steamboats were fragile too, as in *Staffa, Fingal's Cave* (no.131), where one looks vulnerable and small against the might of the natural world, with the famous rock formation, the storm and the waves presided over by an ominous red setting sun. Critics regarded *Wreckers* a work of 'true genius' and *Staffa* sublime.[130] Ten years later, however, *Snow Storm* (no.136), proffered by the artist as an experiential record of a powerful storm, failed to resonate with his audience. Lambasted as having been painted with 'a whole array of kitchen stuff', its primary fault was illegibility: 'where the steamboat is – where the harbour begins, or where it ends … are matters past our finding out,' railed one critic.[131] But in its dizzying confusion lies the key to its understanding: this was not only an image of steam and power versus nature, of the potential fallibility or heroism of man's invention, but also an essay on modernity itself, of life being affected by forces that could never before have been imagined. This shared experience of societal change called for a new mode of painting, one that Turner was only posthumously praised for having developed.

Far harder to assimilate into the exalted realm of oil painting was the most controversial aspect of steam power: the railway. If the steamboat's setting was a natural one – the sea – and its course heavily affected by the elements, the railway posed an altogether more artificial presence in the landscape, travelling on iron

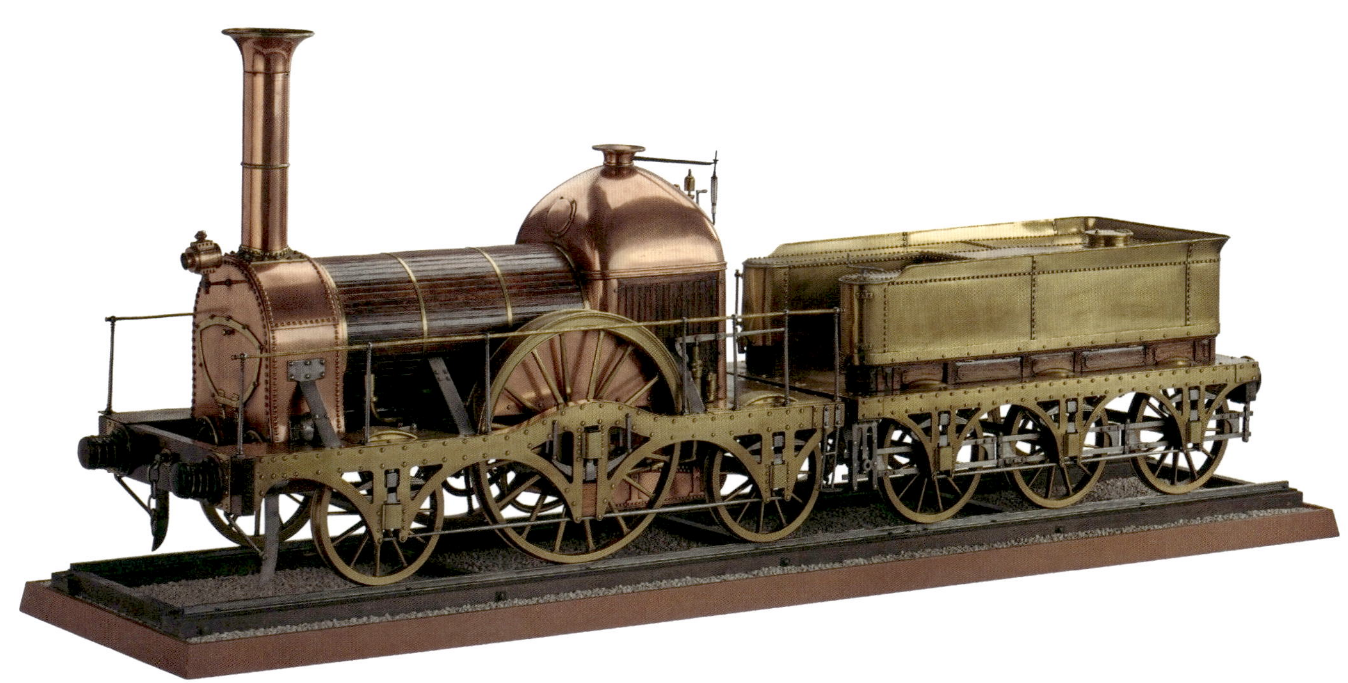

130 Joseph Clement, *Model of 'Firefly' class locomotive* 1838. Metal and wood, 66 × 159.5 × 41.5, Science Museum Group Collection

rails through man-made cuttings, on viaducts or through land cleared of vegetation. Again, diagrammatic prints depicting steam railways abounded, but their informative aesthetic suggested nothing of the impassioned debate that surrounded this manifestation of steam power. Even ten years before 'railway mania', the speculative frenzy that gripped the 1840s, an MP complained that 'physical objects and private rights were stamped under the chariot wheels of the Fire King', that 'mountains were to be cut through, valleys were to be lifted ... the earth was to be tunnelled; parks, gardens, and ornamental grounds were to be broken into'.[132] A powerful sense of the way in which railways spliced through the landscape is conveyed by Turner's only oil painting of a locomotive, *Rain, Steam, and Speed – The Great Western Railway* (no.135). Linking London and the port city of Bristol and developed by notable engineer Isambard Kingdom Brunel, the Great Western Railway was one of the most high-profile routes, boasting the Maidenhead Viaduct, a celebrated feat of engineering, and from 1841 a new class of engine, the Firefly (no.130), which with its larger boilers could reach previously unprecedented speeds of between 50 and 60 miles per hour. Turner may have hoped to garner royal interest, since the premier patron of the arts, Prince Albert, had, like Queen Victoria, travelled along this line in the early 1840s. Taking the most exalted iteration of the railway as its subject, *Rain, Steam, and Speed* manifests a sophisticated answer to the problem of depicting the railway in action, centring this 'ugly' modern subject within a composition rich in allegorical allusion. Bridges old and new bracket the scene, while man-made and natural speed is juxtaposed in the race between the hurtling steam train – perhaps the *Greyhound*, which travelled the route – and the tiny hare that darts in front of it. Technologies old and new are contrasted too, as the train passes a horse-drawn plough on the far right. 'God speed the plough' was the centuries-old refrain of hope for agricultural prosperity; of the railway it was said that Britain had 'a new power over nature ... a new source of national wealth'.[133] This was not just a modern, novel subject, but a milestone achievement in the nation's life.

As much as it was celebrated, however, the railway was feared. One writer observed how passengers would 'pretend to be at their ease', opining that 'where the journey may end, whether at Bristol or in the other world, is the problem'.[134] Such remarks were justified by reports of accidents, like that which took place on Christmas Eve, 1841, on the Great Western Railway line at Sonning Cutting, 10 miles from the location depicted in Turner's painting. Meeting a landslide caused by heavy rain, a train derailed, killing eight and injuring seventeen third-class passengers who were travelling in carriages like those Turner depicts in his painting – simple carts without seats that were open to the elements. Though Turner did not depict the disaster itself, his title, *Rain, Steam, and Speed*, evokes the potent combination of forces that led to the loss of human life on the Great Western Railway that day, of which the public would have been reminded in 1844, the year of the painting's exhibition, when legislation inspired by the Sonning Cutting tragedy was passed to improve third-class passenger safety. It was perhaps the advent of this legislation that motivated Turner to produce a painting that has since been lauded as a powerful emblem of the early days of steam power. As time went on, the irrevocable changes to society and the landscape wrought by steam power were more keenly felt: in 1877 the French writer Théophile Gautier personified Turner's white-hot speeding railway engine as the 'Beast of the Apocalypse'.[135]

One story would have it that one of Turner's boldest paintings of steam power, *Rockets and Blue Lights* (no.142), fell foul of this 'Beast' on its way to the Manchester Art Treasures Exhibition of 1857. Apparently wary of having his Turners transported by rail, the then owner had his valued cargo shipped to Manchester by road, only for the coach containing the paintings to be hit by a train at a level crossing. That it has now been proven that *Rockets and Blue Lights* was not, in fact, among those exhibited in Manchester does not alter the irony of the fact that work by the hand of the artist most equated with the advent of the steam age in Britain collided with the very object of his fascination.[136]

Atmospheres

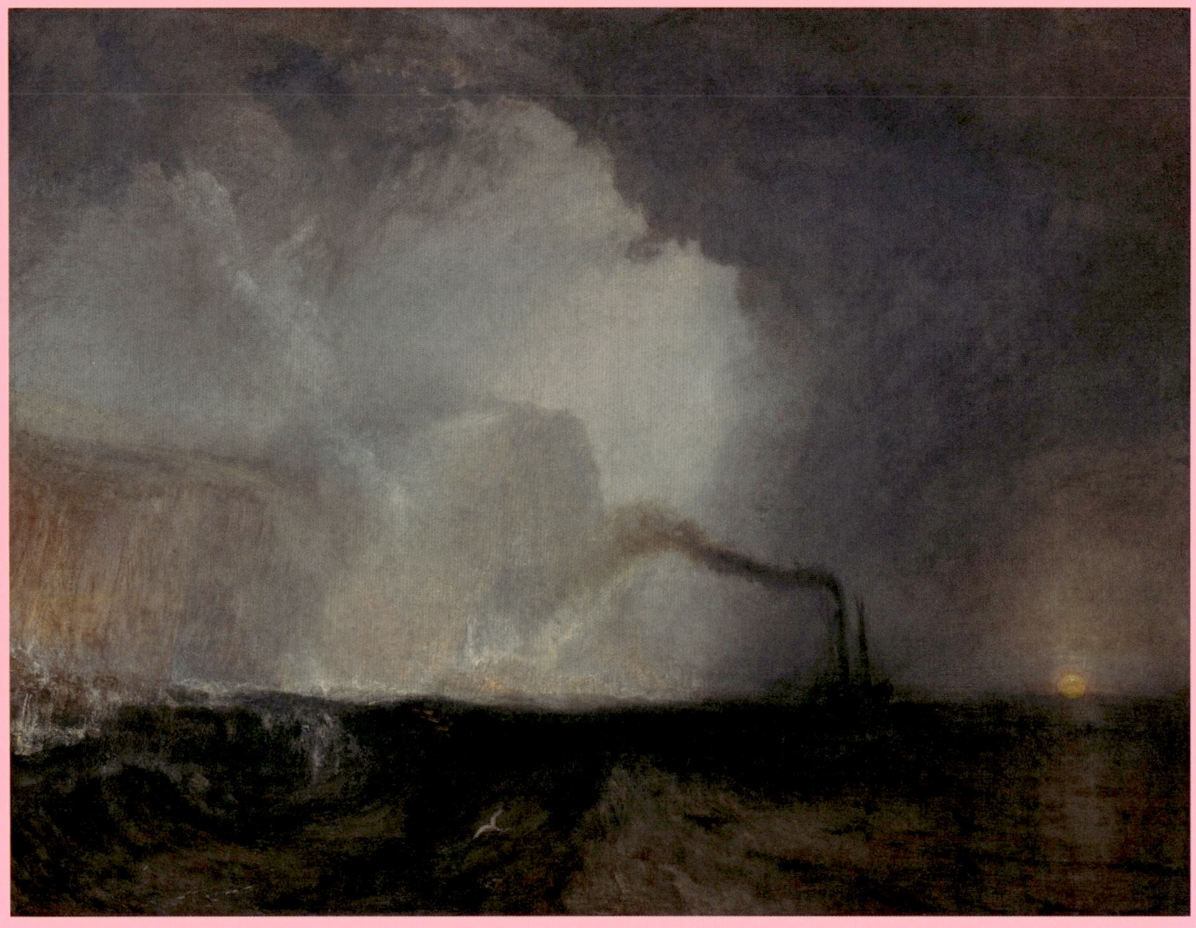

 131 *Staffa, Fingal's Cave* 1832. Oil paint on canvas, 90.8 × 121.3, Yale Center for British Art, Paul Mellon Collection, New Haven

The eruption of Mount Tambora in the Dutch East Indies (Indonesia) in April 1815 was the largest volcanic event in recorded history. Besides killing around 10,000 people outright, it filled the earth's stratosphere with gases, ash and sulphate particulates that caused havoc in weather systems and many thousands more deaths from famine and disease. A sign of things to come was the torrential storm that broke over the Battle of Waterloo in June 1815, turning the field into a quagmire as well as a bloodbath. Appalling weather and social upheaval in Europe in 1816, the 'year without a summer', deterred Turner from visiting Waterloo until 1817. Confined to a villa beside Lake Geneva in 1816, Mary Shelley wrote her novel *Frankenstein* and Byron his poem *Darkness* about environmental apocalypse, 'a dream, which was not all a dream'.

Tambora's after-effects coincided with attempts to understand and classify cloud formations and factors affecting weather and atmosphere, whether in Luke Howard's book *The Climate of London* (1818) and *Seven Lectures on Meteorology* (1837), John Constable's systematic 'skying' or Turner's own *Skies* sketchbook (c.1816–18; Tate). The sun in *Staffa, Fingal's Cave* (no.131) is ringed by a nimbus, indicating impending rain. Turner knew about such phenomena from scientists like Sir David Brewster, but did he understand that the crimson sunsets he painted in other later pictures resulted from atmospheric pollution? While Howard was the first to recognise the impact of cities like London on their local climate, little attention was given to man-made domestic and industrial emissions for which Britain, the world's worst polluter at the time, was exceptionally responsible. Effects on climate in the future were hardly considered. London's smoke and fogs even had admirers like the painter B.R. Haydon, who saw the sooty canopy – fuelled by Newcastle coal – as signifying energy and power.

Turner's *London* (no.90) views the capital's 'murky veil' and 'doubtful air' (his words) from Greenwich Park. In *Leeds* (no.105), his first detailed image of an industrial city, mill chimneys hardly darken a fine day on Beeston Hill, where tentermen hang newly woven and washed cloth outdoors to dry. Having supplied spun woollens for uniforms and flax for rope and sail-cloth to the army and navy, Leeds deserved sympathetic treatment so soon after the war, but Turner immersed Midlands cities like Dudley or Birmingham in their smoky haze (no.132). In an unfinished picture of London (no.133) looking towards John Rennie's Waterloo Bridge (completed in 1817), the air is thick and sulphurous. A government enquiry into air-borne pollution

and public health had begun in 1829 and the picture includes some of
Turner's smokiest steamboats. A more immediate concern in 1831–2
was a cholera epidemic. Fear of this still-mysterious disease confined
Turner to his studio, and perhaps the sickly vapour in his picture
alludes to current theories that cholera spread through 'miasma'
from dirty streets and contaminated rivers like the Thames, a filthy
soup constantly churned by steamers' paddle-wheels. In 1828 Turner
had served on a commission investigating a plan by the painter John
Martin to divert sewage and supply London with clean water from
the River Lea. DBB

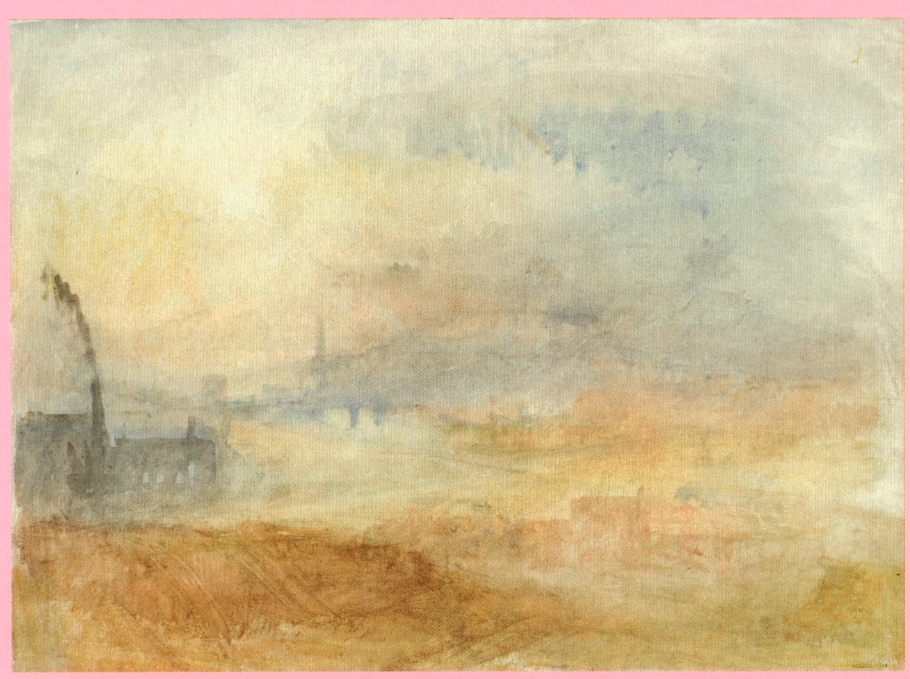

    132 *An Industrial Town at Sunset, Probably Birmingham or Dudley* c.1830–2. Watercolour on paper, 34.8 × 48.2, Tate

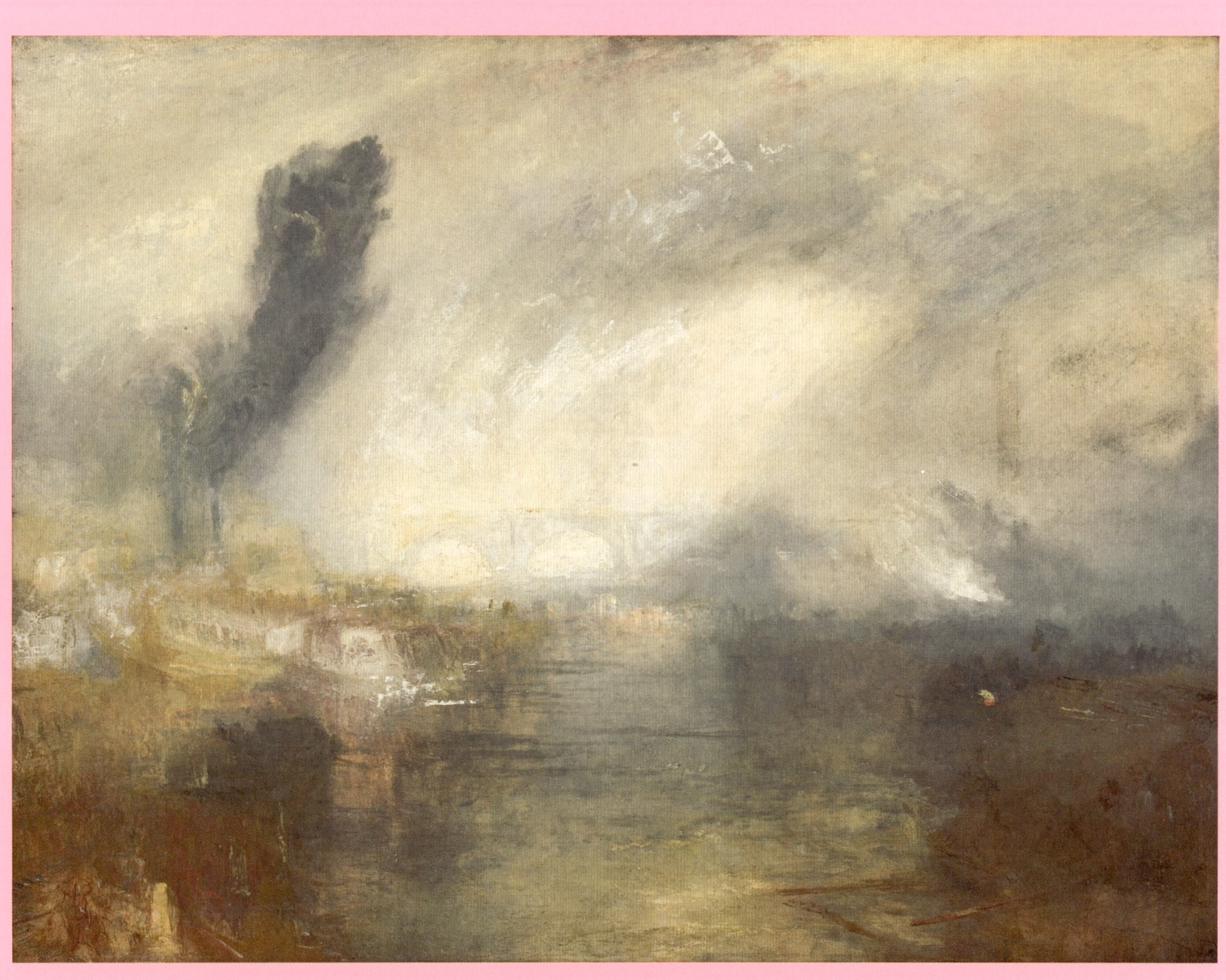

133 *The Thames above Waterloo Bridge* c.1835–40. Oil paint on canvas, 90.5 × 121, Tate

Sail, Rail and Wheels:
Modern Metamorphoses

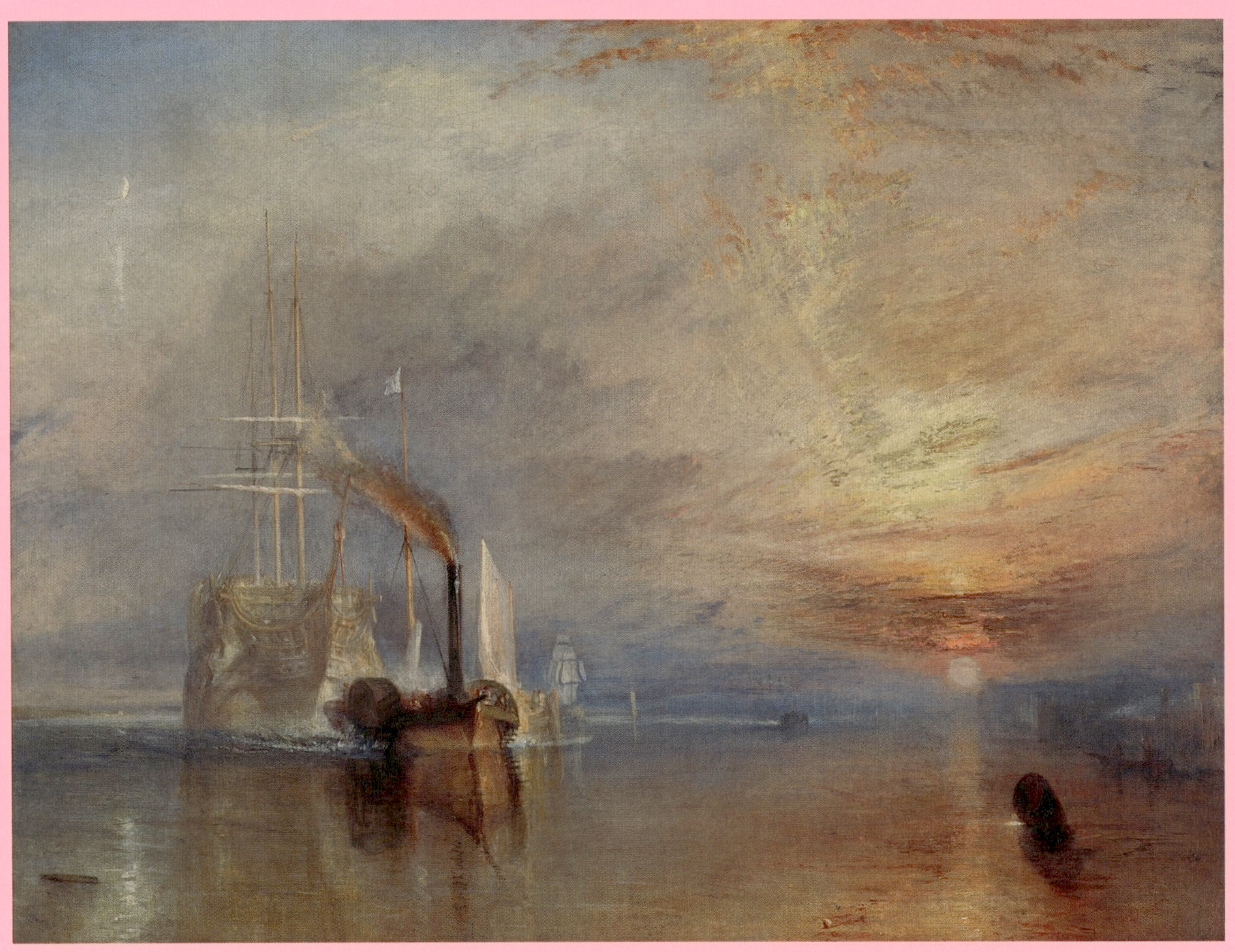

  134 *The Fighting Temeraire Tugged to her Last Berth To Be Broken Up* 1839. Oil paint on canvas, 90.7 × 121.6, The National Gallery, London

Sail and steam, juxtaposed in *The Fighting Temeraire* (no.134), had already appeared in Turner's views of the River Seine like *Between Quilleboeuf and Villequier* (no.143). His watercolour *Dover Castle from the Sea* (no.139), made around the time the first iron steamboat was built at Dudley, includes a vessel converted from sail to steam. *Staffa, Fingal's Cave* (no.131), recalling a stormy trip from Tobermory, was his first oil painting of a steamboat.

Steamboats became commonplace in Turner's work. Carts on elevated iron rails, known as 'hurries', deliver coal to colliers in *Shields, on the River Tyne* (no.137), but *Rain, Steam, and Speed* (no.135) was unprecedented as a picture of a passenger train. An engine of the Firefly class (no.130) operated by the Great Western Railway advances in driving rain across the Thames on Isambard Kingdom Brunel's Maidenhead bridge (1838). The line was the fastest and the bridge's brick arches the widest and flattest in existence at the time. The older road bridge, like sail vessels in other pictures, recalls slower movement in the past. The train's speed – 50 or 60 miles per hour – is emphasised by its diagonal approach, the three puffs of steam receding behind it and a hare trying to outrun it on the track.

Ruskin saw *Rain, Steam, and Speed* during a Royal Academy preview, at the same time as the poet Samuel Rogers, but only ever mentioned it as an 'ugly subject', blinded by his dislike of trains and public transport to how Turner raised these features of modern life to High Art. Introducing a collection of Turner's views of the English coast in 1856, Ruskin admitted 'very little sympathy for people who want to *go* anywhere'.[137] For the Great Western, serving them was a noble cause. It named some of its engines after figures from classical mythology. Asking 'is Turner's train just a train', Inigo Thomas has noted how Orion the Hunter with three stars in his belt, like the engine's puffs of steam, is positioned in the night sky above Lepus (the Hare). He associates the dancing figures by the Thames with the Pleiades, sisters pursued by Orion until Zeus turned them into stars.[138] These insights offset more literal interpretations such as Lady Simon's report to Ruskin and the painter George Richmond that she had seen Turner put his head outside a carriage to observe a rainstorm while returning from Devonshire.[139] Even if this happened, was it on a train? Turner's claim to have witnessed the weather he painted in *Snow Storm – Steam-Boat off a Harbour's Mouth* (no.136) while tied to the mast of a steamer called *Ariel* is probably fiction. In the picture's full title he describes himself as the 'Author'. Ariel's identities as angel and spirit of air, fire and water, and appearance in Shakespeare's *Tempest* promising a 'sea-change into something rich and strange', should leave us unsurprised by the absence of a vessel with this name from timetables of steamers operating out of Harwich, Turner's alleged point of departure. Stories of painters, storms and masts go back centuries. DBB

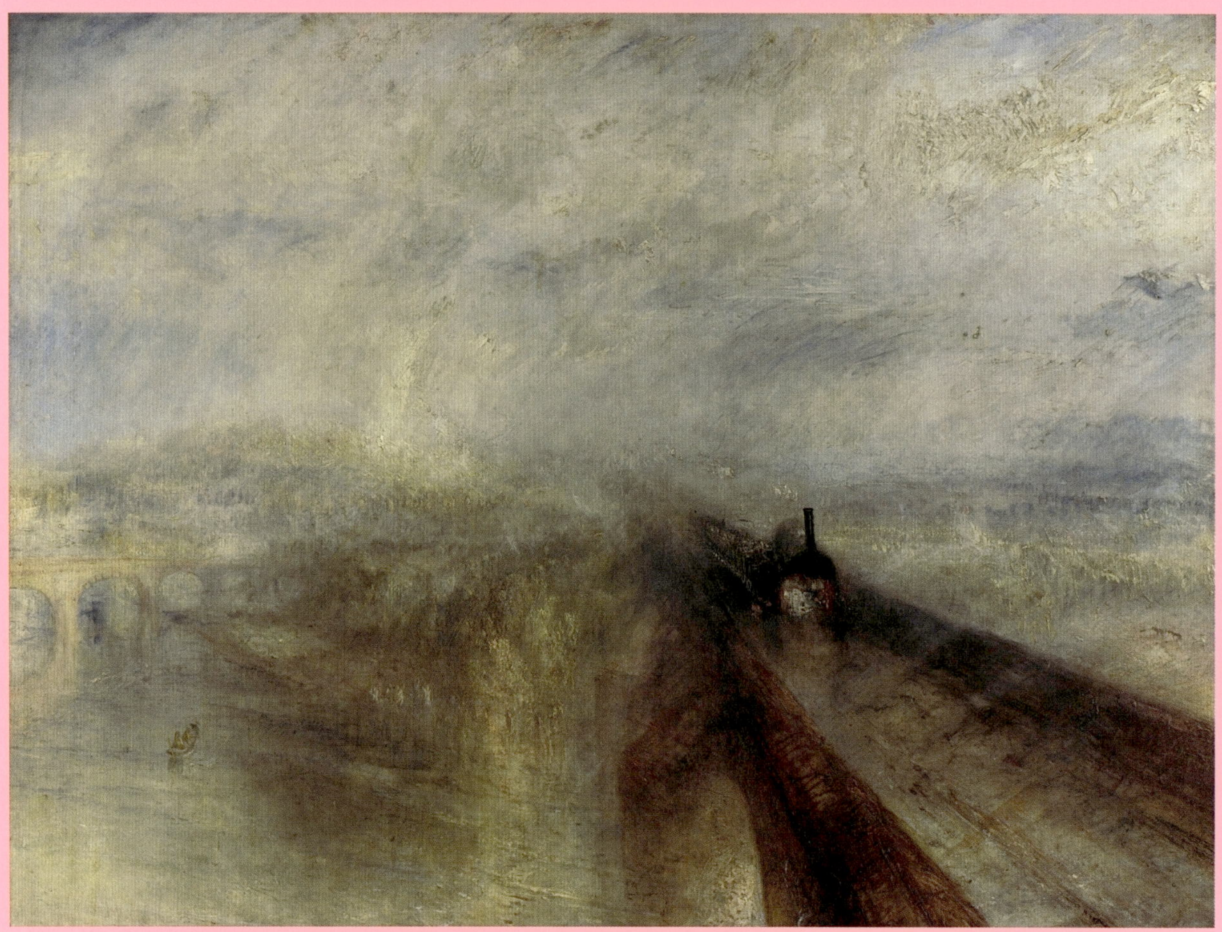

 135 *Rain, Steam, and Speed – The Great Western Railway* 1844. Oil paint on canvas, 91 × 121.8, The National Gallery, London

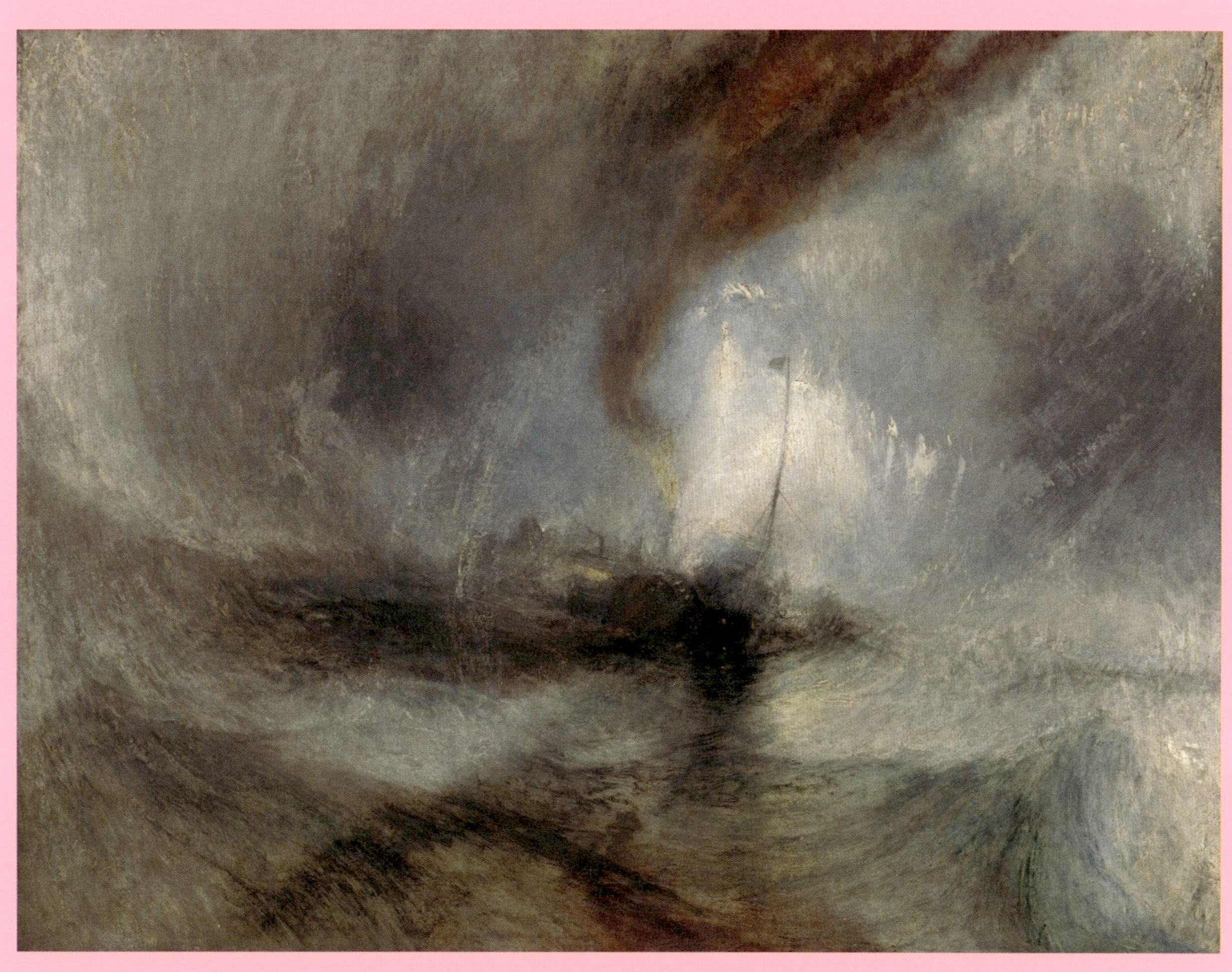

136 *Snow Storm – Steam-Boat off a Harbour's Mouth* exh. 1842. Oil paint on canvas, 91.4 × 121.9, Tate

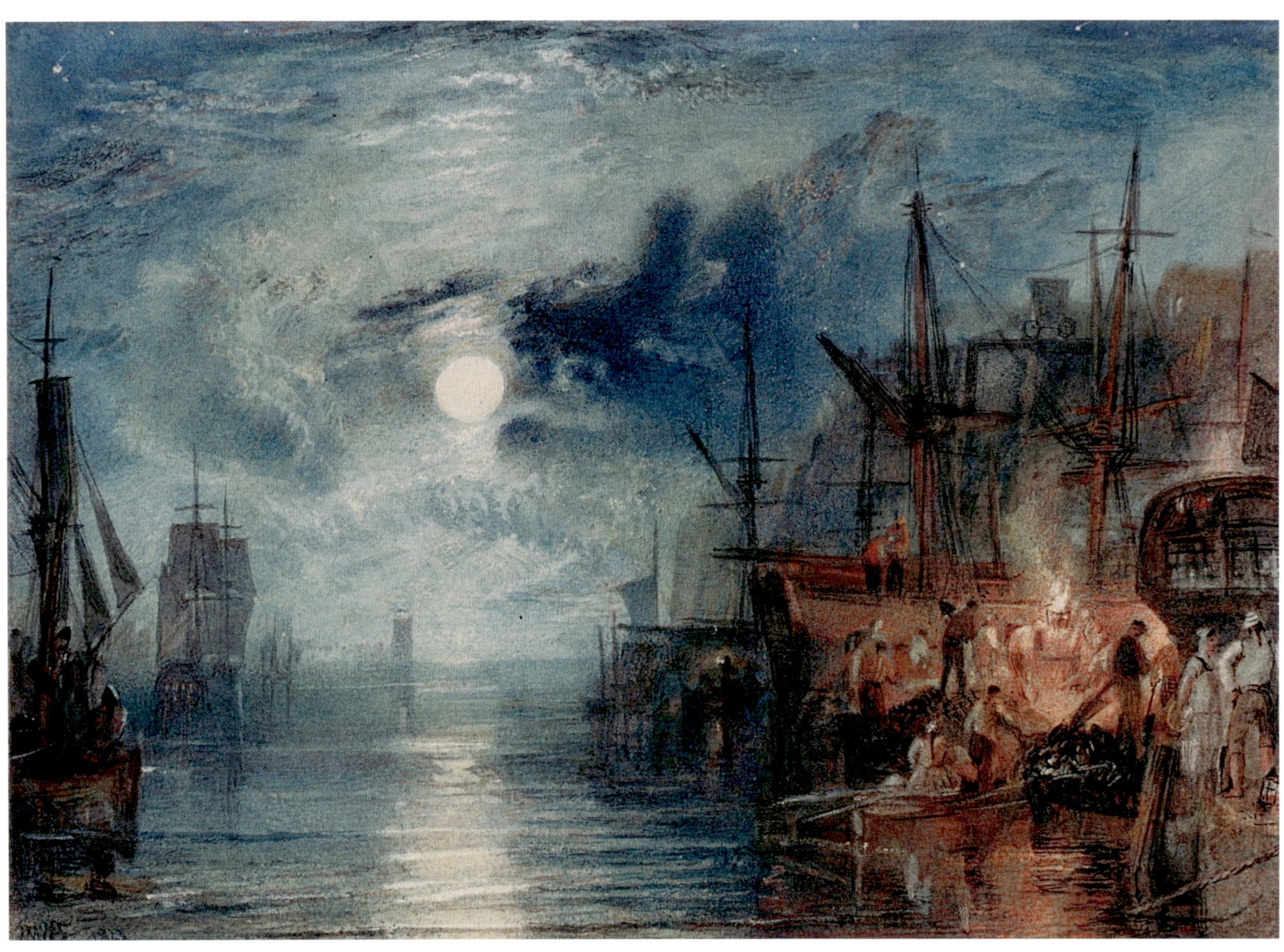

     137 *Shields, on the River Tyne* 1823. Watercolour on paper, 15.4 × 21.6, Tate

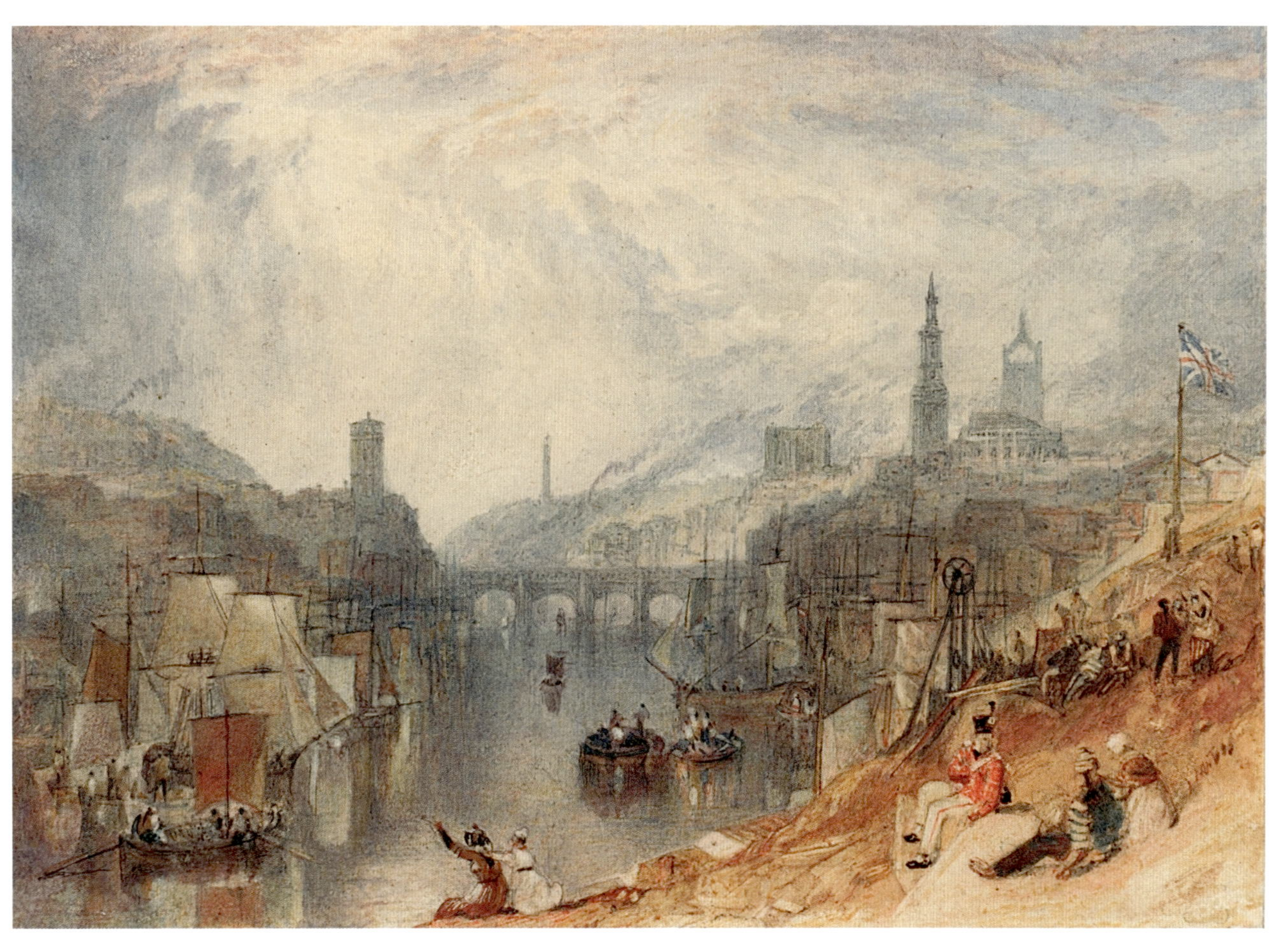

138 *Newcastle-on-Tyne* c.1823. Watercolour on paper, 15.2 × 21.5, Tate

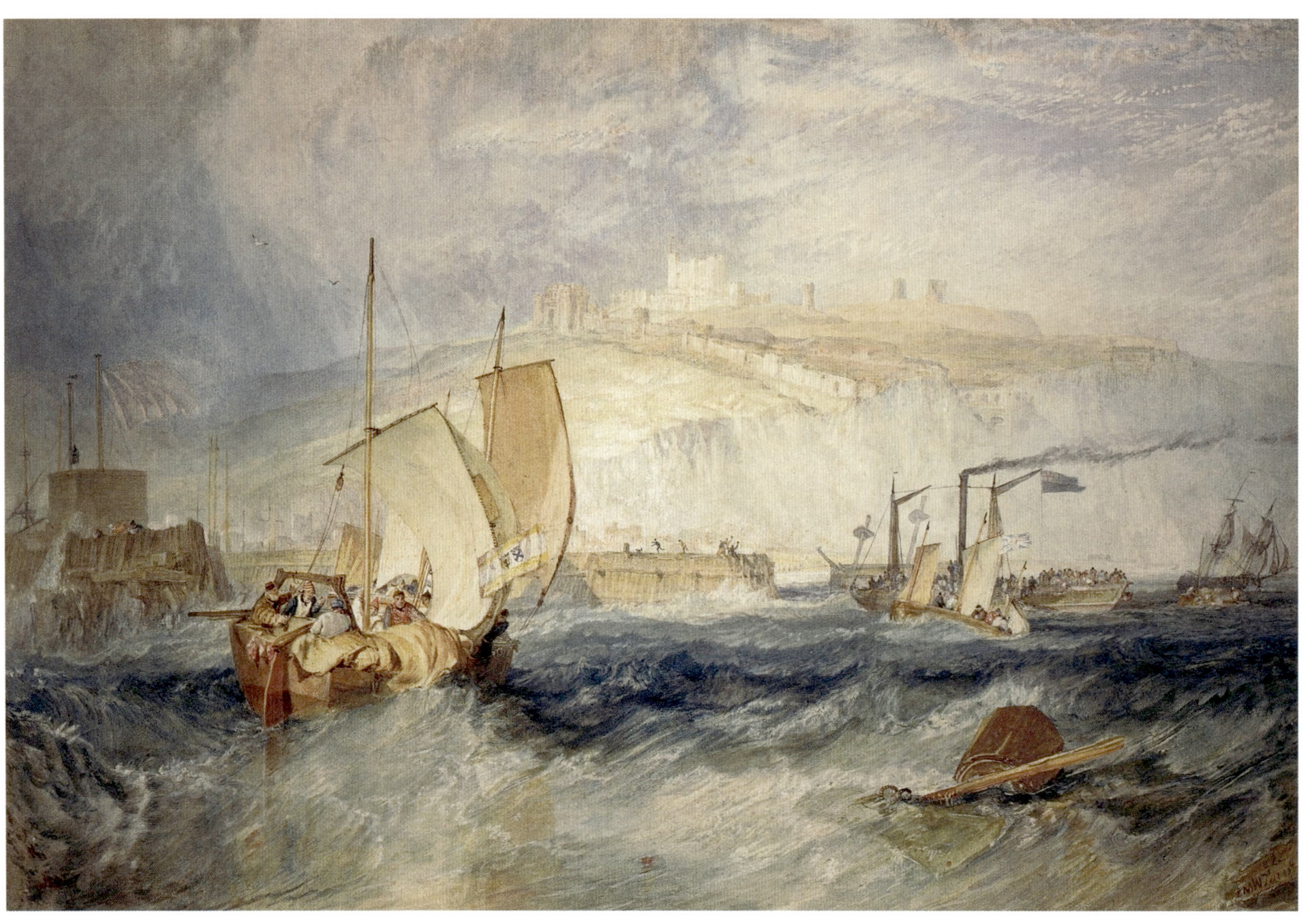

 139 *Dover Castle from the Sea* 1822. Watercolour on paper, 40.5 × 60, Museum of Fine Arts, Boston

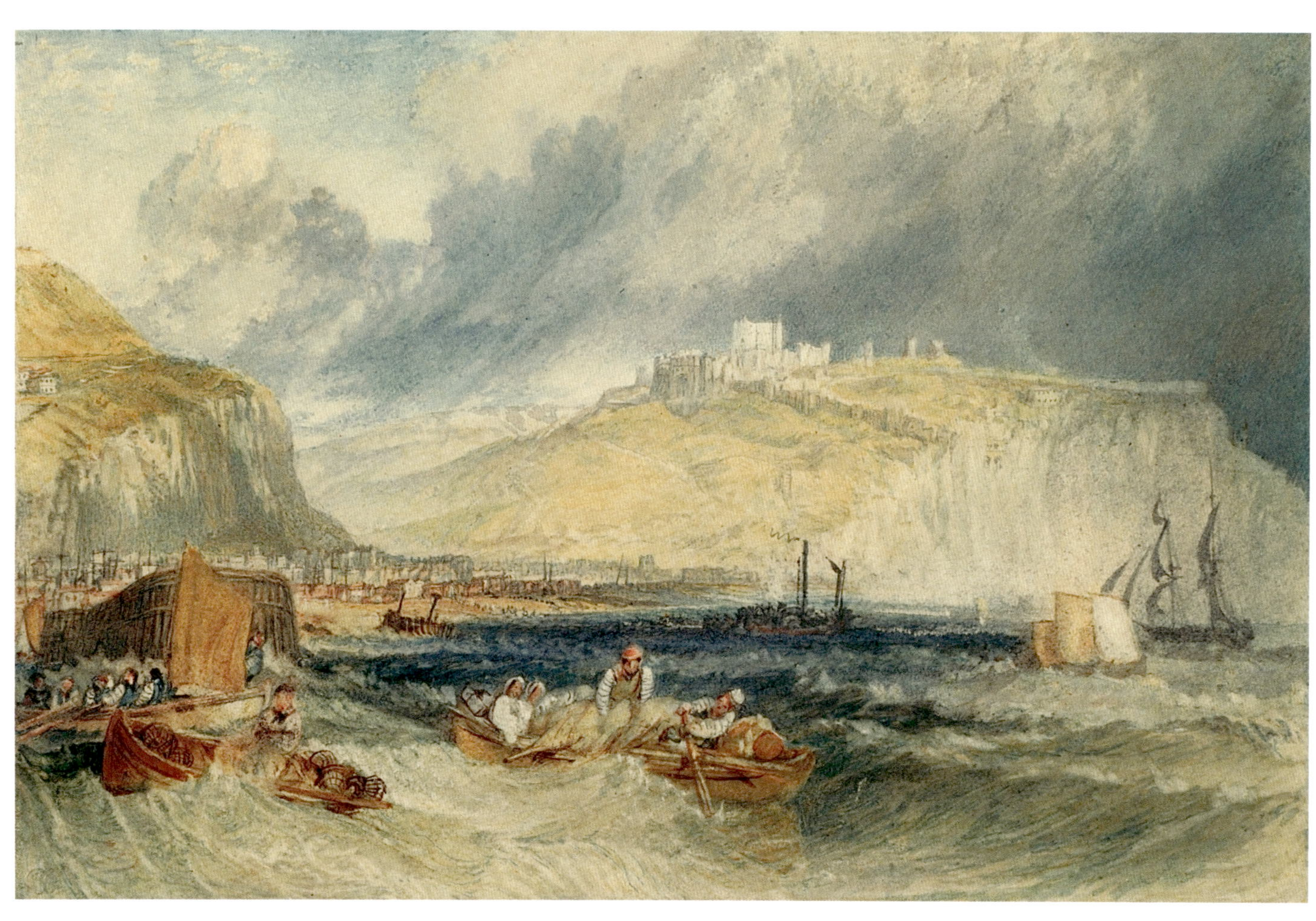

140 *Dover* c.1825. Watercolour on paper, 16.1 × 24.5, Tate

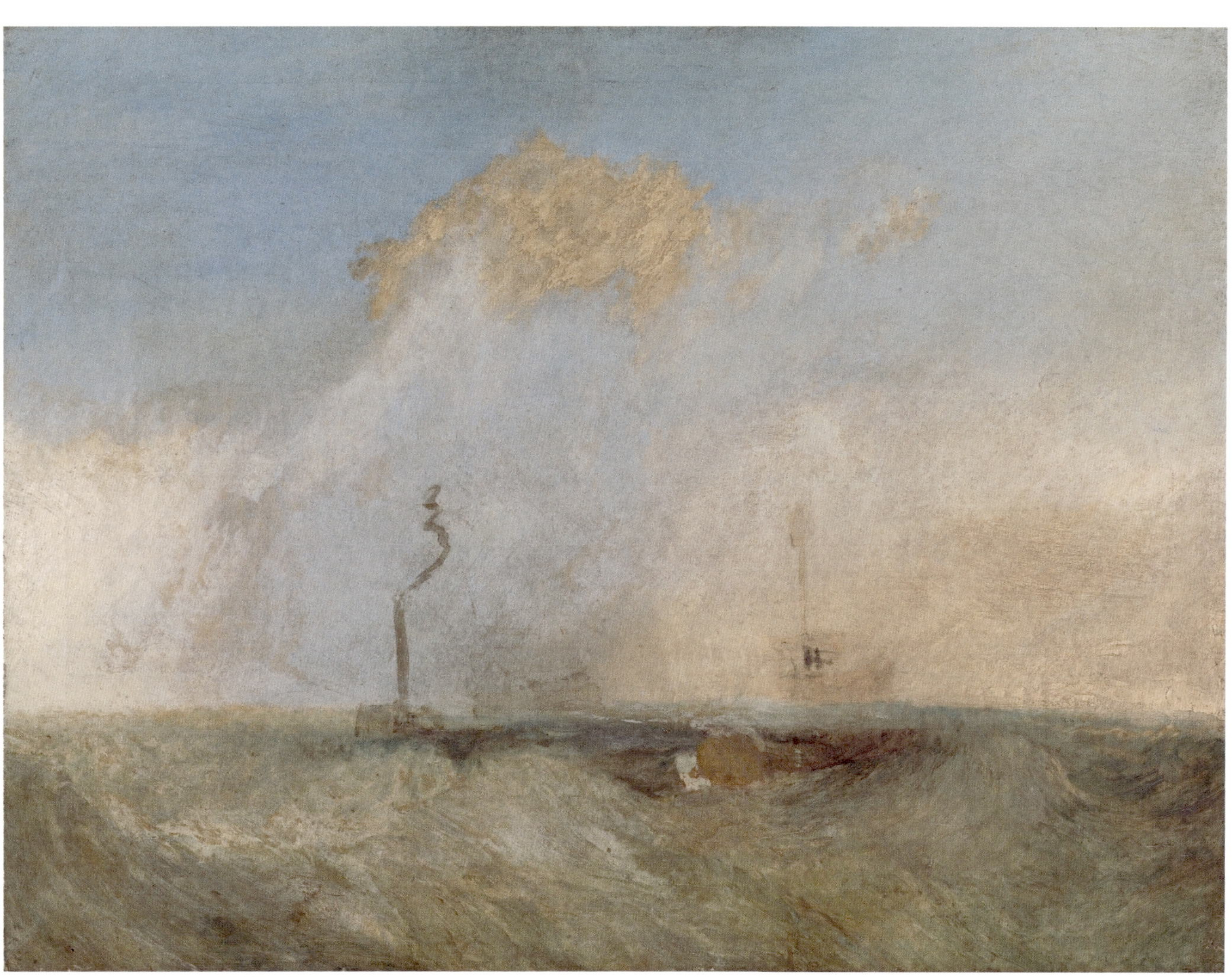

  141 *Steamer and Lightship; a study for 'The Fighting Temeraire'* c.1838–9. Oil paint on canvas, 91.4 × 119.7, Tate

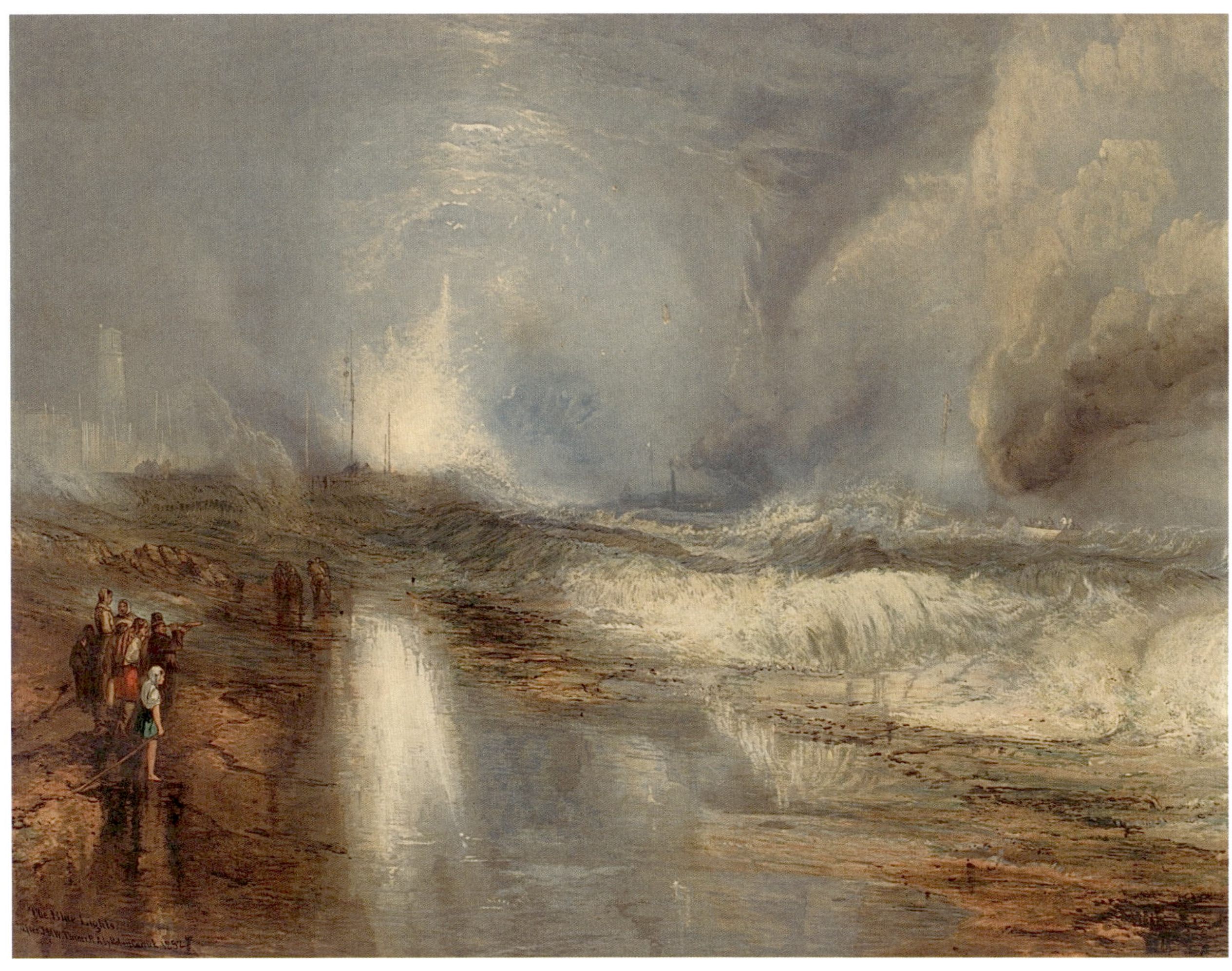

142 Robert Carrick after Joseph Mallord William Turner, *Rockets and Blue Lights* 1852. Lithograph on paper, 56.2 × 75.8 (image), Tate

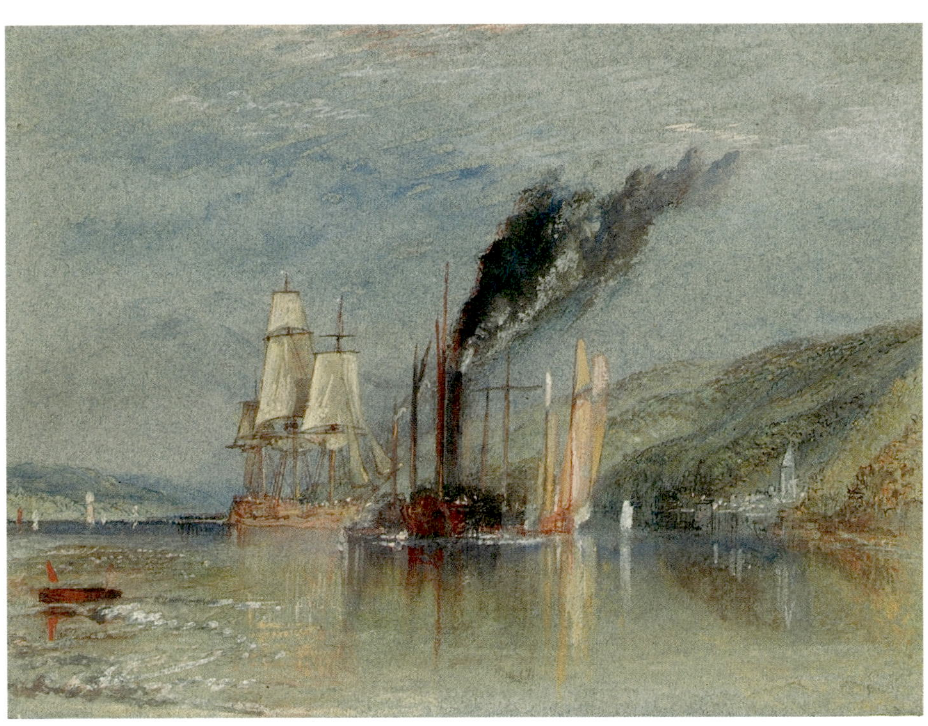

  143 *Between Quilleboeuf and Villequier* c.1832. Gouache and watercolour on paper, 13.7 × 19.1, Tate

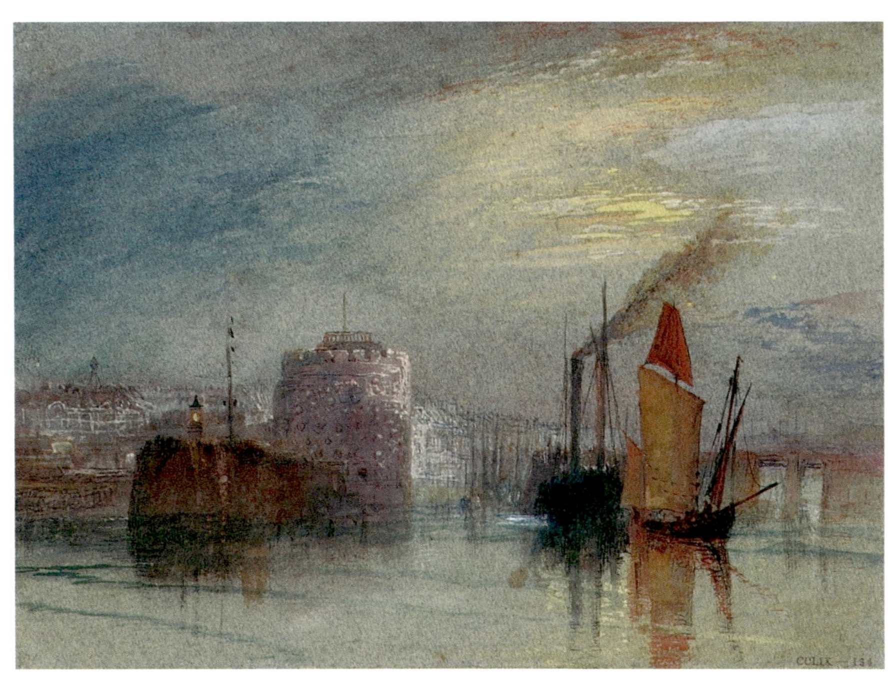

144 *Le Havre: Tour de François 1er* c.1832. Watercolour, goauche and chalk on paper, 14 × 19.2, Tate

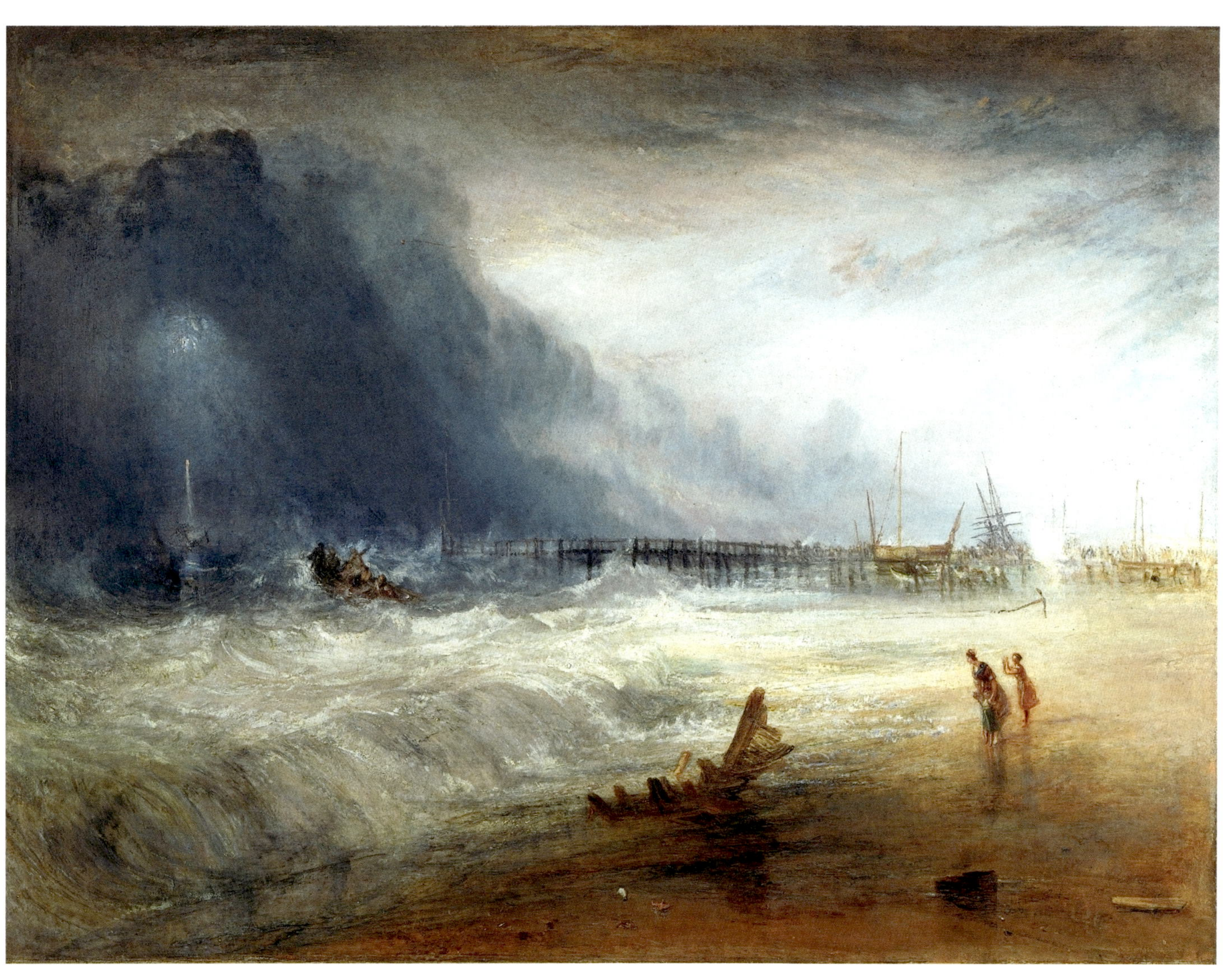

  145 *Life-Boat and Manby Apparatus Going Off to a Stranded Vessel Making Signal (Blue Lights) of Distress* c. 1831,
Oil paint on canvas, 91.4 × 122, Victoria and Albert Museum, London

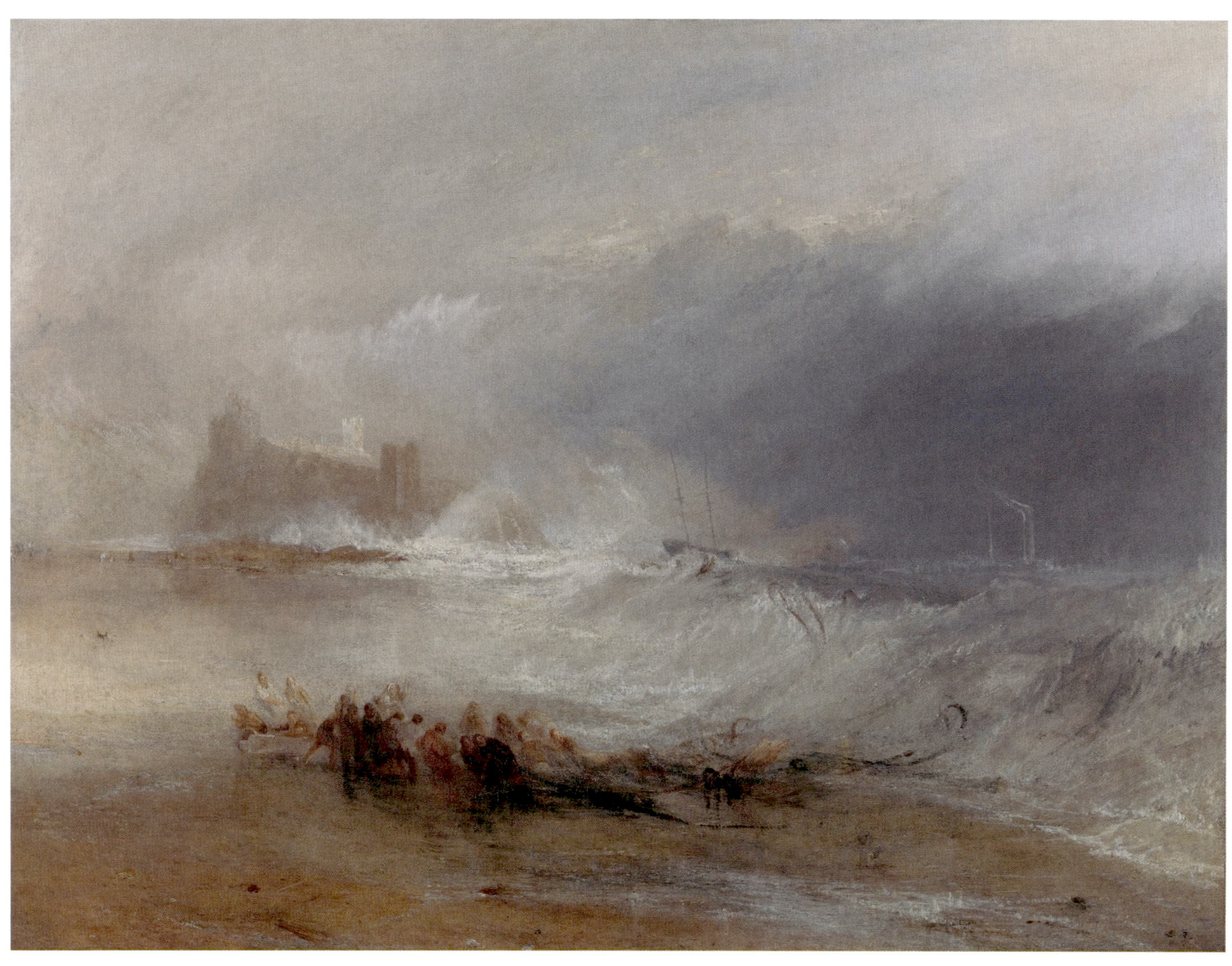

146 *Wreckers – Coast of Northumberland, with a Steam-Boat Assisting a Ship off Shore* 1833–4.
Oil paint on canvas, 90.5 × 120.8, Yale Center for British Art, Paul Mellon Collection, New Haven

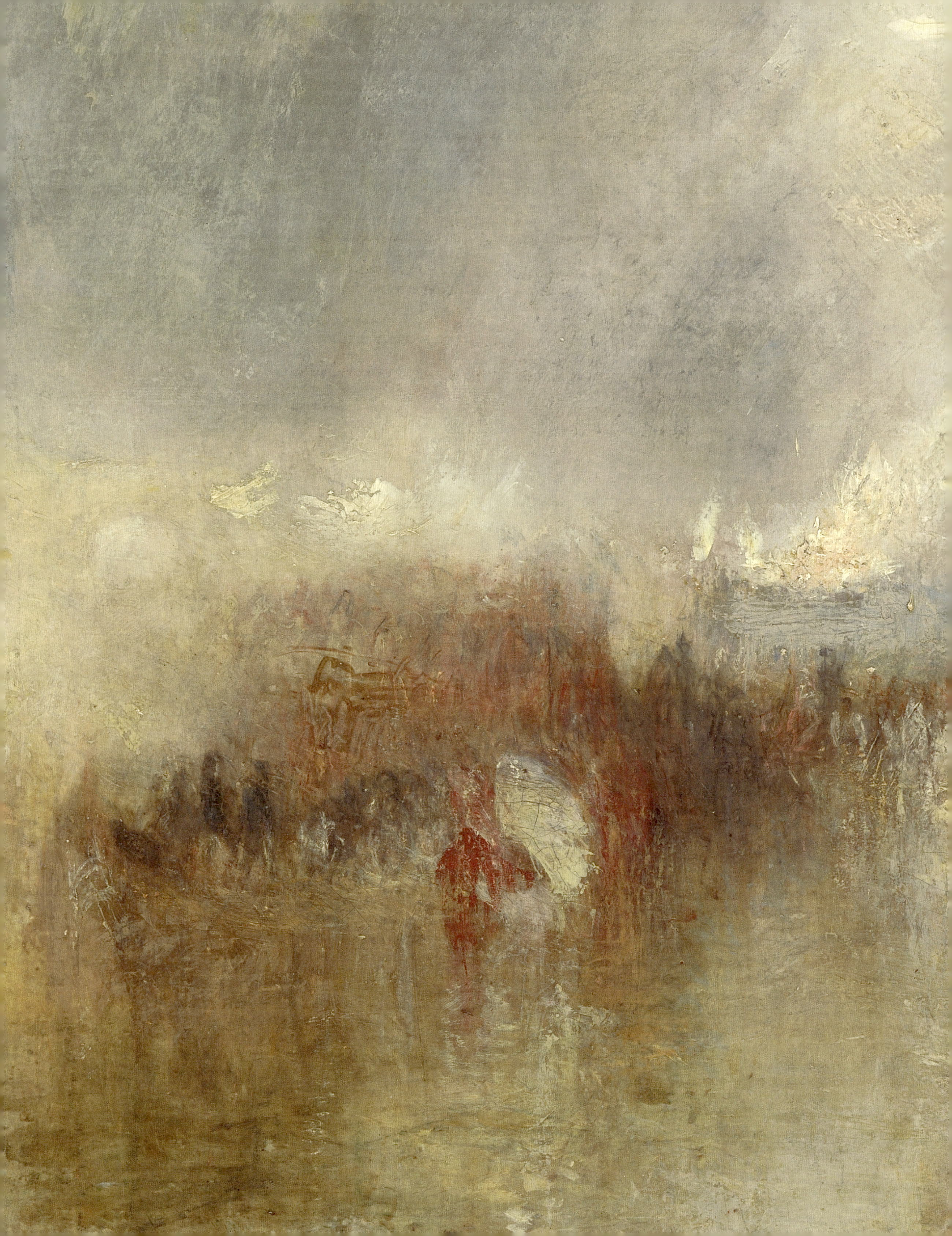

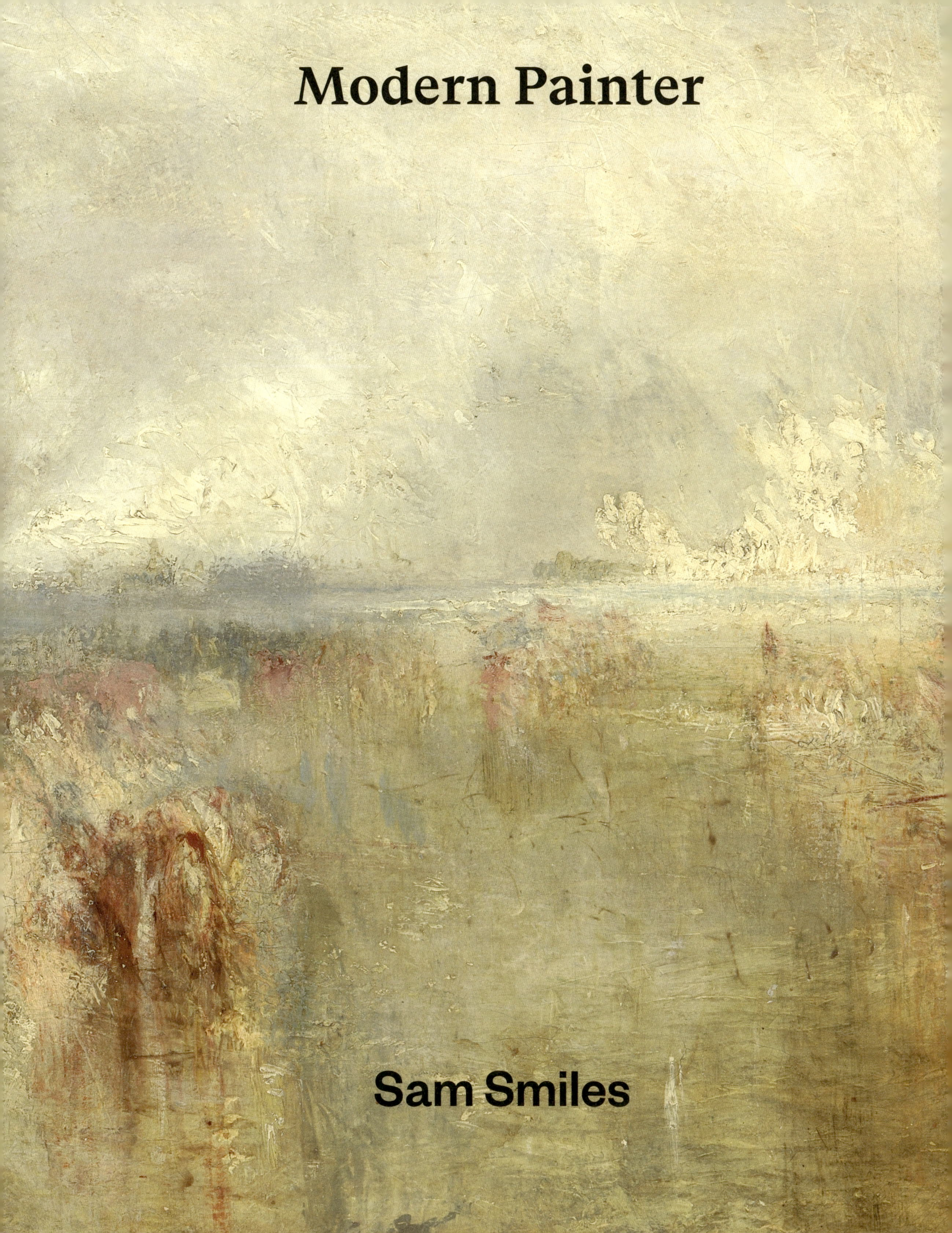

Modern Painter

Sam Smiles

By the time Turner was in his sixties many traditional views of self and society were being undermined by the new economic and social reality of modern Britain. Speaking in 1848 of the bourgeoisie's ceaseless revolutionising of production and the uncertainty, agitation and profound disturbance of social conditions that followed from it, Marx and Engels famously declared: 'All that is solid melts into air.'[140] The new social and industrial paradigm of the nineteenth century also challenged existing standards of artistic representation, whose methods were ill equipped to capture the novelty of modern life; new times called for new methods. Of all his contemporaries, only Turner may be said to have taken up that challenge. He can be characterised as a modern painter not because some of his paintings have modern subjects, nor because his late works look, to some, as though they foreshadow modernism in their 'impressionistic' or even 'abstract' qualities,[141] but because he showed resolutely and consistently how painting might accommodate itself to an innovative age.

In his last decade of work Turner continued to respond to current events. Perhaps prompted by the Treaty of London (April 1839) that established Luxembourg's independence, he revisited the duchy that summer, sketching the city and making a number of studies in gouache. (no.147) Queen Victoria married Prince Albert of Saxe-Coburg and Gotha in February 1840 and in September of that year Turner sketched the prince's birthplace of Schloss Rosenau, near Coburg, showing his oil painting of the subject at the Royal Academy in 1841 (nos.148, 149). In 1843 he exhibited a painting commemorating the opening in 1842 of a new German cultural landmark, the Walhalla, near Regensburg in Bavaria (no.81). In two unfinished oil paintings he captured the state visit to Britain of the French king Louis-Philippe in October 1844 (nos.157–9), and in one of his very last watercolours he reflected on the revolt in Naples that had broken out in May 1848 (no.150). He also painted meditations on the current cults of celebrity surrounding Napoleon (no.160) and his nemesis the Duke of Wellington (no.12), and he explored

the whaling industry, whose oil was so important for machinery and lighting in this era (nos.153–6).

This responsiveness to current issues was unusual, for the idea of the modern artist as an individual engaged with modern experience had not yet taken root in Britain. When John Ruskin published his great defence of Turner, the first volume of *Modern Painters* (1843), its subtitle referred not to the contemporary scene but the timeless qualities of 'the True, the Beautiful, and the Intellectual'.[142] Likewise, in its last volume (1860) Ruskin contrasted Turner's upbringing in modern London with Giorgione's in Renaissance Venice but did not conclude that Turner's early experiences predisposed him to address modernity *per se*, rather that they encouraged him to look beyond the ugliness and banality of everyday existence to treat the bigger themes of nature, life and the human condition: 'He must be a painter of the strength of nature, there was no beauty elsewhere than in that; he must paint also the labour and sorrow and passing away of men: this was the great human truth visible to him.'[143]

Ruskin's inability to see modern life as a compelling subject for artists was not unique. During Turner's career art critics commented regularly on the subject, style and sentiment of the paintings they reviewed, but no English art writer of the time articulated a view of painting and modernity comparable to the one that would be adopted in Charles Baudelaire's famous essay 'The Painter of Modern Life' (1863). Yet by the same token, Baudelaire's concentration on the artist as *flâneur*, registering the ephemeral quality of modern experience and distilling the essence of the urban scene, does not capture how Turner's works physically assert their modernity. Turner's willingness throughout his career to rethink his practice as a painter saw repeated innovations in approach, whether to modern or traditional subjects, especially in his later years. The 1840s, for example, saw him experimenting with the presentation of his ideas, sometimes using shaped formats (square, circular or octagonal frames), exhibiting paired subjects or working in larger series. In adopting new standards of handling and finish he was forging a new language

   Previous page: *The Arrival of Louis-Philippe at the Royal Clarence Yard, Gosport, 8 October 1844* c.1844–5 (no.157)

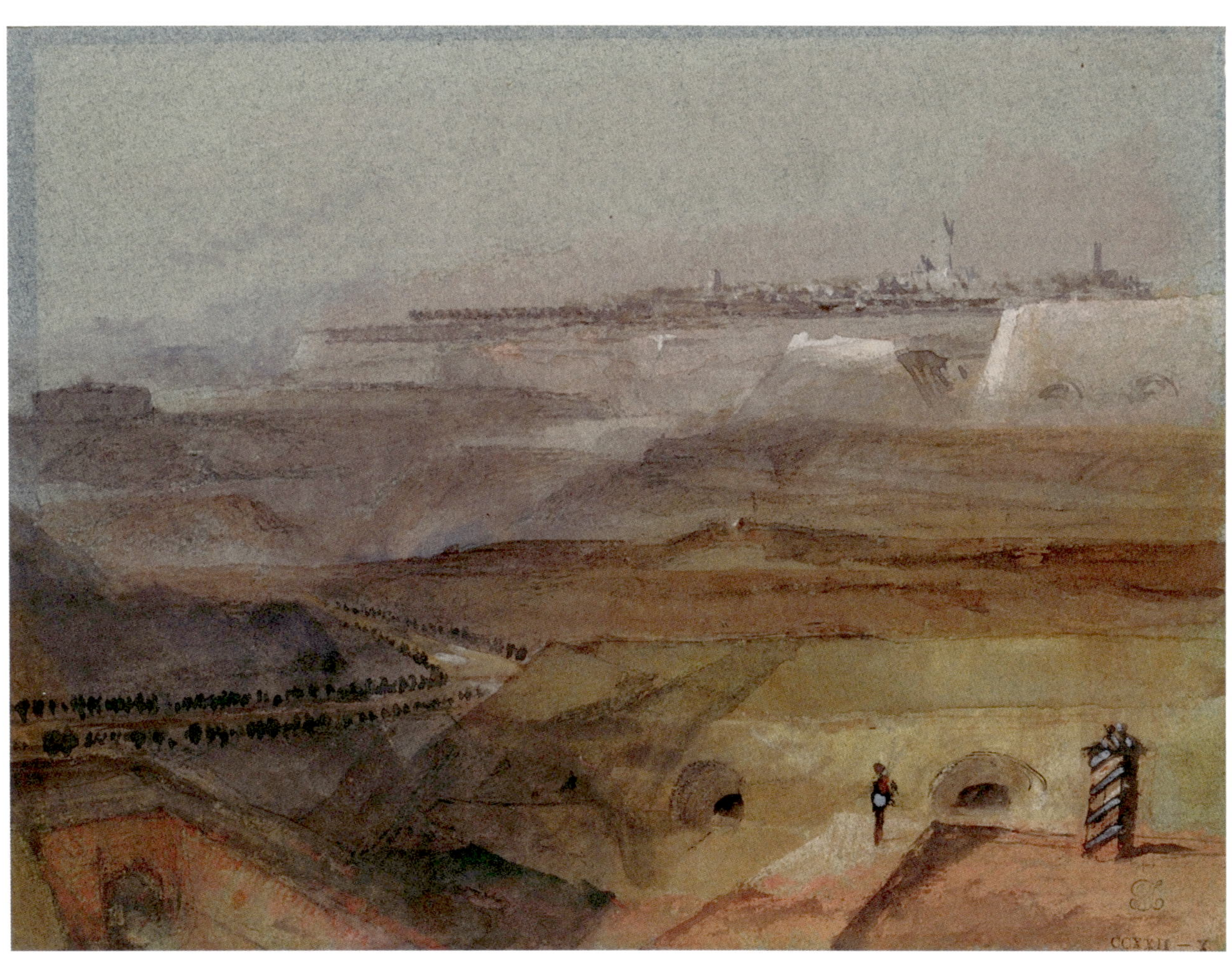

147 *Distant View of Luxembourg from the Bourbon Plateau* c.1839. Gouache, graphite and watercolour on paper, 13.7 × 18.8, Tate

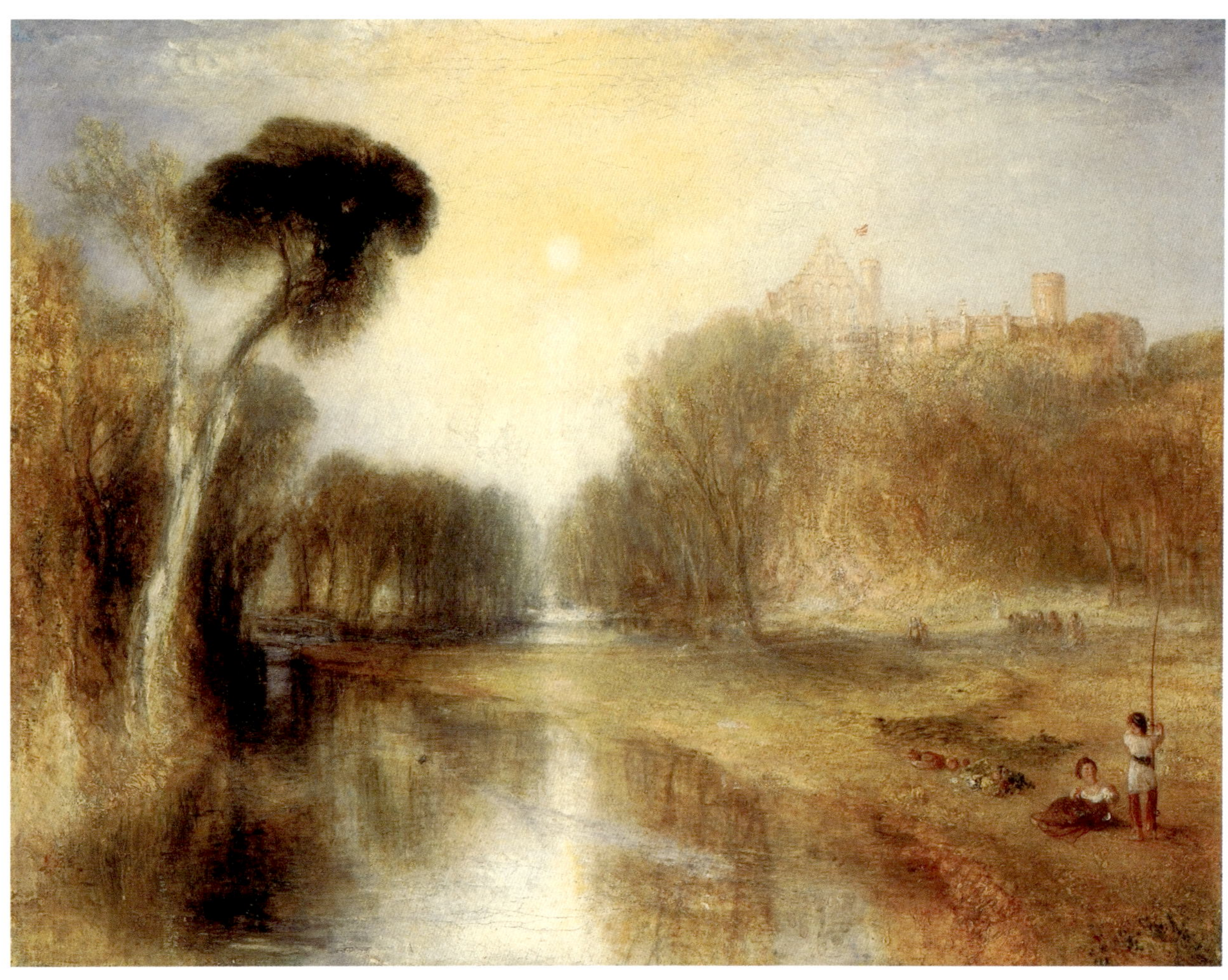

148 *Schloss Rosenau, Seat of HRH Prince Albert of Coburg, near Coburg, Germany* 1841.
Oil paint on canvas, 97 × 124.8, National Museums Liverpool, Liverpool

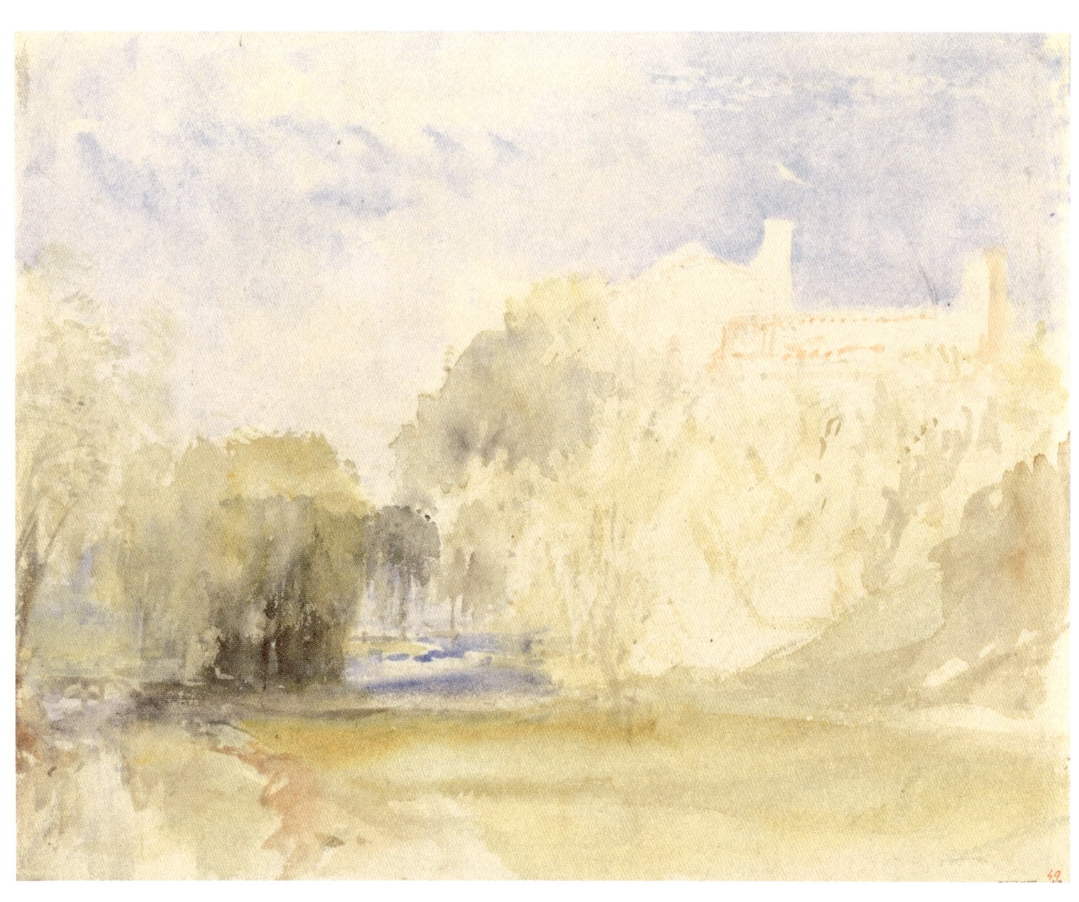

149 *Schloss Rosenau, near Coburg* c.1840. Watercolour on paper, 24.4 × 30.6, Tate

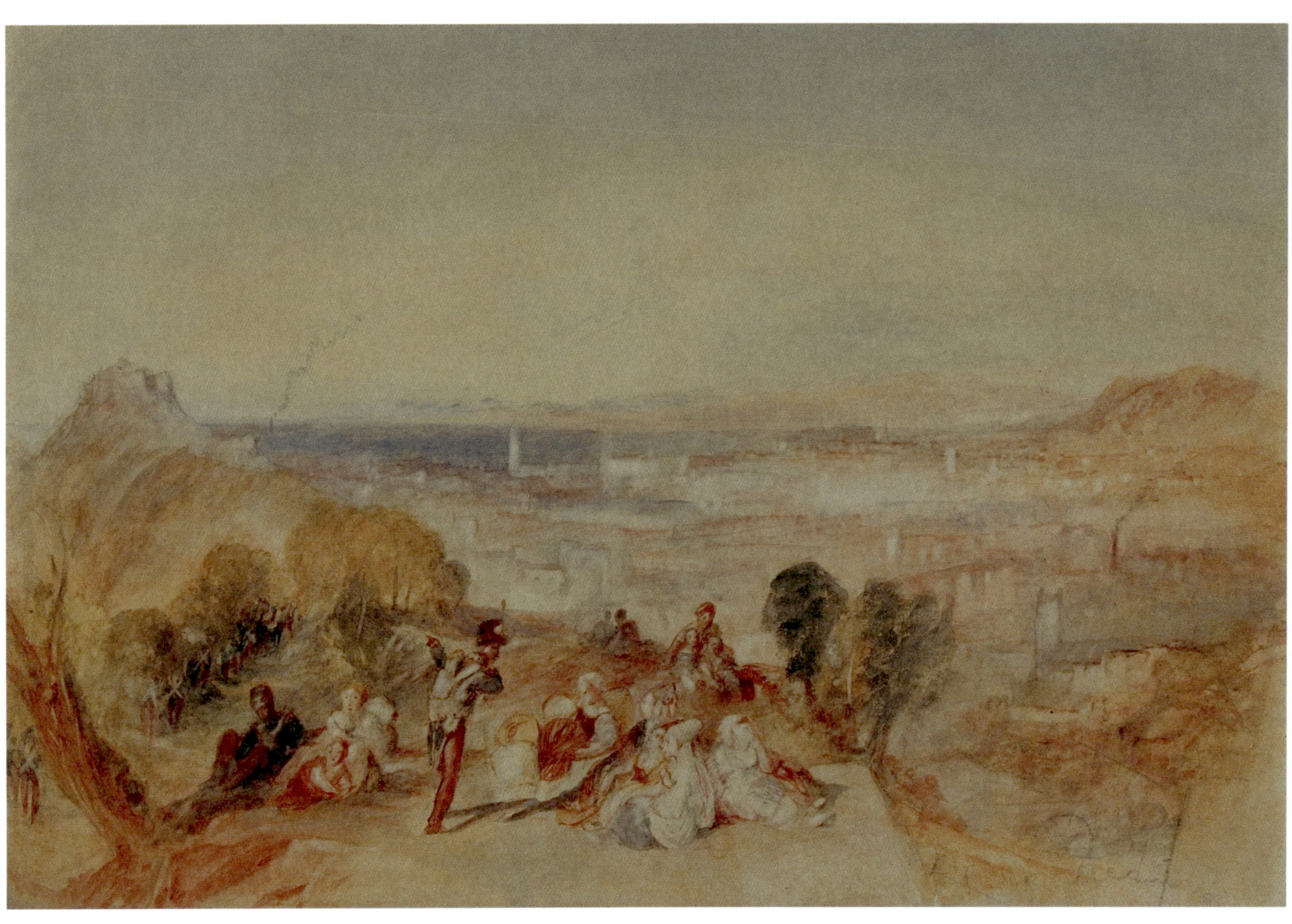

  150 *Naples* c.1851. Watercolour and pencil on paper, 37.1 × 54.3, Manchester Art Gallery

of representation, dispensing with the hard outlines, the separation of individual pictorial motifs and the artificial divisions of the visual field that characterised more traditional approaches.

By the later 1830s Turner's position within the English school was recognised by every critic, friendly or hostile, as offering a completely distinctive approach to painting, utterly unlike his predecessors and contemporaries. As is well known, his enemies regularly took him to task for what they characterised as his excesses, but his supporters championed those very same qualities, too.[144] In 1836, for example, his pictures were praised for their singularity: 'His miraculous conception and daring and master pencil have produced pictorial effects, of a nature to place him in a station unequalled and alone.'[145] The same judgement is found in a review of 1840: 'The truth is, that Mr. Turner ventures to portray those effects of nature which the most daring artists have never thought of attempting.'[146] His supporters' endorsement of his achievement is summed up in a review of the paintings he showed at the Royal Academy in 1843: 'No painter of the present day dare attempt such pictures as Mr. Turner produces.'[147] Sympathetic reviews like these emphasised the artist's idiosyncratic stylistic devices, his 'pictorial effects', which enabled him to portray phenomena, 'effects of nature', hitherto impossible to capture on canvas. Ruskin, too, tended to concentrate on Turner's detailed understanding of the natural world and the fundamental truths his art conveyed as a result of his disciplined observation. This kind of criticism presented Turner as a supremely talented painter of natural phenomena and was not wrong to do so, but it is also evident that it represented Turner's achievement inadequately in two key respects.

First, it promoted the idea that before Turner no artist was capable of exploring nature so comprehensively, while at the same time presuming that nature was permanent and unchanging. However, one might argue differently, that Turner's approach in his last years was not merely a matter of registering complex phenomena more exactly, it also captured

something of the spectator's interaction with the world, not so much offering disciplined scrutiny of an unchanging nature as showing how our perception shapes what we experience. This was very much a modern point of view, indebted to new scientific discoveries about the physiology and psychology of vision.[148] Likewise, his later works seem to elide the distinctions between diverse physical objects and, more generally, to meld the material with the immaterial. This essentially holistic presentation of the world also echoes contemporary thinking. In her best-selling book *On the Connexion of the Physical Sciences* (1834) Mary Somerville, one of Turner's scientific acquaintances, had discussed the universal application of scientific laws, celebrating the 'bond of union' between different physical realms: 'Any one who has observed the reflection of the waves from a wall on the side of a river … after the passage of a steam-boat, will have a perfect idea of the reflection of sound and of light.'[149] This enlarged conception of nature surely informs Turner's later paintings that incorporate his understanding of a world where the rigid separation of objects and phenomena no longer seemed appropriate.

Second, in choosing to approach Turner as a painter of nature above all, his critics downplayed an important aspect of his practice: his response to the times in which he lived. Take, for example, his paintings of Venice. In his watercolours and later oil paintings Turner treats it principally as a city dissolved in light, its topography blurred and obscured by fugitive effects of atmosphere, but this almost mirage-like quality is held in tension with another truth that Venice, once the dominant military and trading power in the eastern Mediterranean, had lost its independence as it declined in significance and now lay under Austrian control. While Venice slipped into picturesque impotence, Britain's industrial and commercial might had seen it rise to economic prominence and become a leader in world trade, which Turner drove home in the contrast between the languorous beauty of *Venice* (no.151) and the round-the-clock energy of the coal trade in Tyneside shown in *Keelmen Heaving in Coals by Moonlight* (no.6). Both canvases were painted for a member of the new entrepreneurial class, the textile manufacturer Henry McConnell, and were surely intended as companion pictures.

Turner's ambitions for landscape painting embraced aspects of the social, political and technological nineteenth century. With respect to that social world, it is clear that he was particularly interested in the spectacle of modernity, delighting in painting contemporary figures thronging the places he depicted. This interest in the social side of landscape had deep roots in his practice, as can be seen in his watercolours of English towns and their citizens from the 1790s to the 1830s and extending to his depictions of fashionably dressed crowds in some of his studies of European locations (nos.17, 84, 88, 114, 152). Even in the more cursory style of his later years this sense of a public witness of contemporary events is a marked feature of many of his works, as in his depiction of the mass of spectators watching the destruction of the Houses of Parliament in 1834 (no.109), the crowds attending the opening of the Walhalla

in 1842 (no.81) or the onlookers caught up in the excitement of Louis Philippe's arrival at Gosport in 1844 (nos.157, 159).

As regards technology, Turner's omnivorous visual appetite saw him represent mills, iron forges, stagecoaches, rockets and ships, especially men-of-war. But what makes his record exceptional is his readiness to take on the new motive power of the age. For evident reasons there was no artistic standard for depicting steam-powered transport, but nor is it obvious, even with the benefit of hindsight, that the means adopted by Turner were inevitable. Had he responded to his times in a more conventional pictorial idiom, he would now have a reputation as a highly proficient observer of nature and a chronicler of the new industrial world, but his artistic standing would not be as high. Instead, he used the challenge presented by modern technological developments as a stimulus to his practice as an artist. Turner's rendition of the locomotive in *Rain, Steam, and Speed* (no.135) provides a good example of how he developed

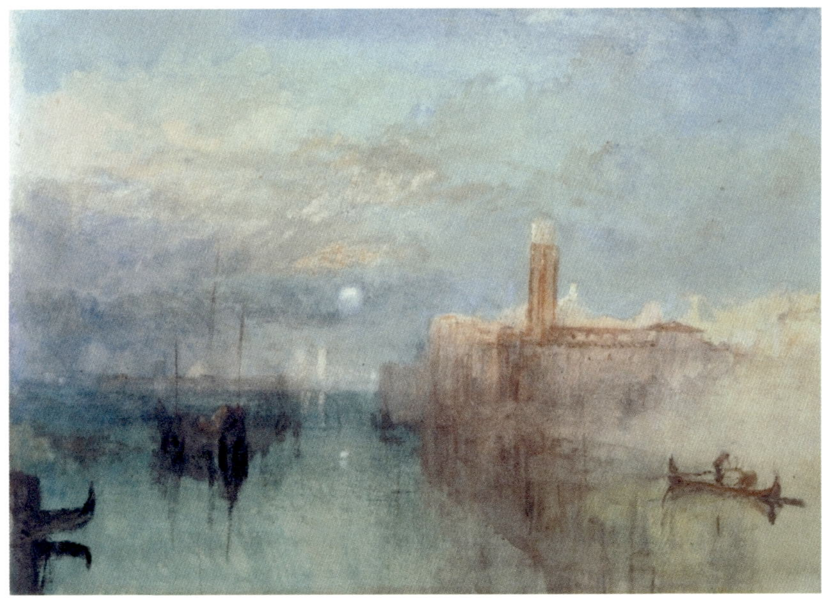

151
Venice by Moonlight, with Boats off a Campanile 1840.
Watercolour on paper,
22 × 31.9, Tate

innovative procedures to represent the new technology. Although illustrated in print media, the railways had not yet stimulated serious painting in Europe and they were new for Turner, too. He does not seem to have studied trains regularly and those few sketches that may possibly do so are slight and ambiguous.[150] The painting's title has speed as its third element, but representing the train's velocity posed a problem without precedent. Turner solved it by including puffs of smoke receding into the background and most obviously by disintegrating the front of the engine with touches of impasto, letting colour advance to indicate the train's closing speed towards the spectator. The formal audacity of the picture was noted by Thackeray, among other critics:

> He has made a picture with real rain, behind which is real sunshine, and you expect a rainbow every minute. Meanwhile, there comes a train down upon you, really moving at the rate of fifty miles an hour ... All these wonders are performed with means not less wonderful than the effects are. The rain ... is composed of dabs of dirty putty *slapped* on to the canvass with a trowel; the sunshine scintillates out of very thick, smeary lumps of chrome yellow. The shadows are produced by cool tones of crimson lake, and

quiet glazings of vermilion, although the fire in the steam-engine *looks* as if it were red. I am not prepared to say that it is not painted with cobalt and pea-green.

Thackeray ended with the words with which this book began: 'The world has never seen anything like this picture.'[151]

Many of Turner's later paintings are equally innovative. This was not merely experiment for its own sake but can be seen as his endeavour to widen the scope of landscape painting in terms of the subjects it treated and the sophisticated means it needed to adopt if it was to come to terms with the wholesale mental rearrangement that seemed necessary to take the measure of the age. The images that result are often elusive and hard to interpret fully, employing a complex interplay of pigment and handling that sometimes frustrates easy comprehension. Yet in developing such an uncompromising style, he was perhaps suggesting that this approach was the only adequate response to the more complex world that confronted him. Turner did not so much illustrate his times as illuminate them, by dint of making the new era a fit subject for the highest reaches of creative endeavour.

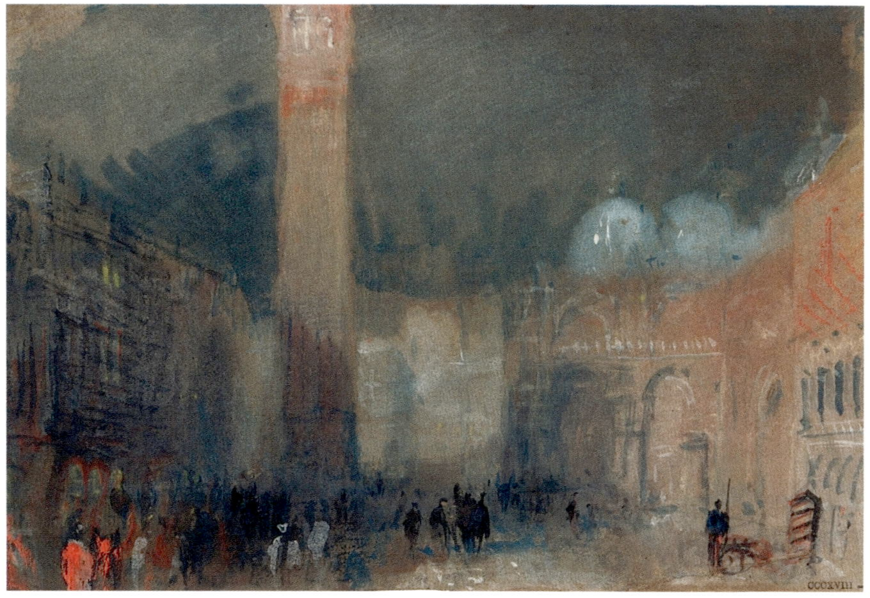

152
Figures in the Piazzetta, Venice, at Night, with the Basilica and Campanile of San Marco (St Mark's)
1840. Watercolour and bodycolour on paper, 15 × 22.8, Tate

Whalers

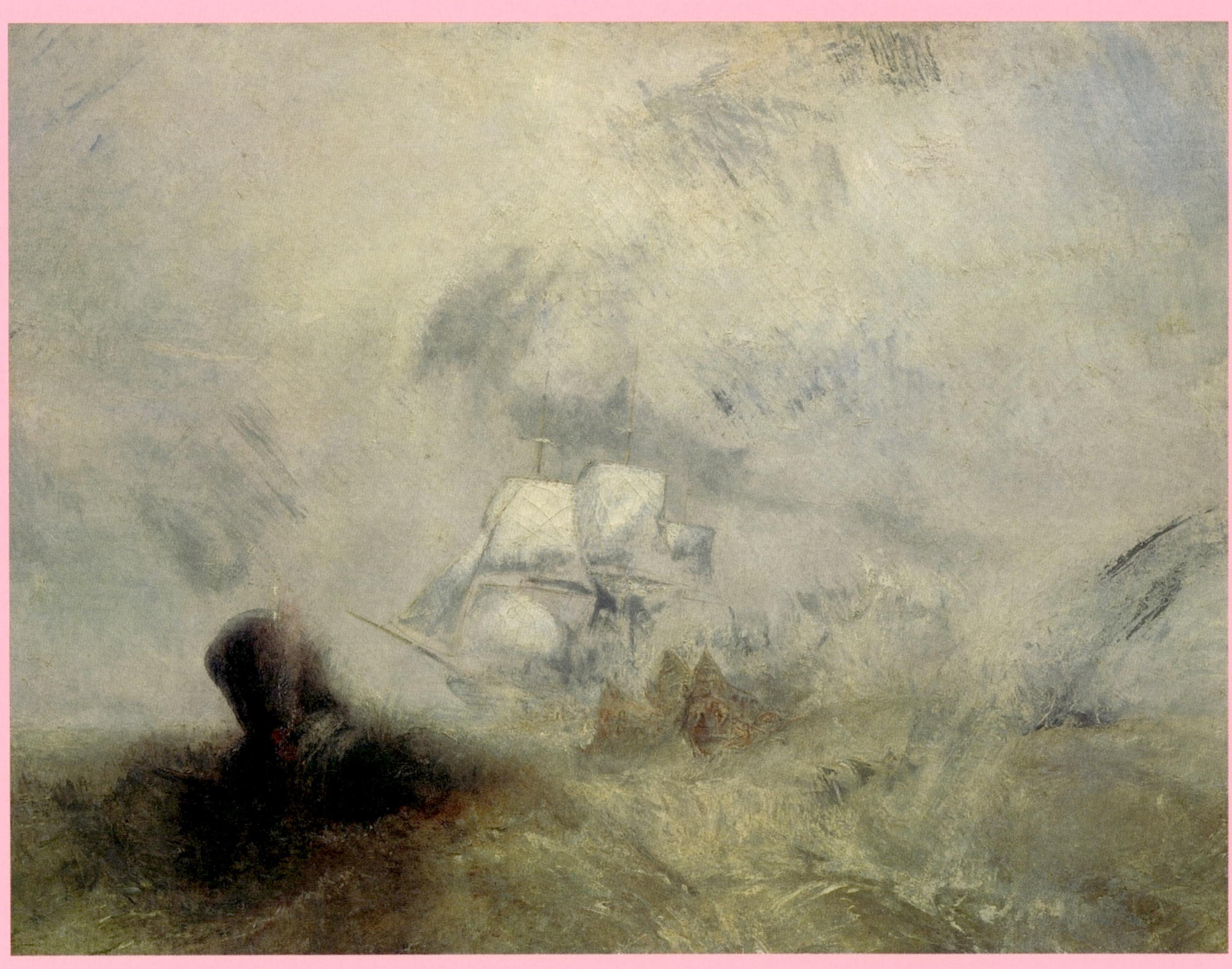

  153 *Whalers* c.1845. Oil paint on canvas, 91.8 × 122.6, The Metropolitan Museum of Art, New York City

The products derived from the nineteenth-century whaling industry, principally whalebone and spermaceti oil, have been justifiably compared to the ubiquity of plastic and hydrocarbon oil in our culture. However, because whaling took place far from land, few artists had depicted it. With the exception of some Dutch paintings of the 1600s, it was typically illustrated in engravings rather than paintings, although some of Turner's contemporaries, including John Ward, John Wilson Carmichael and William Huggins had tackled the subject.

One of Turner's patrons was Elhanan Bicknell, a partner in a firm refining spermaceti oil from the Pacific sperm whale fishery.[152] He had become an important client, buying eight paintings in 1844, and Turner's four paintings of whaling (nos.153–6) were surely designed to attract his interest. To help Turner imagine his subject, Bicknell probably lent him Thomas Beale's *Natural History of the Sperm Whale* and showed him his painting by Huggins, *A Whaler in the South Sea Fishery* (c.1830–5), which bears a similarity to Turner's *Whale Ship*.[153]

In January 1845 Turner invited Bicknell to visit his gallery in Queen Anne Street 'for I have a whale or two on the canvas'.[154] Bicknell briefly acquired *The Whale Ship* but fell out with Turner over its finish. As Ruskin's father reported: 'Bicknell is quarrelling with Turner … he found Water Colour in Whalers and rubbed out some with Handky. He went to Turner who looked Daggers and refused to do anything but at last he has taken it back to alter.'[155] The picture was not returned to Bicknell, who probably disliked its style.

Bicknell's picture shows a bleeding whale rising out of the sea at the left, while in the centre whale boats are capsizing as another resists attack. *Whalers*, also shown in 1845, records a successful hunt, with a harpooned and bleeding whale. The two paintings exhibited in 1846 are less dramatic. *Hurrah! for the Whaler Erebus! Another Fish!* shows a whale being cut up for blubber, its head and jaw hanging from the main mast. The name 'Erebus' probably derives from HMS *Erebus*, which with the *Terror* had explored Antarctica in 1839–43. The warm colours dominant in *Hurrah! for the Whaler Erebus!* are replaced with a cooler palette in *Whalers (Boiling Blubber)*, the sun merely a pallid presence in the sky. The dead whale is being sawn into pieces on the ice at the right, with the ovens used to render the blubber into oil on the left.

The relative novelty of the subject seems to have disarmed Turner's critics. *The Times*, for example, in its critique of *Whalers* praised its 'free, vigorous, fearless embodiment of a moment. To do justice to Turner, it should always be remembered that he is the painter, not of reflections, but of immediate sensations.'[156] A critic of all Turner's exhibits in 1846 concluded: 'So entirely is the eye carried away by a sort of indistinct and harmonious magic, that we seem to consent to abandonment of solid truth and real nature altogether, and allow dark ships to be chrome yellow, whales glistening pink, human beings sun or moon beams, and little thick dabs of paint ethereal clouds.'[157]
SS

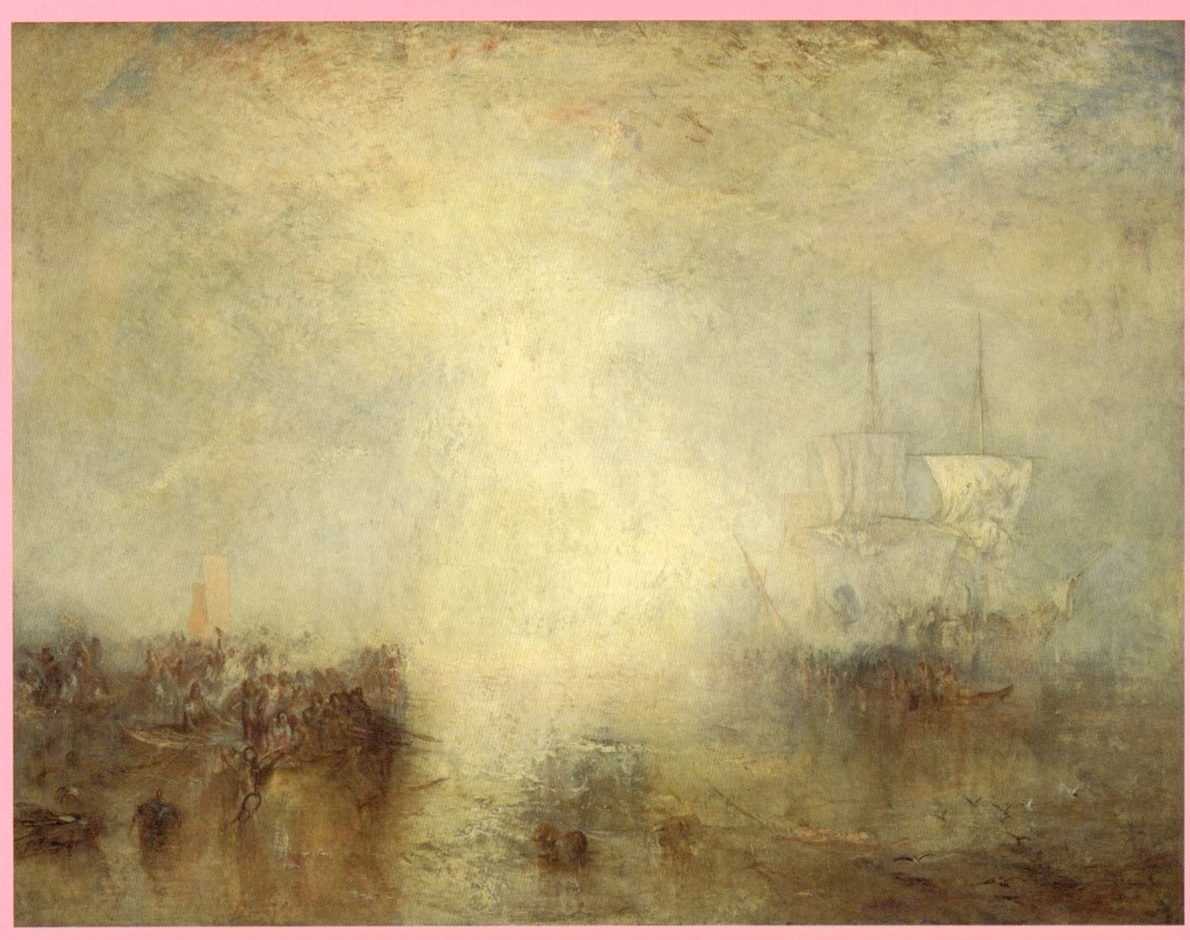

154 *'Hurrah! for the Whaler Erebus! Another Fish!'* exh. 1846. Oil paint on canvas, 90.2 × 120.6, Tate

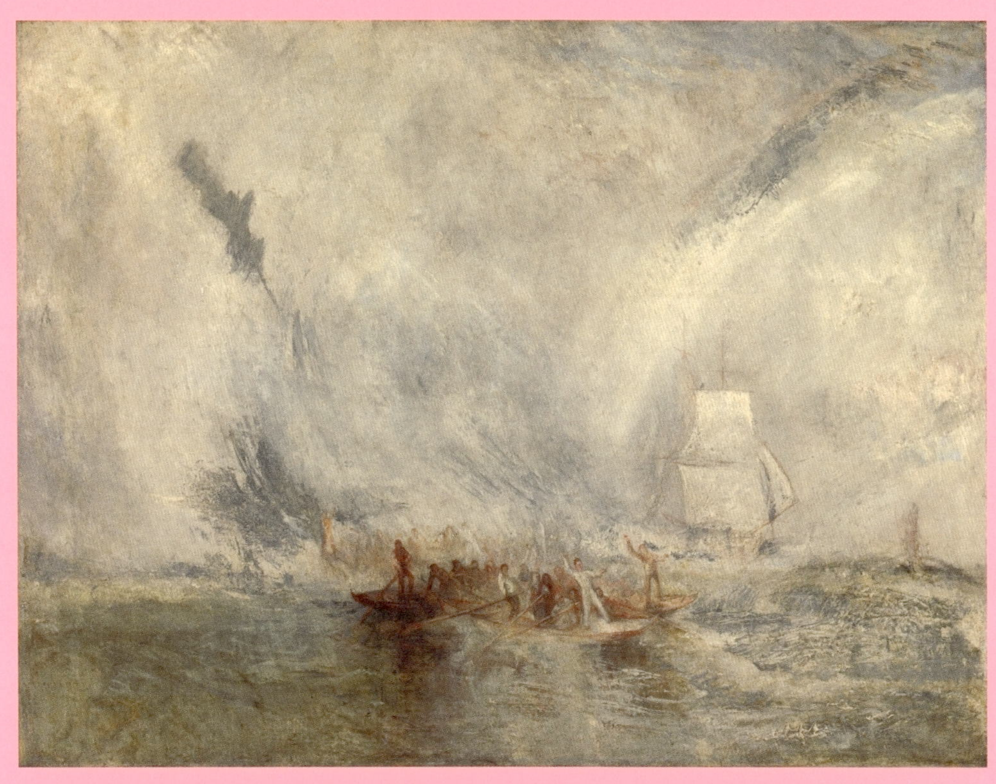

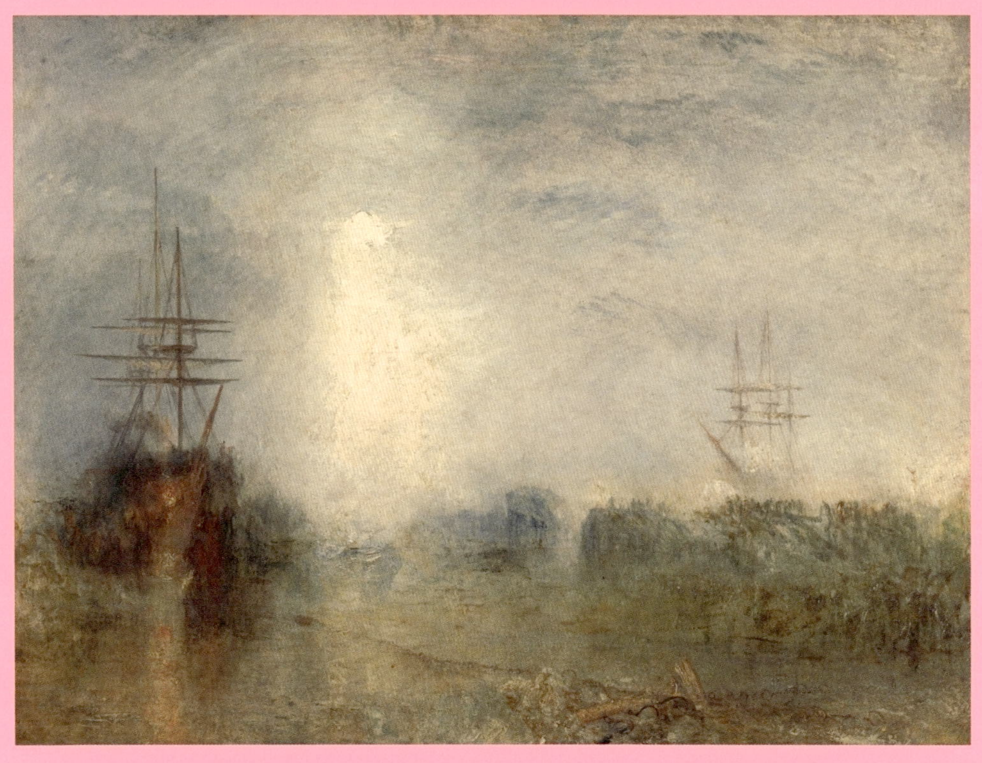

155 *Whalers* exh. 1845. Oil paint on canvas, 91.1 × 121.9, Tate
156 *Whalers (Boiling Blubber) Entangled in Flaw Ice, Endeavouring to Extricate Themselves* exh. 1846. Oil paint on canvas, 89.9 × 120, Tate

Pomp and Circumstance

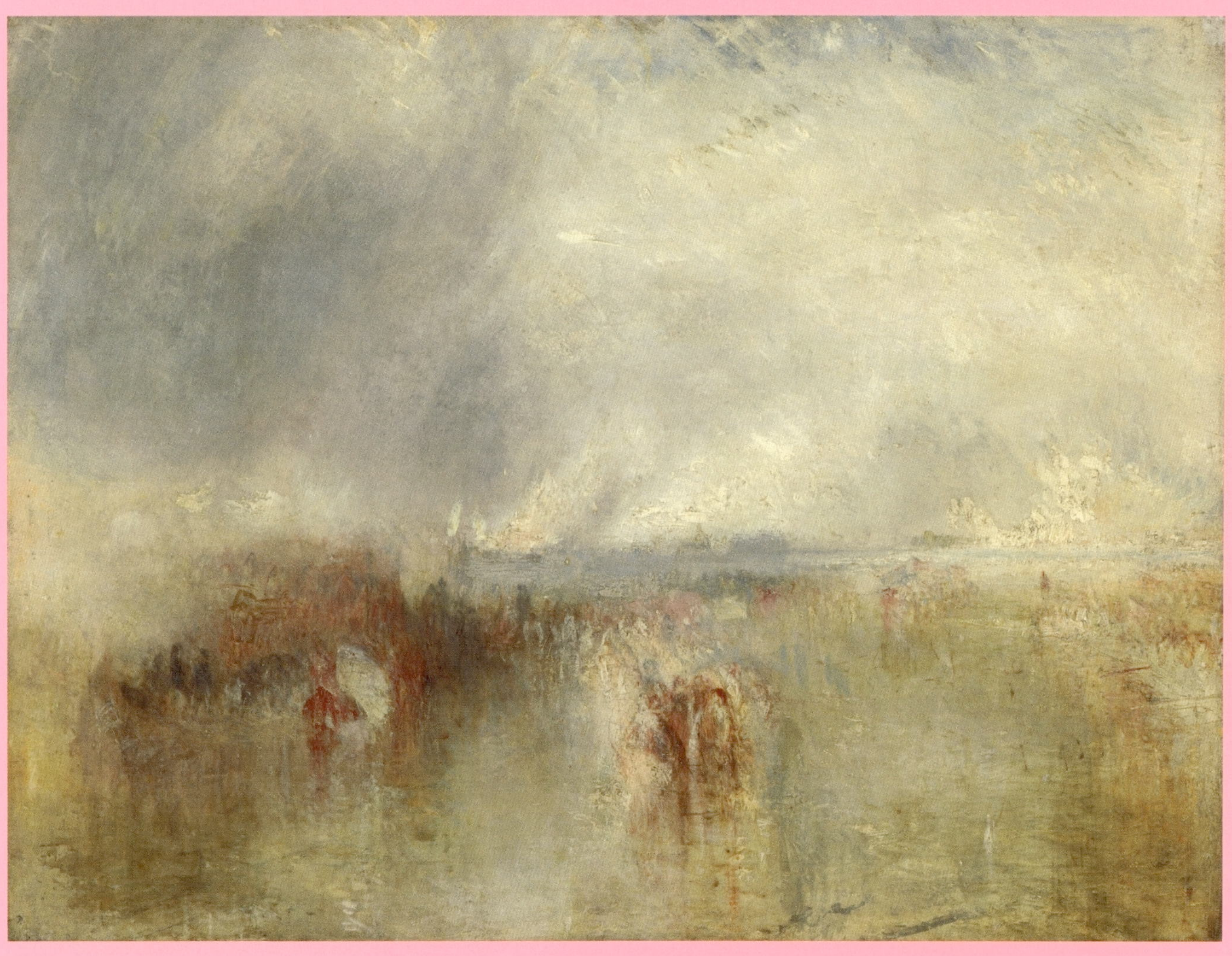

 157 *The Arrival of Louis-Philippe at the Royal Clarence Yard, Gosport, 8 October 1844* c.1844–5. Oil paint on canvas, 90.2 × 120.6, Tate

Turner's response to contemporary royal events did not result in numerous works, but they show that he felt the monarchy provided some potential for possible subjects. His major painting *England: Richmond Hill on the Prince Regents' Birthday* (no.84) captures something of the centrality of the monarchy to public life. In August 1822 he travelled north to record the visit of George IV, as he now was, to Edinburgh. Turner's sketchbook record of the occasion suggests that he planned a series of related works, perhaps hoping for royal favour. The project was abandoned, probably for commercial reasons. Nevertheless, the Turner Bequest includes four oil paintings on mahogany, none of which were completed, two showing the king variously at St Giles's Cathedral and attending a banquet at the Parliament House (no.104), and two depicting the *Royal George* state barge.

Two decades later, Turner travelled to Gosport on 8 October 1844 to witness the arrival of the French king Louis Philippe on the *Gomer*.[158] As well as extending his interest in royal events, and perhaps again hoping for royal patronage, there was a personal association. Turner had known the king in the 1810s when he was in exile and living at Twickenham. In 1836 he sent Turner a medal and received in return a set of prints (probably proof engravings of *The Rivers of France*).[159] Turner was also presented with a jewelled snuffbox, perhaps in 1838. And in September 1845 he was requested to dine with the king at his chateau at Eu (no.164). As this was around the time Queen Victoria was due to visit, it seems possible the king was hoping to engineer a rapprochement with an artist she is said to have regarded as 'mad'.[160]

Queen Victoria's invitation to Louis Philippe was designed to improve relations between France and England and among other tokens of this new entente she invested him as a Knight of the Order of the Garter at Windsor Castle. Turner's pencil sketches of the king's arrival indicate that he viewed it from a boat. He also developed some eleven watercolour studies (for example no.158) and a pen and ink sketch, which show ships decorated with flags and a multitude of small boats surrounding them. This sense of atmosphere, with eager crowds witnessing the ceremonial proceedings, is what his two oil paintings of the event also depict (nos.157, 159). However, these were left unfinished and their subjects were only recently identified. The uncompromising style Turner was using in the mid-1840s usually baffled his critics, and even if he had completed these paintings, this depiction of Louis Philippe's arrival would almost certainly have been ridiculed in the press.

Turner's concentration on the crowd surrounding the *Gomer*, not only recapitulates his interest in the pageantry surrounding George IV's barge (no.103) in 1822 but may also have been intended to contrast with the boat-borne spectators surrounding Napoleon on the *Bellerophon* in 1815, a subject Turner had illustrated in a vignette for Walter Scott's *Life of Napoleon* in the early 1830s (no.64). Together, these representations of national leaders and the crowds surrounding them speak of the celebrity surrounding heads of state, whether monarchs in their prime or notorious enemies in their decline. SS

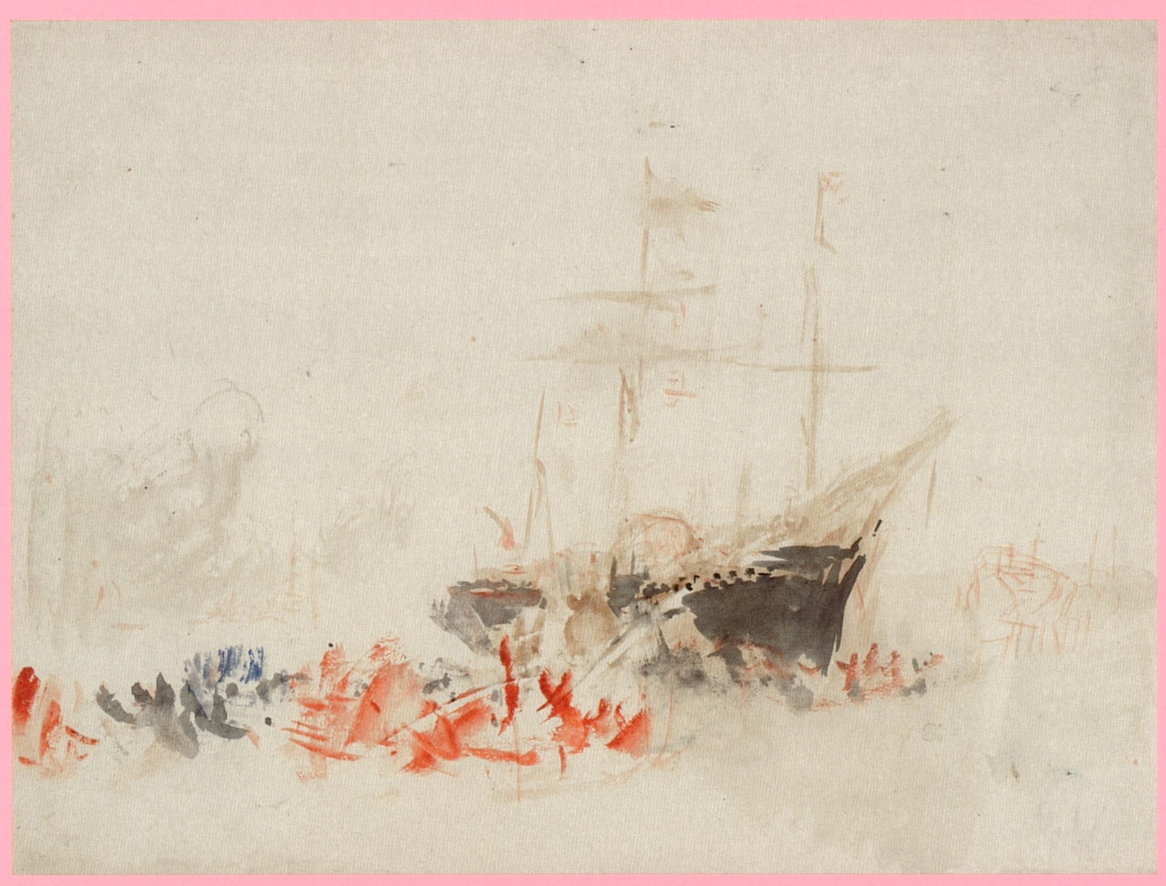

 158 *The Arrival of Louis-Philippe: The 'Gomer' in Portsmouth Harbour* 1844. Watercolour on paper, 23.7 × 31.8, Tate

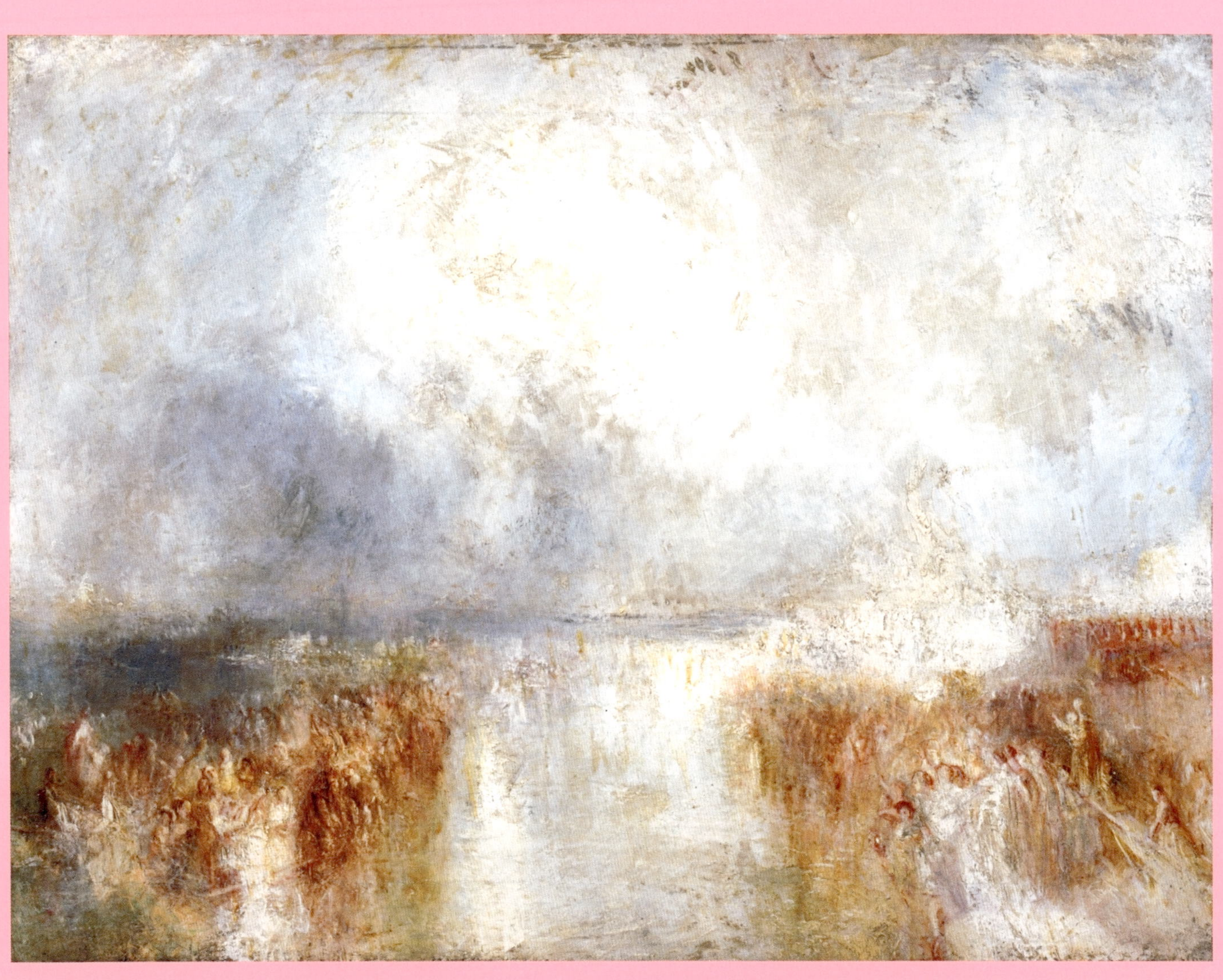

159 *The Disembarkation of Louis-Philippe at the Royal Clarence Yard, Gosport, 8 October 1844* c.1844–5. Oil paint on canvas, 90.8 × 121.3, Tate

Retrospects: Peace and War

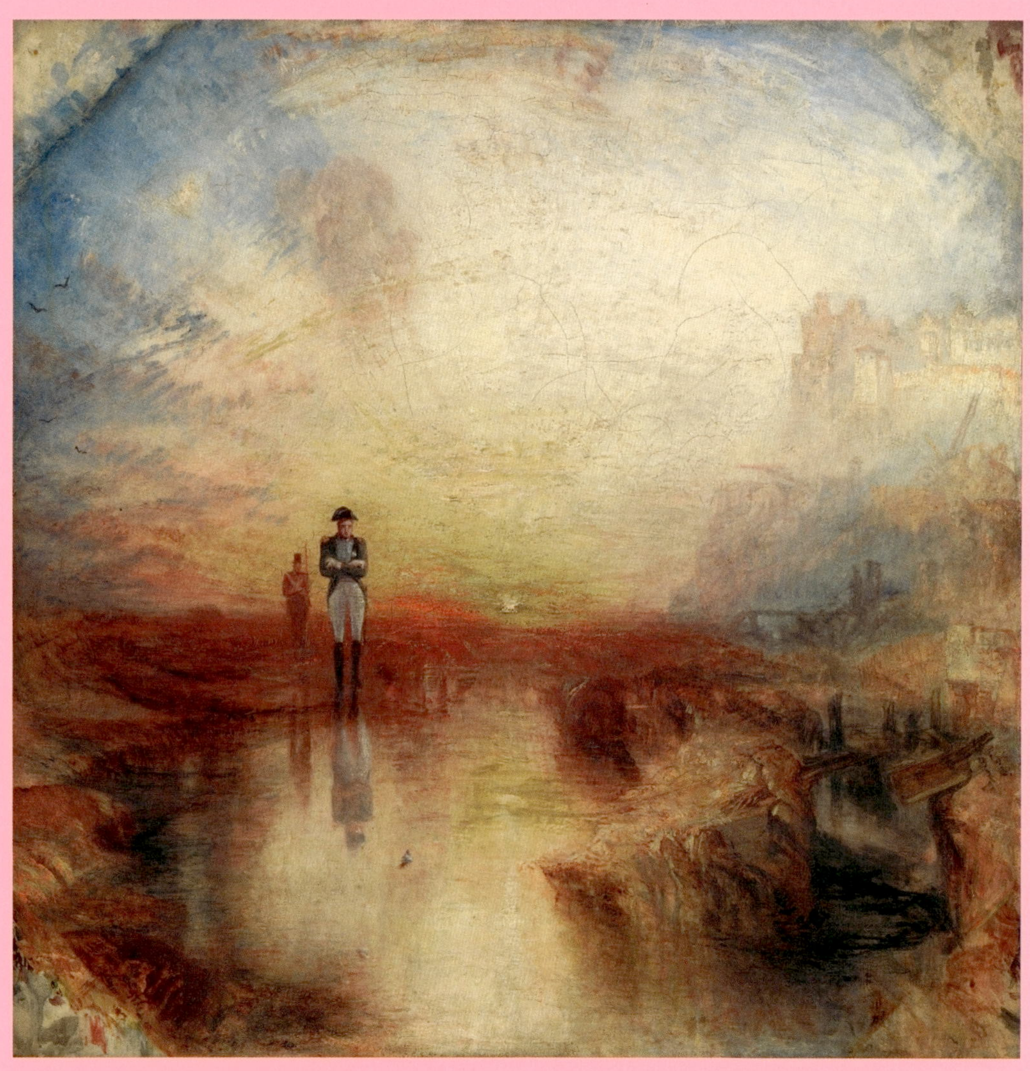

 160 *War. The Exile and the Rock Limpet* exh. 1842. Oil paint on canvas, 79.4 × 79.4, Tate

In the early 1840s Turner experimented with paired paintings,
framed as squares, tondos or octagons. Although not always exhibited
side by side, they were intended to work together in a dialogue of
theme and presentation. *Peace – Burial at Sea* (no.162) depicts
the burial of Turner's colleague, Sir David Wilkie, who had died
of typhoid on his return from the Holy Land in 1841. Fearful of a
typhoid outbreak, the Governor of Gibraltar refused permission
to allow the body ashore and Wilkie was buried at sea, although
Turner has placed a funeral carriage on deck to stand for the public
interment and associated ceremony that never was. Quizzed about
the unnaturally black sails, he replied that he wished he could make
them blacker, revealing how he was personally affected by Wilkie's
premature death. The line Turner attached to the catalogue, 'Merit's
corse [corpse] was yielded to the tide', indicates his feelings not just
for Wilkie, but more generally about the beneficial contribution of
the arts to modern society.

The painting paired with it was *War. The Exile and the Rock Limpet.*
Watched over by a British sentry, Napoleon stands in his island exile
on St Helena, meditating on his fall from power where even a lowly
sea creature has more self-determination than a former emperor.
The bathos of his predicament as Turner depicts it may have been
intended as an emphatic riposte to the glorification of Napoleon seen
in his state funeral and the transfer of his remains to Les Invalides
in December 1840. The lurid sky and, on the right, a sluice gate in the
shape of a butcher's cleaver evoke carnage and bloodshed, the deaths
of thousands being the price of Napoleon's overweening ambition.

Turner's compositions on the subject of Napoleon and his various
campaigns, painted from the 1810s, comprise twenty watercolours
exploring the social and economic impact of the Napoleonic wars
on England, two finished oils of Trafalgar, an oil, a watercolour
and three engravings of Waterloo, and at least a dozen other oils,
watercolours or engravings of other battles and their aftermath,
a dozen images exploring Napoleon's biography and further
compositions contrasting the peace of contemporary Europe with the
ravages of the Napoleonic wars (nos.163, 165–6). Painting Napoleon's
final appearance on the world stage was a natural extension of this
interest. It is possible, indeed, that Turner had originally intended to
paint the ship that brought Napoleon's remains back from St Helena,
La Belle Poule, but then repurposed it for Wilkie's ship *Oriental* when
he heard of his colleague's death. If so, this involved a change from
sail to steam.

Turner's last painting alluding to Napoleon, *The Opening of the Wallhalla, 1842* (no.81), was shown with verse celebrating the restoration of the arts and learning to Germany after the war. Emblems of these and of the *Freiheitskrieg* (liberation war) occupy the foreground of a picture that condenses in one image what *Peace* and *War* represent as a pair. Similarly, in one of Turner's finest late watercolours, *Oberwesel* (no.161), contented families, children and fruitful vineyards crowd the banks of the Rhine, plied by a modern steamboat at the point where the Prussian general Blücher crossed on his way to join Wellington at Waterloo. SS

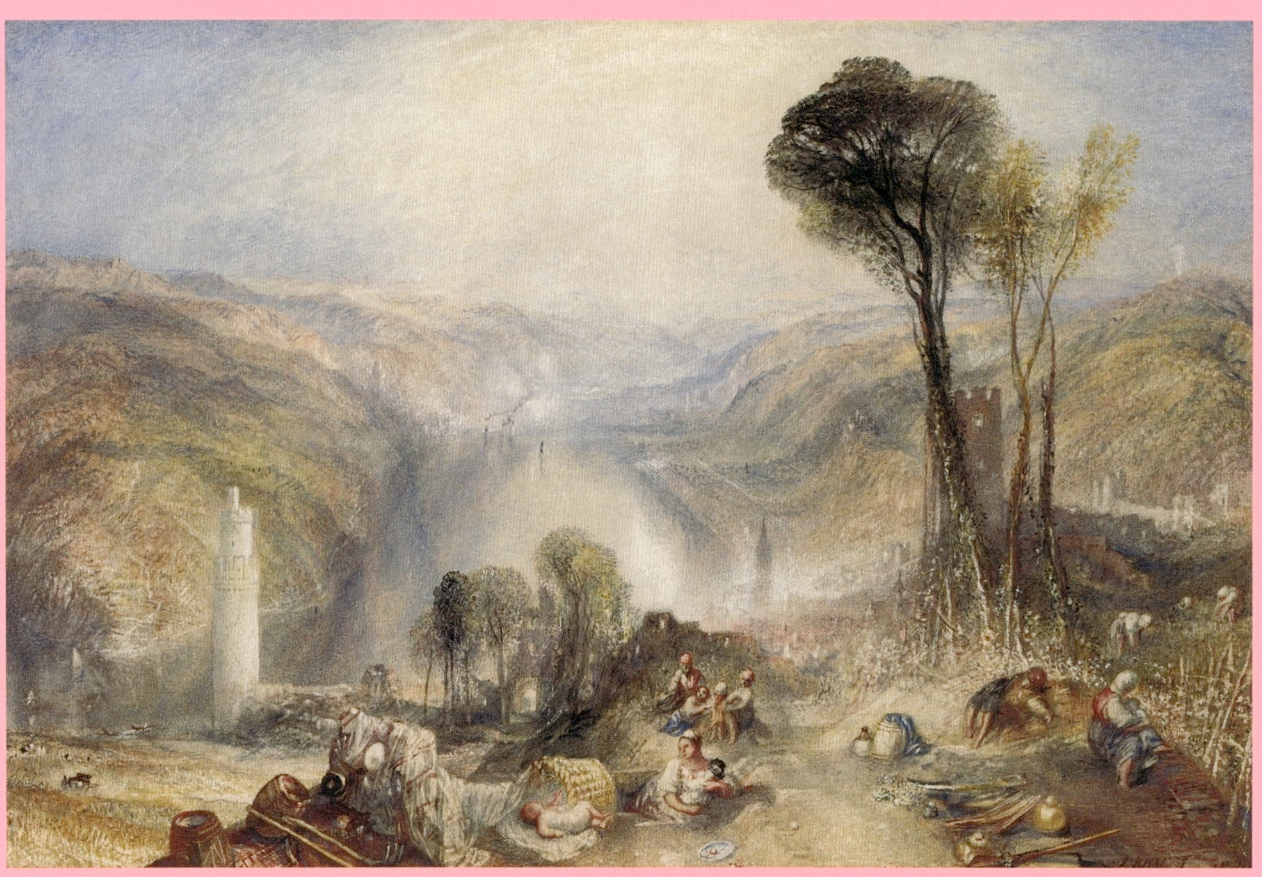

    161 *Oberwesel* 1840. Watercolour, gouache and graphite on paper, 35.4 × 53.3, National Gallery of Art, Washington, DC

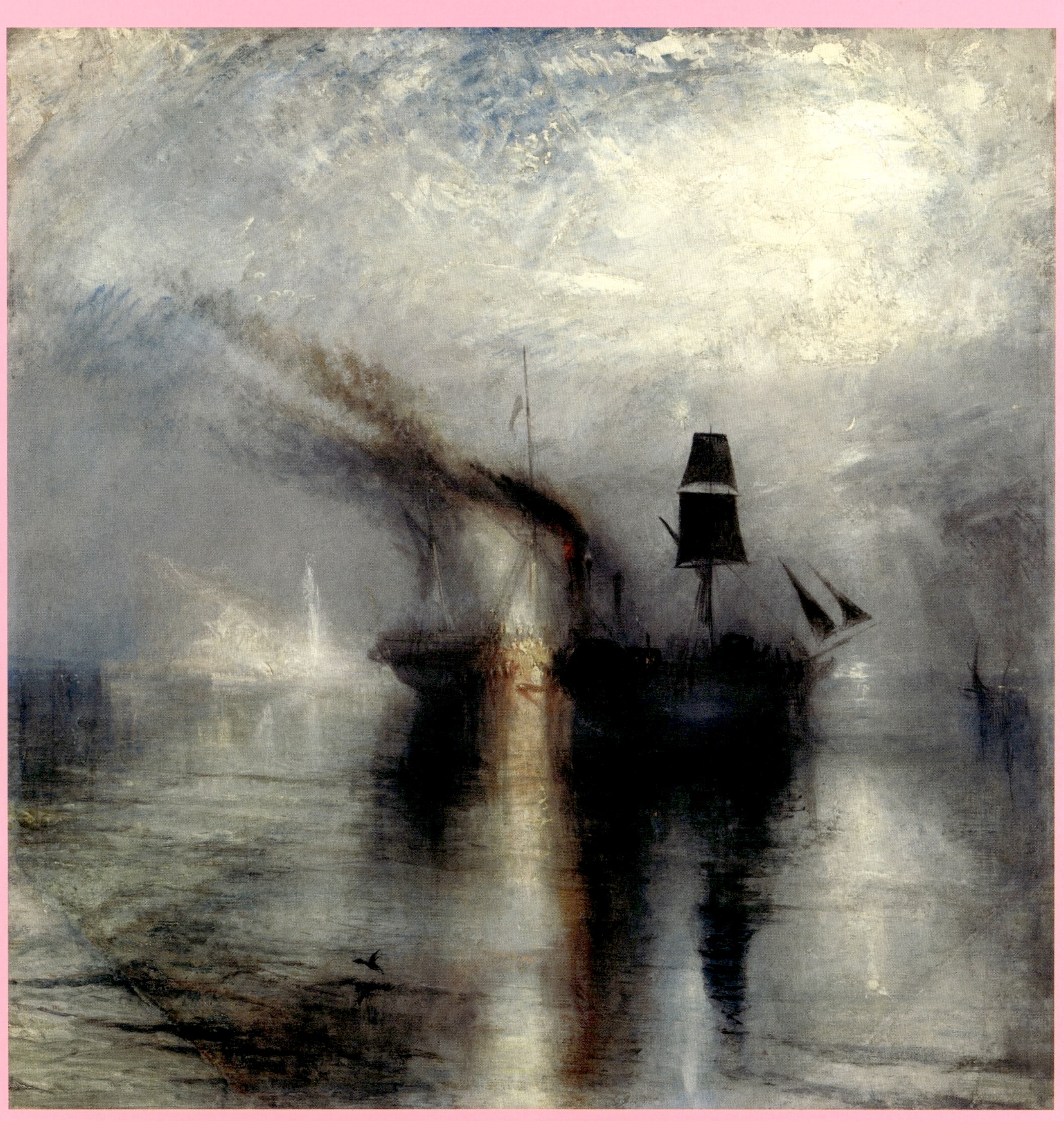

162 *Peace – Burial at Sea* exh. 1842. Oil paint on canvas, 87 × 86.7, Tate

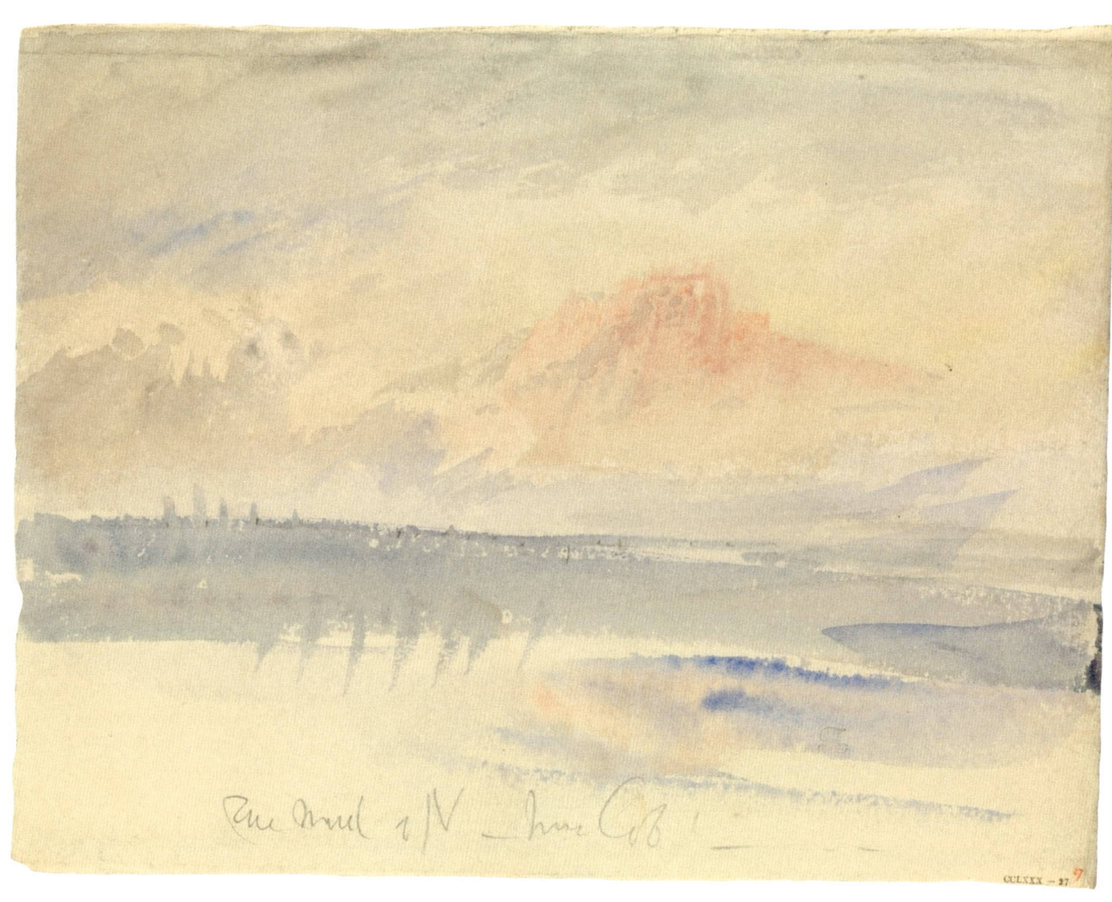

163 *Ehrenbreitstein: 'The March of N from Cob[lenz]'* c.1841–2. Graphite and watercolour on paper, 22 × 29.2, Tate

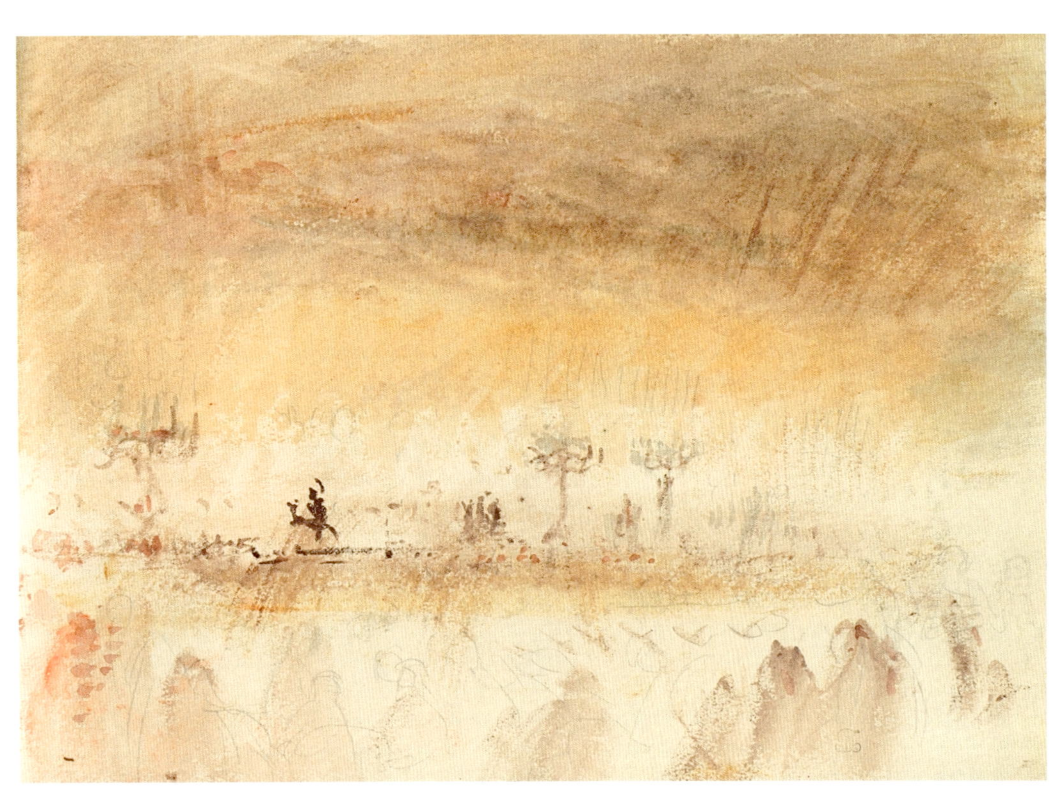

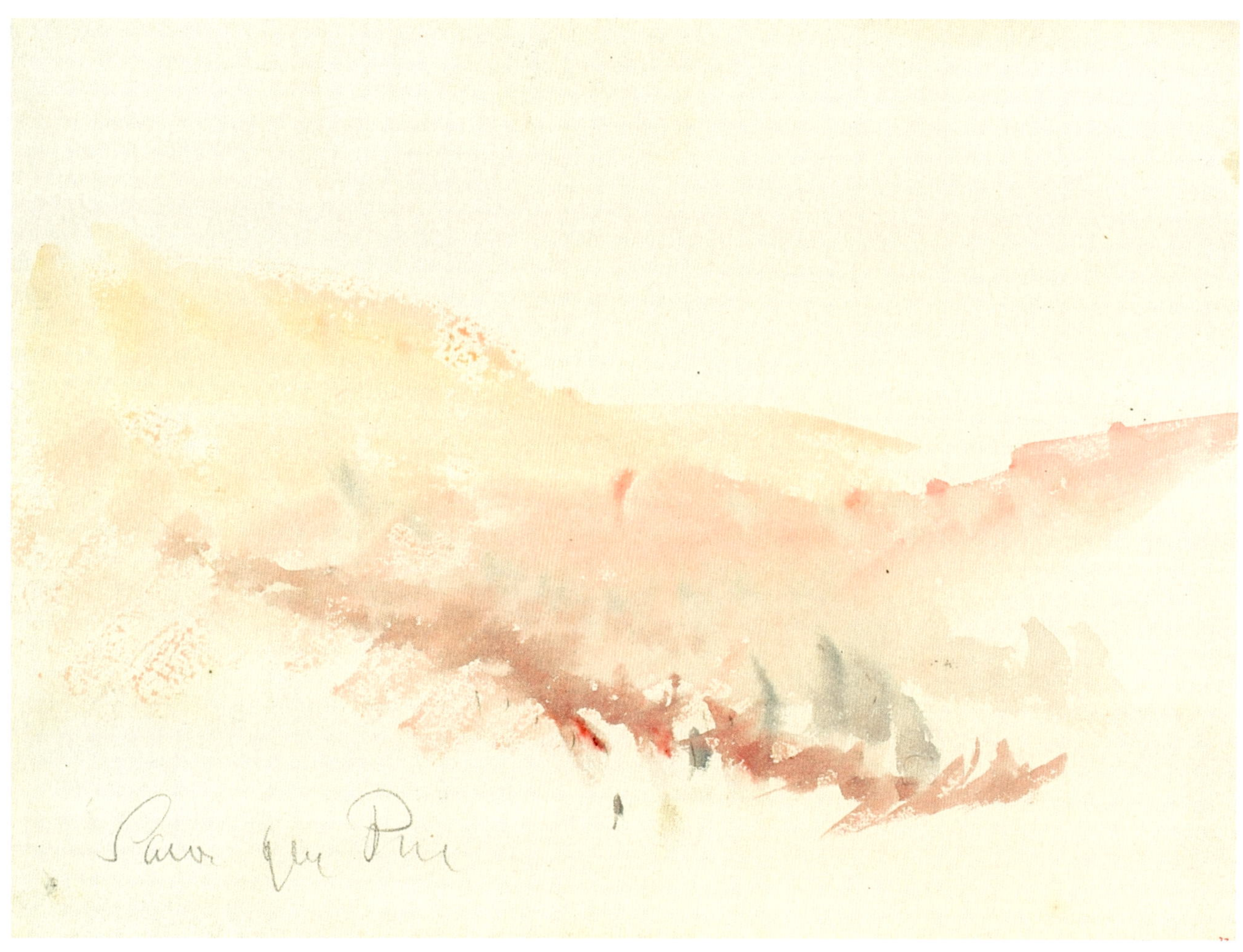

165 *'Sauve Qui Peut': Column of Red Figures, Some on Horseback* c.1841–2. Watercolour on paper, 21.6 × 29, Tate

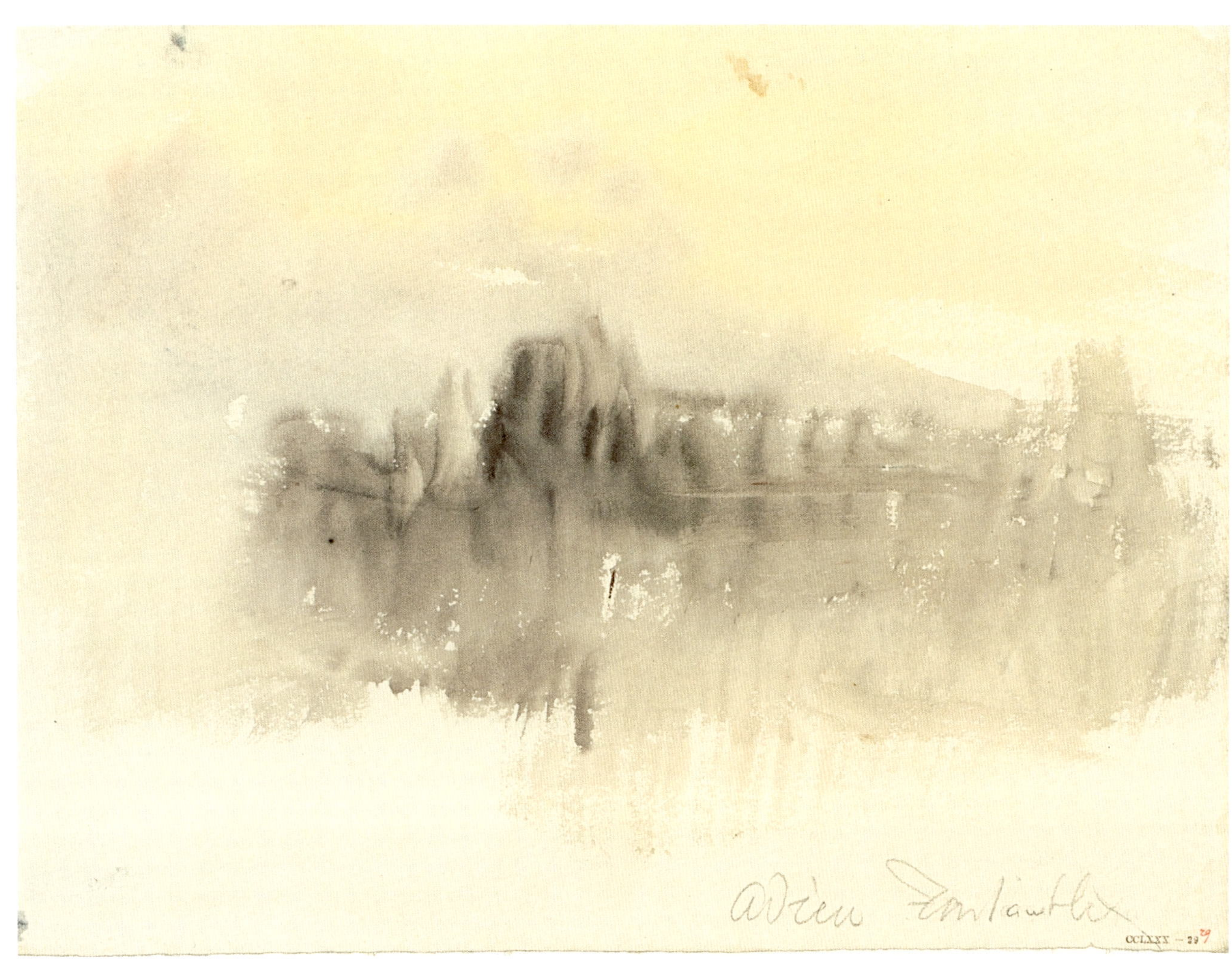

166 *Adieu Fontainebleau* c.1841–2. Graphite and watercolour on paper, 22.1 × 29.2, Tate

Notes

1   *Fraser's Magazine*, June 1844, p.713.
2   John Stuart Mill, 'The Spirit of the Age, No.1', *Examiner*, 9 January 1831, p.20.
3   Test and Corporation Acts repealed, 1828; Roman Catholic Relief Act, 1829; Great Reform Act, 1832; Factory Acts, 1819, 1833, 1844; Slave Trade Act, 1807; Slavery Abolition Act, 1833.
4   Poor Law Amendment Act, 1834; Corn Laws repealed, 1846; Navigation Acts repealed, 1849.
5   William Hazlitt, 'Mr. Coleridge', in E.D. Mackerness (ed.), *The Spirit of the Age*, London and Glasgow 1969, p.54.
6   Mill 1831, p.20; Thomas Carlyle, Article VII, *Edinburgh Review*, vol.49, June 1829, pp.439–59.
7   Constable to Maria Bicknell, June 1813, in R.B. Beckett (ed.), *John Constable's Correspondence*, 6 vols, Ipswich 1962–8, vol.2, 1964, p.110.
8   John Ruskin, *Modern Painters*, vol.1, in E.T. Cook and Alexander Wedderburn (eds.), *The Works of John Ruskin*, 39 vols, London 1903–12, vol.3, p.231.
9   Indigo Jones, 'Letters on Art, no.1', *Worcestershire Chronicle*, 4 September 1850.
10 Cook and Wedderburn 1903–12, vol.7, p.386.
11 Cook and Wedderburn 1903–12, vol.12, p.389.
12 Diary, 5 July 1856, in Ford Madox Hueffer, *Ford Madox Brown*, 1896, pp.127–8.
13 Bernard Richards, review of the BBC 2 programme *The Genius of Turner: Painting the Industrial Revolution* in *Turner Society News*, no.120 (Autumn 2013), p.23.
14 Sam Smiles, 'Turner and the slave trade: speculation and representation, 1805–1840', *British Art Journal*, vol.7, no.3 (Winter 2007–8), pp.47–54.
15 Mackerness 1969, p.139.
16 George Jones, 'Recollections of J.M.W. Turner', in John Gage (ed.), *Collected Correspondence of J.M.W. Turner*, Oxford 1980, p.9.
17 John Landseer in Luke Herrmann, 'John Landseer on Turner: Reviews of Exhibitions in 1808, 1839 and 1840', *Turner Studies*, vol.7, no.1 (Summer 1987), pp.26–33.
18 *London Packet*, 29 April–1 May 1799.
19 *Monthly Magazine*, 1 June 1806.
20 *Repository of Art*, 1 June 1818.
21 *Annals of the Fine Arts*, 1818.
22 *Literary Gazette*, 9 May 1835.
23 *Morning Chronicle*, 7 May 1839.
24 *Spectator*, 11 May 1839.
25 *Art Union*, 15 May 1839.
26 R.C. Leslie to Ruskin, 15 June 1884, in Cook and Wedderburn 1903–12, vol.35, p.576.
27 Ralph Waldo Emerson, *English Traits*, 1857, pp.47–8.
28 Mary Somerville, *Physical Geography*, Philadelphia 1848, p.374.
29 Constable to his brother, George, 12 May 1836, in Beckett 1962–8, vol.5: *Various Friends, with Charles Boner and the Artist's Children*, Ipswich 1967, pp. 32–3.
30 *The Times*, 8 May 1844.
31 *Literary Gazette*, 11 May 1839.
32 *Examiner*, 17 October 1834, p.659.
33 Turner in Andrew Wilton and Rosalind Mallord Turner, *Painting and Poetry: Turner's 'Verse Book' and his Work of 1802–1812*, exh. cat., Tate Gallery, London 1990, p.99.
34 Mackerness 1969, pp.138–9.
35 John Ruskin, *Modern Painters*, in Cook and Wedderburn 1903–12, vol.7, pp.385–6.
36 Walter Scott (ed.), *The Poetical Works of Anna Seward, with Extracts from her Literary Correspondence*, Edinburgh 1810, vol.2, p.218.
37 *The Times*, 23 July 1795.
38 Eric Shanes, 'Britain at Peace and War; J.M.W. Turner's Four "State of the Nation" Surveys, 1793–1836', in *Windows on that World: Essays on British Art Presented to Brian Allen*, London 2012, pp.212–17.
39 David Hill, *Turner in the North*, London and New Haven 1996, p.16, suggests these depict Walker's foundry in Conisborough, while John Gage, *J.M.W. Turner: 'A Wonderful Range of Mind'*, New Haven and London 1987, p.229, supposes that *The Interior of a Cannon Foundry* (no.13) may relate to drawings of the Cyfarthfa ironworks commissioned by Anthony Bacon.
40 Hill 1996, p.16.
41 https://www.tate.org.uk/art/artworks/turner-the-interior-of-a-tilt-forge-d01735, accessed 22 April 2020.
42 A.J. Finberg, The *Life of J.M.W. Turner*, Oxford 1939, p.20.
43 Finberg 1939, p.21.
44 *Reminiscences of Henry Angelo*, London 1830, vol.I, p.94.
45 F.H.W. Sheppard (ed.), 'The Pantheon', *Survey of London: Volumes 31 and 32, St James Westminster, Part 2*, London 1963, pp.268–83: *British History Online*, http://www.british-history.ac.uk/survey-london/vols31-2/pt2/pp268-283, accessed 12 May 2020.
46 Judith Milhous, Gabriella Dideriksen and Robert D. Hume, *Italian Opera in Late Eighteenth-Century London, vol.II: The Pantheon Opera and its Aftermath 1789–1795*, Oxford 2001, pp.133–4; Curtis Price, 'Turner at the Pantheon Opera House, 1791–2', *Turner Studies*, vol.7, no.2 (Winter 1987), p.7.
47 http://blackcountryhistory.org/collections/getrecord/WAGMU_W102/, accessed 22 April 2020.
48 Anon., 'Mr. Robert Ker Porter', in *Public Characters of 1800–1801*, Dublin 1801, p.140.

49 John Landseer, *Review of Publications of Art*, 1808, pp.83–5.

50 Jan Piggott, 'The Symbolism of Turner's Rockets in *The Field of Waterloo*', *Turner Society News*, no.125 (Spring 2016), pp.12–13.

51 Francisco de Goya, *Disasters of War (Los desastres de la guerra)*, 1810–20 (published 1863).

52 Cecilia Powell, '*The Field of Waterloo*: Turner's *Guernica*', *Turner Society News*, no.123 (Spring 2015), pp.16–18.

53 John Landseer in Herrmann 1987, p.32.

54 Byron to Hobhouse, 22 April 1820, in Leslie A. Marchand (ed.), *Byron's Letters and Journals, Volume VII: 'Between two worlds', 1820*, p.81.

55 Jan Piggott, *Turner's Vignettes*, exh. cat., Tate Gallery, London 1993, p.59.

56 Cook and Wedderburn 1903–12, vol.34, p.341.

57 Sam Smiles, '*The Fall of Anarchy*: Politics and Anatomy in an Enigmatic Painting by J.M.W. Turner', in *Tate Papers*, no.25, Spring 2016: https://www.tate.org.uk/research/publications/tate-papers/25/fall-of-anarchy-politics-anatomy-turner, accessed 2 September 2020.

58 *Morning Post*, 1844.

59 John Gage, *Rain, Steam and Speed*, London 1972; David Blayney Brown, 'Rule, Britannia? Patriotism, Progress and the Picturesque in Turner's Britain', in Michael Lloyd (ed.), *Turner*, exh. cat., National Gallery of Australia, Canberra 1996, pp.49–50.

60 Cecilia Powell, 'Shipwreck and Scandal: Turner and the *Amphitrite*', *Turner Society News*, no.128 (Autumn 2017), pp.5–8.

61 Alaric Watts, *The Literary Souvenir*, London 1831, pp.219–21.

62 Yale Center for British Art, New Haven, Connecticut.

63 In William Combe's satire of 'picturesque' connoisseurship *The Tour of Doctor Syntax Through London* (1820), the painting inspires the protagonist's wife to visit Richmond Hill and admire the view depicted by Turner (p.152).

64 Shanes 2012, pp.211–30.

65 His actual birthday was on 12 August, outside of the London season.

66 The painting was exhibited with lines from the 'Summer' section of James Thomson's poem *The Seasons* (1727), a celebration of the English landscape.

67 The guns were of the sort fired at the garden party given by the Dowager Countess of Cardigan in 1817 that the picture was based on: Jean Golt, 'Beauty and Meaning on Richmond Hill: New Light on Turner's Masterpiece of 1819', *Turner Studies*, vol. 7, no. 2 (Winter 1987), pp.9–20.

68 Shanes 2012, p.225; Anthony Bailey, *Standing in the Sun: A Life of J.M.W. Turner*, London 2013, p.2.

69 See Gerald Finley, *Turner and George IV in Edinburgh 1822*, London and Edinburgh 1981.

70 Bailey 2013, p.174.

71 The paintings were possibly planned in conjunction with a series of engravings and abandoned when discussion with publishers foundered. See Finley 1981, pp.45, 49.

72 Finley 1981, p.13

73 See Turner's 1795 sketch of the building (Tate inv. no. D02356) and c.1799 colour study (Tate inv. no. D02357).

74 The soldiers' outmoded headwear (the 'cocked hat' worn in the watercolour was replaced by the 'shako' at the start of the nineteenth century) suggests that Turner was not working from direct observation. My thanks to Tony Field and colleagues at the Rifles (Berkshire and Wiltshire) Museum for their assistance on this point.

75 Opponents of the bill calculated that every horse employed in husbandry would cost an additional 12 shillings a year as a result. Sam Smiles, *The Turner Book*, London and New York 2006, p.67

76 Christina Payne, *Toil and Plenty: Images of the Agricultural Landscape in England, 1780–1890*, exh. cat., Nottingham University Art Gallery 1993, pp.88–9.

77 See Shanes 2012, pp.219–23.

78 The word Slough may itself have triggered associations with the 'Slough of despond' in John Bunyan's *Pilgrim's Progress*. See Shanes 2012, p.219.

79 George III converted large portions of the royal parks at Richmond and Windsor into farms on which the latest agricultural methods were employed. See Michelle L. Miller, 'J.M.W. Turner's *Ploughing Up Turnips, Near Slough*: The Cultivation of Cultural Dissent', *The Art Bulletin*, vol.77, no.4 (December 1995), p.575.

80 Shanes 2012, p.219. This was also partly the result of a long-standing tradition linking the vegetable with the Hanoverian kings: Miller 1995, p.577.

81 John Barrell, *The Dark Side of the Landscape: The Rural Poor in English Painting, 1730–1840*, Cambridge (1980) 2009, p.153.

82 Richard Johns, 'From the Nore: Turner at the Mouth of the Thames' in Satish Padiyar, Philip Shaw and Philippa Simpson (eds.), *Visual Culture and the Revolutionary and Napoleonic Wars*, London 2016, p.91.

83 Turner to Sir John Fleming Leicester, 12 December 1810. See Gage 1980, p.44.

84 Seventy-four Martello towers were built along the coast between 1796 and 1812, in addition to towers built more sparingly elsewhere in Great Britain.

85 Gillian Forrester, *Turner's 'Drawing Book': The Liber Studiorum*, London 1996, p.93.

86 The text is transcribed in full in Wilton and Turner 1990, pp.170–76.

87 Gage 1980, p.55n.

88 See Gage 1987, pp.195–7.

89 James Purdon, 'Grand union – how canals have captivated British artists for centuries', *Apollo*, 21 March 2020: https://www.apollo-magazine.com/canals-british-art/, accessed 22 April 2020.

90 The print is derived from Turner's painting *Grand Junction Canal at Southall Mill* (exh. 1810).

91 David Hill, *Turner and Leeds: Image of Industry*, Huddersfield 2008, p.179.

92 By 1830 some thirty stagecoaches and forty mail coaches passed through the town every day on the Great North Road. See Eric Shanes, *Turner's England, 1810–38*, London 1990a, p.194.

93 Eric Shanes, *Turner's Human Landscape*, London 1990b, p.112.

94 Shanes 1990a, p.226.

95 An engraving of the picture that Turner included in his *Liber Studiorum* series of prints was classed as an 'Architectural' subject, confirming the hospital buildings as the focus of the composition.

96 Turner exhibited paintings with accompanying verses on forty-six occasions between 1800 and 1850. Shanes 1990b, p.72.

97 Gage 1987, p.188.

98 Eric Shanes, 'Turner's "Unknown" London Series', *Turner Studies*, vol. 1, no. 2 (Winter 1981), pp.36–42.

99 John Bonehill and Stephen Daniels, 'Projecting London: Turner and Greenwich', *Oxford Art Journal*, vol.35, no.2 (2012), pp.171–194.

100 William Cobbett, *Rural Rides*, vol.1, London 1912, p.237.

101 Tate inv. no. T05260.

102 John Ruskin, *Notes by Mr. Ruskin*, London 1878, p.38.

103 See Elizabeth K. Helsinger, *Rural Scenes and National Representation: Britain, 1815–1850*, Princeton, MJ, 1997, p.32.

104 For a further discussion of Turner's working staffage, see Sam Smiles, *Eye Witness: Artists and Visual Documentation in Britain 1770–1830*, Aldershot and Brookfield, VT, 2000, pp.169–77.

105 See Stephen Daniels 'The Implications of Industry: Turner and Leeds', *Turner Studies*, vol.6, no.1 (Summer 1983), pp.10–17.

106 See Eric Shanes, *Young Mr. Turner*, New Haven and London 2016, p.198.

107 See Eric Shanes, *Turner's England, 1810–38*, London 1990, pp.138–9.

108 See Smiles 2016.

109 See Shanes 1990, pp.198–9.

110 For an extensive discussion see Stephen Daniels, 'Reforming Landscape: Turner and Nottingham', in P. de Bolla et al. (eds.), *Land, Nation and Culture, 1740–1840: Thinking the Republic of Taste*, Basingstoke 2005, pp.12–36.

111 Cecilia Powell, 'Turner's Women: The Painted Veil', *Turner Society News*, no.63 (March 1993), pp.12–15.

112 *Chronicles of the Sea or, Faithful narratives of shipwrecks, fires, famines and disasters*, no.14, 24 March 1838, pp.105–6.

113 Originally established in 1823 as the Society for the Mitigation and Gradual Abolition of Slavery, it became the Anti-Slavery Society in 1827; see Gelien Matthews, *Caribbean Slave Revolts and the British Abolitionist Movement*, Baton Rouge 2006.

114 See John McCoubrey, 'Turner's Slave Ship: Abolition, Ruskin, and Reception', *Word and Image*, vol.4, no.4, Oct.–Dec. 1998, pp.319–53.

115 One slave managed to climb back on board undetected, the remaining 132 drowned. The ship's underwriters disputed the claim and the ensuing court case in 1783 brought the incident to public attention. See Ian Baucom, *Specters of the Atlantic: Finance Capital, Slavery, and the Philosophy of History*, Durham 2005, and F.O. Shyllon, *Black Slaves in Britain*, London 1974, pp.184–209.

116 See Sam Smiles, 'Turner and the slave trade: speculation and representation, 1805–1840', *British Art Journal*, vol.7, no.3 (Winter 2007–8), pp.47–54.

117 'Steam to India', *Tait's Edinburgh Magazine*, May 1839, p.293.

118 Mary Somerville, *Physical Geography*, Philadelphia 1848, p.374.

119 *Mechanics' Magazine*, vol.1, no.3 (March 1833), p.118–19.

120 Mrs [Barbara] Hofland, *River Scenery, by Turner and Girtin, with Descriptions by Mrs. Hofland. Engraved by Eminent Engravers, from Drawings by J.M.W. Turner, R.A. and the Late Thomas Girtin*, London 1827, p.4.

121 *Gentleman's Magazine*, vol.97, part 1 (March 1827), p.528. The reviewer makes the suggestion that a row of Lombardy poplars and fir would conceal the works.

122 *Blackwood's Magazine*, April 1830, quoted in William S. Rodner, *J.M.W. Turner: Romantic Painter of the Industrial Revolution*, Berkeley and London 1997, p.124.

123 George Head, *A Home Tour in the Manufacturing Districts of England in the Summer of 1835*, London 1835, p.344, quoted in Rodner 1997, p.100.

124 Quoted in Martin Butlin and Evelyn Joll, *The Paintings of J.M.W. Turner*, rev. edn, New Haven and London 1984, no.277, p.230.

125 The publication bears a printed date of 1834 but was issued in the autumn of 1833 in time for the Christmas trade: *Tate Gallery: Illustrated Catalogue of Acquisitions 1986–88*, London 1996.

126 Quoted in Rodner 1997, p.30.

127 'Thomas Campbell's Poetical Works', in *Quarterly Review* 57, Dec. 1836, pp.360–1; *Arnold's Magazine of the Fine Arts and Journal of Literature and Science*, London and

Edinburgh 1834, vol.3, p.269.

128 Francis Greenacre, 'James Baker Pyne (1800–1870)', in *Oxford Dictionary of National Biography*, online edition, Oxford 2012: http://www.oxforddnb.com/view/article/22931, accessed 31 December 2019; quoted in Diana Villar, *John Wilson Carmichael 1799–1868*, Portsmouth 1995, p.67.

129 See reviews and John Ruskin quoted in Butlin and Joll 1984, vol.1, p.257.

130 Butlin and Joll 1984, vol.1, pp.199, 207.

131 *Athenaeum*, 14 May 1842.

132 Quoted in Stephen Daniels, 'Images of the railway in nineteenth century paintings and prints', in *Trainspotting – Images of the Railway in British Art*, exh. cat., Nottingham Castle Museum, 1985, p.12.

133 That Turner may have had this phrase in mind was first suggested by his contemporary, George Leslie. See Butlin and Joll 1984, vol.1, p.256; *Blackwood's Edinburgh Magazine*, vol.23 (1828), p.93.

134 *Blackwood's Edinburgh Magazine*, vol.23 (1828), p.92.

135 Théophile Gautier, *Histoire de Romantisme*, Paris 1877, quoted in John Gage, *Turner: Rain, Steam and Speed*, London 1972, p.33.

136 The incident was described by William Day in a letter written in the 1890s to the painting's then owner James Orrock. See https://media.clarkart.edu/1955.37_EuroCat.pdf, accessed 22 December 2019.

137 John Ruskin, *The Harbours of England*, 1856, in Cook and Wedderburn 1903–12, vol.13, p.26.

138 Inigo Thomas, 'The Chase ... Turner's "Rain, Steam and Speed"', *London Review of Books*, vol.38, no.20 (20 October 2016), pp.15–18.

139 See John Gage, *Turner: Rain, Steam and Speed*, Oxford 1972, p.16.

140 Karl Marx and Frederick Engels, *Manifesto of the Communist Party* [1848], in A.J.P. Taylor (ed.), *The Communist Manifesto* (Harmondsworth: Penguin Books, 1967), p.83.

141 For a critique of the idea of Turner as a proto-modern painter, see Sam Smiles, *J.M.W. Turner: The Making of a Modern Artist*, Manchester 2007.

142 Complete title: *Modern Painters: their superiority in the art of landscape painting to all the Ancient Masters proved by examples of the True, the Beautiful, and the Intellectual, from the works of modern artists, especially from those of J. M. W. Turner, Esq., R.A.*

143 John Ruskin, 'The Two Boyhoods', *Modern Painters*, vol.5, in Cook and Wedderburn 1903–12, vol.7, pp.385–6.

144 See Sam Smiles, *The Late Works of JMW Turner: The Artist and his Critics*, New Haven and London 2020.

145 *New Monthly Magazine and Literary Journal*, vol.46, no.184 (April 1836), p.517.

146 *Polytechnic Journal*, vol.2, no.6 (June 1840), p.461.

147 *Morning Advertiser*, 9 May 1843.

148 For a wide-ranging discussion of 'subjective vision' in this period, see Jonathan Crary, *Techniques of the Observer: On Vision and Modernity in the Nineteenth Century*, Cambridge, Mass., 1990.

149 Mary Somerville, *On the Connexion of the Physical Sciences*, London 1834, p.150.

150 See, for example, 'Worcester and Shrewsbury' sketchbook (1831?), Turner Bequest CCXXXIX 25, 58a, 84.

151 [William Makepeace Thackeray], 'May Gambols; or, Titmarsh in the Picture-Galleries', *Fraser's Magazine*, June 1844, pp.712–13.

152 Langton and Bicknell was a firm of whaling-ship owners and candle manufacturers.

153 See Peter Bicknell, 'Turner's *The Whale Ship*: A Missing Link?', *Turner Studies*, vol. 5, no.2 (Winter 1985), pp.20–3.

154 John Gage (ed.), *Collected Correspondence of J.M.W. Turner*, Oxford 1980, p.205.

155 Harold I. Shapiro, *Ruskin in Italy: Letters to his Parents, 1845*, Oxford 1972, p.248.

156 *The Times*, 6 May 1845, quoted in Butlin and Joll 1984, p.261.

157 *Literary Gazette*, 9 May 1846, quoted in Butlin and Joll 1984, p.261.

158 See Ian Warrell, '"I saw Louis Philippe land at Portsmouth": Fixing Turner's Presence at the Arrival of the King of the French, 8 October 1844', *Turner Society News*, no.120 (Autumn 2013), pp.8–15.

159 Turner's letter acknowledging his receipt of the medal is dated 26 April 1836. A précis is published in John Gage, 'Further Correspondence of J.M.W. Turner', *Turner Studies*, vol.6, no.1 (Summer 1986), p.4.

160 David Blayney Brown, 'Turner et le voyage de Louis-Philippe en Angleterre', in Valérie Bajou (ed.), *Louis-Philippe et Versailles*, exh. cat., Château de Versailles 2019, pp.120–1.

Selected Bibliography

Anthony Bailey, *Standing in the Sun: A Life of J.M.W. Turner*, London 2013.

John Barrell, *The Dark Side of the Landscape: The Rural Poor in English Painting, 1730–1840*, Cambridge (1980) 2009.

Ian Baucom, *Specters of the Atlantic: Finance Capital, Slavery, and the Philosophy of History*, Durham 2005.

R.B. Beckett (ed.), *John Constable's Correspondence*, 6 vols, Ipswich 1962–8.

Peter Bicknell, 'Turner's *The Whale Ship*: A Missing Link?', *Turner Studies*, vol. 5, no.2 (Winter 1985).

David Blayney Brown, *Turner and Byron*, exh. cat., Tate Gallery, London 1992

David Blayney Brown, 'Rule, Britannia? Patriotism, Progress and the Picturesque in Turner's Britain', in Michael Lloyd (ed.), *Turner*, exh. cat., National Gallery of Australia, Canberra 1996.

David Blayney Brown, 'Turner et le voyage de Louis-Philippe en Angleterre', in Valérie Bajou (ed.), *Louis-Philippe et Versailles*, exh. cat., Château de Versailles 2019.

David Blayney Brown and Sam Smiles, *Light into Colour: Turner in the South West*, exh. cat., Tate St Ives, 2006.

Blackwood's Edinburgh Magazine, vol.23 (1828).

Martin Butlin and Evelyn Joll, *The Paintings of J.M.W. Turner*, rev. edn, New Haven and London 1984.

E.T. Cook and Alexander Wedderburn (eds.), *The Works of John Ruskin*, 39 vols, London 1903–12.

Leo Costello, *J.M.W. Turner and the Subject of History*, Farnham 2012.

Jonathan Crary, *Techniques of the Observer: On Vision and Modernity in the Nineteenth Century*, Cambridge, Mass., 1990.

Stephen Daniels, 'The Implications of Industry: Turner and Leeds', *Turner Studies*, vol.6, no.1 (Summer 1983).

Stephen Daniels, 'Images of the railway in nineteenth century paintings and prints', in *Trainspotting – Images of the Railway in British Art*, exh. cat., Nottingham Castle Museum, 1985.

Stephen Daniels, 'Reforming Landscape: Turner and Nottingham', in P. de Bolla et al. (eds.), *Land, Nation and Culture, 1740–1840: Thinking the Republic of Taste*, Basingstoke 2005.

Ralph Waldo Emerson, *English Traits*, 1857.

A.J. Finberg, The *Life of J.M.W. Turner*, Oxford 1939.

Gerald Finley, *Turner and George IV in Edinburgh 1822*, London and Edinburgh 1981.

Gillian Forrester, *Turner's 'Drawing Book': The Liber Studiorum*, London 1996.

John Gage, *Rain, Steam and Speed*, London 1972.

John Gage (ed.), *Collected Correspondence of J.M.W. Turner*, Oxford 1980.

John Gage, 'Further Correspondence of J.M.W. Turner', *Turner Studies*, vol.6, no.1 (Summer 1986).

John Gage, *J.M.W. Turner: 'A Wonderful Range of Mind'*, New Haven and London 1987.

Jean Golt, 'Beauty and Meaning on Richmond Hill: New Light on Turner's Masterpiece of 1819', *Turner Studies*, vol. 7, no. 2 (Winter 1987).

Francis Greenacre, 'James Baker Pyne (1800–1870)', in *Oxford Dictionary of National Biography*, online edition, Oxford 2012: http://www.oxforddnb.com/view/article/22931, accessed 31 December 2019.

James Hamilton, *Turner and the Scientists*, exh. cat., Tate Gallery, London 1998.

James Hamilton, *Turner's Britain*, London 2003.

Hazlitt, 'Mr. Coleridge', in E.D. Mackerness (ed.), *The Spirit of the Age*, London and Glasgow 1969.

Elizabeth K. Helsinger, *Rural Scenes and National Representation: Britain, 1815–1850*, Princeton, MJ, 1997.

Luke Herrmann, 'John Landseer on Turner: Reviews of Exhibitions in 1808, 1839 and 1840', *Turner Studies*, vol.7, no.1 (Summer 1987), pp.26–33.

David Hill, *Turner in the North*, London and New Haven 1996.

David Hill, *Turner and Leeds: Image of Industry*, Huddersfield 2008.

Ford Madox Hueffer, *Ford Madox Brown*, 1896.

Richard Johns, 'From the Nore: Turner at the Mouth of the Thames', in Satish Padiyar, Philip Shaw and Philippa Simpson (eds.), *Visual Culture and the Revolutionary and Napoleonic Wars*, London 2016, pp.87–101.

John McCoubrey, 'Turner's Slave Ship: Abolition, Ruskin, and Reception', *Word and Image*, vol.4, no.4, Oct.–Dec. 1998.

Gelien Matthews, *Caribbean Slave Revolts and the British Abolitionist Movement*, Baton Rouge 2006.

Judith Milhous, Gabriella Dideriksen and Robert D. Hume, *Italian Opera in Late Eighteenth-Century London, vol.II: The Pantheon Opera and its Aftermath 1789–1795*, Oxford 2001.

Michelle L. Miller, 'J.M.W. Turner's *Ploughing Up Turnips, Near Slough*: The Cultivation of Cultural Dissent', *The Art Bulletin,* vol.77, no.4 (December 1995), pp.572–83.

Christina Payne, *Toil and Plenty: Images of the Agricultural Landscape in England, 1780–1890*, exh. cat., Nottingham University Art Gallery 1993.

Jan Piggott, 'The Symbolism of Turner's Rockets in *The Field of Waterloo*', *Turner Society News*, no.125 (Spring 2016).

Cecilia Powell, 'Turner's Women: The Painted Veil', *Turner Society News*, no.63 (March 1993).

Cecilia Powell, '*The Field of Waterloo*: Turner's *Guernica*', *Turner Society News*, no.123 (Spring 2015).

Cecilia Powell, 'Shipwreck and Scandal: Turner and the *Amphitrite*', *Turner Society News*, no.128 (Autumn 2017).

Curtis Price, 'Turner at the Pantheon Opera House, 1791–2', *Turner Studies*, vol.7, no.2 (Winter 1987), pp.2–8.

James Purdon, 'Grand union – how canals have captivated British artists for centuries', *Apollo*, 21 March 2020: https://www.apollo-magazine. com/canals-british-art/, accessed 22 April 2020.

Bernard Richards, review of the BBC 2 programme *The Genius of Turner: Painting the Industrial Revolution* in *Turner Society News*, no.120 (Autumn 2013).

William S. Rodner, *J.M.W. Turner: Romantic Painter of the Industrial Revolution*, Berkeley and London 1997.

John Ruskin, *Notes by Mr. Ruskin*, London 1878.

Eric Shanes, *Turner's Picturesque Views in England and Wales 1825–1838*, London 1979.

Eric Shanes, 'Turner's "Unknown" London Series', *Turner Studies*, vol. 1, no. 2 (Winter 1981), pp.36–42.

Eric Shanes, *Turner's England, 1810–38*, London 1990a.

Eric Shanes, *Turner's Human Landscape*, London 1990b.

Eric Shanes, 'Britain at Peace and War; J.M.W. Turner's Four "State of the Nation" Surveys, 1793–1836', in *Windows on that World: Essays on British Art Presented to Brian Allen*, London 2012, pp.211–30.

Eric Shanes, *Young Mr. Turner*, New Haven and London 2016.

Harold I. Shapiro, *Ruskin in Italy: Letters to his Parents, 1845*, Oxford 1972.

F.O. Shyllon, *Black Slaves in Britain*, London 1974.

Sam Smiles, *Eye Witness: Artists and Visual Documentation in Britain 1770–1830*, Aldershot and Brookfield, VT, 2000.

Sam Smiles, *The Turner Book*, London and New York 2006.

Sam Smiles, *J.M.W. Turner: The Making of a Modern Artist*, Manchester 2007.

Sam Smiles, 'Turner and the slave trade: speculation and representation, 1805–1840', *British Art Journal*, vol.7, no.3 (Winter 2007–8), pp.47–54.

Sam Smiles, '*The Fall of Anarchy*: Politics and Anatomy in an Enigmatic Painting by J.M.W. Turner', in *Tate Papers*, no.25, Spring 2016, https://www.tate.org.uk/ research/publications/tate-papers/25/ fall-of-anarchy-politics-anatomy-turner, accessed 2 September 2020.

Tate Gallery: Illustrated Catalogue of Acquisitions 1986–88, London 1996.

A.J.P. Taylor (ed.), *The Communist Manifesto*, Harmondsworth 1967.

[William Makepeace Thackeray], 'May Gambols; or, Titmarsh in the Picture-Galleries', *Fraser's Magazine*, June 1844.

Inigo Thomas, 'The Chase … Turner's "Rain, Steam and Speed"', *London Review of Books*, vol.38, no.20 (20 October 2016).

Diana Villar, *John Wilson Carmichael 1799–1868*, Portsmouth 1995.

Ian Warrell, '"I saw Louis Philippe land at Portsmouth": Fixing Turner's Presence at the Arrival of the King of the French, 8 October 1844', *Turner Society News*, no.120 (Autumn 2013).

Ian Warrell, *Turner's Wessex: Architecture and Ambition*, London 2015.

Andrew Wilton, *Turner in his Time*, London 1987.

Andrew Wilton, *Painting and Poetry: Turner's Verse Book and his Work of 1804–1812*, London 1990.

Andrew Wilton and Rosalind Mallord Turner, *Painting and Poetry: Turner's 'Verse Book' and his Work of 1802–1812*, exh. cat., Tate Gallery, London 1990.

List of Exhibited Works

All works by J.M.W. Turner unless otherwise stated.
Measurements are in centimetres, height before width, before depth.
Information is correct at time of printing but subject to change.

Introduction

*The Hero of a Hundred
Fights* c.1800–10, reworked and
exhibited 1847
Oil paint on canvas
90.8 × 121.3
Tate. Accepted by the nation as part
of the Turner Bequest 1856
TATE ONLY

The Chain Pier, Brighton c.1828
Oil paint on canvas
71.1 × 136.5
Tate. Accepted by the nation as part
of the Turner Bequest 1856

Chichester Canal c.1828
Oil paint on canvas
65.4 × 134.6
Tate. Accepted by the nation as part
of the Turner Bequest 1856

Signs of the Time

Philip James de Loutherbourg
(1740–1812)
*The Boiler House and Casting House
of a Furnace, Probably Bedlam Furnace,
at Coalbrookdale* 1786 or 1800
Pen and ink, graphite and watercolour
on paper
7.3 × 9.5
Tate. Accepted by the nation as part
of the Turner Bequest 1856
TATE ONLY

Philip James de Loutherbourg
(1740–1812)
*Near View of the Resolution Steam-
Engine, Coalbrookdale* 1786 or 1800
Pen and ink and graphite on paper
8 × 12.4
Tate. Accepted by the nation as part
of the Turner Bequest 1856
TATE ONLY

Philip James de Loutherbourg
(1740–1812)
*The Resolution Steam-Engine,
Coalbrookdale, Seen from the New Pool*
1786 or 1800
Pen and ink and graphite on paper
8 × 12.3
Tate. Accepted by the nation as part
of the Turner Bequest 1856
TATE ONLY

*The Pantheon, the Morning after the
Fire* 1792
Graphite and watercolour on paper
39.5 × 51.5
Tate. Accepted by the nation as part
of the Turner Bequest 1856

*Shipwreck on a Rocky Coastline with a
Ruined Castle* 1792–3
Watercolour and pencil on paper
16.9 × 23.6
The Whitworth, The University
of Manchester

*Llanstephan Castle by Moonlight,
with a Kiln in the Foreground* c.1795

Graphite and watercolour on paper
23.1 × 28.1cm
Tate. Accepted by the nation as part
of the Turner Bequest 1856

*Fishermen Hauling a Boat through Surf
on a Windlass* 1796–7
Watercolour and gouache on paper
19.4 × 26.9
Tate. Accepted by the nation as part
of the Turner Bequest 1856

High Green, Wolverhampton 1796
Watercolour on paper
31.8 × 41.9
Wolverhampton Arts & Culture

*Interior of a Forge: Making
Anchors* 1796–7
Gouache, graphite and watercolour
on paper
11.3 × 18.6
Tate. Accepted by the nation as part
of the Turner Bequest 1856

Small Boats beside a Man-o'-War 1796–7
Watercolour and gouache on paper
35.4 × 61.7
Tate. Accepted by the nation as part
of the Turner Bequest 1856

The Interior of a Cannon Foundry 1797–8
Graphite and watercolour on paper
24.7 × 34.7
Tate. Accepted by the nation as part
of the Turner Bequest 1856

*Imaginary Landscape with Windsor
Castle on a Cliff and a Distant Plain* c.1798
Gouache, graphite and watercolour
on paper
45.7 × 73.6
Tate. Accepted by the nation as part
of the Turner Bequest 1856

*General View of Cyfarthfa Ironworks
from the Brecon Road* 1798
Graphite on paper
28.9 × 45.6
Tate. Accepted by the nation as part
of the Turner Bequest 1856

*View of Cyfarthfa Ironworks ?from the
North-West* 1798
Graphite on paper
28.8 × 45.7
Tate. Accepted by the nation as part
of the Turner Bequest 1856

The Interior of a Tilt Forge c.1798
Graphite on paper
17.4 × 25
Tate. Accepted by the nation as part
of the Turner Bequest 1856

A Lime Kiln by Moonlight c.1799
Watercolour on paper
16.5 × 24
Herbert Art Gallery and Museum,
Coventry. Purchased with support
from the Arts Council England / V&A
Purchase Grant Fund

Edward Dayes (1763–1804)
Bedlam Furnace, Coalbrookedale
date not known
Gouache, graphite and watercolour
on paper
31.6 × 44
Tate. Accepted by the nation as part
of the Turner Bequest 1856
TATE ONLY

Philip James de Loutherbourg
(1740–1812)
The Battle of the Nile 1800
Oil paint on canvas
152.4 × 214
Tate. Purchased with assistance from
the Friends of the Tate Gallery 1971
TATE ONLY

Paul Sandby Munn (1773–1845)
*Bedlam Furnace, Madeley Dale,
Shropshire* 1803
Watercolour on paper
32.5 × 54.8
Tate. Purchased 1986
TATE ONLY

Edinburgh, from Caulton-hill exh. 1804
Graphite and watercolour on paper
66 × 100
Tate. Accepted by the nation as part
of the Turner Bequest 1856

Donkeys beside a Mine Shaft c.1805–7
Gouache, graphite and watercolour
on paper
57.7 × 78
Tate. Accepted by the nation as part
of the Turner Bequest 1856

Frederick Christian Lewis (1779–1856)
after J.M.W. Turner (1775–1851)
Colebrooke Dale 1825
Mezzotint on paper
13.6 × 19.8 (image)
Tate. Purchased 1986
TATE ONLY

War and Peace

*The Fortress of Seringapatam, from the
Cullaly Deedy Gate* 1800
Graphite and watercolour on paper
47.5 × 67.7
Nirmalya Kumar Collection

The Siege of Seringapatam c.1800
Graphite, watercolour and gouache
on paper
42.1 × 64.7
Tate. Purchased 1986

The Devil's Bridge, St Gotthard 1803
Oil paint on canvas
76.8 × 62.8
Schorr Collection
TATE ONLY

Study for 'The Battle of Trafalgar, as
Seen from the Mizen Starboard Shrouds
of the Victory' 1805
Graphite on paper
11.4 × 18.4
Tate. Accepted by the nation as part
of the Turner Bequest 1856

*The 'Victory': From Quarterdeck to
Poop* 1805
Pen and ink, graphite and watercolour
on paper
42.4 × 56.5
Tate. Bequeathed by
Henry Vaughan 1900

*The Battle of Trafalgar, as Seen from the
Mizen Starboard Shrouds of the Victory*
1806–8
Oil paint on canvas
170.8 × 238.8
Tate. Accepted by the nation as part
of the Turner Bequest 1856

Description of The Battle of Trafalgar,
as Seen from the Mizen Starboard
Shrouds of the Victory, 1806
Pen and ink on paper
18.7 × 23.4
Tate. Accepted by the nation as part
of the Turner Bequest 1856

Key to 'The Battle of Trafalgar, as Seen
from the Mizen Starboard Shrouds of
the Victory' 1806
Pen and ink and watercolour on paper
18.6 × 23.4
Tate. Accepted by the nation as part
of the Turner Bequest 1856

Lake of Thun c.1806–7
Graphite and watercolour on paper
18.5 × 26.4
Tate. Accepted by the nation as part
of the Turner Bequest 1856

*Spithead: Boat's Crew Recovering an
Anchor* 1807–9
Oil paint on canvas
171.4 × 233.7
Tate. Accepted by the nation as part
of the Turner Bequest 1856

*The 'Victory' Coming up the Channel
with the Body of Nelson* c.1807–19
Graphite and watercolour on paper
20 × 28.5
Tate. Bequeathed by
Henry Vaughan 1900
TATE ONLY

Charles Turner (1774–1857) after
J.M.W. Turner (1775–1851) *The Fifth
Plague of Egypt* 1808
Etching and mezzotint on paper
18 × 26 (image)
TATE ONLY

The Wreck of a Transport Ship c.1810
Oil paint on canvas
173 × 245
Calouste Gulbenkian Museum, Lisbon
TATE ONLY

*Snow Storm: Hannibal and his Army
Crossing the Alps* exh. 1812
Oil paint on canvas
146 × 237.5
Tate. Accepted by the nation as part
of the Turner Bequest 1856

*The Battle of Fort Rock, Val d'Aouste,
Piedmont, 1796* exh. 1815
Watercolour and gouache on paper

69.6 × 101.5
Tate. Accepted by the nation as part
of the Turner Bequest 1856

*Lake of Lucerne, from the Landing Place
at Fleulen, Looking towards Bauen and
Tell's Chapel, Switzerland* 1815
Watercolour, gouache and gum arabic
on paper
66 × 100
Clode Collection
TATE ONLY

*Printed Handkerchief entitled
'The Battle of Waterloo'* c.1815
White cotton printed in red, spiral
twist border
63 × 54
On Loan from the Council of the
National Army Museum, London
TATE

Plymouth with Mount Batten c.1816
Watercolour on paper
14.6 × 23.5
Victoria and Albert Museum.
William Smith Bequest
TATE AND KAM ONLY

*(1) Diagram of the Disposition of British
Forces at Waterloo; (2) La Haye Sainte
from the South* 1817
Graphite on paper
15 × 9.4
Tate. Accepted by the nation as part
of the Turner Bequest 1856

The Field of Waterloo 1817
Watercolour and graphite on paper
28.8 × 20.5
The Syndics of the Fitzwilliam Museum,
University of Cambridge
TATE ONLY

A Mounted Soldier c.1817–18
Graphite on paper
6.9 × 10.3
Tate. Accepted by the nation as part
of the Turner Bequest 1856

The Field of Waterloo exh. 1818
Oil paint on canvas
147.3 × 238.8
Tate. Accepted by the nation as part
of the Turner Bequest 1856

A First Rate Taking in Stores 1818
Watercolour and graphite on paper
28.6 × 39.7
Trustees of the Cecil Higgins Art Gallery
(The Higgins Bedford)
TATE ONLY

The Loss of an East Indiaman c.1818
Watercolour and graphite on paper
28 × 39.5
Trustees of the Cecil Higgins Art Gallery
(The Higgins Bedford)
TATE ONLY

Second Sketch for 'The Battle of
Trafalgar' c.1823
Oil paint on canvas
90.2 × 121.3
Tate. Accepted by the nation as part
of the Turner Bequest 1856

William Raymond Smith (1818–1848)
after J.M.W. Turner (1775–1851)
Saltash, Cornwall 1827
Line engraving on paper
16.4 × 23.3 (image)
Tate. Purchased 1986
TATE ONLY

Thomas Jeavons (1795–1867) after
J.M.W. Turner (1775–1851) *Devonport
and Dock Yard, Devonshire* 1830
Line engraving on paper
16.2 × 24.4 (image)
Tate. Purchased 1986
TATE ONLY

*Calais Sands at Low Water: Poissards
Collecting Bait* 1830
Oil paint on canvas
68.8 × 103.8
Bury Art Museum, Greater Manchester
TATE ONLY

*Ship models including small craft for
cross-Channel invasion, with the sea and
background painted by Turner* c.1804
Wood and mixed media
45.9 × 29.8 × 21
Tate Archive
TATE ONLY

Modern Thought

*Ehrenbreitstein, During the Demolition
of the Fortress* 1819–20
Watercolour on paper
17.5 × 28.4
Bury Art Museum, Greater Manchester

Charles Mottram (1807–1876) after
John Doyle (1797–1868) *Samuel Rogers
at his Breakfast Table*, c.1823
Mezzotint and engraving on paper
58 × 86.6 (image)
Tate. Presented by Dr David Blayney
Brown 1987
TATE ONLY

Marengo, for Rogers's 'Italy' c.1826–7
Graphite, watercolour and gouache
on paper
21.4 × 29.8
Tate. Accepted by the nation as part
of the Turner Bequest 1856

Edward Goodall (1795–1870) after
J.M.W. Turner (1775–1851) *Marengo,
in Samuel Rogers,* 'Italy: A Poem' 1830
Line engraving on paper
5.1 × 8.9 (image)
Tate Library and Archive
TATE ONLY

*Ship-building (An Old Oak Dead),
for Rogers's* 'Poems' c.1830–2
Graphite and watercolour on paper
19.1 × 24.8
Tate. Accepted by the nation as part
of the Turner Bequest 1856
TATE ONLY

John Cousen (1804–1880) after
J.M.W. Turner (1775–1851)
The Acropolis, Athens 1832
Line engraving on paper

18.2 × 25 (image)
Tate. Transferred from the British
Museum 1988
TATE ONLY

Ehrenbreitstein c.1832
Watercolour on paper
29.5 × 43.5
Bury Art Museum, Greater Manchester

Edward Finden (1791–1857) after
J.M.W. Turner (1775–1851) *The Field
of Waterloo. From Hougoumont* 1833
Line engraving on paper
5 × 9 (image)
Tate. Transferred from the
British Museum 1988
TATE ONLY

Edward Finden (1791–1857) after
J.M.W. Turner (1775–1851) *Scio (Fontana
di Melek Mehmet, Pasha)* 1833
Line engraving on paper
23.3 × 17.6 (platemark)
Tate. Transferred from the British
Museum 1988
TATE ONLY

Edward Goodall (1795–1870) after
J.M.W. Turner (1775–1851)
Traitor's Gate, Tower of London 1834
Line engraving on paper
9 × 8.7 (image)
Tate Library and Archive
TATE ONLY

William Miller (1796–1882) after
J.M.W. Turner (1775–1851)
Fontainebleau 1834–6
Line engraving on paper
9.5 × 7.5 (image)
Tate. Purchased 1987
TATE ONLY

John Horsburgh (1791–1869) after
J.M.W. Turner (1775–1851) *Napoleon's
Logement, Quai Conti* 1834–6
Line engraving on paper
11.5 × 7 (image)
Tate. Purchased 1987
TATE ONLY

Edward Goodall (1795–1870) after
J.M.W. Turner (1775–1851)
St Anne's Hill (I) 1834
Line engraving on paper
29.2 × 15 (sheet)
Tate. Transferred from the
British Museum 1988
TATE ONLY

James Tibbitts Willmore (1800–1883)
after J.M.W. Turner (1775–1851)
Fire at Sea 1835
Line engraving on paper
12.5 × 8.8 (image)
Tate. Purchased 1986
TATE ONLY

William Miller (1796–1882) after
J.M.W. Turner (1775–1851)
Vincennes 1835
Line engraving on paper
7.7 × 8 (image)
Tate. Purchased 1987
TATE ONLY

*Vignette Study for 'Kosciusko', for
Campbell's 'Poetical Works'* c.1835–6
Watercolour on paper
17.8 × 22.5
Tate. Accepted by the nation as part
of the Turner Bequest 1856

Edward Goodall (1795–1870) after
J.M.W. Turner (1775–1851)
The Bellerophon, Plymouth Sound 1836
Line engraving
11 × 8.5 (image)
Tate. Purchased 1987
TATE ONLY

Henry Griffiths (d.1849) after
J.M.W. Turner (1775–1851)
The Wreck 1836
Line engraving on paper
11 × 8 (image)
Tate. Purchased 1986
TATE ONLY

Edward Goodall (1795–1870) after
J.M.W. Turner (1775–1851)
Battle of the Baltic 1837
Line engraving on paper
8.3 × 7 (image)
Tate. Purchased 1986
TATE ONLY

Robert Wallis (1794–1878) after
J.M.W. Turner (1775–1851)
Hohenlinden 1837
Line engraving on paper
10.4 × 7.4
Tate. Purchased 1986
TATE ONLY

Edward Goodall (1795–1870) after
J.M.W. Turner (1775–1851)
Prague – Kosciusko 1837
Line engraving on paper
8.4 × 8 (image)
Tate. Purchased 1986
TATE ONLY

James Tibbitts Willmore (1800–1883)
after J.M.W. Turner (1775–1851)
The Sea! The Sea! 1837
Line engraving on paper
12.5 × 9.6 (image)
Tate. Purchased 1988
TATE ONLY

Venice, the Bridge of Sighs exh. 1840
Oil paint on canvas
68.6 × 91.4
Tate. Accepted by the nation as part
of the Turner Bequest 1856

The Opening of the Wallhalla, 1842
exh. 1843
Oil paint on mahogany
112.7 × 200.7
Tate. Accepted by the nation as part
of the Turner Bequest 1856

Home Front

The New Council Room, Salisbury 1805
Watercolour on paper
30 × 39
Trustees of the Cooper Gallery,
Barnsley

*A Country Blacksmith Disputing upon the
Price of Iron, and the Price Charged to the
Butcher for Shoeing his Poney* exh. 1807
Oil paint on mahogany
54.9 × 77.8
Tate. Accepted by the nation as part
of the Turner Bequest 1856

London from Greenwich Park exh. 1809
Oil paint on canvas
90.2 × 120
Tate. Accepted by the nation as part
of the Turner Bequest 1856

*Ploughing Up Turnips, near Slough
('Windsor')* exh. 1809
Oil paint on canvas
101.9 × 130.2
Tate. Accepted by the nation as part
of the Turner Bequest 1856

Martello Towers near Bexhill, Sussex 1811
Etching on paper
17.6 × 25.7 (image)
Tate. Presented by A. Acland Allen
through the Art Fund 1925
TATE ONLY

Windmill and Lock 1811
Etching and watercolour on paper
17.7 × 25.8 (image)
Tate. Presented by W.G. Rawlinson 1913

*England: Richmond Hill, on the Prince
Regent's Birthday* exh. 1819
Oil paint on canvas
180 × 334.6
Tate. Accepted by the nation as part
of the Turner Bequest 1856

*Designs for the 'Royal Progress' Series;
Two Scotch Bonnets* 1822
Graphite on paper
11.1 × 37.6
Tate. Accepted by the nation as part
of the Turner Bequest 1856
TATE ONLY

*Frontispiece to Volume Two of The
Provincial Antiquities and Picturesque
Scenery of Scotland* c.1822–5
Graphite and wash on paper
25.7 × 17.6
Tate. Accepted by the nation as part
of the Turner Bequest 1856
TATE ONLY

*George IV's Departure from the 'Royal
George'* 1822
Oil paint on mahogany
75.2 × 92.1
Tate. Accepted by the nation as part
of the Turner Bequest 1856

*George IV at the Provost's Banquet in
the Parliament House, Edinburgh* c.1822
Oil paint on mahogany
68.6 × 91.8
Tate. Accepted by the nation as part
of the Turner Bequest 1856

*More Park, near Watford, on the
River Colne* c.1823
Watercolour and gouache on paper
15.8 × 22.1
Tate. Accepted by the nation as part
of the Turner Bequest 1856

Rye, Sussex c.1823
Watercolour on paper
14.7 ×23.1
Lent by Amgueddfa Cymru –
National Museum Wales.
Bequest: Gwendoline Davies, 1952
TATE ONLY

Hythe, Kent 1824
Watercolour on paper
14 × 22.9
Guildhall Art Gallery, City of London

Kirkstall Lock, on the River Aire 1824–5
Watercolour on paper
15.9 × 23.5
Tate. Accepted by the nation as part
of the Turner Bequest 1856

James Charles Allen (1790?–1833)
after J.M.W. Turner (1775–1851)
St. Mawes, Cornwall 1824
Line engraving on paper
14.6 × 22.3 (image)
Tate. Purchased 1986
TATE ONLY

Robert Wallis (1794–1878) after
J.M.W. Turner (1775–1851) *Lancaster
from the Aqueduct Bridge* 1827
Line engraving on paper
16.5 × 23.2 (image)
Tate. Purchased 1986
TATE ONLY

Stamford, Lincolnshire c.1828
Watercolour on paper
23.9 × 42
Usher Gallery, Lincoln
TATE ONLY

Samuel Fisher (active 1830–55) after
J.M.W. Turner (1775–1851)
Coventry, Warwickshire 1833
Line engraving on paper
16.5 × 24.4 (image)
Tate. Transferred from the
British Museum 1988
TATE ONLY

Causes and Campaigns

Wycliffe, near Rokeby c.1816
Watercolour and bodycolour on paper
29.2 × 43
Board of Trustees of the National
Museums and Galleries on Merseyside,
Walker Art Gallery, National Museums
Liverpool, Liverpool. Bequeathed by
Miss Eva Melly, 1944
TATE ONLY

Sidmouth, Devon 1825–7
Watercolour on paper
18.4 × 26.3
The Whitworth, The University
of Manchester

Salisbury, from Old Sarum c.1827–8
Watercolour on paper
27.2 × 41
On loan from The Salisbury Museum
TATE ONLY

John P. Quilley (active 1812–1842) after
J.M.W. Turner (1775–1851)
The Deluge 1828
Mezzotint on paper
37.9 × 57.7
Tate. Purchased 1986
TATE ONLY

The Northampton Election,
6 December 1830 c.1830–1
Watercolour, gouache and ink on paper
29.2 × 43.8
Tate. Purchased 2007

James Baylis Allen (1803–1876) after
J.M.W. Turner (1775–1851)
Stoneyhurst, Lancashire 1830
Line engraving on paper
16.1 × 23.5 (image)
Tate. Purchased 1988
TATE ONLY

Nottingham 1831
Watercolour on paper
31 × 47
Nottingham City Museums
TATE ONLY

The Prince of Orange, William III,
Embarked from Holland, and Landed
at Torbay, November 4th, 1688, after a
Stormy Passage exh. 1832
Oil paint on canvas
90.2 × 120
Tate. Presented by Robert Vernon 1847

Chetham & Robinson/Chesworth
& Robinson
Reform Mug c.1832
Pink lusterware with transfer print
8.2 × 10.8
The Syndics of the Fitzwilliam Museum,
University of Cambridge
TATE ONLY

Thomas Higham (1796–1844) after
J.M.W. Turner (1775–1851)
Ely Cathedral, Cambridgeshire 1833
Line engraving on paper
16.8 × 22.9 (image)
Tate. Purchased 1988
TATE ONLY

The Fall of Anarchy (?) c.1833–4
Oil paint on canvas
59.7 × 75.6
Tate. Accepted by the nation as part
of the Turner Bequest 1856

The Burning of the Houses of
Parliament c.1834–5
Watercolour and gouache on paper
30.2 × 44.4
Tate. Accepted by the nation as part
of the Turner Bequest 1856
TATE ONLY

The Temple of Poseidon at Sounion
(Cape Colonna) c.1834
Graphite, watercolour and gouache
on paper
38.2 × 58.8
Accepted by HM Government
in lieu of tax and allocated to the
Tate Gallery 1999

A Disaster at Sea ?c.1835
Oil paint on canvas
171.4 × 220.3
Tate. Accepted by the nation as part
of the Turner Bequest 1856

Joseph Davis (active 1825–1857)
British & Foreign Anti-Slavery
Society Medal 1840
White metal
5.2 × 5.2
National Maritime Museum, Greenwich,
London, Michael Graham-Stewart
Slavery Collection. Acquired with the
assistance of the Heritage Lottery Fund
TATE ONLY

Henry Melville (active 1826–1841) after
Thomas Hosmer Shepherd (1793–1864)
Exeter Hall. The great Anti-Slavery
Meeting, 1841 1841, in Joseph Mead,
London Interiors with their Costumes
& Ceremonies from Drawings made
by permission of the Public Offices
(Proprietors & Trustees of the
Metropolitan Buildings)
Line engraving on paper
13 × 17.8
Private collection
TATE ONLY

Steam and Speed

William Daniell (1769–1837)
Steam Boat on the Clyde near
Dumbarton 1817
Etching and aquatint on paper
16.2 × 24.1
Tate. Presented by Tate Gallery
Publications 1979
TATE ONLY

Newcastle-on-Tyne c.1823
Watercolour on paper
15.2 × 21.5
Tate. Accepted by the nation as part
of the Turner Bequest 1856

Shields, on the River Tyne 1823
Watercolour on paper
15.4 × 21.6
Tate. Accepted by the nation as part
of the Turner Bequest 1856

Dover c.1825
Watercolour on paper
16.1 × 24.5
Tate. Accepted by the nation as part
of the Turner Bequest 1856

An Industrial Town at Sunset, Probably
Birmingham or Dudley c.1830–2
Watercolour on paper
34.8 × 48.2
Tate. Accepted by the nation as part
of the Turner Bequest 1856

The Thames above Waterloo
Bridge c.1835–40
Oil paint on canvas
90.5 × 121
Tate. Accepted by the nation as part
of the Turner Bequest 1856

Life-Boat and Manby Apparatus Going
Off to a Stranded Vessel Making Signal
(Blue Lights) of Distress c.1831
Oil paint on canvas
91.4 × 122
Victoria and Albert Museum, London
Given by John Sheepshanks, 1857
TATE ONLY

William Miller (1796–1882) after
J.M.W. Turner (1775–1851)
The Tower of London 1831
Line engraving on paper
9.4 × 14.7 (image)
Tate. Transferred from the
British Museum 1988
TATE ONLY

Le Havre: Tour de François Ier c.1832
Watercolour and gouache on paper
14 × 19.2
Tate. Accepted by the nation as part
of the Turner Bequest 1856

Between Quilleboeuf and Villequier 1832
Watercolour and gouache on paper
13.7 × 19.1
Tate. Accepted by the nation as part
of the Turner Bequest 1856

Robert Brandard (1805–1862) after
J.M.W. Turner (1775–1851)
Between Quilleboeuf and Villequier 1834
Line engraving on paper
9.5 × 13.8
Tate. Transferred from the British
Museum 1988
KAM AND BOSTON ONLY

Seascape with a Boat 1835
Watercolour, bodycolour and chalk
on paper
14.2 × 19.3
Lent by Museums Sheffield
TATE ONLY

Steamer and Lightship; a study for
'The Fighting Temeraire' c.1838–9
Oil paint on canvas
91.4 × 119.7
Tate. Accepted by the nation as part
of the Turner Bequest 1856

The Fighting Temeraire Tugged to her
Last Berth To Be Broken Up 1838–9
Oil paint on canvas
90.7 × 121.6
The National Gallery, London.
Turner Bequest, 1856
TATE ONLY

Joseph Clement (1779–1844)
Model of 'Firefly' class locomotive 1838
Metal and wood
66 × 159.5 × 41.5
On Loan from the Science
Museum Group
TATE ONLY

Snow Storm – Steam-Boat off a
Harbour's Mouth exh. 1842
Oil paint on canvas
91.4 × 121.9
Tate. Accepted by the nation as part
of the Turner Bequest 1856

Rain, Steam, and Speed – The Great
Western Railway 1844
Oil paint on canvas
91 × 121.8
The National Gallery, London.
Turner Bequest, 1856
TATE ONLY

A Steamer Leaving Harbour c.1845
Chalk and watercolour
on paper
22.1 × 33.2
Tate. Accepted by the nation as part
of the Turner Bequest 1856

James Tibbitts Willmore (1800–1883)
after J.M.W. Turner (1775–1851)
Dover 1851
Line engraving on paper
40.6 × 59.5 (image)
Tate. Purchased 1990
TATE ONLY

Robert Carrick (1820–1905) after
J.M.W. Turner (1775–1851)
Rockets and Blue Lights 1852
Lithograph on paper
56.2 × 75.8 (image)
Tate. Purchased 1992
TATE ONLY

Modern Painter

The Bock and the Rham, Luxembourg,
above the Alzette Valley c.1839
Gouache, pen and ink and watercolour
on paper
14.2 × 19.1
Tate. Accepted by the nation as part
of the Turner Bequest 1856

Distant View of Luxembourg from the
Bourbon Plateau c.1839
Gouache, graphite and watercolour
on paper
13.7 × 18.8
Tate. Accepted by the nation as part
of the Turner Bequest 1856

Figures in the Piazzetta, Venice, at Night,
with the Basilica and Campanile of
San Marco (St Mark's) 1840
Watercolour and bodycolour on paper
15 × 22.8
Tate. Accepted by the nation as part
of the Turner Bequest 1856

The Market Place at Coburg 1840
Watercolour and gouache on paper
19.2 × 27.9
Tate. Accepted by the nation as part
of the Turner Bequest 1856

Schloss Rosenau, near Coburg c.1840–1
Watercolour on paper
24.4 × 30.6
Tate. Accepted by the nation as part
of the Turner Bequest 1856

Venice by Moonlight, with Boats off a
Campanile 1840
Watercolour on paper
22 × 31.9
Tate. Accepted by the nation as part
of the Turner Bequest 1856

Adieu Fontainebleau c.1841–2
Graphite and watercolour on paper
22.1 × 29.2
Tate. Accepted by the nation as part
of the Turner Bequest 1856

*Ehrenbreitstein: 'The March
of N from Cob[lenz]'* c.1841–2
Graphite and watercolour on paper
22 × 29.2
Tate. Accepted by the nation as part
of the Turner Bequest 1856

*'Sauve Qui Peut': Column of Red Figures,
Some on Horseback* c.1841–2
Watercolour on paper
21.6 × 29
Tate. Accepted by the nation as part
of the Turner Bequest 1856

*Schloss Rosenau, Seat of HRH Prince
Albert of Coburg, near Coburg,
Germany* 1841
Oil paint on canvas
97 × 124.8
Board of Trustees of the National
Museums and Galleries on Merseyside,
Sudley House, National Museums
Liverpool, Liverpool
TATE ONLY

James Tibbitts Willmore (1800–1883)
after J.M.W. Turner (1775–1851)
Oberwesel 1842
Line engraving on paper
22.7 × 34 (image)
Private collection
TATE ONLY

Peace – Burial at Sea exh. 1842
Oil paint on canvas
87 × 86.7
Tate. Accepted by the nation as part
of the Turner Bequest 1856

War. The Exile and the Rock Limpet
exh. 1842
Oil paint on canvas
79.4 × 79.4
Tate. Accepted by the nation as part
of the Turner Bequest 1856

Burning Blubber 1844–5
Pastel and watercolour on paper
21.8 × 33
Tate. Accepted by the nation as part
of the Turner Bequest 1856

*The Arrival of Louis-Philippe: The
'Gomer' in Portsmouth Harbour* 1844
Watercolour on paper
23.7 × 31.8
Tate. Accepted by the nation as part
of the Turner Bequest 1856

*The Arrival of Louis-Philippe at
the Royal Clarence Yard, Gosport,
8 October 1844* c.1844–5
Oil paint on canvas
90.2 × 120.6
Tate. Accepted by the nation as part
of the Turner Bequest 1856

*The Disembarkation of Louis-Philippe
at the Royal Clarence Yard, Gosport,
8 October 1844* c.1844–5
Oil paint on canvas
90.8 × 121.3
Tate. Accepted by the nation as part
of the Turner Bequest 1856

*A Grand Interior with Candelabra ?at the
Château d'Eu* 1845
Graphite, gouache and watercolour
on paper
23.2 × 33.2
Tate. Accepted by the nation as part
of the Turner Bequest 1856

Whalers exh. 1845
Oil paint on canvas
91.1 × 121.9
Tate. Accepted by the nation as part
of the Turner Bequest 1856

*'Hurrah! for the Whaler Erebus!
Another Fish!'*, exh. 1846
Oil paint on canvas
90.2 × 120.6
Tate. Accepted by the nation as part
of the Turner Bequest 1856

*Whalers (Boiling Blubber) Entangled
in Flaw Ice, Endeavouring to Extricate
Themselves* exh. 1846
Oil paint on canvas
89.9 × 120
Tate. Accepted by the nation as part
of the Turner Bequest 1856

Naples c.1851
Watercolour and pencil on paper
37.1 × 54.3
Manchester Art Gallery
Mr James Thomas Blair bequest, 1917

*The Bridge of Sighs, Venice, on a
Starlit Night* 1840
Watercolour and bodycolour on paper
22.7 × 15.4
Tate. Accepted by the nation as part
of the Turner Bequest 1856
KIMBELL AND BOSTON ONLY

*A Gondola beneath the Ponte Ca' di Dio,
Venice, with the Palazzo Ducale (Doge's
Palace) and Campanile of San Marco in
the Distance* 1840
Watercolour on paper
24.5 × 30.5
Tate. Accepted by the nation as part
of the Turner Bequest 1856
KIMBELL AND BOSTON ONLY

*Lightning near the Campanile of San
Marco (St Mark's), Venice, from the
Hotel Europa (Palazzo Giustinian) at
Night* 1840
Watercolour and gouache on paper
15.8 × 23.2
Tate. Accepted by the nation as part
of the Turner Bequest 1856
KIMBELL AND BOSTON ONLY

*Moonlight on the Lagoon near
Venice* 1840
Watercolour and bodycolour on paper
24.5 × 30.4
Tate. Accepted by the nation as part
of the Turner Bequest 1856
KIMBELL AND BOSTON ONLY

*Sunset over the Lagoon near
Venice* 1840
Gouache on paper
18.5 × 28
Tate. Accepted by the nation as part
of the Turner Bequest 1856
KIMBELL AND BOSTON ONLY

*Venice by Moonlight, with Boats off
a Campanile*, 1840
Watercolour on paper
22 × 31.9
Tate. Accepted by the nation as part
of the Turner Bequest 1856
KIMBELL AND BOSTON ONLY

Venice with the Salute c.1840–5
Oil paint on canvas
79.2 × 108.5
Tate. Accepted by the nation as part
of the Turner Bequest 1856
KIMBELL AND BOSTON ONLY

Venice Quay, Ducal Palace exh. 1844
Oil paint on canvas
62.2 × 92.7
Tate. Accepted by the nation as part
of the Turner Bequest 1856
KIMBELL AND BOSTON ONLY

Image Credits

© Bury Art Museum, Greater Manchester, UK 56, 75, 76
© Calouste Gulbenkian Foundation, Lisbon Calouste Gulbenkian Museum – Founder's Collection. photo: Catarina Gomes Ferreira 42
© 2020 Cleveland Museum of Art / Scala Image Bank 5
© The Clode Collection 52
Collection of the Duke of Northumberland 121
© The Collection: Art and Archaeology in Lincolnshire (Usher Gallery, Lincoln) 88
© The Fitzwilliam Museum, Cambridge 50, 110
Guildhall Art Gallery, City of London 95
Harvard Art Museums/Fogg Museum. Photo: ©President and Fellows of Harvard College 96
Hastings Museum & Art Gallery 122
Herbert Art Gallery and Museum, Coventry / Bridgeman Images 22
Nirmalya Kumar Collection 45
© Manchester Art Gallery / Bridgeman Images 150
© The Metropolitan Museum, New York City 91, 153
Musée des Beaux-Arts, Bordeaux/ Bridgeman Images 59
Museum of the City of Athens, Athens Vouros-Eutaxias 58
Museum of Fine Arts, Boston 47, 86, 119, 139
Museum of Fine Arts, Houston Museum 87
Museums Sheffield 127

© The National Gallery, London 134, 135
© National Gallery of Art, Washington 6, 161
© National Maritime Museum, Greenwich, London 9, 34, 118
Image Courtesy National Museums Liverpool 125, 148
© National Museum of Wales 94
National Railway Museum/Science & Society Picture Library 130
By permission of Nottingham City Museums & Galleries 115
Photo (C) RMN-Grand Palais (musée des châteaux de Malmaison et de Bois-Préau) / Franck Raux 30
Photo (C) RMN-Grand Palais (musée du Louvre) / Michel Urtado 117
© Royal Academy of Art, London 106
Salisbury and South Wiltshire Museum / Bridgeman Images 112
Schorr Collection 48
Science Museum/Science & Society Picture Library 10
© Tate, 2020 3, 8, 11, 12, 13, 15, 16, 19, 20, 21, 23, 24, 25, 26, 27, 28, 31, 32, 35, 37, 38, 40, 41, 43, 44, 49, 51, 55, 57, 61, 62, 63, 65, 67, 68, 69, 70, 71, 72, 77, 78, 79. 80, 81, 84, 85, 90, 92, 97, 100, 101, 102, 103, 104, 109, 111, 113, 114, 116, 124, 126, 128, 132, 133, 137, 138, 140, 141, 142, 143, 144, 147, 151, 152, 155, 156, 158, 159, 160, 162, 164, 165, 166; /Oliver Cowling 4, 14, 83; /Mark Heathcote 136; /Ambrose Hickman 7, 46, 60, 64, 66, 73, 74, 89, 99, 123, 129, 149; /Joe Humphrys 154, 157; / David Lambert 39, 163; /Rod Tidnam

and Oliver Cowling 120
© The Trustees of the British Museum 2, 107
Trustees of the Cecil Higgins Art Gallery (The Higgins Bedford) 53, 54
Courtesy of the Trustees of the Cooper Gallery, Barnsley 82
© Victoria and Albert Museum, London 98, 145
Wellcome Collection 1
Courtesy of The Whitworth, The University of Manchester 18, 108
Wolverhampton Art Gallery, Wolverhampton / Bridgeman Images 17
Yale Center for British Art, Paul Mellon Collection 29, 33, 36, 93, 105, 131, 146

Index

Supporting Tate

Tate relies on a large number of supporters – individuals, foundations, companies and public sector sources – to enable it to deliver its programme of activities, both on and off its gallery sites. This support is essential in order for Tate to acquire works of art for the Collection, run education, outreach and exhibition programmes, care for the Collection in storage and enable art to be displayed, both digitally and physically, inside and outside Tate. Please contact us at:

Development Office
Tate
Millbank
London SW1P 4RG
Tel: +44 (0)20 7887 4900
Fax: +44 (0)20 7887 8098

Tate Americas Foundation
520 West 27 Street Unit 404
New York, NY 10001
USA
Tel: 001 212 643 2818
Fax: 001 212 643 1001

Donations, no matter the size, are gratefully received, either to support particular areas of interest, or to contribute to general activity costs.

Legacies

A legacy to Tate may take the form of a residual share of an estate, a specific cash sum, or an item of property such as a work of art. Legacies to Tate are free of inheritance tax and help to secure a strong future for the Collection and galleries. For further information please contact the Development Office.

Offers in lieu of tax

Inheritance Tax can be satisfied by transferring to the Government a work of art of outstanding importance. In this case the amount of tax is reduced. It can be made a condition of the offer that the work of art is allocated to Tate. Please contact us for details.

Tate Members

Tate Members enjoy unlimited free admission throughout the year to all exhibitions at Tate, as well as a number of other benefits such as exclusive use of our Members' Rooms and a free annual subscription to *Tate Etc*. Whilst enjoying the exclusive privileges of membership, members also help secure Tate's position at the very heart of British and modern art. Members support actively contributes towards new purchases of important art, ensuring that Tate's collection continues to be relevant and comprehensive, as well as funding projects in London, Liverpool and St Ives that increase access and understanding for everyone.

Tate Patrons

Tate Patrons share a passion for art and are committed to supporting Tate on an annual basis. The Patrons help enable the acquisition of works across Tate's broad collecting remit and support the staging of major exhibitions in the galleries. They also give their support to vital conservation, learning and research projects. The scheme provides a forum for Patrons to share their interest in art and meet curators, artists and one another in an enjoyable environment through a regular programme of events. These events take place both at Tate and beyond and encompass curator-led exhibition tours, visits to artists' studios and private collections, art trips both in the UK and abroad, and access to art fairs. The scheme welcomes supporters from outside the UK, giving the programme a truly international scope.

Corporate Membership

Corporate Membership at Tate offers companies opportunities for corporate entertaining and the chance for a wide variety of employee benefits. These include special private views, special access to paying exhibitions, out-of-hours visits and tours, invitations to VIP events and talks at members' offices.

Corporate Investment

Tate has developed a range of imaginative partnerships with the corporate sector, ranging from international interpretation and exhibition programmes to local outreach and staff development programmes. We are particularly known for high-profile business to business marketing initiatives and employee benefit packages. Please contact the Corporate Partnerships team for further details.

Charity Details

The Tate Gallery is an exempt charity; the Museums & Galleries Act 1992 added the Tate Gallery to the list of exempt charities defined in the 1960 Charities Act. Tate Foundation is a registered charity (number 1085314).

Tate Americas Foundation

Tate Americas Foundation is an independent charity based in New York that supports the work of Tate in the United Kingdom. It receives full tax exempt status from the IRS under section 501(c)(3) allowing United States taxpayers to receive tax deductions on gifts towards annual membership programmes, exhibitions, scholarship and capital projects. For more information please contact the Tate Americas Foundation office.

This information is correct as of the beginning of June 2020

Hamiltons Gallery
Catriona Jeffries and
    Duane Linklater
Pamela J Joyner and
    Alfred J Giuffrida
Isaac Julien, in honour of
    Maria Balshaw
Peter and Maria Kellner
J. Patrick Kennedy and
    Patricia A. Kennedy
Kettle's Yard
Rasha Khawaja
Ku-lim Kim
David Knaus
Samuel H. Kress Foundation
David Kronn
Kurimanzutto Gallery
Lachaise Foundation
Catherine Lagrange
The Estate of Sheila Lanyon
Fondation Walter &
    Nicole LeBlanc
Agnès and Edward Lee
    Acquisition Fund
Legacy Trust UK
Kiyoko Lerner
The Linbury Trust
James Lindon
The London Community
    Foundation
Andrew Lugg
LUMA Foundation
Lyndsey Ingram Ltd
The Estate of Sir Edwin Manton
Manton Foundation
Agnes Martin Foundation
Matt's Gallery
Dóra Maurer
Lord McAlpine of West Green
The Estate of
    Kenneth McGowan
Steve McQueen
The Mead Family Foundation
The Andrew W. Mellon
    Foundation
Adrian Mibus
Helen Mignano
Barry Miles
Naomi Milgrom Foundation
Ronald Moody Trust
Henry Moore Foundation
Mottahedan Family
Philip Mould & Company
National Heritage
    Memorial Fund
The National Lottery
    Heritage Fund
The National Trust
The Paul Neagu Estate (UK)
Mike Nelson
New Carlsberg Foundation
Hélène Nguyen-Ban
Nicholas and Judith's
    Charitable Settlement
Hermann Nitsch and
    Nitsch Foundation
Ordnance Survey
Outset Contemporary Art Fund
Maureen Paley
Simon and Midge Palley
William Palmer
Martin Parr
Paul Hamlyn Foundation
Paul Mellon Centre for
    Studies in British Art
Yana and Stephen Peel

Catherine Petitgas
Patricia Phelps de Cisneros
The Stanley Picker Trust
The Pivovarov Family
The Porthmeor Fund
David W. Posnett, OBE
Serena Prest Fund
Pretzel Gallery
Stephen Prina
Emilio Prini
Fiona Rae, in honour of
    Sir Nicholas Serota
Carla Rapoport
Rea Family
Robert Rennie
Chris Rokos
Emmanuel Roman
The Estate of Eugene and
    Penelope Rosenberg
Rothschild Foundation
Roland Rudd
Edward Ruscha
Sean Ryerson
The Estate of Simon Sainsbury
Gillian and Simon Salama-Caro
Jean and Melanie Salata
Anders and Yukiko Schroeder
Karsten Schubert
Jake and Hélène Marie Shafran
Jack Shear
Gene Sherman
Leo Shih
The Estate of Sylvia Sleigh
Matthew Slotover and
    Emily King
Jay Smith and Laura Rapp
Douglas So
Rimma Solod-Iankilevski
Southard Reid
Lord Stevenson of
    Coddenham, CBE
Emile Stipp
The Estate of Michael Stoddart
Mercedes and Ian Stoutzker
Maria Sukkar
Surgo Donor Advised Fund
Beth Swofford
Tamares Real Estate Holdings
    Inc. in collaboration with the
    Zabludowicz Collection
Tanya Bonakdar Gallery
Tate 1897 Circle
Tate Africa Acquisitions
    Committee
Tate Americas Foundation
Tate Asia-Pacific
    Acquisitions Committee
Tate European Collection Circle
Tate International Council
Tate Latin American
    Acquisitions Committee
Tate Members
Tate Middle East and
    North Africa
    Acquisitions Committee
Tate and Museum of
    Contemporary Art
    Australia, donated
    through the Australian
    Government's Cultural
    Gifts Program by Martin
    Gascoigne, and with the
    support of the Qantas
    Foundation
Tate North American
    Acquisitions Committee

Tate Patrons
Tate Photography
    Acquisitions Committee
Tate Russia and Eastern
    Europe Acquisitions
    Committee
Tate South Asia Acquisitions
    Committee
Terra Foundation for
    American Art
The Estate of
    Mr Nicholas Themans
Thomas Dane Gallery
Sandra Thompson
Imants Tillers and Michael
    Nelson Jagamara
Wolfgang Tillmans, in honour
    of Sir Nicholas Serota
Russell Tovey
Bill and Ruth True
Luc Tuymans
Lance Uggla
Dr Suzanne Ullmann
V-A-C Foundation
The Estate of
    Mollie Winifred Vickers
Marie-Louise von Motesiczky
    Charitable Trust
Kemang Wa Lehulere
Wagner Foundation
Mark Wallinger
Michael Werner, in honour of
    Sir Nicholas Serota
White Cube Ltd
Rachel Whiteread
Jane and Michael Wilson
The Lord Leonard and
    Lady Estelle Wolfson
    Foundation
Zhang Xiaogang
The Estate of
    Mr Anthony Zambra
Qiao Zhibing, in honour of
    Gregor Muir
Roman Zubal
and those who wish to remain anonymous

Platinum Patrons
Eric Abraham
Ghazwa Mayassi Abu-Suud
Maria Adonyeva
Mr Shane Akeroyd
Basil Alkazzi
Celia and Edward Atkin, CBE
The Estate of Francis Bacon
Lars Bane
Alex Beard
Beecroft Charitable Trust
Francesca Bellini Joseph and
    Allan Hennings
Jacques Boissonnas
Natalia Bondarenko
John Booth
Rory and Elizabeth Brooks
The Lord Browne of
    Madingley, FRS, FREng
Karen Cawthorn Argenio
XiaoMeng Cheng
Victoria Chu
Mr Stephane Custot
Pascale Decaux
Ladi Delano
Sophie Diedrichs
Valentina Drouin
Ashiya Dudhia
Eykyn Maclean Ltd

Mr David Fitzsimons
Edwin Fox Foundation
Stephen Friedman
Hugh Gibson
Olga Grishina
Mr Florian Gutzwiller
Alexis and Anne-Marie Habib
Andrew Harcourt
David Herro
Misha and Theresa Horne
Mr and Mrs Yan Huo
Mr Phillip Hylander
Natascha Jakobs-Linssen
Maria and Peter Kellner
Luigi Mazzoleni and Jose Graci
Scott and Suling Mead (Chair)
Emma Menell
Mary Moore
Afsaneh Moshiri
Hussam Otaibi
Simon and Midge Palley
Jan-Christoph Peters
Alexander and Bella Petrov
Mr and Mrs Paul Phillips
Mr Gilberto and
    Mrs Daniela Pozzi
Frances Reynolds
Sir Paul and Lady Ruddock
Ralph Segreti
Jake and Hélène Marie Shafran
Andrée Shore
Maria and Malek Sukkar
Ann Tang Chiu
Pierre Tollis and
    Alexandra Mollof
Annie Vartivarian
Saffron Wace
Michael and Jane Wilson
Lady Wolfson of Marylebone
Chizuko Yashiro
Meng Zhou
Jessica Zirinis
and those who wish to remain anonymous

Gold Patrons
Jose Alcantara
Ms Mila Askarova
Guya Bertoni
Louise and Charlie Bracken
Liza Cawthorn
Angela Choon
Beth and Michele Colocci
Harry G David
Ms Miel de Botton
Mr Frank Destribats
Mrs Maryam Eisler
Jennifer Ellis
Sarah Fischel
Giovanna Gromo
Tudor Havriliuc
Michael Herzog
Henry Highley
Mr M J Margulies
Alison Myners
Mariela Pissioti
Mathew Prichard
Garance Primat
Valerie Rademacher
Jordana Reuben
Sybil Robson Orr
Almine Ruiz-Picasso
Franz Schwarz
Carol Sellars
Raksha Sriram
Rebecca Taylor
Mr and Mrs Stanley S Tollman

Manuela and Iwan Wirth
and those who wish to remain anonymous

Silver Patrons
Geoffrey and Julian Agnew
    Charitable Trust
Sharis Alexandrian
Ryan Allen and Caleb Kramer
Mrs Malgosia Alterman
The Anson Charitable Trust
Toby and Kate Anstruther
Mr and Mrs Zeev Aram
Hannah Armstrong
James Arnell
Shalni Arora
Mrs Charlotte Artus
Aspect Charitable Trust
Tracy Barakat
Peter Barham
Mrs Jane Barker
Oliver Barker
Victoria Barnsley, OBE
Hazel Barratt
Jim Bartos
Dr Amelie Beier
Ms Anne Berthoud
Madeleine Bessborough
Shoshana Bloch
David Blood and Beth Bisso
Bruno Boesch
Harry and Fabiana Bond
Brigid Bose
Elena Bowes
Alina Boyko
Viscountess Bridgeman
Laura Brimson
Ben and Louisa Brown
Michael Burrell
Mrs Marlene Burston
Mrs Aisha Cahn
Sarah Caplin
Timothy and Elizabeth Capon
Mr Francis Carnwath and Ms
    Caroline Wiseman
Roger Cazalet
Lord and Lady Charles Cecil
Dr Peter Chocian
Paris Christofferson
John F Clappier
Andres Clase
Frank Cohen
Mrs Jane Collins
Dr Judith Collins
Terrence Collis
Mr and Mrs Oliver Colman
Mayte Comin
Giles and Sonia Coode-Adams
Cathy Corbett
Pilar Corrias
Tommaso Corvi-Mora
Mr and Mrs Bertrand Coste
Kathleen Crook and
    James Penturn
Richard Cyzer
Fiona Davies
Sir Howard Davies
Sir Roger and Lady De Haan
Elisabeth De Kergorlay
Giles de la Mare
Mr Damon and
    The Hon Mrs de Laszlo
Jean-Annet de Saint Rapt
Anne Chantal Defay Sheridan
Pier-Luigi del Renzio
Paula Diaz
Jackie Donnelly Russell

Joan Edlis
Lord and Lady Egremont
Margaret Erbe
John Erle-Drax
Dr Nigel Evans
Stuart and Margaret Evans
Carl Faker
Mrs Heather Farrar
David Fawkes
Mrs Margy Fenwick
Laurie Fitch
The Sylvie Fleming Collection
Lt Commander Paul Fletcher
Mr and Mrs Laurent Ganem
Mala Gaonkar
Elena Geuna
Mr Mark Glatman
Ms Emily Goldner and Mr
    Michael Humphries
Aphrodite Gonou
Kate Gordon
Dimitri Goulandris
Penelope Govett
Martyn Gregory
Richard and Odile Grogan
Carol Grose
Professor John Gruzelier
Mrs Helene Guerin-Llamas
Jill Hackel Zarzycki
Alex Haidas
Arthur Hanna
Mark Harris
Michael and Morven Heller
Cherine Helmy
Christian Hernandez and
    Michelle Crowe Hernandez
Paul Higgins
Muriel Hoffner
James Holland-Hibbert
Lady Hollick, OBE
Holtermann Fine Art
Jeff Horne
John Huntingford
Helen Janecek
Sarah Jennings
Mr Haydn John
Mr Michael Johnson
Mike Jones
Jay Jopling
Mrs Brenda Josephs
Tracey Josephs
Mr Joseph Kaempfer
Andrew Kalman
Ghislaine Kane
Ivan Katzen
Dr Martin Kenig
Mr David Ker
Mr and Mrs Simon Keswick
Mrs Mae Khouri
David Killick
Mr and Mrs James Kirkman
Brian and Lesley Knox
David P Korn
Kowitz Trust
Mr and Mrs Herbert Kretzmer
Linda Lakhdhir
Simon Lee
Tiina Lee
Leonard Lewis
Sharron Lewis
Sophia and Mark Lewisohn
Mr Gilbert Lloyd
Mrs Elizabeth Louis
Jeff Lowe
Alison Loyd
Kate MacGarry

Fiona Mactaggart
Sir John Mactaggart
Audrey Mandela
Lali Marganiya
Marsh Christian Trust
Daniele Mattogno
Ms Fiona Mellish
Mrs R W P Mellish
Professor Rob Melville
Dr Helen Metcalf
Vincent Meyer
Victoria Miro
Mrs Bona Montagu
Mrs William Morrison
Ms Deborah Norton
Julian Opie
Pilar Ordovás
Desmond Page
Maureen Paley
Sir Michael Palin
Mrs Kathrine Palmer
Mathieu Paris
Mrs Véronique Parke
Trevor Pickett
Frederique Pierre-Pierre
Professor Richard Portes,
    CBE, FBA
Graham Powell
Susan Prevezer, QC
Mr and Mrs Ryan Prince
Ivetta Rabinovich
Patricia Ranken
Carla Rapoport
Mrs Phyllis Rapp
Lady Ritblat
David Rocklin
Frankie Rossi
Mr David V Rouch
Mr James Roundell
Mr Charles Roxburgh
Hakon Runer and Ulrike
    Schwarz-Runer
Mr Alex Sainsbury and
    Ms Elinor Jansz
Mr Richard Christo Salmon
Tatiana Salomon
Cherrill and Ian Scheer
Sylvia Scheuer
Mrs Cara Schulze
Melissa Sesana
The Hon Richard Sharp
Neville Shulman, CBE
Simon C Dickinson Ltd
David Solo
Louise Spence
Mr Nicos Steratzias
Marie-Claude Stobart
Mrs Patricia Swannell
Mr James Swartz
The Lady Juliet Tadgell
Tot Taylor
Isadora Tharin
Elaine Thomas
Anthony Thornton
Marita Thurnauer
Ian Tollett
Victoria Tollman O'Hana
Karen Townshend
Andrew Tseng
Melissa Ulfane
Mrs Jolana Vainio and
    Dr Petri Vainio
Celine Valligny
Mrs Cecilia Versteegh
Gisela von Sanden
Andreas Vourecas-Petalas

Audrey Wallrock
Linda Waterhouse
Offer Waterman
Michael Webber
Sian West
Miss Cheyenne Westphal
Professor Sarah Whatmore
Derek James Wilson
Mr Douglas Woolf
Adam Wurr
and those who wish to remain anonymous

Young Patrons
10 Hanover
Samira Abdelmalek
Paulo Abecasis
Nadine Adams
Estelle Akeroyd Hunt
Nadia Akpinar
Hugo Alcantara
Miss Noor Al-Rahim
HRH Princess Alia Al-Senussi
Fiona Amitai
Mihai Anca
Tamim Antoniades
Gulru Arvas
Nur Arvas
Lucy Attwood
Miss Olivia Aubry
Charles and Tetyana Banner
Federica Baretta
Dehlia Barman
Lucy Barry
Katrina Beechey
Penny Johanna Beer
Eleni Beveratou
Dr Maya Beyhan
Dorothee Boissonnas
Erin Booth
Kit Brennan
David Carpenter
Lauren Carpenter
Thibaud Chaligne
Matthew Charlton
Aidan Christofferson
Bianca Chu
Niamh Conneely
Thamara Corm
Stephanie Courmont
Huguette Craggs
Averil Curci
Helena Czernecka
Henry Danowski
Veronika Dapunt
Mr Joshua Davis
Countess Charlotte
    de la Rochefoucauld
Émilie De Pauw
Agnes de Royere
Aliya de Tiesenhausen
Emie Diamond
Indira Dyussebayeva
Alexandra Economou
Eleanor A Edelman
Kate Finefrock
Thomas Forwood
Jane and Richard Found
Sylvain Fresia
Brian Fu
Mr Andreas Gegner
Mr Taymour Grahne
Beth Greenacre
Miles Greenberg
Jiafeng He
Ari Helgason
Patrick Hennessey

Max Edouard Friedrich Hetzler
Alexander Hollinshead
Simona Houldsworth
Stefan Idowu-Bello
Phoebus Istavrioglu
Ning Jiang
Aled Jones
Miss Meruyert Kaliyeva
Mrs Vasilisa Kameneva
Zoe Karafylakis Sperling
Tamila Kerimova
Ms Chloe Kinsman
Maria Korolevskaya
Daria Kravchenko
Nattasja Kusuma
Dominic Lamotte
Nicholas M Lamotte
Angélica Lèbre
Hena Lee
Alexandra Lekomtseva
John Lellouche
Alexander Lewis
Georgina Lewis
Ines Leynaud
Yisi Li
Jonathan Lim
Di Liu
Han Lo
Tessa Lord
Mr J Lueddeckens
Amber Mackenzie
Yusuf Macun
Ms Sonia Mak
Dr Christina Makris
Mr Jean-David Malat
Zain Masud
Magnus Mathisen
Charles-Henri McDermott
Frederick McDonald
Edward McGovern
Mary McNicholas
Shahid Miah
Miss Nina Moaddel
Lisa Molodtsova
Mr Fernando Moncho Lobo
Ikenna Obiekwe
Aurore Ogden (Co-Chair,
    Young Patrons
    Ambassador Group)
Reine and Boris Okuliar
Berkay Oncel
Miruna Onofrei
Margot O'Sullivan
Periklis Panagopoulos
Yioryios Papayioryiou
Olympia Pappa
Divya Pathak
Harsha Perera
Alexander V Petalas (Co-
    Chair, Young Patrons
    Ambassador Group)
Victor Petitgas
Robert Phillips
Mr Mark Piolet
Mary Pollock
Ayelén Privato
Christopher Pullen
Ms Catherine Quin
Mr Eugenio Re Rebaudengo
Nour Saleh
Daniel Schwarz
Count Indoo Sella Di Monteluce
Robert Sheffield
Ms Marie-Anya Shriro
Amar Singh
Evgenia Slyusarenko

Alexander Smith
Henry Spethmann
Jana Soin
Katarina Stojanovic
Dominic Stolerman
Marine Tanguy
Melisa Tapan
Nayrouz Tatanaki
Vassan Thavaraja
Mr Leo Thetiot
Soren S K Tholstrup
Omer Tiroche
Charles Towning
Alexandrei Trausch
Nicolas Trausch
Mr Giancarlo Trinca
Mr Philippos Tsangrides
Ms Navann Ty
Giada Vaghi
Mr Lawrence Van Hagen
Sophie van Rappard
Damian Vesey
Alina Voronova
Luning Wang
Samuel Wang
Kim Williams
Thomas Williams
Alexandra Wood
Michelle Wu
Ethan Yip
HRH Princess Eugenie of York
Evgeny Zborovsky
Yuejia Zhou
Marcelo Osvaldo Zimmler
and those who wish to remain anonymous

**International
Council Members**
Staffan Ahrenberg,
    Editions Cahiers d'Art
Mr Geoff Ainsworth, AM
Tiqui Atencio Demirdjian and
    Ago Demirdjian
Michael J. Audain
Petr Aven
Maria Baibakova and
    Adrien Faure
Nicolas Berggruen
Jo and Tom Bloxham
Pontus Bonnier
Paloma Botín O'Shea
Bill Bowness
Ivor Braka
The Deborah Loeb
    Brice Foundation
Elizabeth Brooks
Andrew Cameron, AM
Nicolas and Celia Cattelain
Christina Chandris
Richard Chang (Vice Chair)
Pierre Chen, Yageo
    Foundation, Taiwan
Mr Euisun Chung and
    Mrs Geesun Chung
Mr and Mrs Attilio Codognato
Sir Ronald Cohen and
    Lady Cohen
Dimitris Daskalopoulos
Mr and Mrs Michel David-Weill
Miel de Botton
Suzanne Deal Booth
Robert and Renée Drake
Olga Dreesmann
Füsun and Faruk Eczacibasi
Fares and Tania Fares
Doris Fisher

Wendy Fisher
Amanda and Glenn Fuhrman
Mrs Belma Gaudio and
	The Butters Foundation
Candida and Zak Gertler
Yassmin Ghandehari
Lydia and Manfred Gorvy
Laurence Graff
Xavier Guerrand-Hermès
Mimi and Peter Haas Fund
Margrit and Paul Hahnloser
Susan Hayden
Ydessa Hendeles
Marlene Hess and James D. Zirin
Maja Hoffmann
Vicky Hughes
Ishikawa Foundation
Sangita Jindal
Dakis and Lietta Joannou
Ms Monica Kalpakian
Richard and Pamela Kramlich
Andreas and Ulrike Kurtz
Catherine Lagrange
Pierre Lagrange
The Lauder Foundation -
	Leonard and
	Judy Lauder Fund
Agnès and Edward Lee
Seo Hyun Lee
Jacqueline and Marc Leland
Ms Joyce Liu
Panos and Sandra Marinopoulos
Victoria Mikhelson
Naomi Milgrom, AO
Simon and Catriona Mordant
Mrs Yoshiko Mori
Gael Neeson
Dr Mark Nelson
Mr and Mrs Takeo Obayashi
HRH Princess Firyal of Jordan
Mr and Mrs Eyal Ofer
Andrea and José
	Olympio Pereira
Hideyuki Osawa
Midge and Simon Palley
Irene Panagopoulos
Young-Ju Park
Véronique Parke
Yana and Stephen Peel
Daniel and Elizabeth Peltz
Catherine Petitgas (Chair)
Sydney Picasso
Lekha Poddar
Miss Dee Poon
Ms Miuccia Prada and
	Mr Patrizio Bertelli
Laura Rapp and Jay Smith
Maya and Ramzy Rasamny
Patrizia Sandretto Re
	Rebaudengo and
	Agostino Re Rebaudengo
Frances Reynolds
Michael Ringier
Hanneli M Rupert
Sevil Sabanci
Dame Theresa Sackler, DBE
Mrs Lily Safra
Rajeeb and Nadia Samdani
Alejandro Santo Domingo
Tarana and Tarun Sawhney
Dasha Shenkman, OBE
Dr Gene Sherman, AM
Jon and Kimberly Shirley
Uli and Rita Sigg
Norman C. Stone
John J Studzinski, CBE

Maria and Malek Sukkar
Mr Christen Sveaas
Katja and Nicolai Tangen /
	AKO Foundation
Ms Lorraine Tarabay
Warly Tomei
Richard and Maggie Tsai
Mrs Ninetta Vafeia
Paulo A W Vieira
Mercedes Vilardell
Robert and Felicity
	Waley-Cohen
Angela Westwater and
	David Meitus
Diana Widmaier Picasso
Christen and Derek Wilson
Mrs Sylvie Winckler
The Hon Dame Janet Wolfson
	de Botton, DBE
Terry Wu
Yang Yang
Poju Zabludowicz and Anita
	Zabludowicz, OBE
and those who wish to remain anonymous

**Africa Acquisitions
Committee**
Aki Abiola
Kathy Ackerman Robins
Adnan Bashir
Priti Chandaria Shah
Mrs Kavita Chellaram
Harry G David
Lana de Beer David
Mr and Mrs Michel David-Weill
Ladi Delano
Mrs Wendy Fisher
Diane B. Frankel
Pulane Tshabalala Kingston
Samallie Kiyingi
Othman Lazraq
Gervanne Leridon
Matthias Leridon
Caro Macdonald
Dale Mathias
Pascale Revert Wheeler
Emile Stipp
Josef Vascovitz and
	Lisa Goodman
Mercedes Vilardell (Chair)
Alexa Waley-Cohen
Peter Warwick
and those who wish to remain anonymous

**Asia-Pacific
Acquisitions Committee**
Shane Akeroyd
Jim Amberson
Matthias Arndt
Bonnie and R Derek Bandeen
Lito and Kim Camacho
Mr and Mrs John Carrafiell
David Chau
Mrs Marisa Chearavanont
Adrian Cheng
Jonathan Cheung
Lawrence Chu
Marcel Crespo
Mrs Yassmin Ghandehari
Esther Heer-Zacek
Philippa Hornby
Shareen Khattar Harrison
Mr Jung Wan Kim
Ms Yung Hee Kim
Director of Arario Museum
Ms Ellie Lai

Alan Lau (Co-Chair)
Woon Kyung Lee
Woong-Yeul Lee
Jasmine Li
Lin Qi
Ms Dina Liu
Alan and Yenn Lo
Ms Kai-Yin Lo
Yoonwhe Leo Moon &
	Young Ran Yun
Lynn Ou
Mr John Porter
Arif Suherman
Mr Patrick Sun
Chikako Tatsuuma
Dr Andreas Teoh
Rudy Tseng
Rachel Verghis
Wang Bing
Yang Bin
Jenny Yeh
Fernando Zobel de Ayala
	(Co-Chair)
and those who wish to remain anonymous

**Latin American
Acquisitions Committee**
Monica and Robert Aguirre
José Antonio Alcantara
Francesca Bellini
Celia Birbragher
Countess Nicole
	Brachetti Peretti
Estrellita and Daniel Brodsky
Luis Javier Castro
Simone Coscarelli Parma
HSH the Prince
	Pierre d'Arenberg
Tiqui Atencio Demirdjian
	(Co-Chair)
Marta Regina
	Fernandez-Holmann
Heloisa Genish
Barbara Hemmerle Gollust
Julian Iragorri
Aimee Labarrere de Servitje
José Luis Lorenzo
Sofia Mariscal and Guillermo
	Penso Blanco
Susan McDonald
Gabriela Mendoza
Felipe and Denise Nahas Mattar
Veronica Nutting
Victoria and Isaac Oberfeld
Silvia Paz Illobre
Catherine Petitgas
Claudio Federico Porcel
Thibault Poutrel
Frances Reynolds
Erica Roberts (Co-Chair)
Roberto Ruhman
Alin Ryan Lobo
Catalina Saieh Guzmán
Teresa Sapey
Lilly Scarpetta
Richard Weinstein
and those who wish to remain anonymous

**Middle East and North Africa
Acquisitions Committee**
Abdulla Al Gurg
HRH Princess Alia Al-Senussi
Abdelmonem Bin Eisa Alserkal
Marwan T Assaf
Perihan Bassatne
Family Boghossian

Ms Isabelle de la Bruyère
Füsun Eczacibasi
Maryam Eisler
Shirley Elghanian
Noor Fares
Dr Farhad Farjam
Hossein and Dalia Fateh
Negin Fattahi-Dasmal
Raghida Ghandour Al Rahim
Mareva Grabowski
Aysegül Karadeniz
Mr Elie Khouri
Maha Kutay
Dina Nasser-Khadivi
Mr Moshe Peterburg
Ramzy and Maya Rasamny
Mrs Karen Ruimy
Maria (Co-Chair) and Malek
	Sukkar
Faisal Tamer (Co-Chair)
Mr Zahid and Ms Binladin
Roxane Zand
and those who wish to remain anonymous

**North American Acquisitions
Committee**
Jacqueline Appel and
	Alexander Malmaeus
Abigail Baratta
Dorothy Berwin
Chrissy Taylor Broughton and
	Lee Broughton
Dillon Cohen
Michael Corman and Kevin Fink
James E Diner
Mala Gaonkar
Jill Garcia
Victoria Gelfand-Magalhaes
Shari Glazer
Amy Gold
Pamela J Joyner
Peter Kahng
Patricia Kaneb Kelly
Nancy Kaneb Soule
Christian Keesee
Anna Korshun
Miyoung Lee
Marjorie and Michael Levine
James Lindon
Kathleen Madden and
	Paul Frantz
Stavros Merjos
Gregory R Miller (Co-Chair)
Rachelli Mishori and Leon Koffler
Sami Mnaymneh
Shabin and Nadir Mohamed
Alexander V. Petalas
Holly Peterson
Amy and John Phelan
Laura Rapp and Jay Smith
Mrs. Stephanie Robinson
Carolin Scharpff-Striebich
Ralph Segreti
Komal Shah
Francis and Eleanor Shen
Kimberly and Jon Shirley
Beth Swofford
Ann Tang Chiu
Roberto Toscano and Nadia
	Toscano-Palon
Charlotte Wagner
Christen Wilson (Co-Chair)
	and Derek Wilson
Mary Zlot
and those who wish to remain anonymous

**Photography Acquisitions
Committee**
Ryan Allen and Caleb Kramer
Nicholas Barker
Cynthia Lewis Beck
Carolin Becker
Pierre Brahm
Alla Broeksmit
Elizabeth (Co-Chair) and
	Rory Brooks
Michael A Chesser
Beth and Michele Colocci
Mr and Mrs Michel David-Weill
Mr Hyung-Teh Do
David Fitzsimons
Lisa Garrison
Emily Goldner and
	Mike Humphries
Alexandra Hess
Natascha Jakobs-Linssen
Elizabeth and William Kahane
Jack Kirkland (Co-Chair)
Randall Kroszner and
	David Nelson
Nathalie Lambert-Besseddik
Suling Mead
Sebastien Montabonel
Saadi Soudavar
Nicholas Stanley
Maria and Malek Sukkar
Francois Trausch, in memory
	of Caroline Trausch
Annie Vartivarian
Michael and Jane Wilson
and those who wish to remain anonymous

**Russia and Eastern Europe
Acquisitions Committee**
Dilyara Allakhverdova
	(Co-Chair)
Stella Beniaminova
David and Kathryn Birnbaum
Attila Brezoczki
Francise Hsin-Wen Chang
Marian Gazdik
Jan Hammer
Patrick Hessel
Vilius Kavaliauskas and
	Rita Kavaliauskiene
Peter Kulloi (Co-Chair)
Eniko Leányvári and Gábor Illés
Iveta Manasherova
Danica and Eduard Maták
Luba Michailova
Florin Pogonaru
Petr Pudil
Valeria Rodnyansky
Robert Runták
Ovidiu Sandor
Zsolt Somlói
Mr Laszlo Vago
Veronika Zonabend
Mr Jānis Zuzāns
and those who wish to remain anonymous

**South Asia
Acquisitions Committee**
Krishna Bhupal
Dr Arani and Mrs Shumita Bose
Krishna Choudhary
Akshay Chudasama
Jai Danani
Taimur Hassan
Dr Amin Jaffer
Deepanjana Klein
Simran Kotak and Vir Kotak